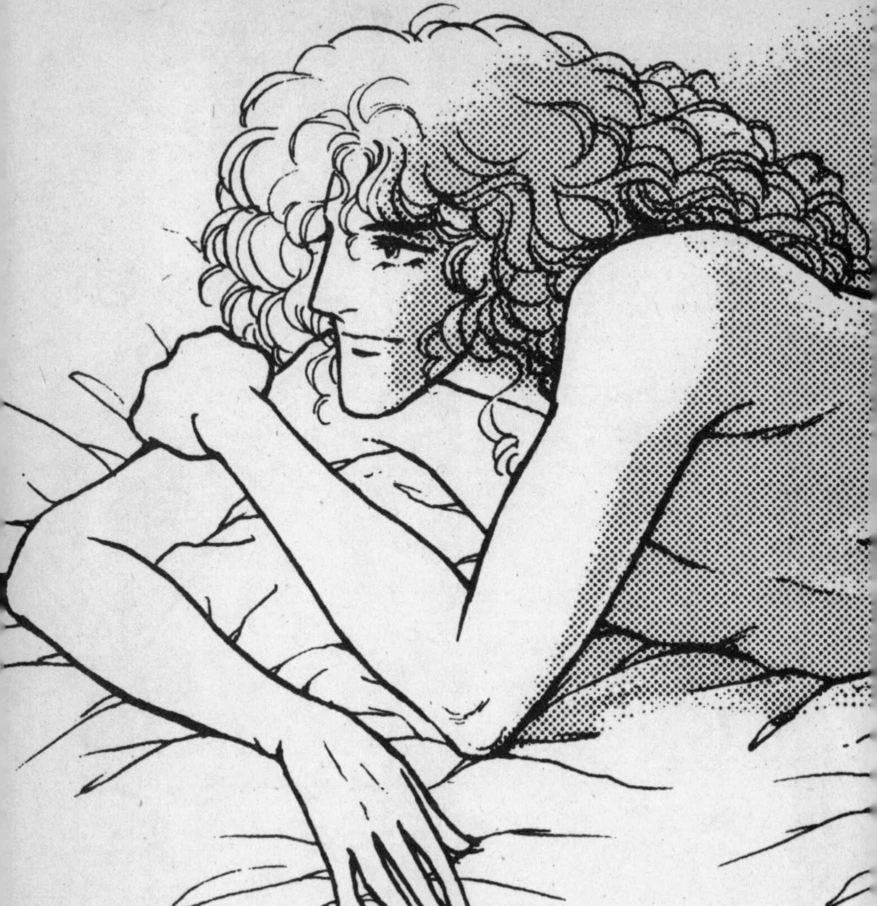

FROM EROICA
LOVE

Volume 7 **By Yasuko Aioke**

CONTENTS

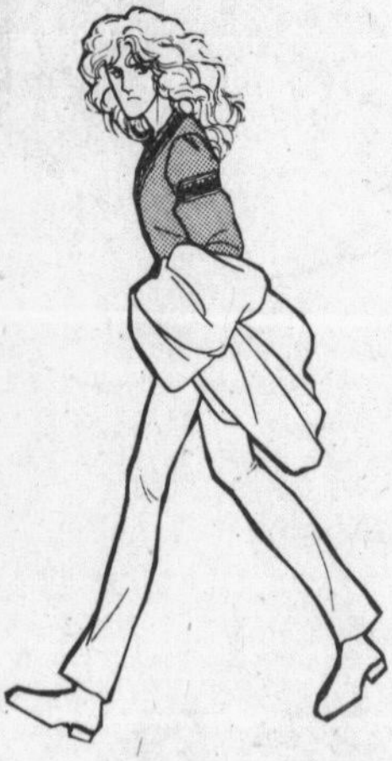

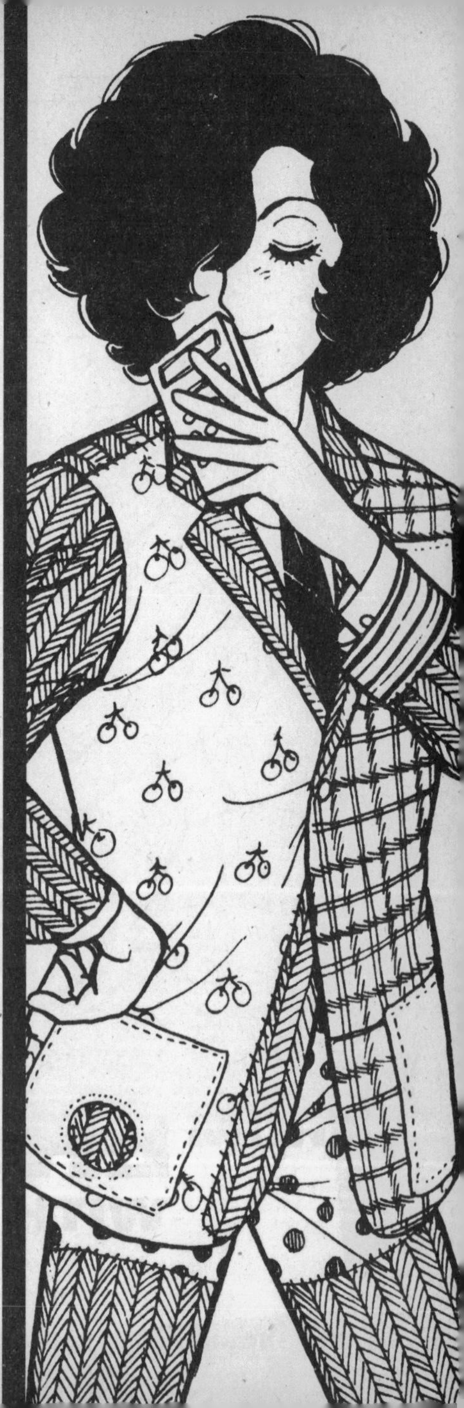

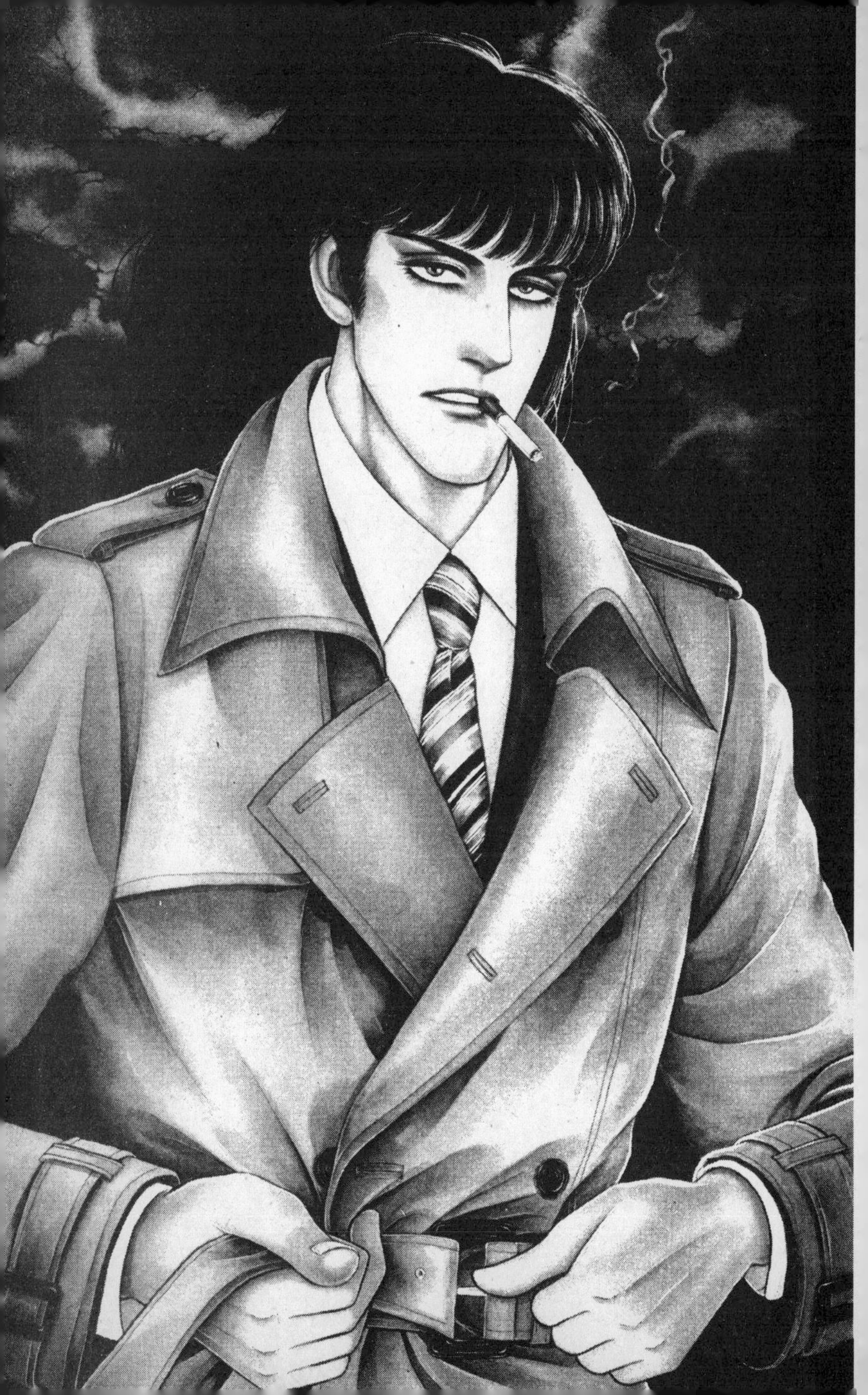

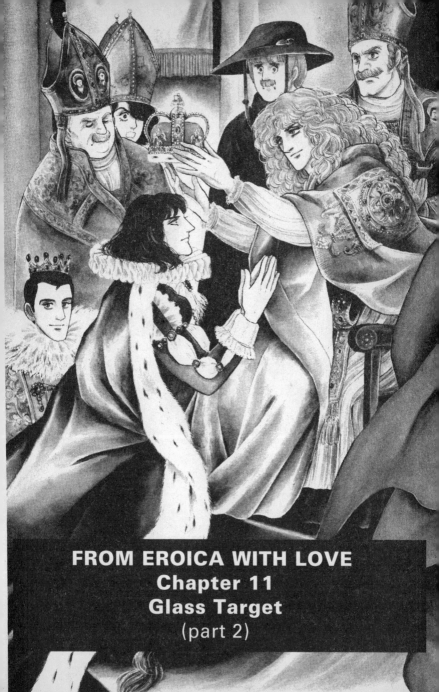

FROM EROICA WITH LOVE
Chapter 11
Glass Target
(part 2)

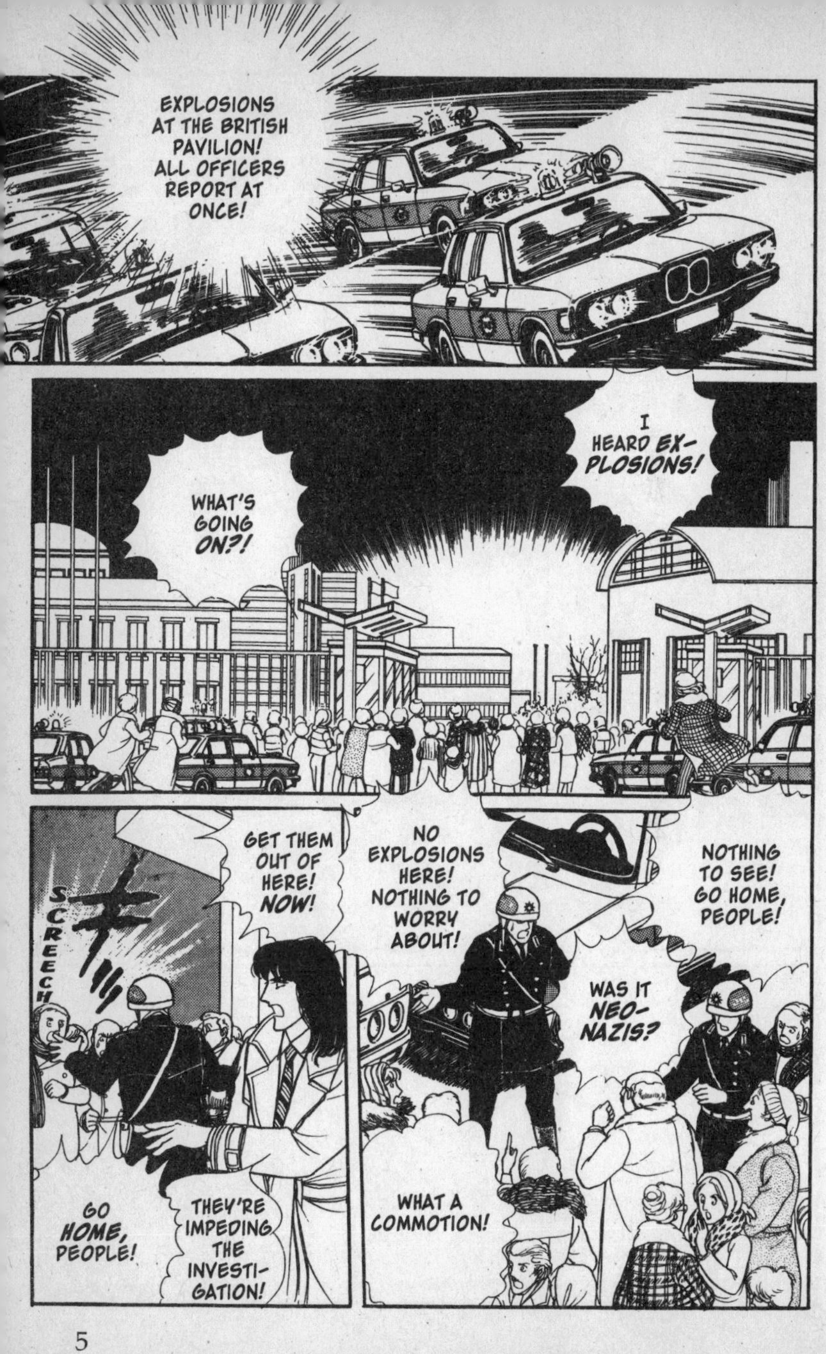
EXPLOSIONS AT THE BRITISH PAVILION! ALL OFFICERS REPORT AT ONCE!
I HEARD EXPLOSIONS!
WHAT'S GOING ON?!
NOTHING TO SEE! GO HOME, PEOPLE!
NO EXPLOSIONS HERE! NOTHING TO WORRY ABOUT!
WAS IT NEO-NAZIS?
WHAT A COMMOTION!
GET THEM OUT OF HERE! NOW!
SCREEECH
THEY'RE IMPEDING THE INVESTIGATION!
GO HOME, PEOPLE!

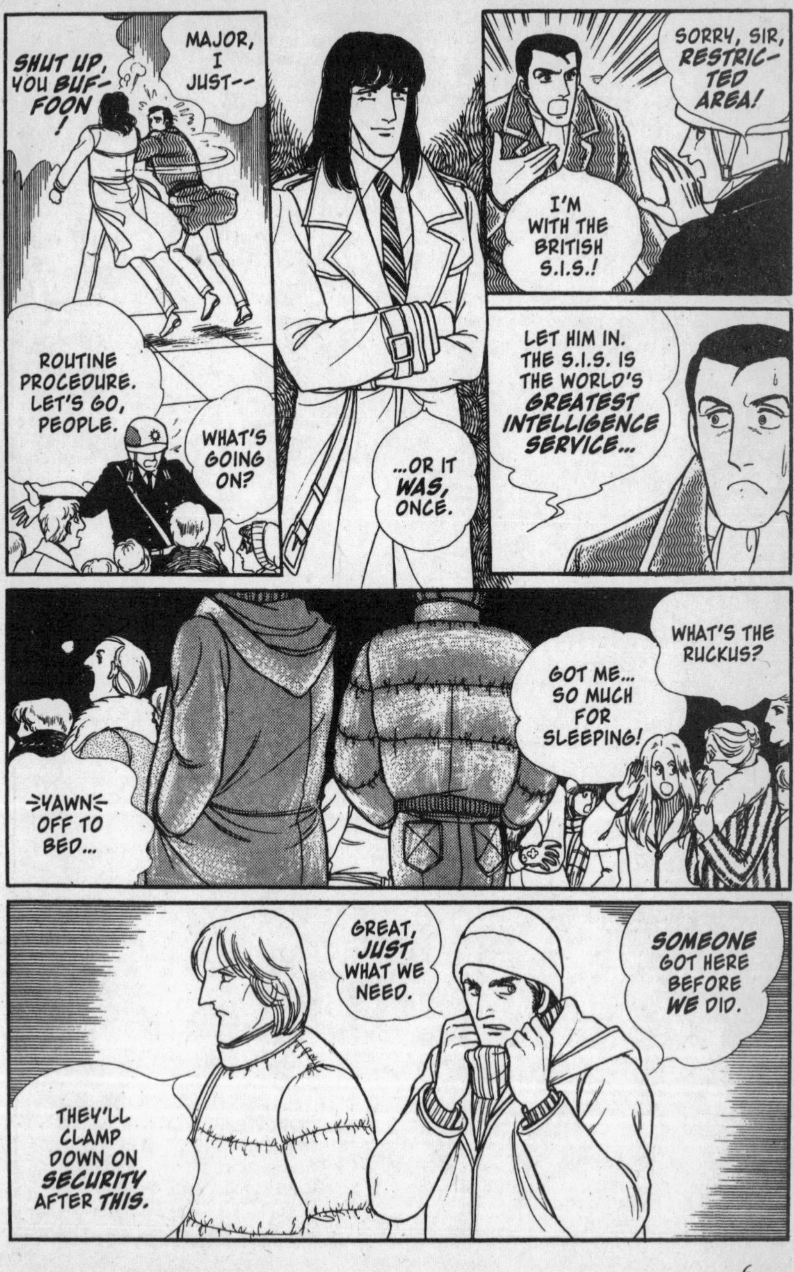
SORRY, SIR, RESTRICTED AREA!
I'M WITH THE BRITISH S.I.S.!
LET HIM IN. THE S.I.S. IS THE WORLD'S GREATEST INTELLIGENCE SERVICE...
...OR IT WAS, ONCE.
MAJOR, I JUST--
SHUT UP, YOU BUFFOON!
WHAT'S GOING ON?
ROUTINE PROCEDURE. LET'S GO, PEOPLE.
WHAT'S THE RUCKUS?
GOT ME... SO MUCH FOR SLEEPING!
YAWN
OFF TO BED...
SOMEONE GOT HERE BEFORE WE DID.
GREAT, JUST WHAT WE NEED.
THEY'LL CLAMP DOWN ON SECURITY AFTER THIS.

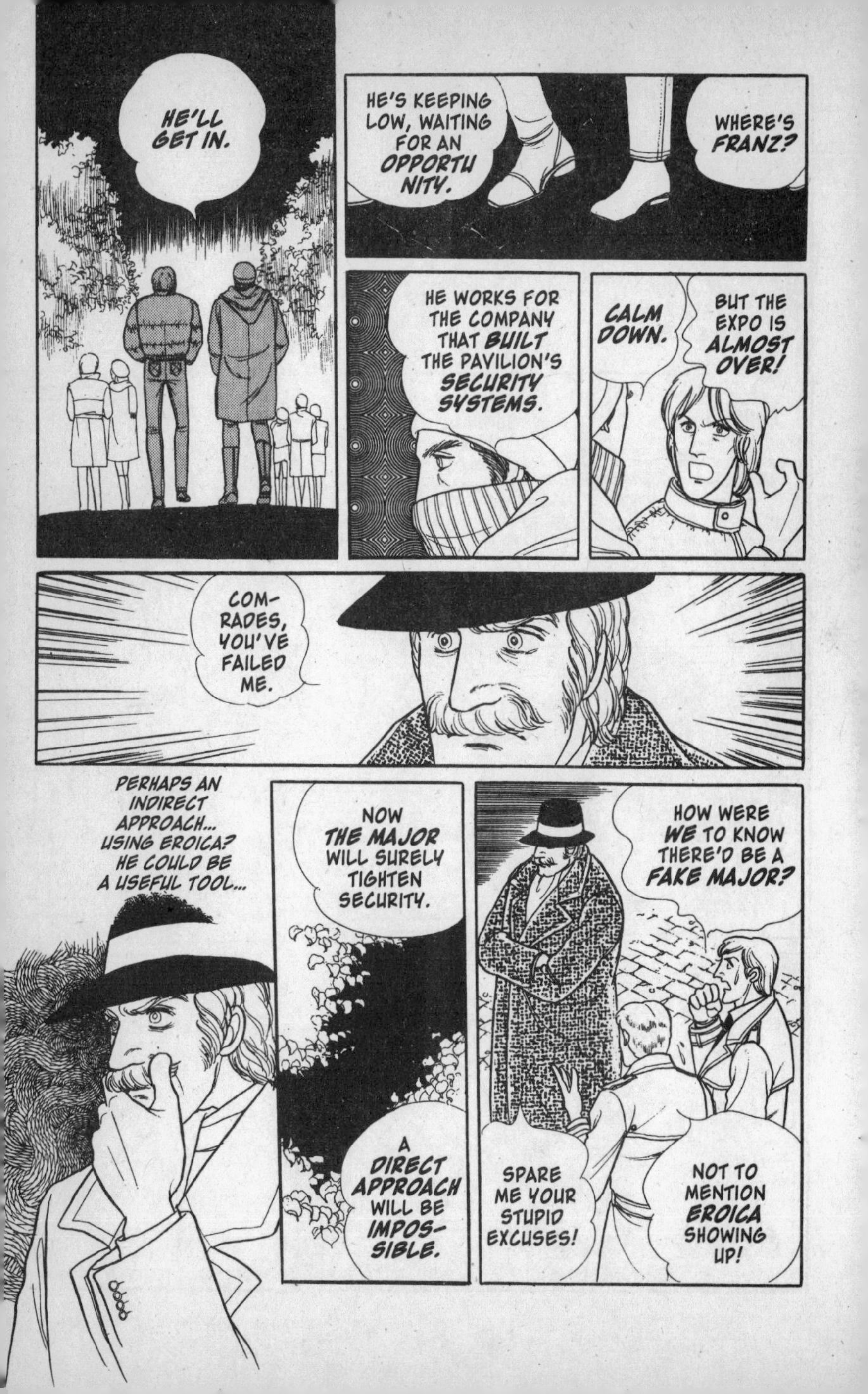
WHERE'S FRANZ?
HE'S KEEPING LOW, WAITING FOR AN OPPORTUNITY.
BUT THE EXPO IS ALMOST OVER!
CALM DOWN.
HE WORKS FOR THE COMPANY THAT BUILT THE PAVILION'S SECURITY SYSTEMS.
HE'LL GET IN.
COMRADES, YOU'VE FAILED ME.
HOW WERE WE TO KNOW THERE'D BE A FAKE MAJOR?
NOT TO MENTION EROICA SHOWING UP!
SPARE ME YOUR STUPID EXCUSES!
NOW THE MAJOR WILL SURELY TIGHTEN SECURITY.
A DIRECT APPROACH WILL BE IMPOSSIBLE.
PERHAPS AN INDIRECT APPROACH... USING EROICA? HE COULD BE A USEFUL TOOL...

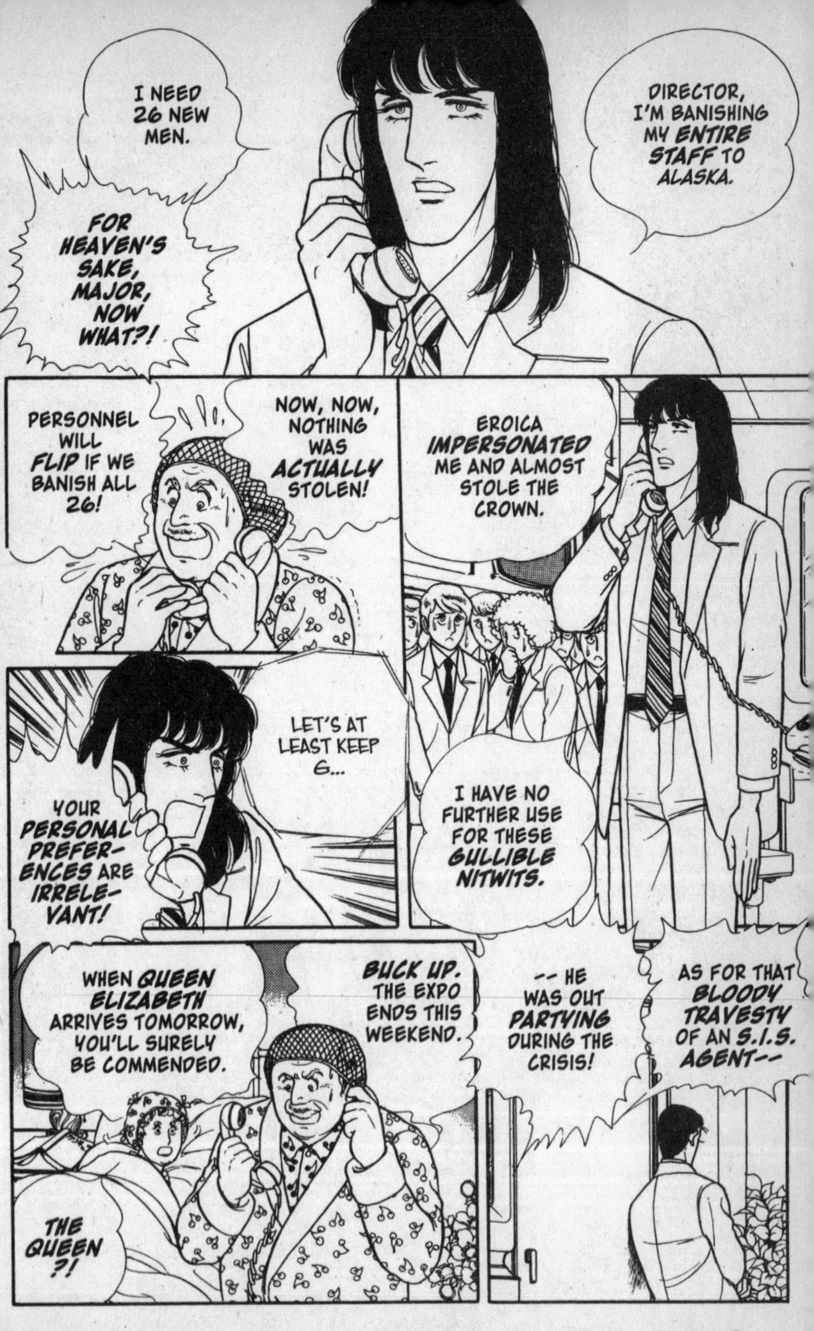
DIRECTOR, I'M BANISHING MY ENTIRE STAFF TO ALASKA.
I NEED 26 NEW MEN.
FOR HEAVEN'S SAKE, MAJOR, NOW WHAT?!
EROICA IMPERSONATED ME AND ALMOST STOLE THE CROWN.
I HAVE NO FURTHER USE FOR THESE GULLIBLE NITWITS.
NOW, NOW, NOTHING WAS ACTUALLY STOLEN!
PERSONNEL WILL FLIP IF WE BANISH ALL 26!
LET'S AT LEAST KEEP 6...
YOUR PERSONAL PREFERENCES ARE IRRELEVANT!
AS FOR THAT BLOODY TRAVESTY OF AN S.I.S. AGENT--
--HE WAS OUT PARTYING DURING THE CRISIS!
BUCK UP. THE EXPO ENDS THIS WEEKEND.
WHEN QUEEN ELIZABETH ARRIVES TOMORROW, YOU'LL SURELY BE COMMENDED.
THE QUEEN?!

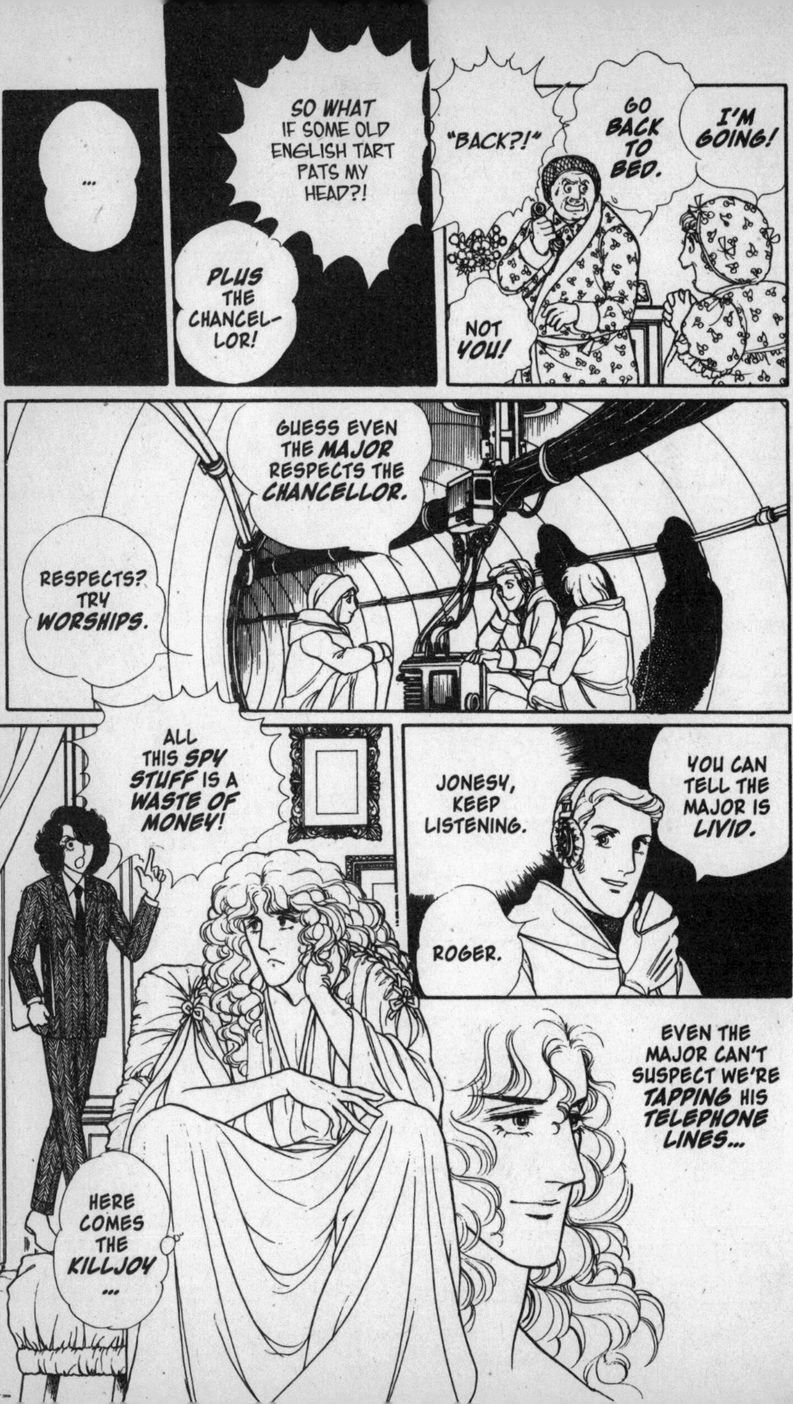
I'M GOING!
GO BACK TO BED.
"BACK?!"
NOT YOU!
SO WHAT IF SOME OLD ENGLISH TART PATS MY HEAD?!
PLUS THE CHANCEL-LOR!
...
GUESS EVEN THE MAJOR RESPECTS THE CHANCELLOR.
RESPECTS? TRY WORSHIPS.
YOU CAN TELL THE MAJOR IS LIVID.
JONESY, KEEP LISTENING.
ROGER.
EVEN THE MAJOR CAN'T SUSPECT WE'RE TAPPING HIS TELEPHONE LINES...
ALL THIS SPY STUFF IS A WASTE OF MONEY!
HERE COMES THE KILLJOY ...

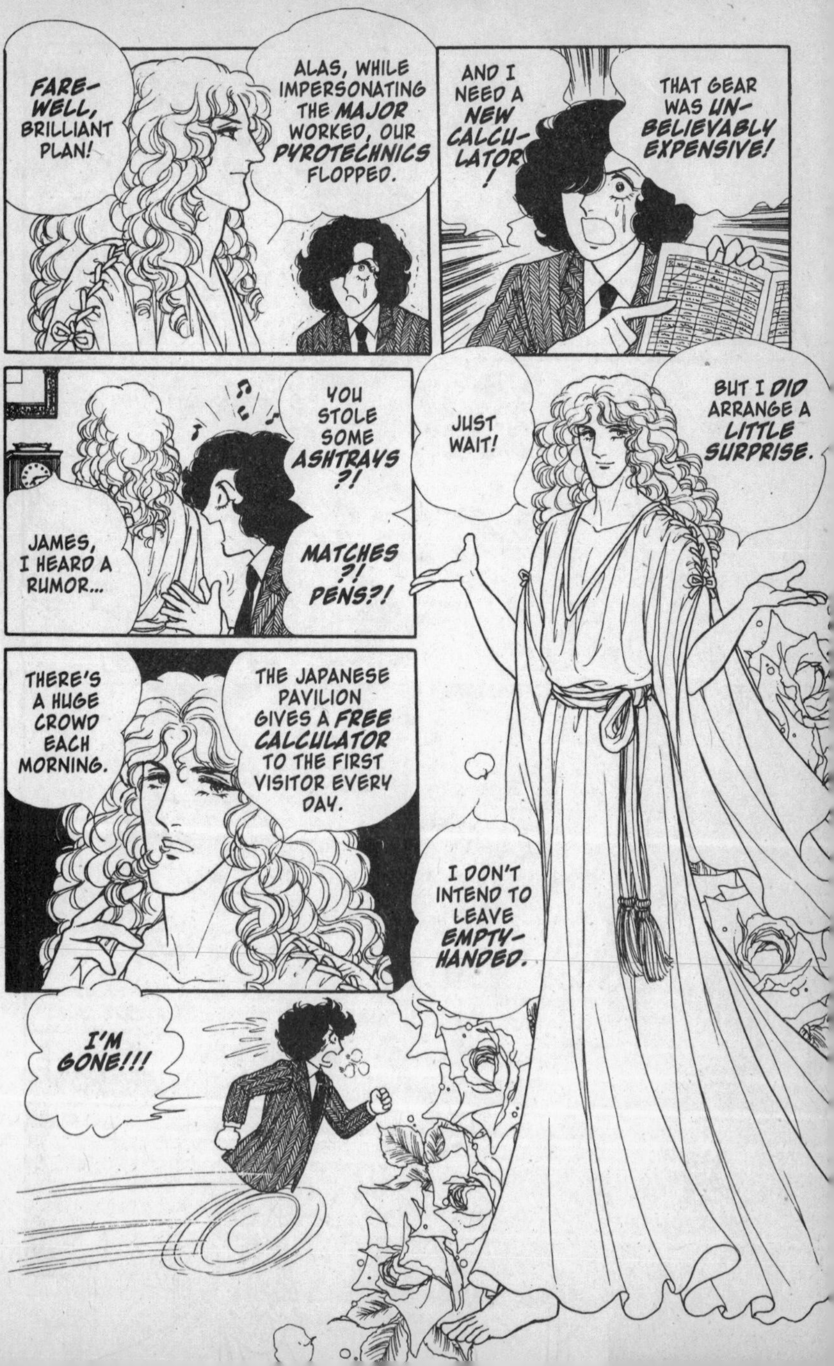
THAT GEAR WAS UN-BELIEVABLY EXPENSIVE!
AND I NEED A NEW CALCULATOR!
ALAS, WHILE IMPERSONATING THE MAJOR WORKED, OUR PYROTECHNICS FLOPPED.
FARE-WELL, BRILLIANT PLAN!
BUT I DID ARRANGE A LITTLE SURPRISE.
JUST WAIT!
I DON'T INTEND TO LEAVE EMPTY-HANDED.
YOU STOLE SOME ASHTRAYS?!
MATCHES?! PENS?!
JAMES, I HEARD A RUMOR...
THE JAPANESE PAVILION GIVES A FREE CALCULATOR TO THE FIRST VISITOR EVERY DAY.
THERE'S A HUGE CROWD EACH MORNING.
I'M GONE!!!

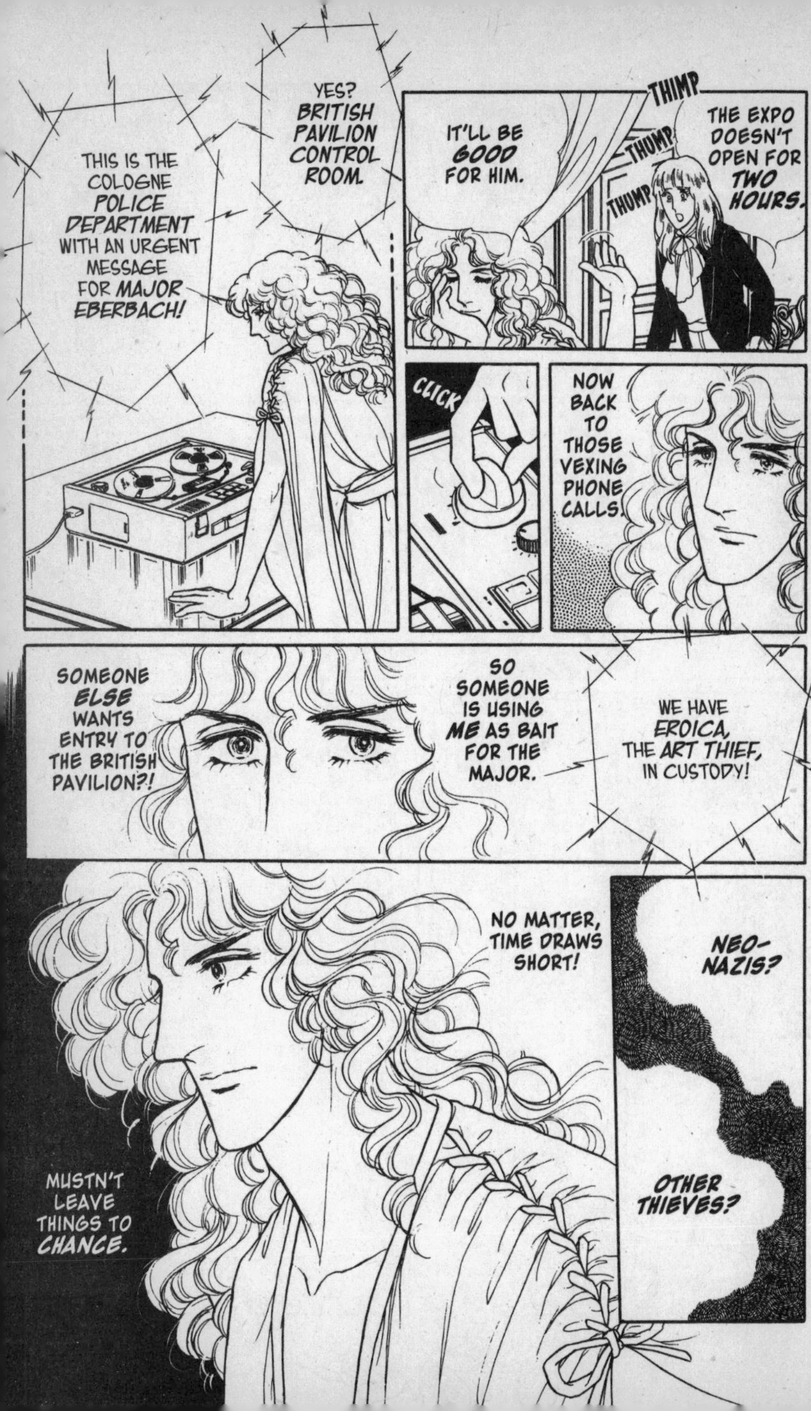
THIMP
THE EXPO DOESN'T OPEN FOR TWO HOURS.
THUMP
THUMP
IT'LL BE GOOD FOR HIM.
NOW BACK TO THOSE VEXING PHONE CALLS.
CLICK
YES? BRITISH PAVILION CONTROL ROOM.
THIS IS THE COLOGNE POLICE DEPARTMENT WITH AN URGENT MESSAGE FOR MAJOR EBERBACH!
WE HAVE EROICA, THE ART THIEF, IN CUSTODY!
SO SOMEONE IS USING ME AS BAIT FOR THE MAJOR.
SOMEONE ELSE WANTS ENTRY TO THE BRITISH PAVILION?!
NEO-NAZIS?
OTHER THIEVES?
NO MATTER, TIME DRAWS SHORT!
MUSTN'T LEAVE THINGS TO CHANCE.

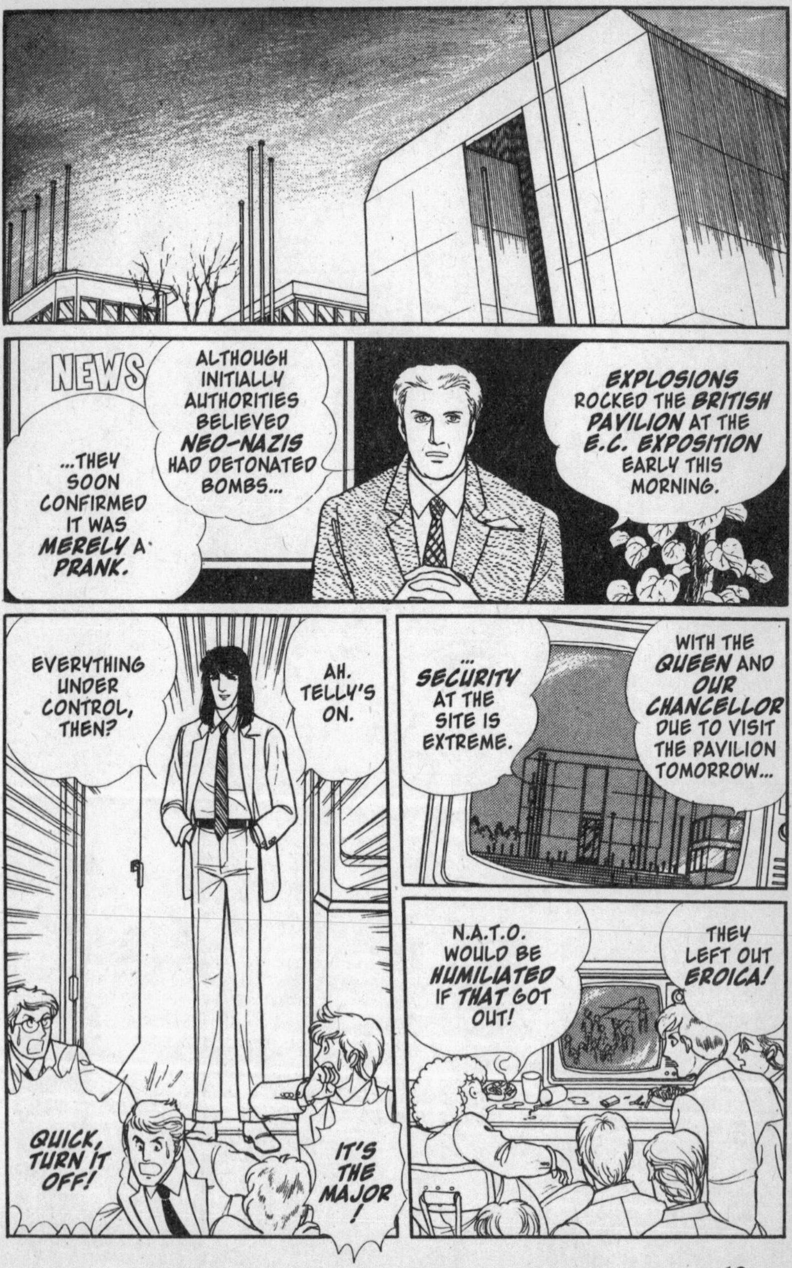
NEWS
EXPLOSIONS ROCKED THE BRITISH PAVILION AT THE E.C. EXPOSITION EARLY THIS MORNING.
ALTHOUGH INITIALLY AUTHORITIES BELIEVED NEO-NAZIS HAD DETONATED BOMBS...
...THEY SOON CONFIRMED IT WAS MERELY A PRANK.
WITH THE QUEEN AND OUR CHANCELLOR DUE TO VISIT THE PAVILION TOMORROW...
...SECURITY AT THE SITE IS EXTREME.
THEY LEFT OUT EROICA!
N.A.T.O. WOULD BE HUMILIATED IF THAT GOT OUT!
AH. TELLY'S ON.
EVERYTHING UNDER CONTROL, THEN?
IT'S THE MAJOR!
QUICK, TURN IT OFF!

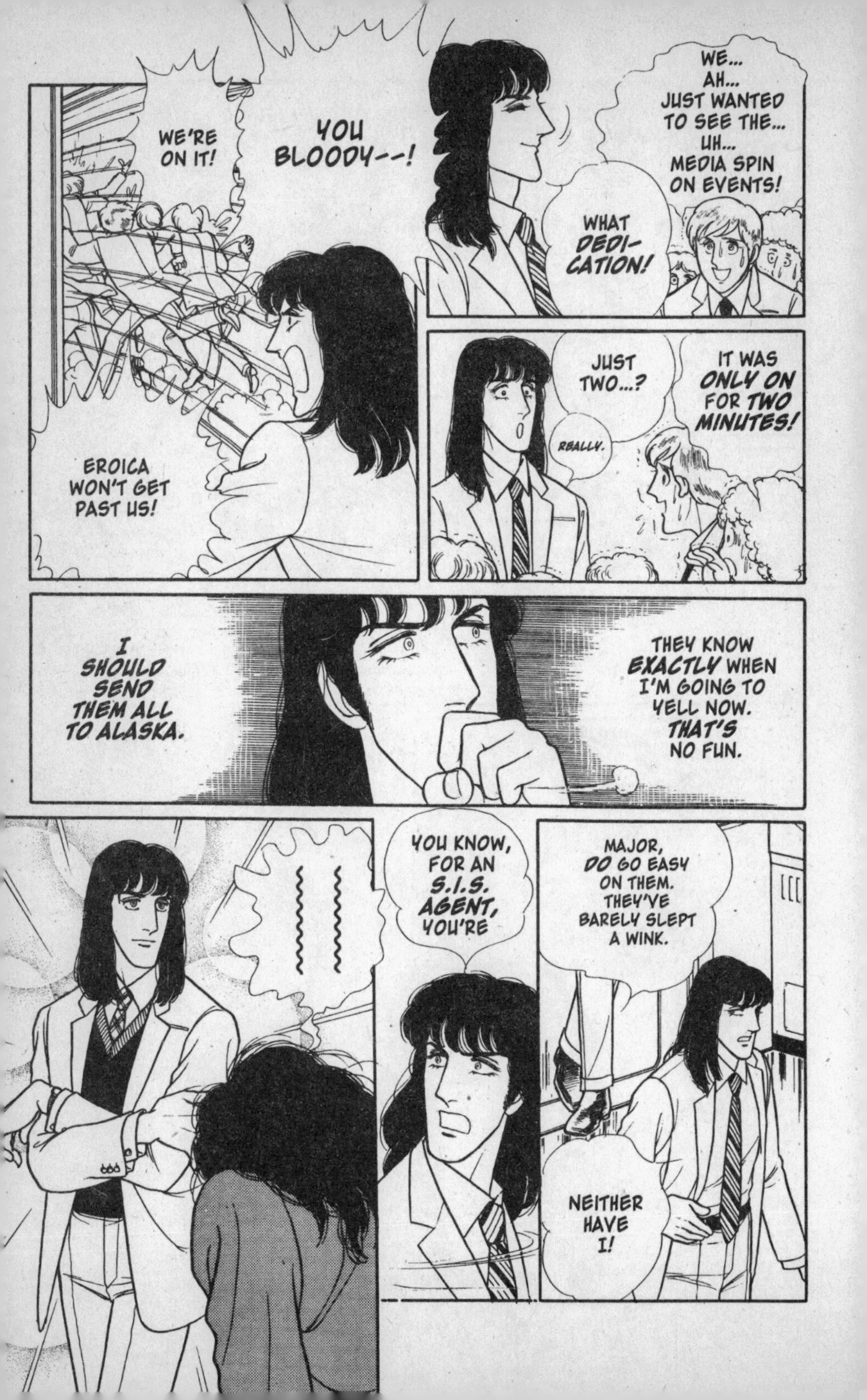
WE... AH... JUST WANTED TO SEE THE... UH... MEDIA SPIN ON EVENTS!
WHAT DEDICATION!
IT WAS ONLY ON FOR TWO MINUTES!
JUST TWO...?
REALLY.
YOU BLOODY--!
WE'RE ON IT!
EROICA WON'T GET PAST US!
THEY KNOW EXACTLY WHEN I'M GOING TO YELL NOW. THAT'S NO FUN.
I SHOULD SEND THEM ALL TO ALASKA.
MAJOR, DO GO EASY ON THEM. THEY'VE BARELY SLEPT A WINK.
NEITHER HAVE I!
YOU KNOW, FOR AN S.I.S. AGENT, YOU'RE

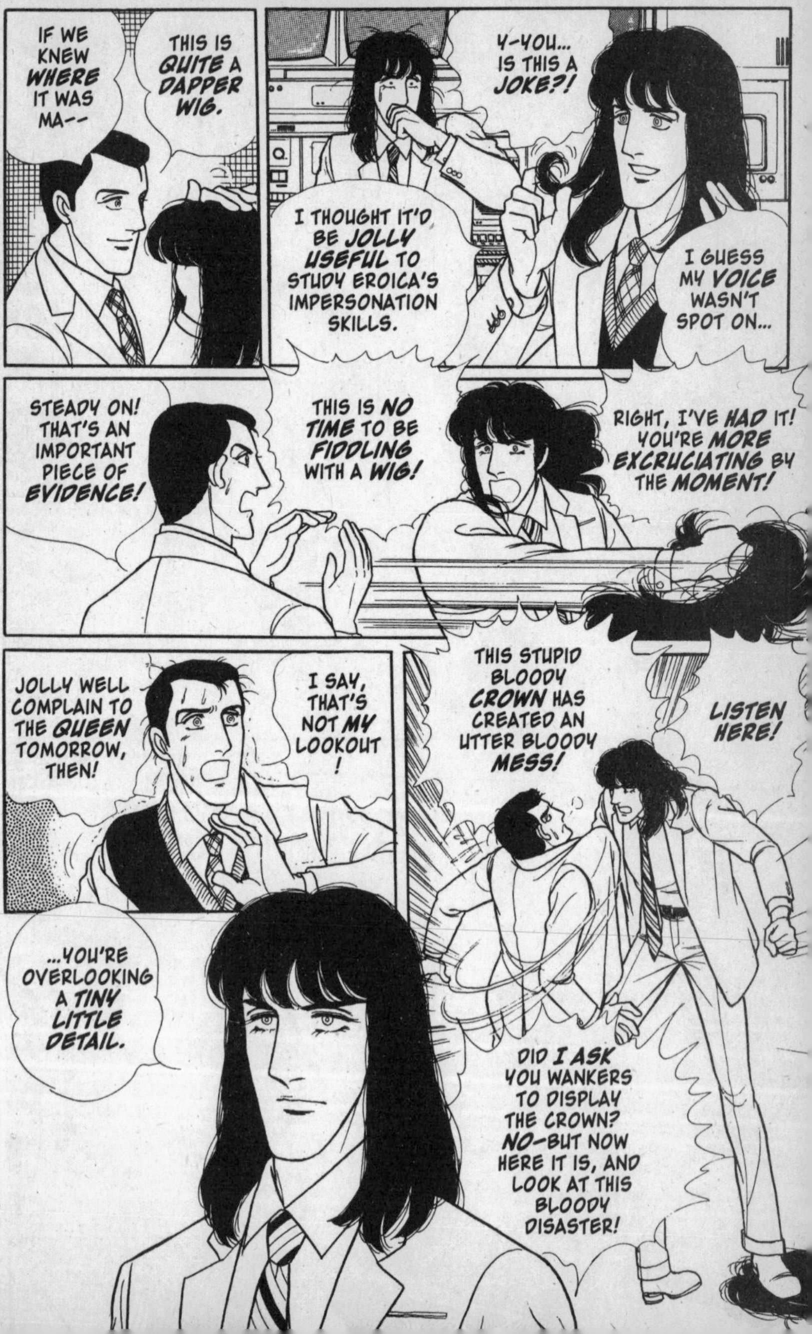
Y-YOU... IS THIS A JOKE?!
I GUESS MY VOICE WASN'T SPOT ON...
I THOUGHT IT'D BE JOLLY USEFUL TO STUDY EROICA'S IMPERSONATION SKILLS.
THIS IS QUITE A DAPPER WIG.
IF WE KNEW WHERE IT WAS MA--
RIGHT, I'VE HAD IT! YOU'RE MORE EXCRUCIATING BY THE MOMENT!
THIS IS NO TIME TO BE FIDDLING WITH A WIG!
STEADY ON! THAT'S AN IMPORTANT PIECE OF EVIDENCE!
LISTEN HERE!
THIS STUPID BLOODY CROWN HAS CREATED AN UTTER BLOODY MESS!
DID I ASK YOU WANKERS TO DISPLAY THE CROWN? NO--BUT NOW HERE IT IS, AND LOOK AT THIS BLOODY DISASTER!
I SAY, THAT'S NOT MY LOOKOUT!
JOLLY WELL COMPLAIN TO THE QUEEN TOMORROW, THEN!
...YOU'RE OVERLOOKING A TINY LITTLE DETAIL.

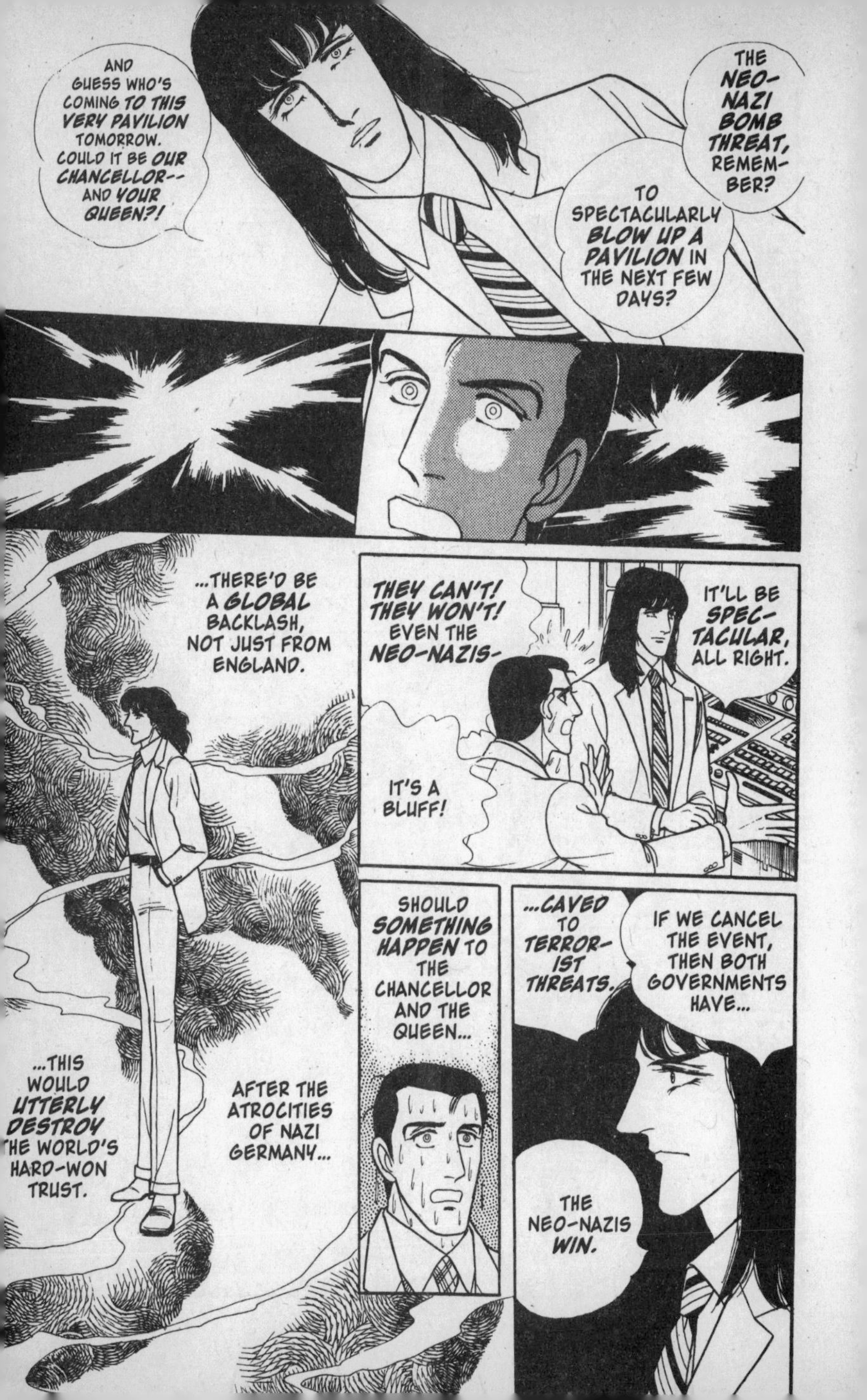
THE NEO-NAZI BOMB THREAT, REMEMBER?
TO SPECTACULARLY BLOW UP A PAVILION IN THE NEXT FEW DAYS?
AND GUESS WHO'S COMING TO THIS VERY PAVILION TOMORROW. COULD IT BE OUR CHANCELLOR--AND YOUR QUEEN?!
IT'LL BE SPECTACULAR, ALL RIGHT.
THEY CAN'T! THEY WON'T! EVEN THE NEO-NAZIS-
IT'S A BLUFF!
IF WE CANCEL THE EVENT, THEN BOTH GOVERNMENTS HAVE...
...CAVED TO TERRORIST THREATS.
THE NEO-NAZIS WIN.
SHOULD SOMETHING HAPPEN TO THE CHANCELLOR AND THE QUEEN...
AFTER THE ATROCITIES OF NAZI GERMANY...
...THIS WOULD UTTERLY DESTROY THE WORLD'S HARD-WON TRUST.
...THERE'D BE A GLOBAL BACKLASH, NOT JUST FROM ENGLAND.

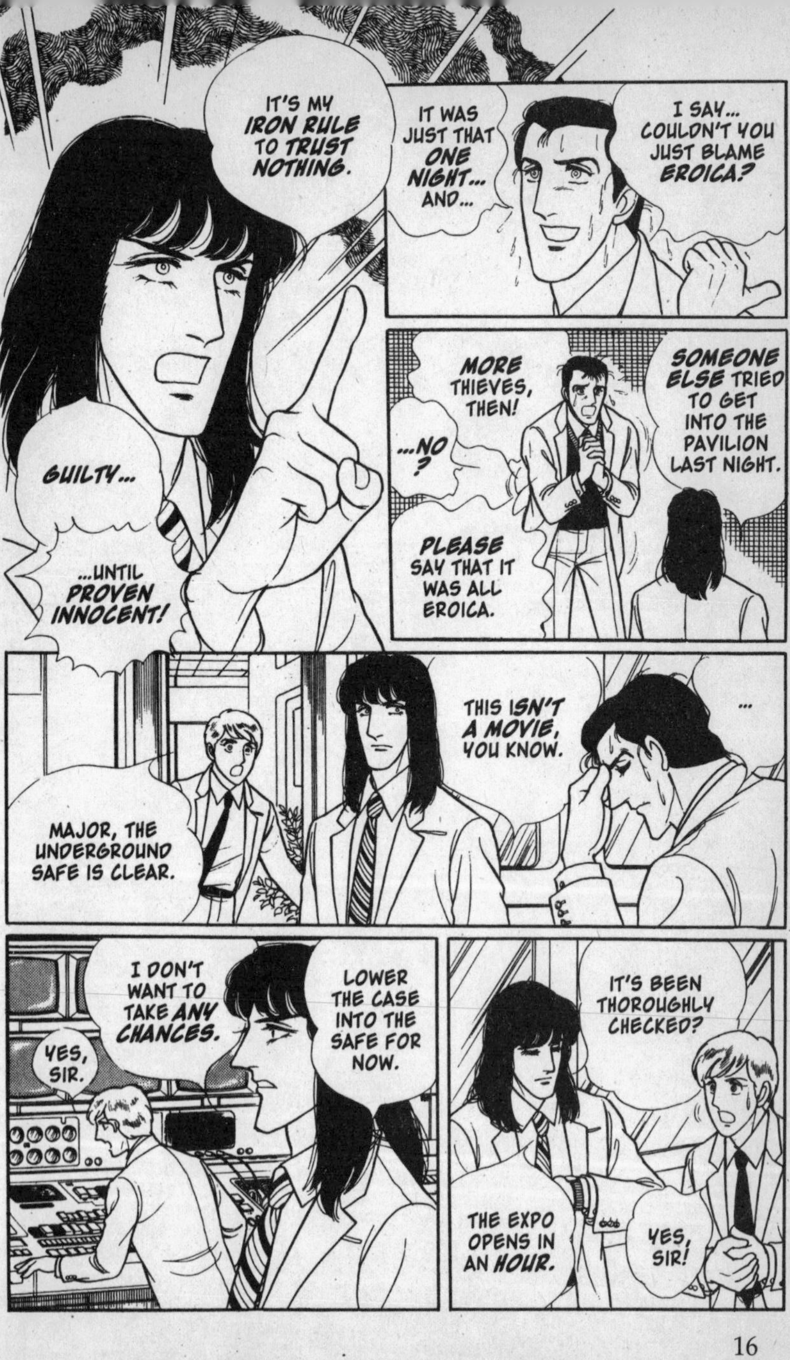
I SAY... COULDN'T YOU JUST BLAME EROICA?
IT WAS JUST THAT ONE NIGHT... AND...
SOMEONE ELSE TRIED TO GET INTO THE PAVILION LAST NIGHT.
MORE THIEVES, THEN!
...NO?
PLEASE SAY THAT IT WAS ALL EROICA.
IT'S MY IRON RULE TO TRUST NOTHING.
GUILTY...
...UNTIL PROVEN INNOCENT!
...
THIS ISN'T A MOVIE, YOU KNOW.
MAJOR, THE UNDERGROUND SAFE IS CLEAR.
IT'S BEEN THOROUGHLY CHECKED?
YES, SIR!
THE EXPO OPENS IN AN HOUR.
LOWER THE CASE INTO THE SAFE FOR NOW.
I DON'T WANT TO TAKE ANY CHANCES.
YES, SIR.

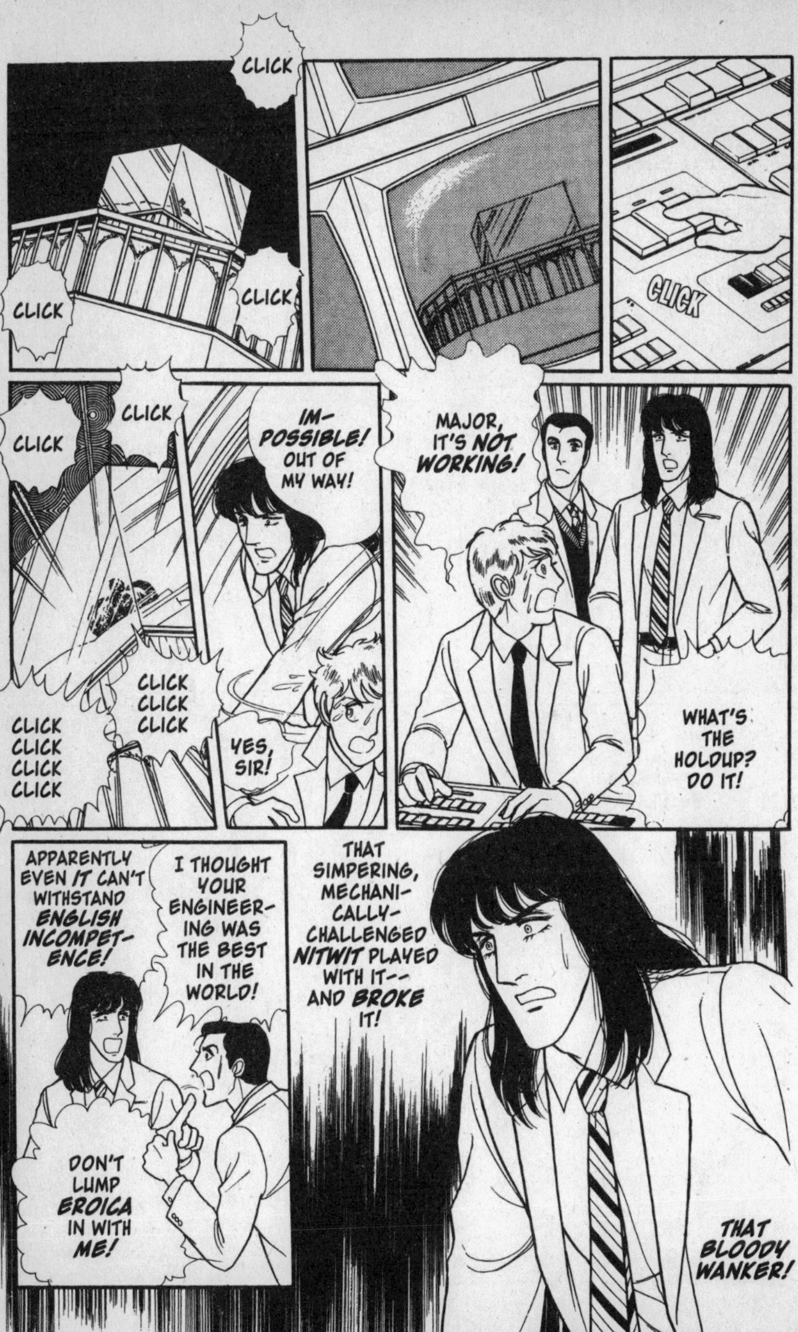
CLICK
CLICK
CLICK
CLICK
MAJOR, IT'S NOT WORKING!
WHAT'S THE HOLDUP? DO IT!
IM-POSSIBLE! OUT OF MY WAY!
CLICK
CLICK
CLICK CLICK CLICK
YES, SIR!
CLICK CLICK CLICK CLICK
THAT SIMPERING, MECHANI-CALLY-CHALLENGED NITWIT PLAYED WITH IT-- AND BROKE IT!
THAT BLOODY WANKER!
I THOUGHT YOUR ENGINEER-ING WAS THE BEST IN THE WORLD!
APPARENTLY EVEN IT CAN'T WITHSTAND ENGLISH INCOMPET-ENCE!
DON'T LUMP EROICA IN WITH ME!

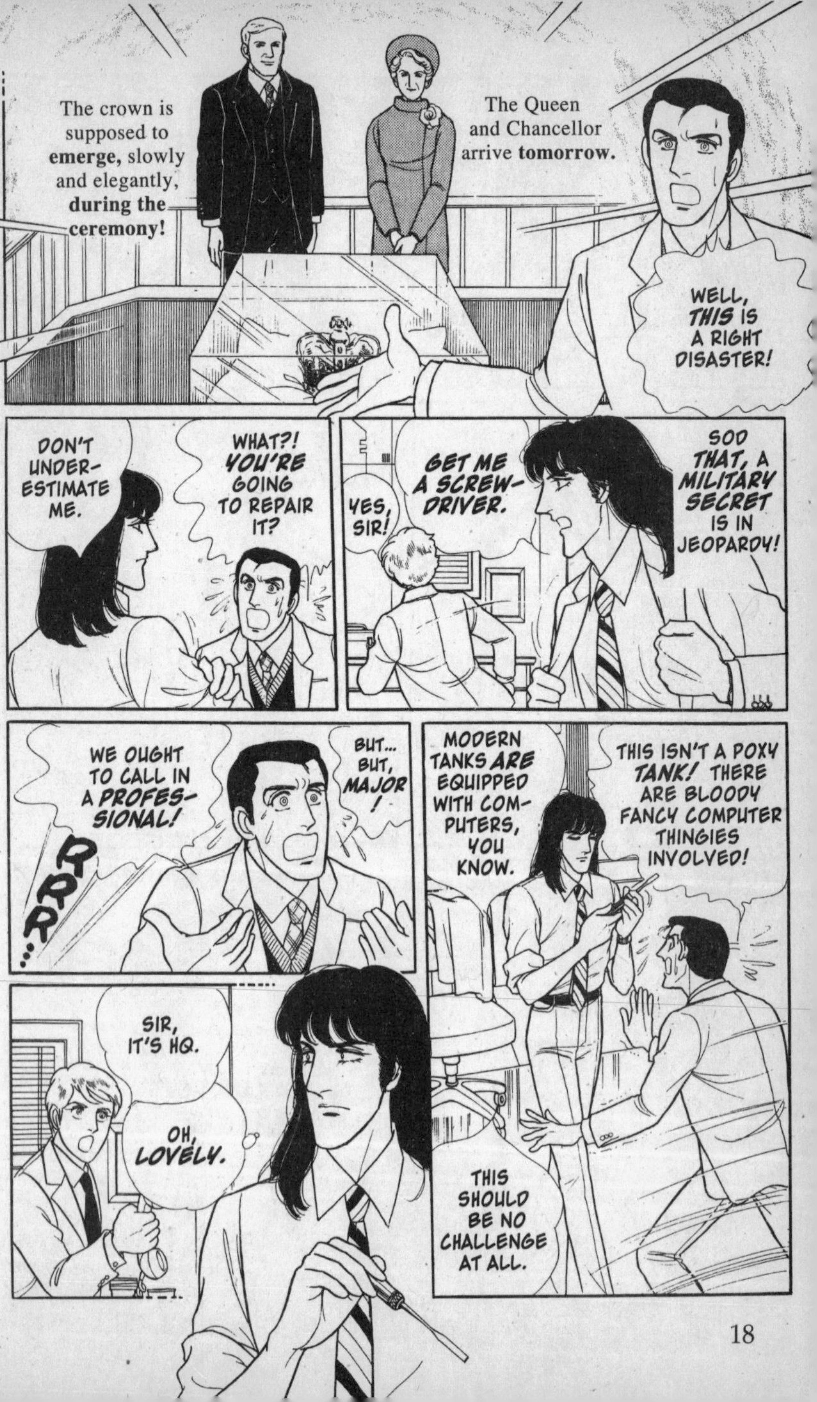
The Queen and Chancellor arrive **tomorrow.**
The crown is supposed to **emerge,** slowly and elegantly, **during the ceremony!**
WELL, *THIS* IS A RIGHT DISASTER!
SOD *THAT,* A *MILITARY SECRET* IS IN JEOPARDY!
GET ME A SCREW-DRIVER.
YES, SIR!
WHAT?! *YOU'RE* GOING TO REPAIR IT?
DON'T UNDER-ESTIMATE ME.
THIS ISN'T A POXY *TANK!* THERE ARE BLOODY FANCY COMPUTER THINGIES INVOLVED!
MODERN TANKS *ARE* EQUIPPED WITH COM-PUTERS, YOU KNOW.
THIS SHOULD BE NO CHALLENGE AT ALL.
BUT... BUT, *MAJOR* !
WE OUGHT TO CALL IN A *PROFES-SIONAL!*
RRR...
SIR, IT'S HQ.
OH, *LOVELY.*

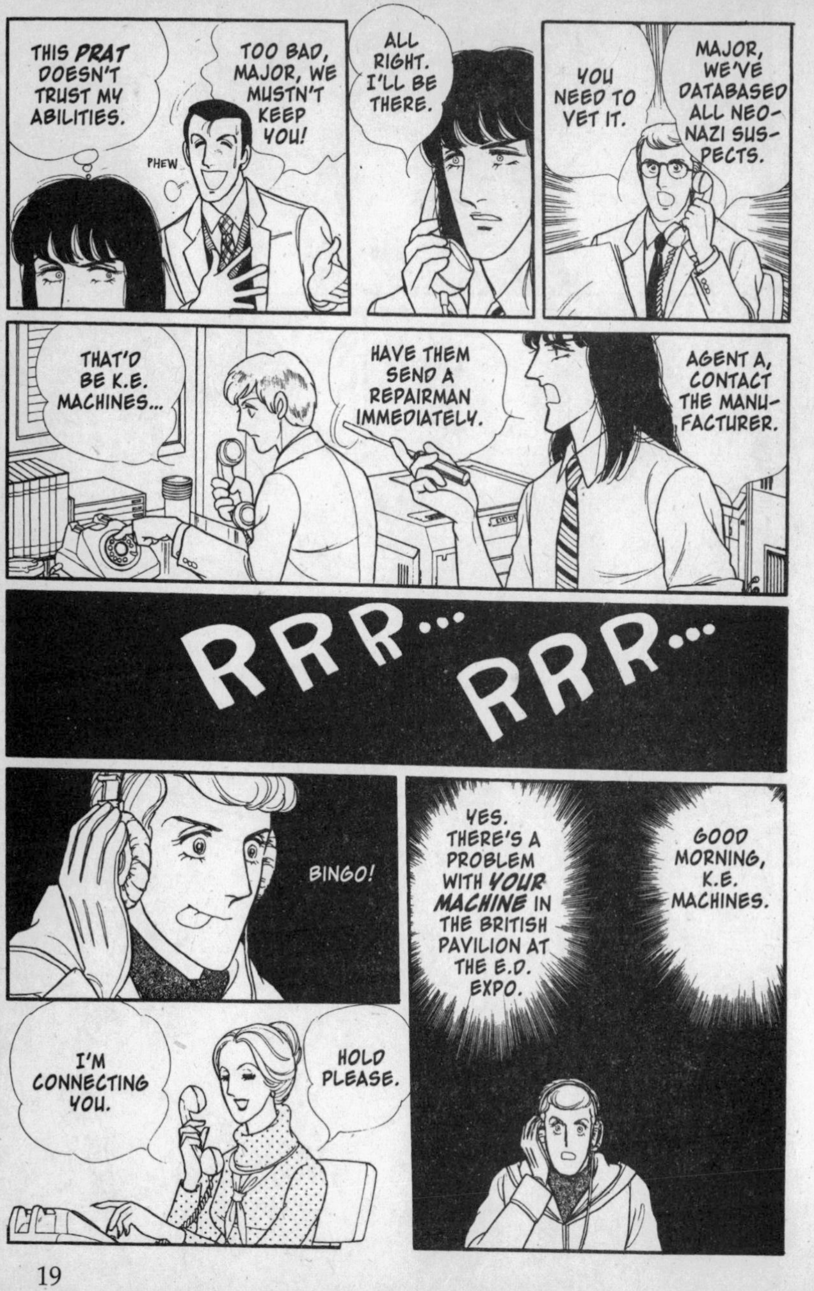
MAJOR, WE'VE DATABASED ALL NEO-NAZI SUSPECTS.
YOU NEED TO VET IT.
ALL RIGHT. I'LL BE THERE.
TOO BAD, MAJOR, WE MUSTN'T KEEP YOU!
PHEW
THIS *PRAT* DOESN'T TRUST MY ABILITIES.
AGENT A, CONTACT THE MANU-FACTURER.
HAVE THEM SEND A REPAIRMAN IMMEDIATELY.
THAT'D BE K.E. MACHINES...
RRR...
RRR...
GOOD MORNING, K.E. MACHINES.
YES. THERE'S A PROBLEM WITH *YOUR MACHINE* IN THE BRITISH PAVILION AT THE E.D. EXPO.
BINGO!
HOLD PLEASE.
I'M CONNECTING YOU.

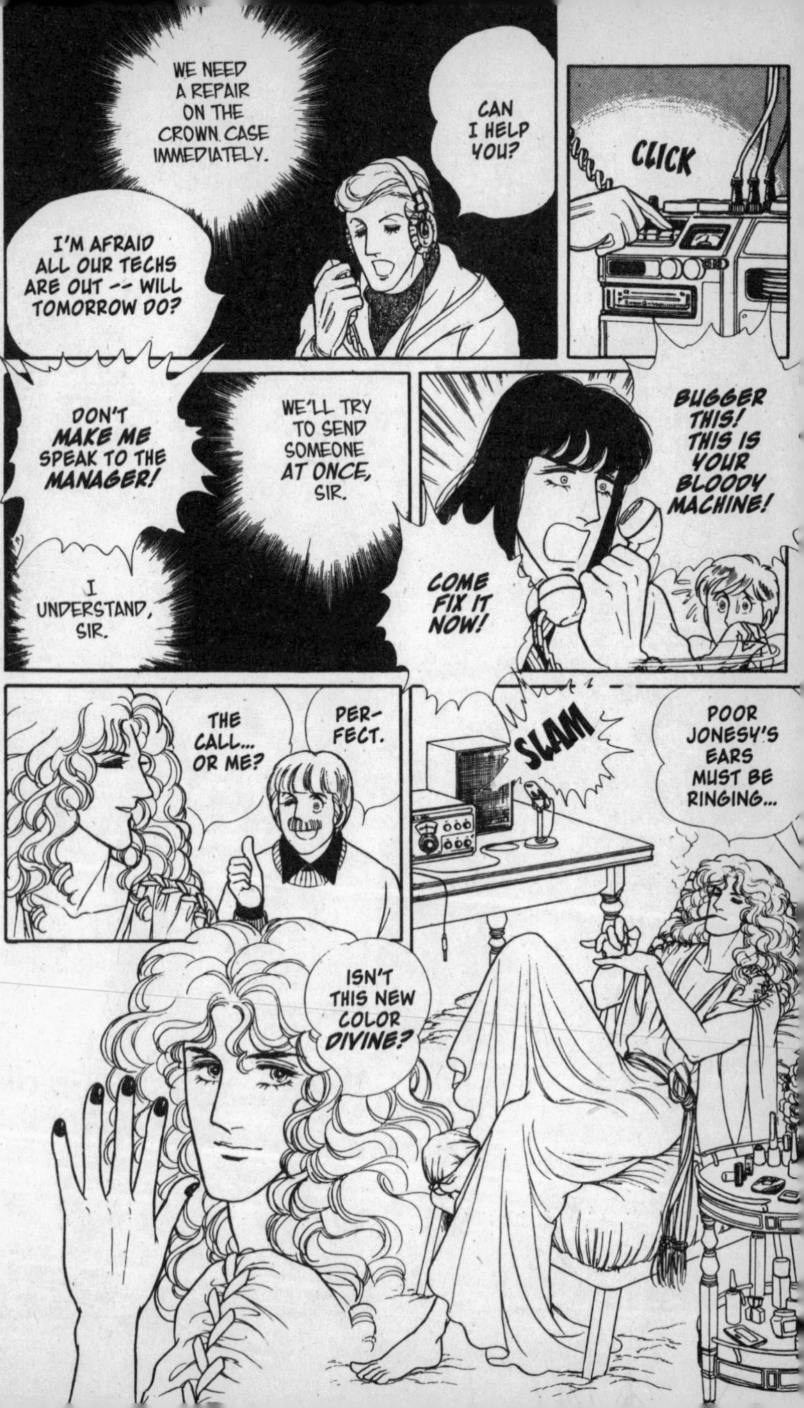
CLICK
CAN I HELP YOU?
WE NEED A REPAIR ON THE CROWN CASE IMMEDIATELY.
I'M AFRAID ALL OUR TECHS ARE OUT -- WILL TOMORROW DO?
BUGGER THIS! THIS IS YOUR BLOODY MACHINE!
COME FIX IT NOW!
WE'LL TRY TO SEND SOMEONE AT ONCE, SIR.
DON'T MAKE ME SPEAK TO THE MANAGER!
I UNDERSTAND, SIR.
SLAM
POOR JONESY'S EARS MUST BE RINGING...
PER-FECT.
THE CALL... OR ME?
ISN'T THIS NEW COLOR DIVINE?

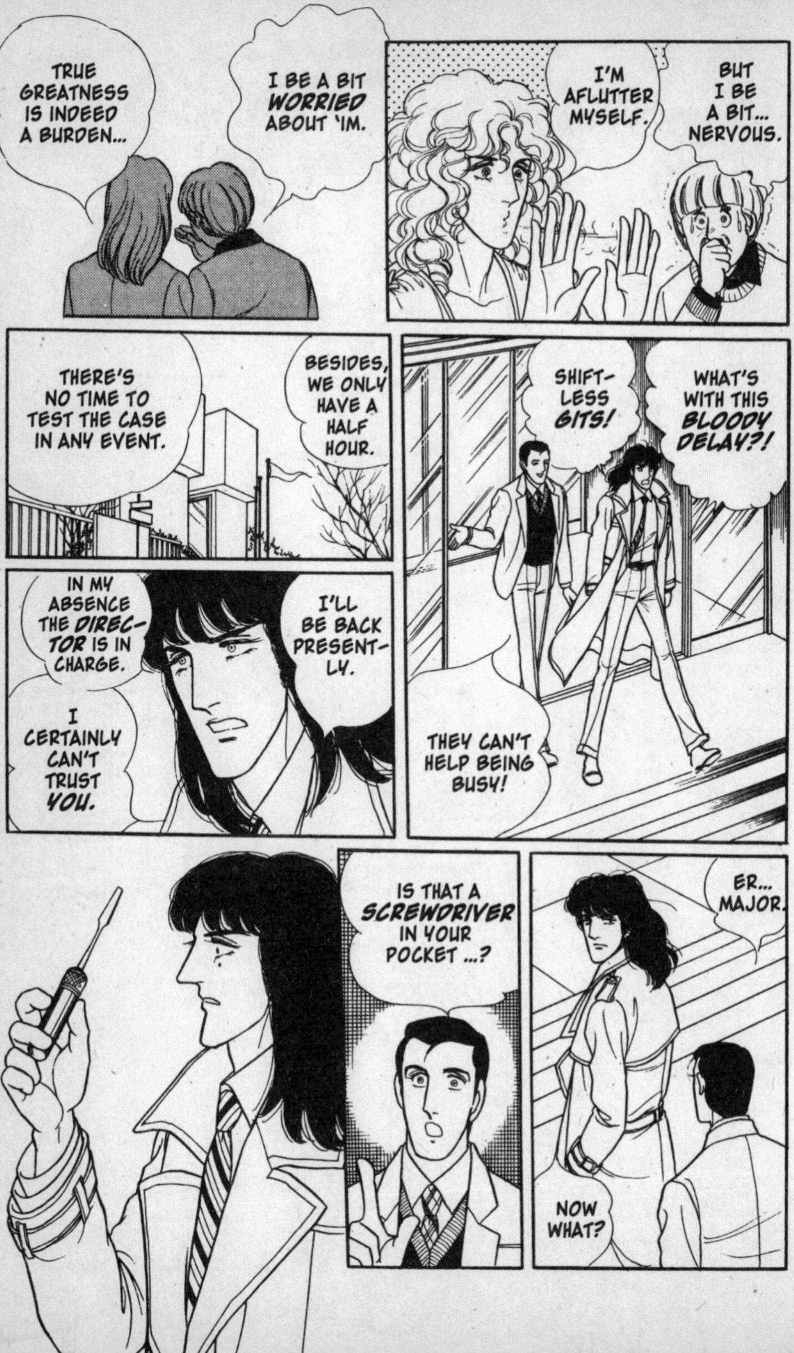
BUT I BE A BIT... NERVOUS.
I'M AFLUTTER MYSELF.
I BE A BIT WORRIED ABOUT 'IM.
TRUE GREATNESS IS INDEED A BURDEN...
WHAT'S WITH THIS BLOODY DELAY?!
SHIFT-LESS GITS!
THEY CAN'T HELP BEING BUSY!
BESIDES, WE ONLY HAVE A HALF HOUR.
THERE'S NO TIME TO TEST THE CASE IN ANY EVENT.
I'LL BE BACK PRESENT-LY.
IN MY ABSENCE THE DIREC-TOR IS IN CHARGE.
I CERTAINLY CAN'T TRUST YOU.
ER... MAJOR.
NOW WHAT?
IS THAT A SCREWDRIVER IN YOUR POCKET ...?

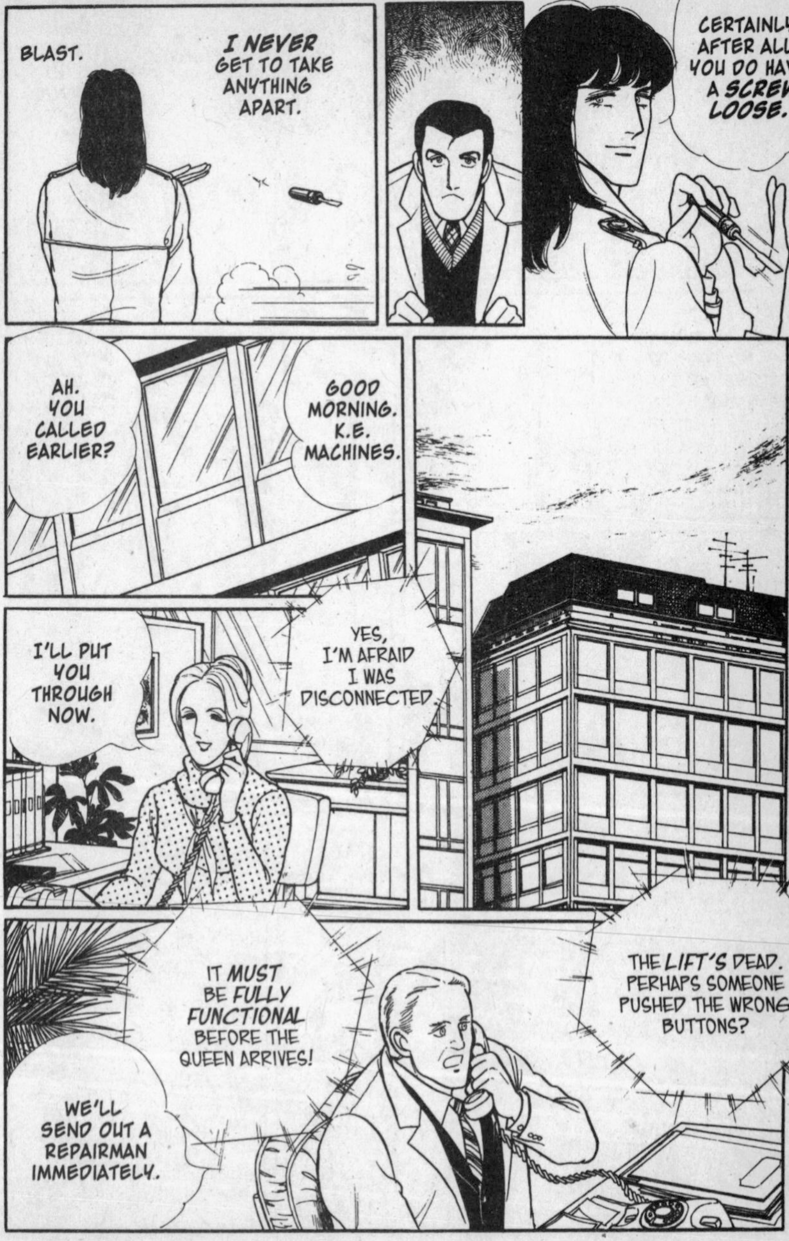
CERTAINLY. AFTER ALL, YOU DO HAVE A *SCREW LOOSE.*
I NEVER GET TO TAKE ANYTHING APART.
BLAST.
GOOD MORNING. K.E. MACHINES.
AH. YOU CALLED EARLIER?
YES, I'M AFRAID I WAS DISCONNECTED.
I'LL PUT YOU THROUGH NOW.
THE *LIFT'S* DEAD. PERHAPS SOMEONE PUSHED THE WRONG BUTTONS?
IT *MUST* BE *FULLY FUNCTIONAL* BEFORE THE QUEEN ARRIVES!
WE'LL SEND OUT A REPAIRMAN IMMEDIATELY.

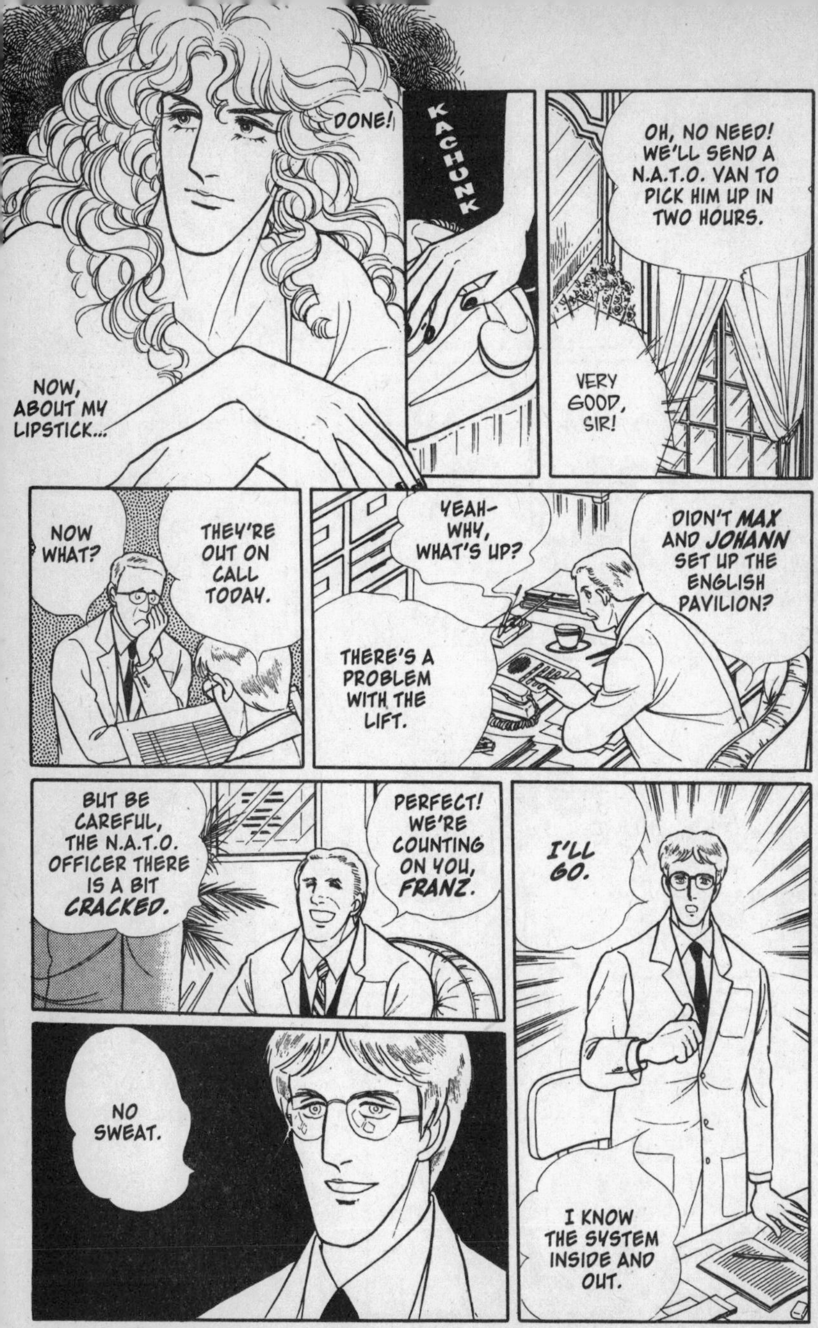
OH, NO NEED! WE'LL SEND A N.A.T.O. VAN TO PICK HIM UP IN TWO HOURS.
VERY GOOD, SIR!
KACHUNK
DONE!
NOW, ABOUT MY LIPSTICK...
DIDN'T MAX AND JOHANN SET UP THE ENGLISH PAVILION?
YEAH- WHY, WHAT'S UP?
THERE'S A PROBLEM WITH THE LIFT.
THEY'RE OUT ON CALL TODAY.
NOW WHAT?
I'LL GO.
I KNOW THE SYSTEM INSIDE AND OUT.
PERFECT! WE'RE COUNTING ON YOU, FRANZ.
BUT BE CAREFUL, THE N.A.T.O. OFFICER THERE IS A BIT CRACKED.
NO SWEAT.

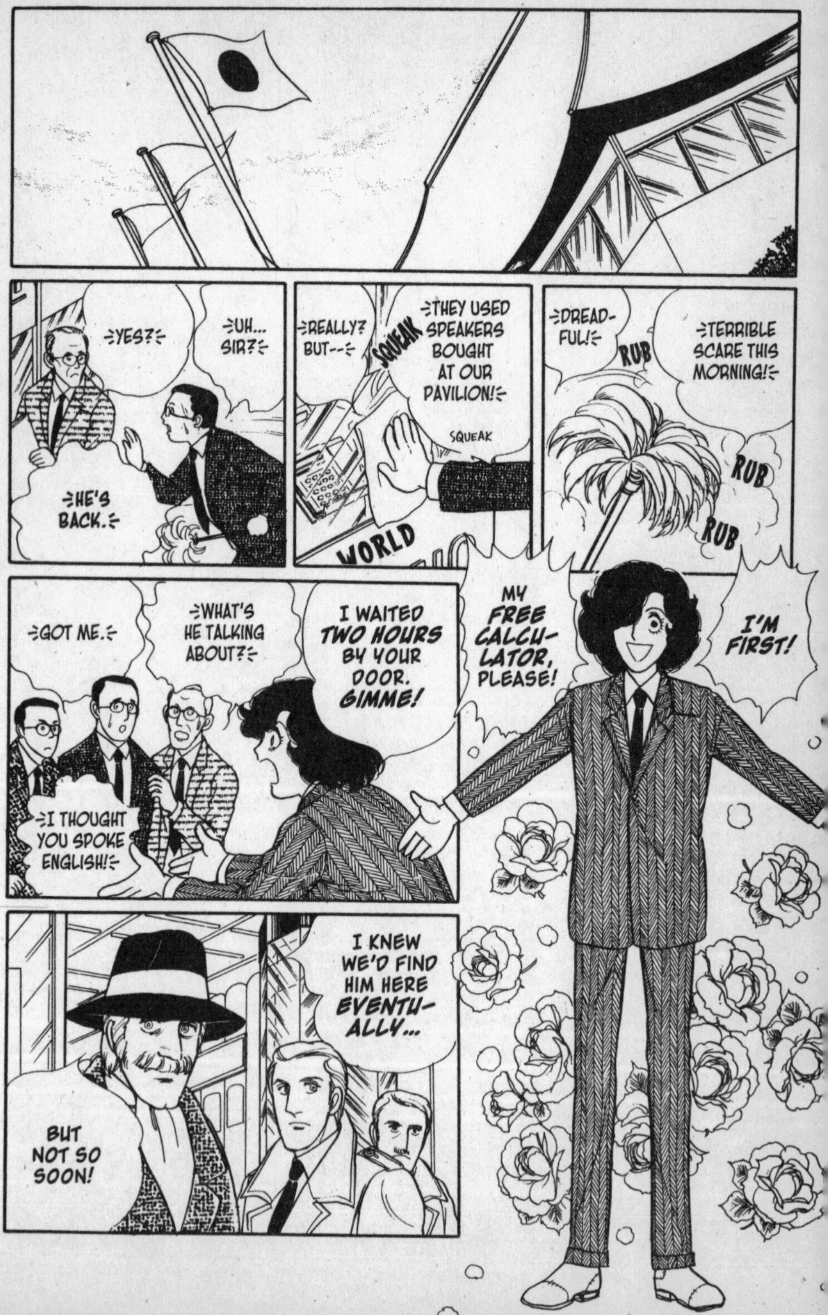
TERRIBLE SCARE THIS MORNING!
DREAD-FUL!
RUB
RUB
RUB
THEY USED SPEAKERS BOUGHT AT OUR PAVILION!
REALLY? BUT--
SQUEAK
SQUEAK
WORLD
UH... SIR?
YES?
HE'S BACK.
I'M FIRST!
MY FREE CALCULATOR, PLEASE!
I WAITED TWO HOURS BY YOUR DOOR. GIMME!
WHAT'S HE TALKING ABOUT?
GOT ME.
I THOUGHT YOU SPOKE ENGLISH!
I KNEW WE'D FIND HIM HERE EVENTUALLY...
BUT NOT SO SOON!

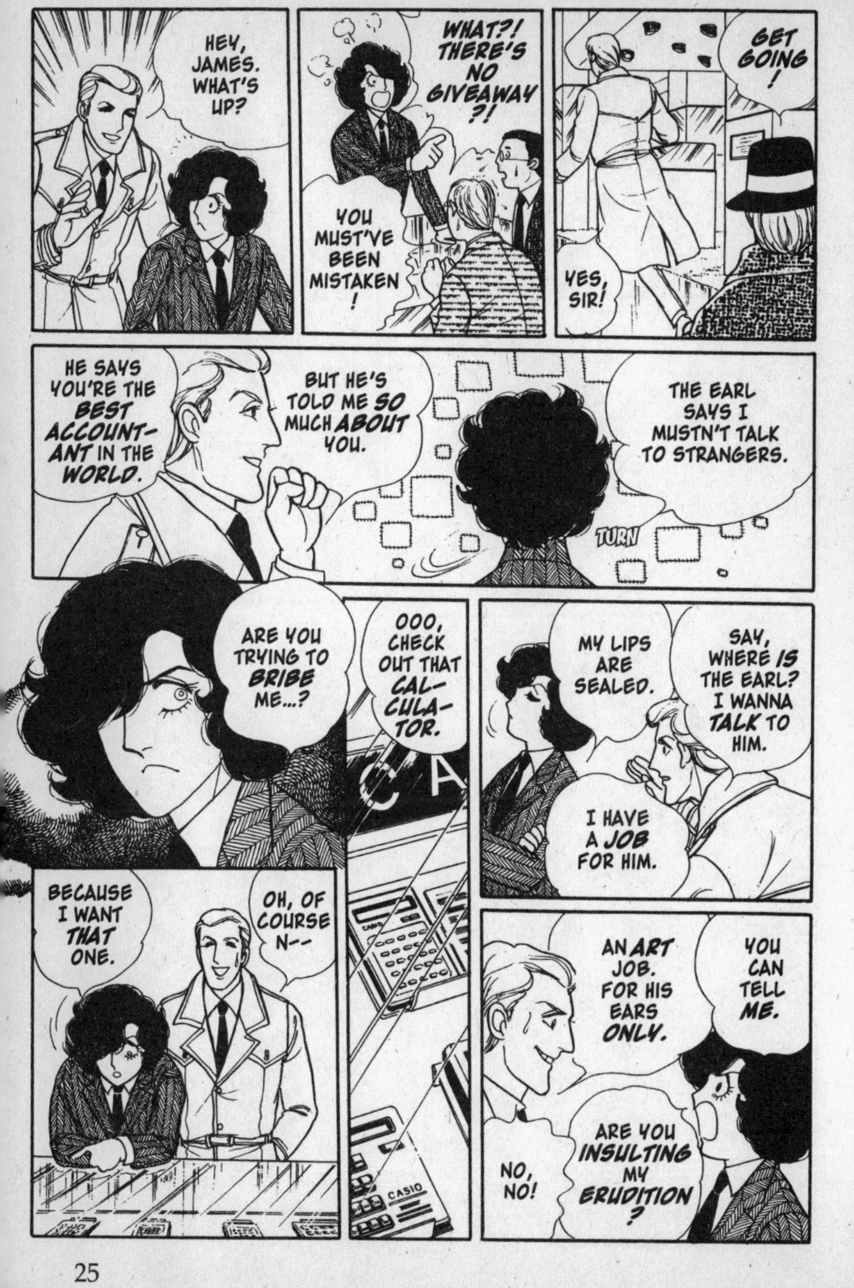
GET GOING!
YES, SIR!
WHAT?! THERE'S NO GIVEAWAY?!
YOU MUST'VE BEEN MISTAKEN!
HEY, JAMES. WHAT'S UP?
THE EARL SAYS I MUSTN'T TALK TO STRANGERS.
TURN
BUT HE'S TOLD ME SO MUCH ABOUT YOU.
HE SAYS YOU'RE THE BEST ACCOUNTANT IN THE WORLD.
SAY, WHERE IS THE EARL? I WANNA TALK TO HIM.
MY LIPS ARE SEALED.
I HAVE A JOB FOR HIM.
YOU CAN TELL ME.
AN ART JOB. FOR HIS EARS ONLY.
ARE YOU INSULTING MY ERUDITION?
NO, NO!
OOO, CHECK OUT THAT CALCULATOR.
CASIO
ARE YOU TRYING TO BRIBE ME...?
OH, OF COURSE N--
BECAUSE I WANT THAT ONE.

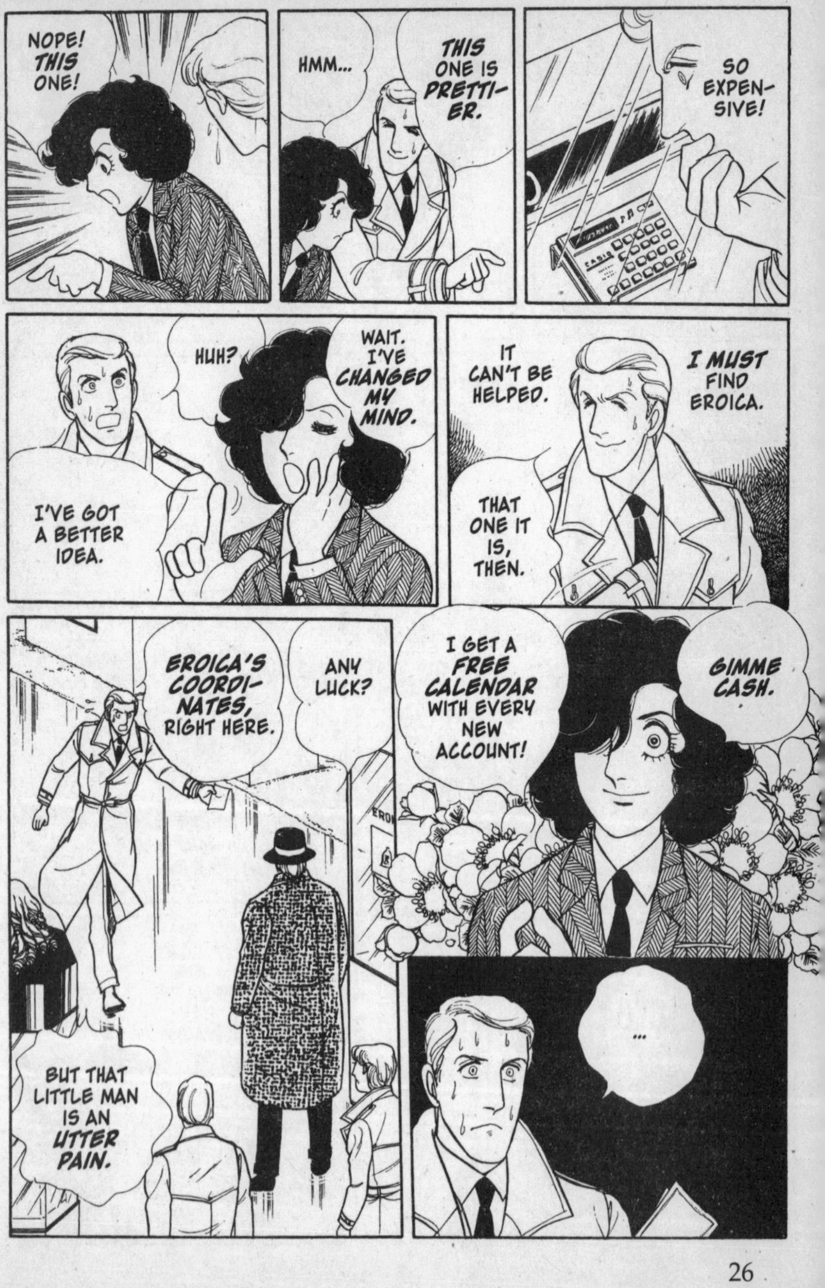
SO EXPEN-SIVE!
THIS ONE IS PRETTI-ER.
HMM...
NOPE! THIS ONE!
I MUST FIND EROICA.
IT CAN'T BE HELPED.
THAT ONE IT IS, THEN.
WAIT. I'VE CHANGED MY MIND.
HUH?
I'VE GOT A BETTER IDEA.
GIMME CASH.
I GET A FREE CALENDAR WITH EVERY NEW ACCOUNT!
...
ANY LUCK?
EROICA'S COORDI-NATES, RIGHT HERE.
BUT THAT LITTLE MAN IS AN UTTER PAIN.

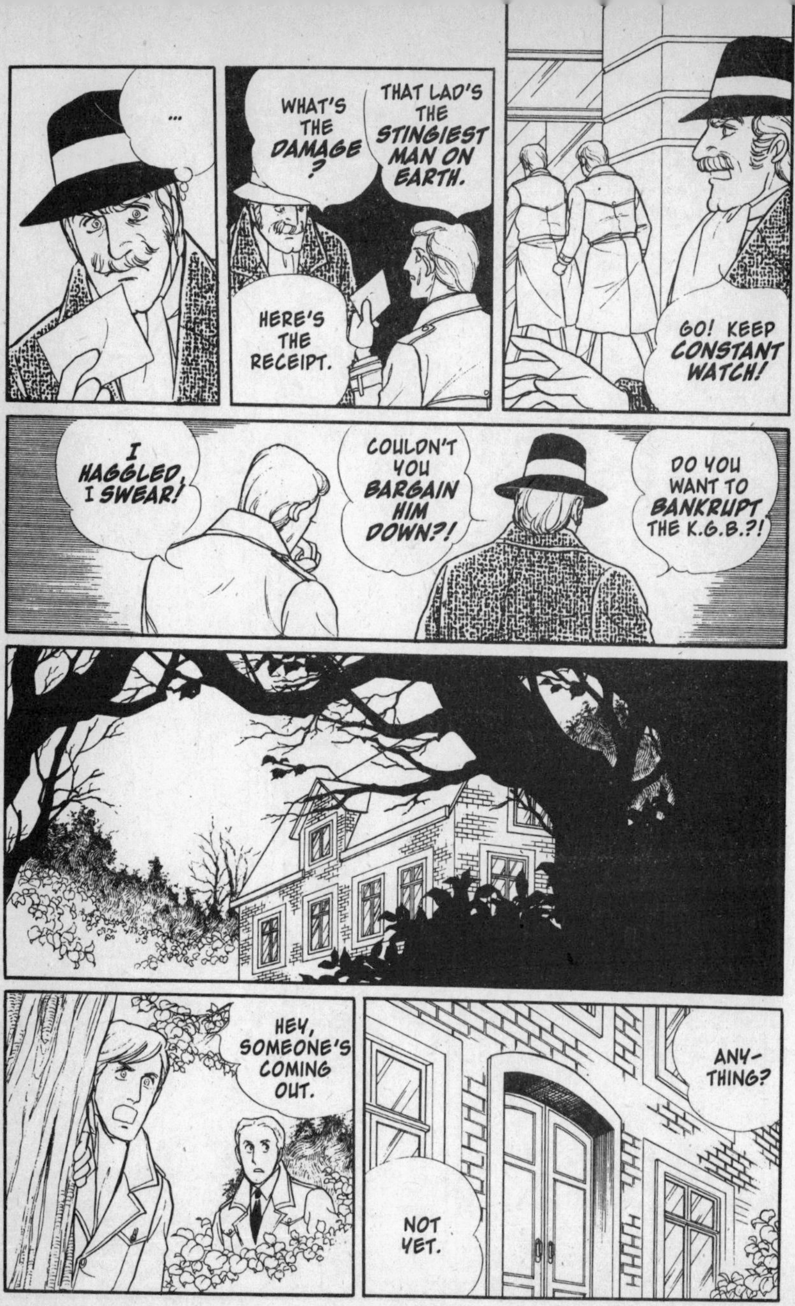
GO! KEEP CONSTANT WATCH!
THAT LAD'S THE STINGIEST MAN ON EARTH.
WHAT'S THE DAMAGE?
HERE'S THE RECEIPT.
...
DO YOU WANT TO BANKRUPT THE K.G.B.?!
COULDN'T YOU BARGAIN HIM DOWN?!
I HAGGLED, I SWEAR!
ANY-THING?
NOT YET.
HEY, SOMEONE'S COMING OUT.

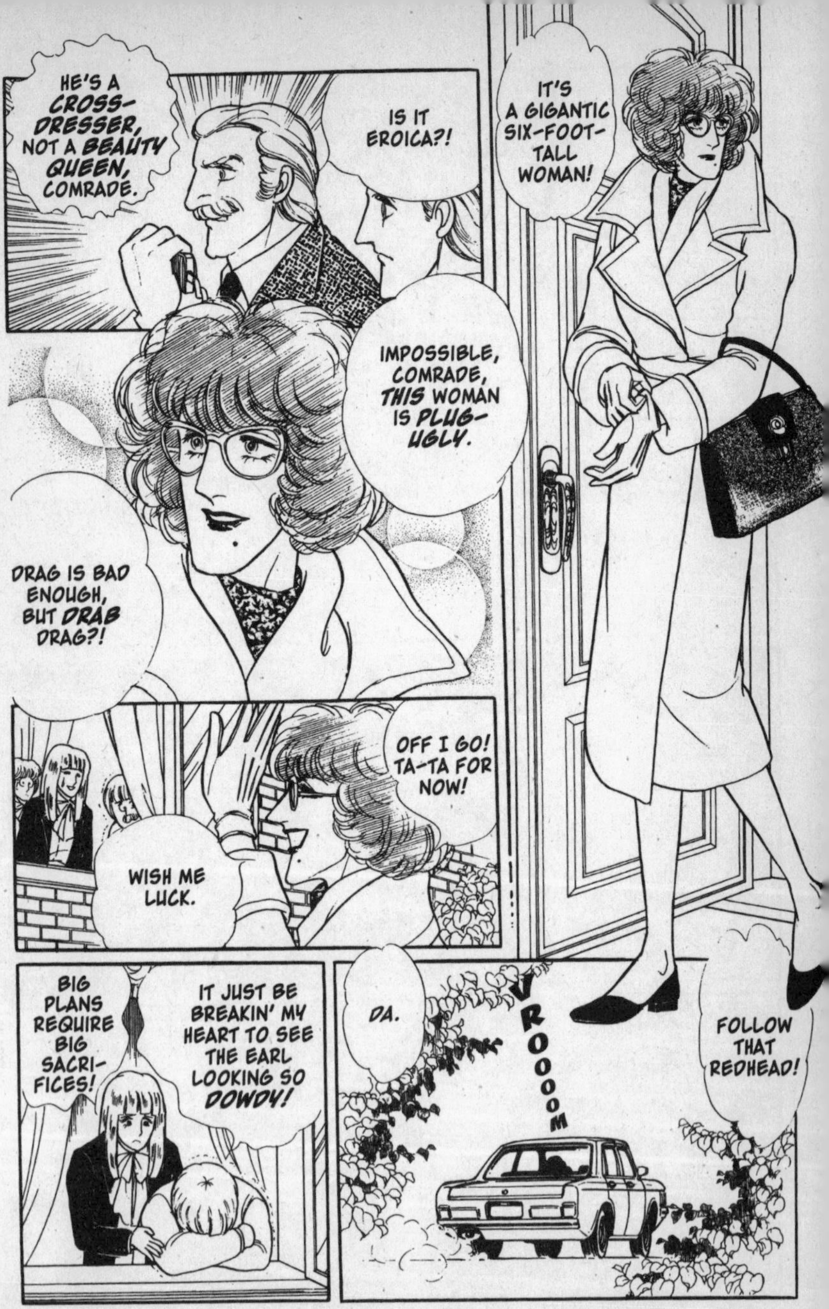
IT'S A GIGANTIC SIX-FOOT-TALL WOMAN!
IS IT EROICA?!
HE'S A CROSS-DRESSER, NOT A BEAUTY QUEEN, COMRADE.
IMPOSSIBLE, COMRADE, THIS WOMAN IS PLUG-UGLY.
DRAG IS BAD ENOUGH, BUT DRAB DRAG?!
OFF I GO! TA-TA FOR NOW!
WISH ME LUCK.
FOLLOW THAT REDHEAD!
DA.
VROOOOM
IT JUST BE BREAKIN' MY HEART TO SEE THE EARL LOOKING SO DOWDY!
BIG PLANS REQUIRE BIG SACRI-FICES!

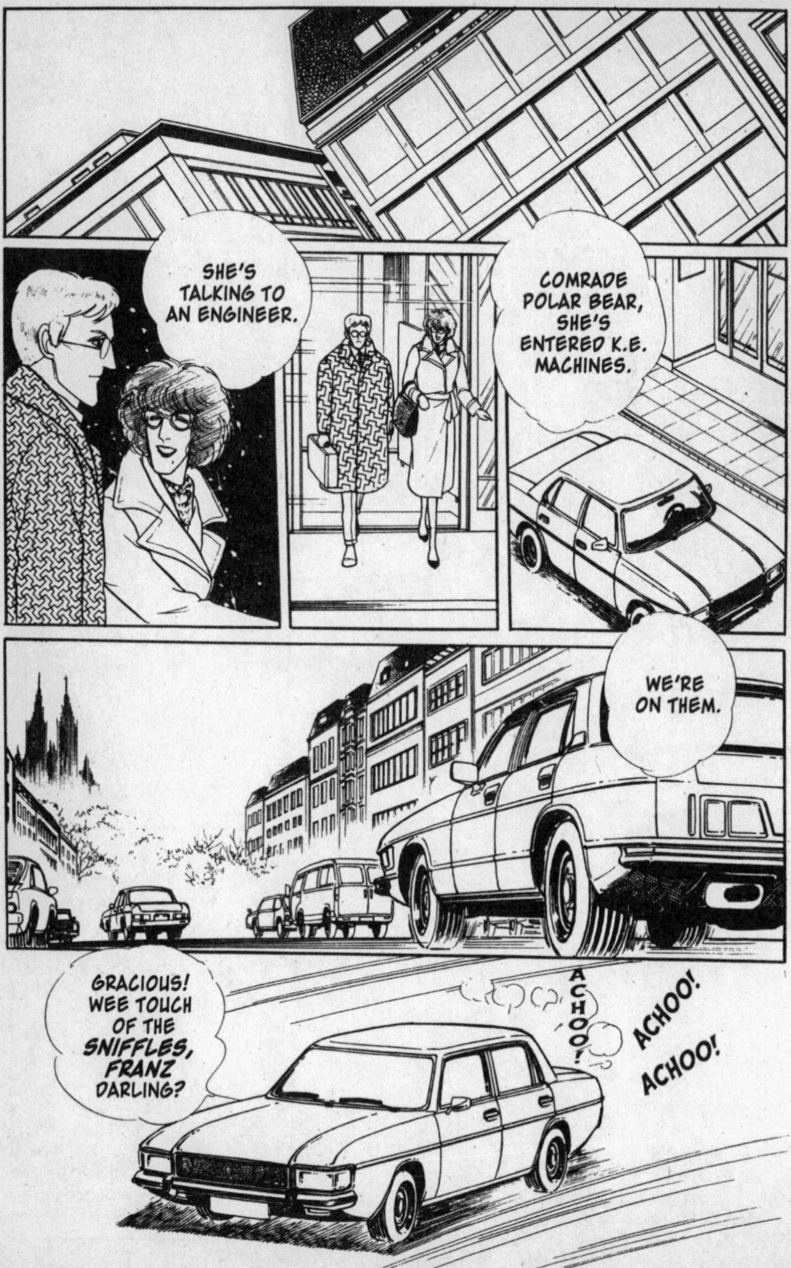
COMRADE POLAR BEAR, SHE'S ENTERED K.E. MACHINES.
SHE'S TALKING TO AN ENGINEER.
WE'RE ON THEM.
ACHOO!
ACHOO!
ACHOO!
GRACIOUS! WEE TOUCH OF THE SNIFFLES, FRANZ DARLING?

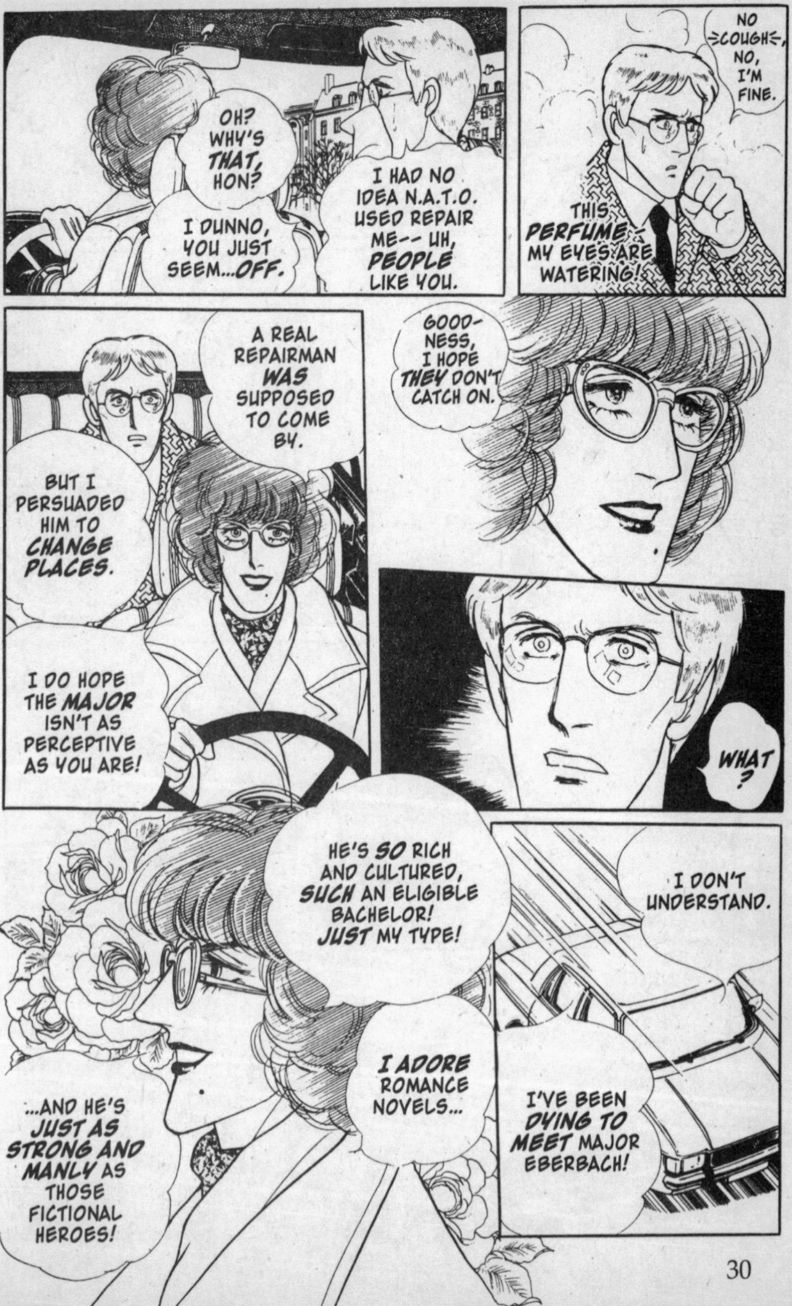
NO =COUGH=, NO, I'M FINE.
THIS PERFUME-- MY EYES ARE WATERING!
I HAD NO IDEA N.A.T.O. USED REPAIR ME-- UH, PEOPLE LIKE YOU.
OH? WHY'S THAT, HON?
I DUNNO, YOU JUST SEEM...OFF.
GOOD-NESS, I HOPE THEY DON'T CATCH ON.
WHAT?
A REAL REPAIRMAN WAS SUPPOSED TO COME BY.
BUT I PERSUADED HIM TO CHANGE PLACES.
I DO HOPE THE MAJOR ISN'T AS PERCEPTIVE AS YOU ARE!
I DON'T UNDERSTAND.
I'VE BEEN DYING TO MEET MAJOR EBERBACH!
HE'S SO RICH AND CULTURED, SUCH AN ELIGIBLE BACHELOR! JUST MY TYPE!
I ADORE ROMANCE NOVELS...
...AND HE'S JUST AS STRONG AND MANLY AS THOSE FICTIONAL HEROES!

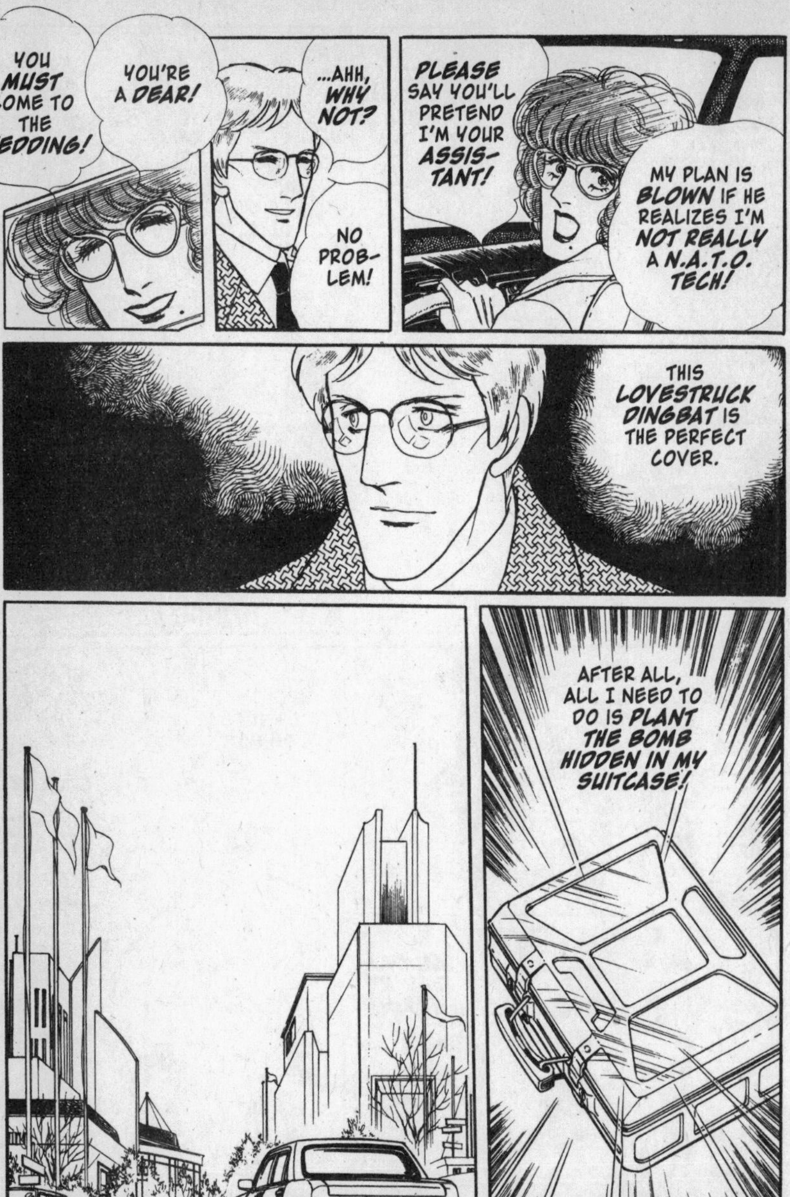
PLEASE SAY YOU'LL PRETEND I'M YOUR ASSISTANT!
MY PLAN IS BLOWN IF HE REALIZES I'M NOT REALLY A N.A.T.O. TECH!
...AHH, WHY NOT?
NO PROBLEM!
YOU'RE A DEAR!
YOU MUST COME TO THE WEDDING!
THIS LOVESTRUCK DINGBAT IS THE PERFECT COVER.
AFTER ALL, ALL I NEED TO DO IS PLANT THE BOMB HIDDEN IN MY SUITCASE!

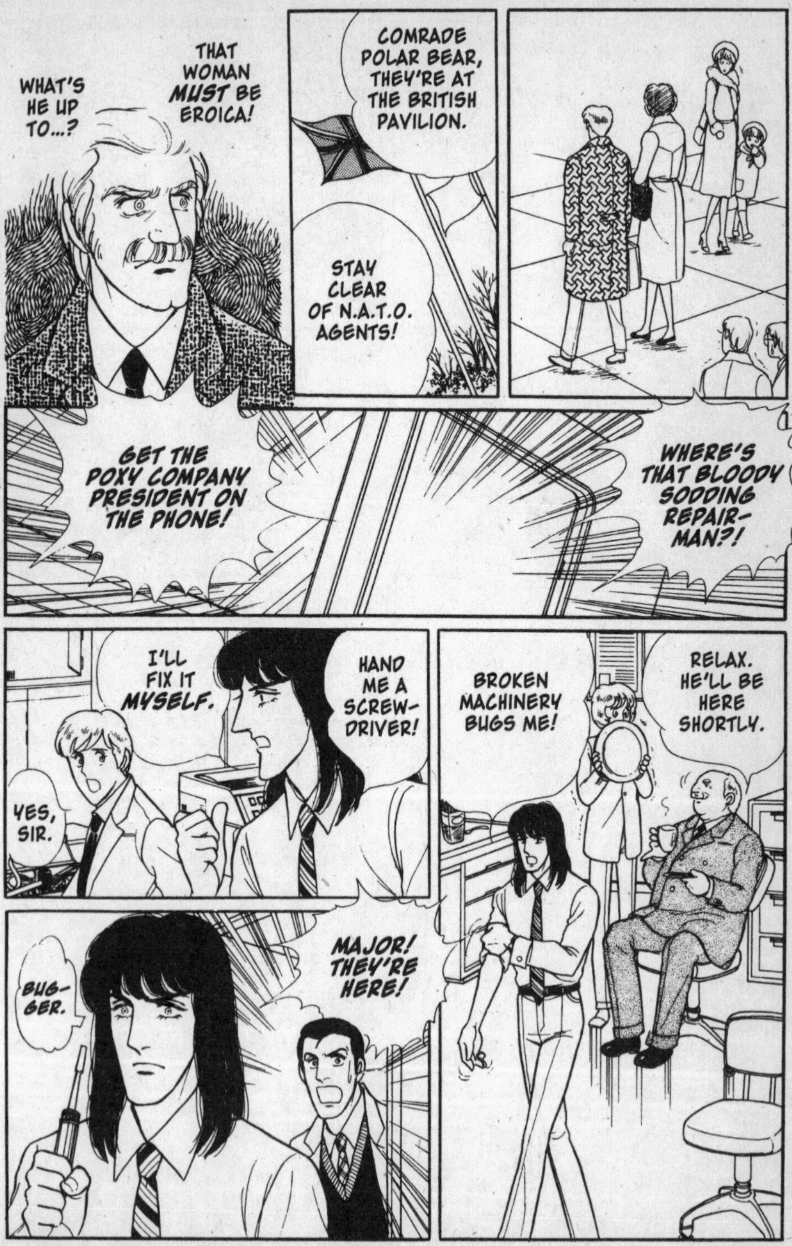
COMRADE POLAR BEAR, THEY'RE AT THE BRITISH PAVILION.
STAY CLEAR OF N.A.T.O. AGENTS!
THAT WOMAN *MUST* BE EROICA!
WHAT'S HE UP TO...?
WHERE'S THAT BLOODY SODDING REPAIR-MAN?!
GET THE POXY COMPANY PRESIDENT ON THE PHONE!
RELAX. HE'LL BE HERE SHORTLY.
BROKEN MACHINERY BUGS ME!
HAND ME A SCREW-DRIVER!
I'LL FIX IT *MYSELF*.
YES, SIR.
MAJOR! THEY'RE HERE!
BUG-GER.

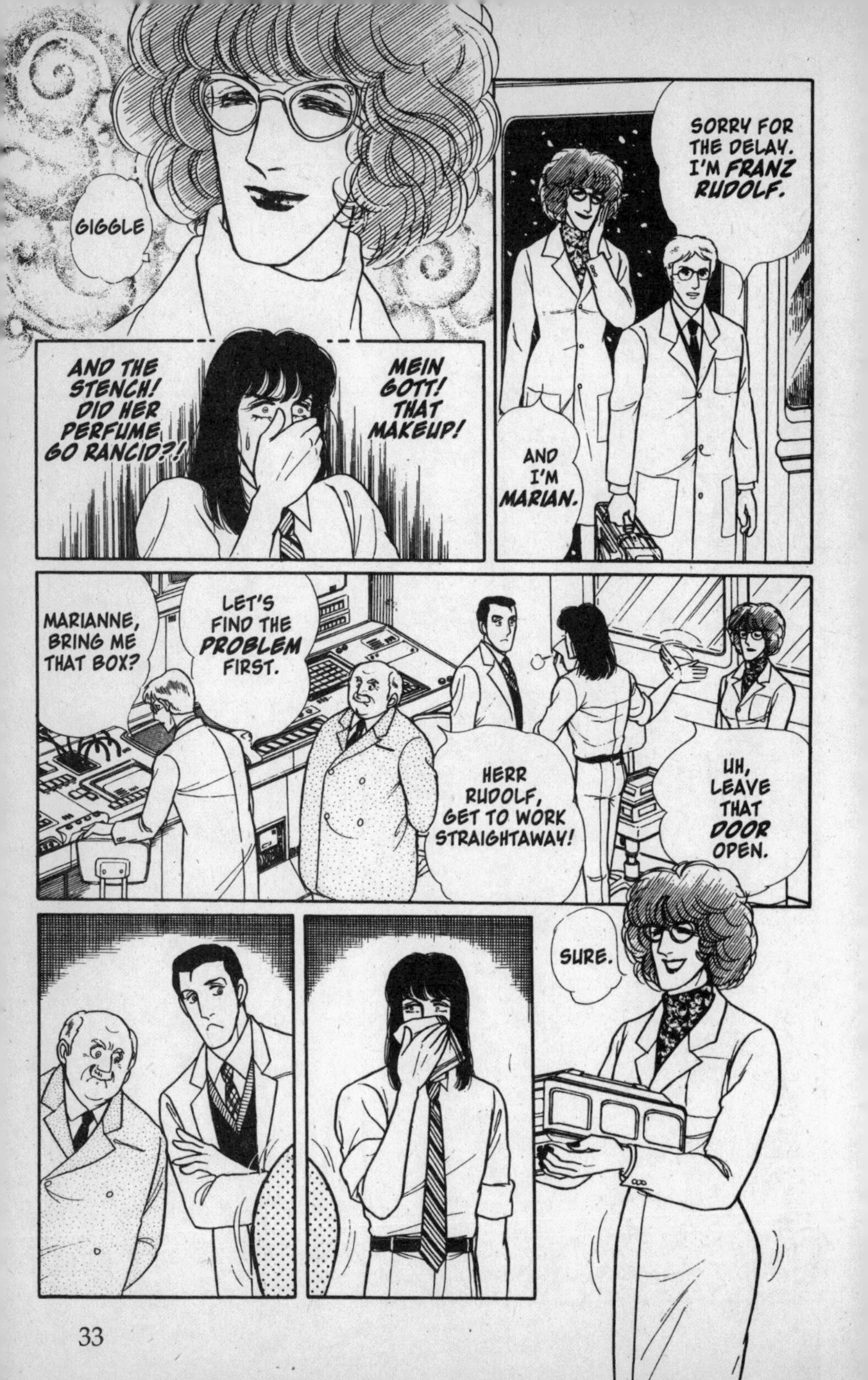
SORRY FOR THE DELAY. I'M FRANZ RUDOLF.
AND I'M MARIAN.
GIGGLE
MEIN GOTT! THAT MAKEUP!
AND THE STENCH! DID HER PERFUME GO RANCID?!
UH, LEAVE THAT DOOR OPEN.
HERR RUDOLF, GET TO WORK STRAIGHTAWAY!
LET'S FIND THE PROBLEM FIRST.
MARIANNE, BRING ME THAT BOX?
SURE.

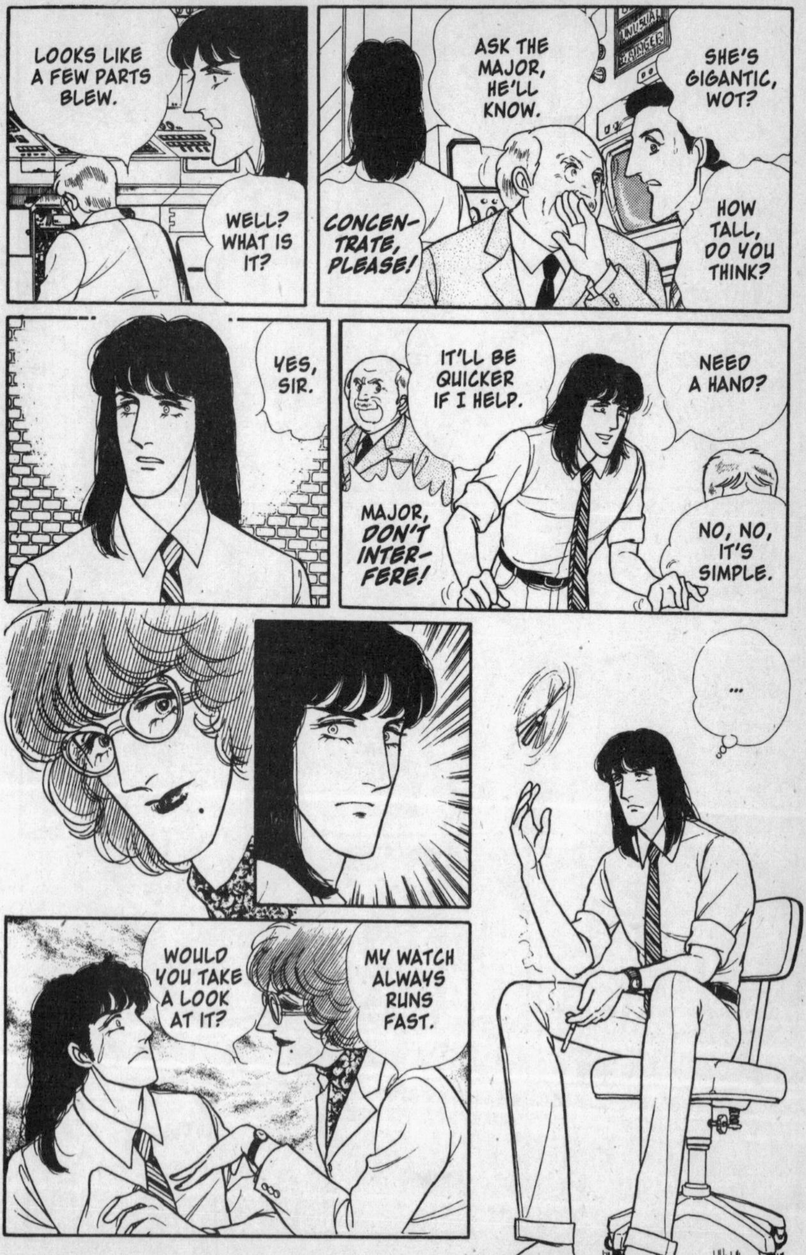
SHE'S GIGANTIC, WOT?
HOW TALL, DO YOU THINK?
ASK THE MAJOR, HE'LL KNOW.
CONCENTRATE, PLEASE!
WELL? WHAT IS IT?
LOOKS LIKE A FEW PARTS BLEW.
NEED A HAND?
NO, NO, IT'S SIMPLE.
IT'LL BE QUICKER IF I HELP.
MAJOR, DON'T INTERFERE!
YES, SIR.
...
MY WATCH ALWAYS RUNS FAST.
WOULD YOU TAKE A LOOK AT IT?

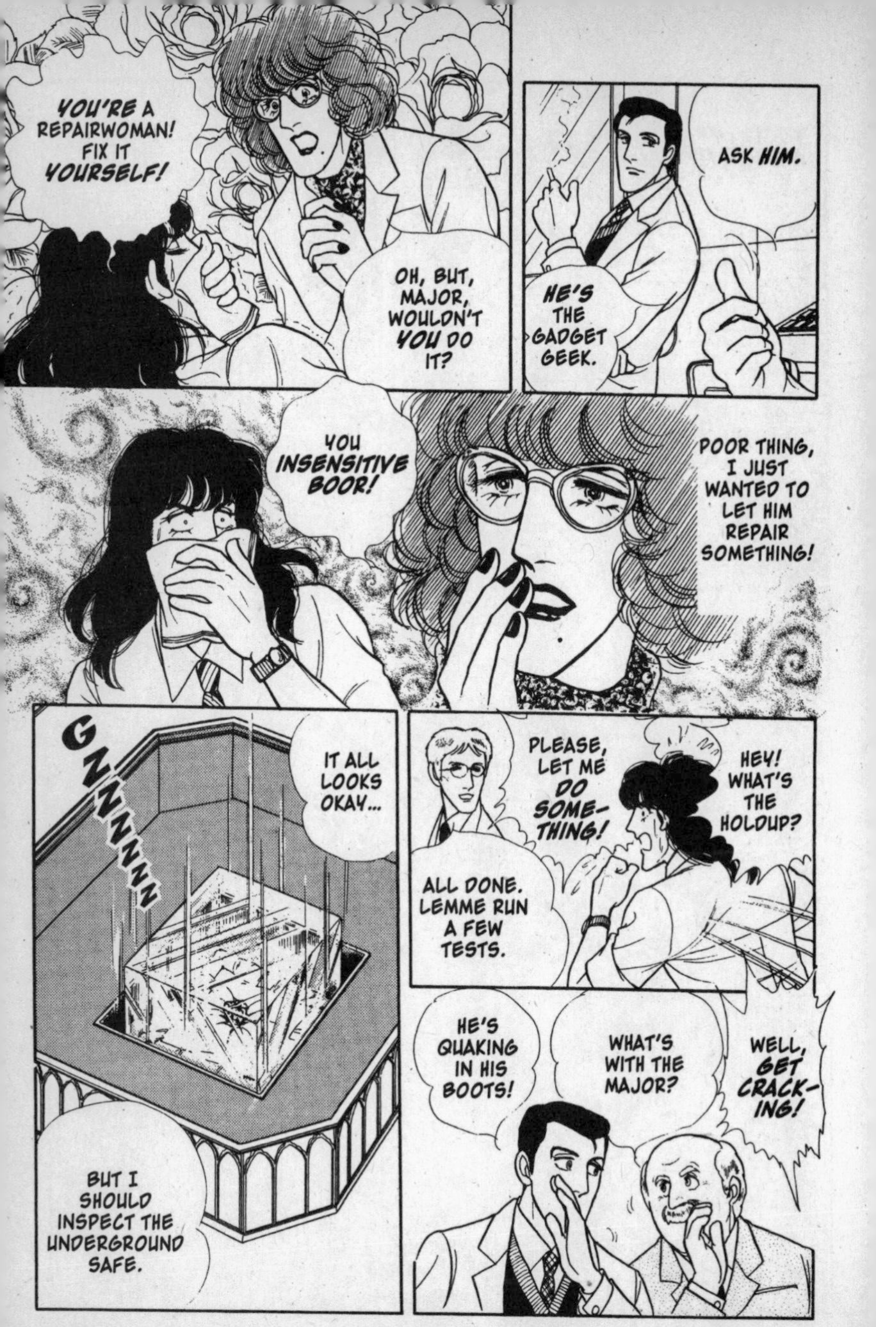
ASK HIM.
HE'S THE GADGET GEEK.
YOU'RE A REPAIRWOMAN! FIX IT YOURSELF!
OH, BUT, MAJOR, WOULDN'T YOU DO IT?
POOR THING, I JUST WANTED TO LET HIM REPAIR SOMETHING!
YOU INSENSITIVE BOOR!
HEY! WHAT'S THE HOLDUP?
PLEASE, LET ME DO SOME-THING!
ALL DONE. LEMME RUN A FEW TESTS.
WELL, GET CRACKING!
WHAT'S WITH THE MAJOR?
HE'S QUAKING IN HIS BOOTS!
IT ALL LOOKS OKAY...
GZZZZZZ
BUT I SHOULD INSPECT THE UNDERGROUND SAFE.

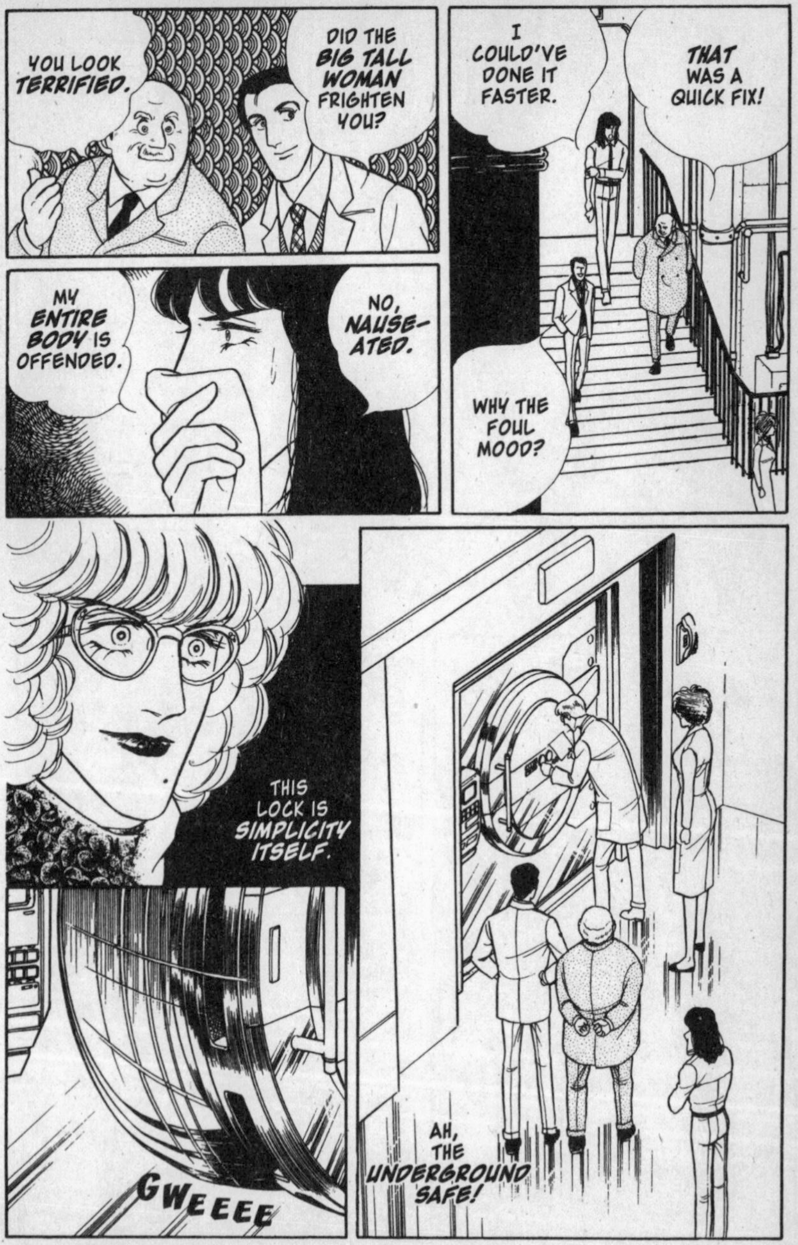
THAT WAS A QUICK FIX!
I COULD'VE DONE IT FASTER.
WHY THE FOUL MOOD?
DID THE BIG TALL WOMAN FRIGHTEN YOU?
YOU LOOK TERRIFIED.
NO, NAUSEATED.
MY ENTIRE BODY IS OFFENDED.
AH, THE UNDERGROUND SAFE!
THIS LOCK IS SIMPLICITY ITSELF.
GWEEEEE

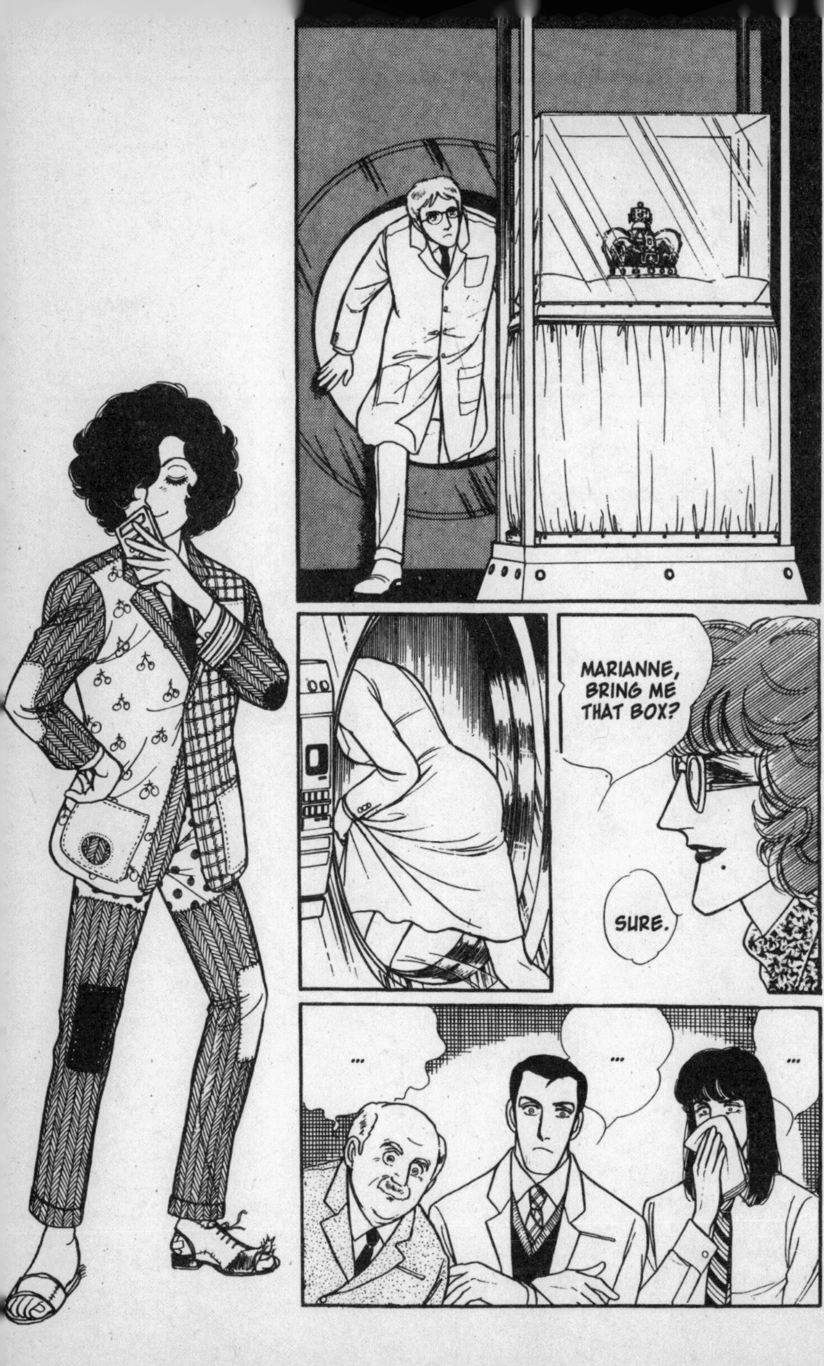
MARIANNE, BRING ME THAT BOX?
SURE.
...
...
...

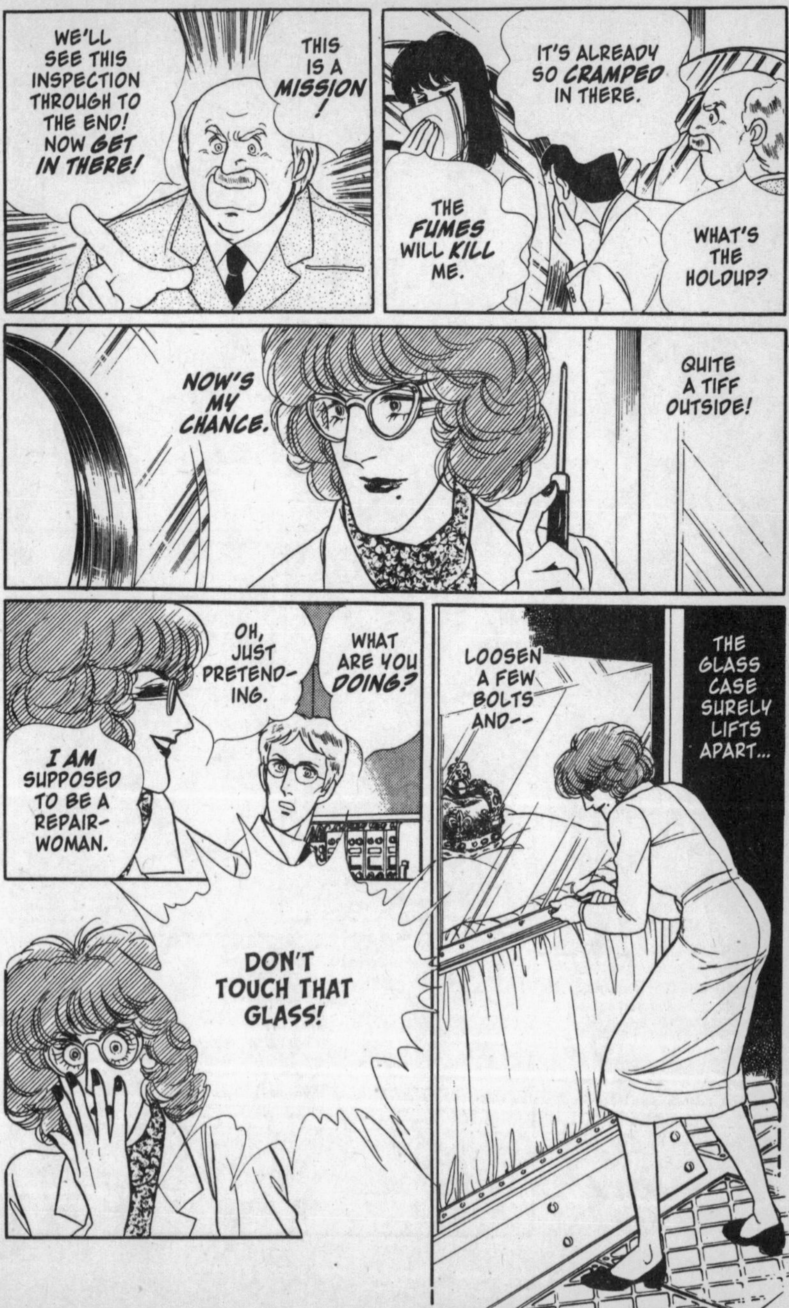

IT'S ALREADY SO CRAMPED IN THERE.
WHAT'S THE HOLDUP?
THE FUMES WILL KILL ME.
THIS IS A MISSION!
WE'LL SEE THIS INSPECTION THROUGH TO THE END! NOW GET IN THERE!
QUITE A TIFF OUTSIDE!
NOW'S MY CHANCE.
THE GLASS CASE SURELY LIFTS APART...
LOOSEN A FEW BOLTS AND--
WHAT ARE YOU DOING?
OH, JUST PRETENDING.
I AM SUPPOSED TO BE A REPAIR-WOMAN.
DON'T TOUCH THAT GLASS!

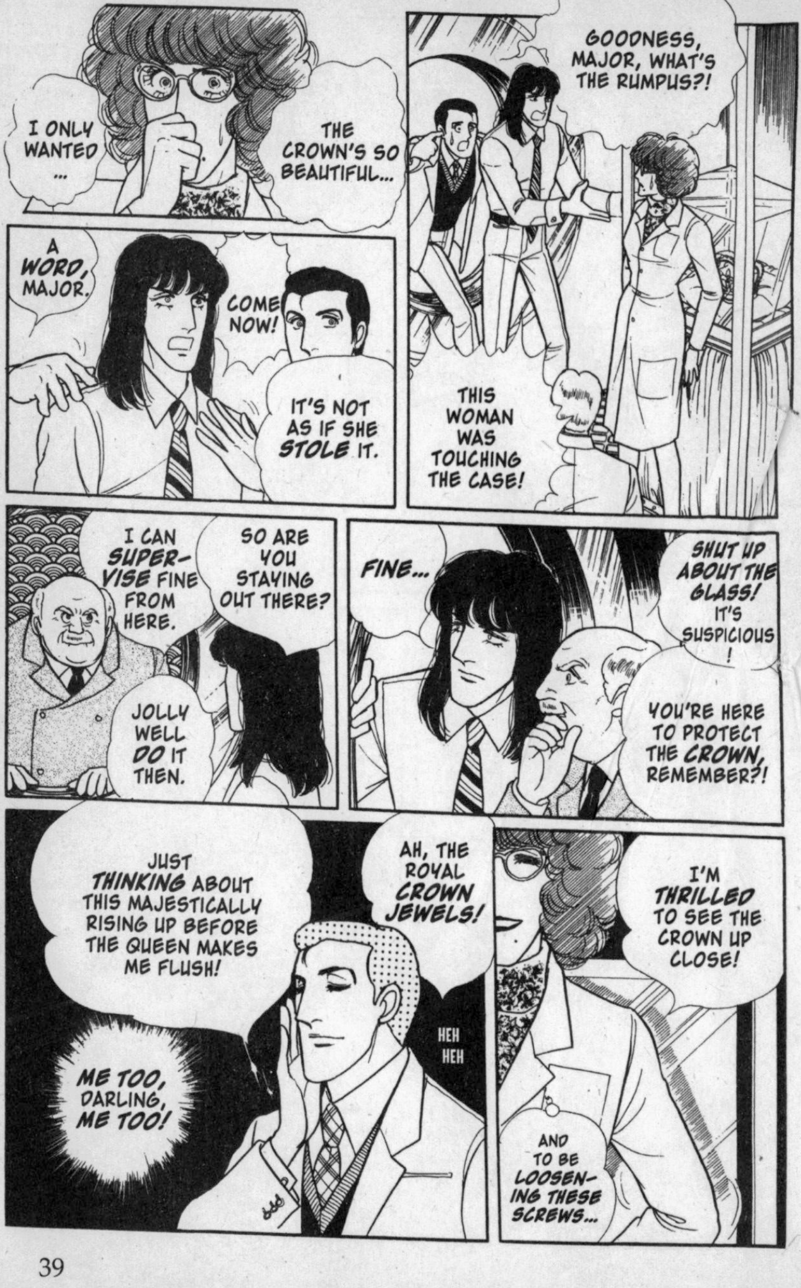
GOODNESS, MAJOR, WHAT'S THE RUMPUS?!
THIS WOMAN WAS TOUCHING THE CASE!
THE CROWN'S SO BEAUTIFUL...
I ONLY WANTED ...
COME NOW!
IT'S NOT AS IF SHE STOLE IT.
A WORD, MAJOR.
SHUT UP ABOUT THE GLASS! IT'S SUSPICIOUS!
YOU'RE HERE TO PROTECT THE CROWN, REMEMBER?!
FINE...
SO ARE YOU STAYING OUT THERE?
I CAN SUPERVISE FINE FROM HERE.
JOLLY WELL DO IT THEN.
I'M THRILLED TO SEE THE CROWN UP CLOSE!
AND TO BE LOOSENING THESE SCREWS...
AH, THE ROYAL CROWN JEWELS!
JUST THINKING ABOUT THIS MAJESTICALLY RISING UP BEFORE THE QUEEN MAKES ME FLUSH!
HEH HEH
ME TOO, DARLING, ME TOO!

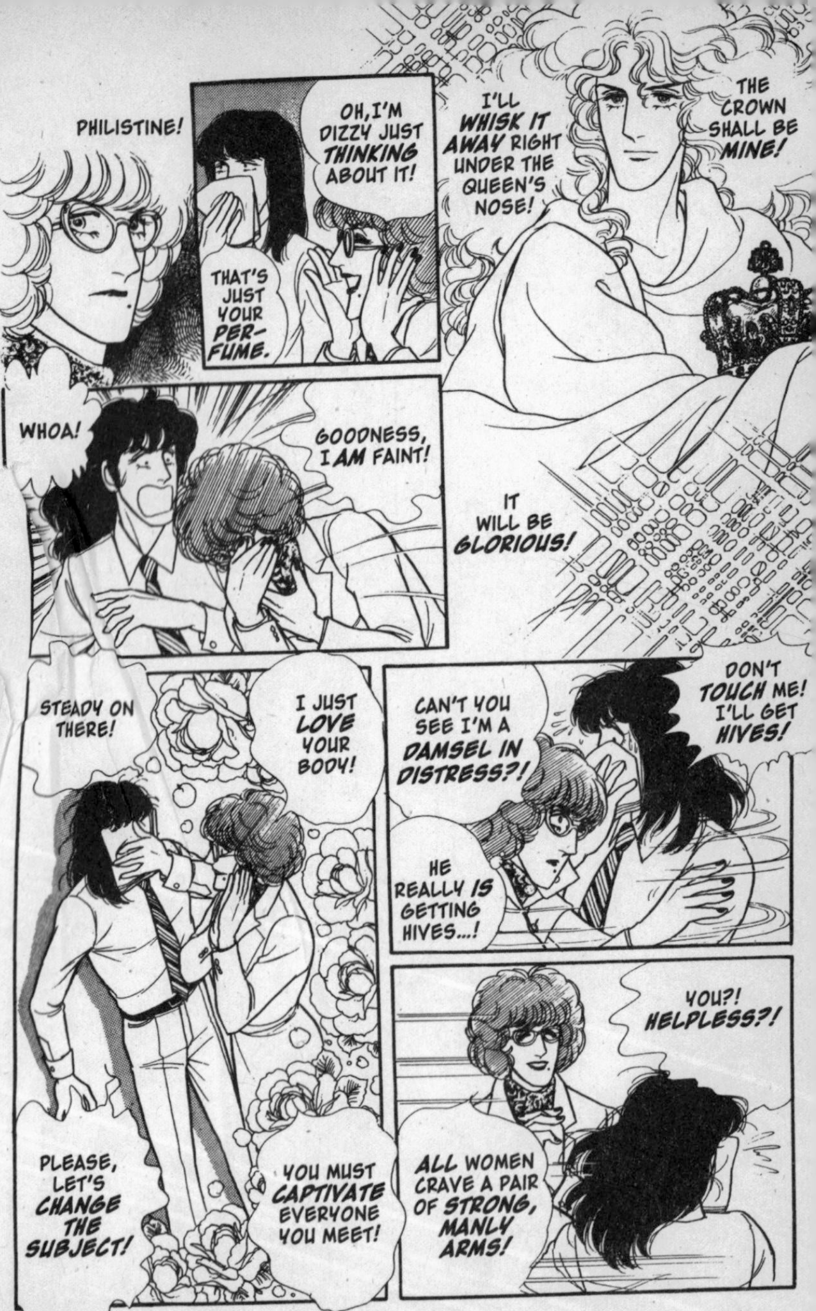
THE CROWN SHALL BE MINE!
I'LL WHISK IT AWAY RIGHT UNDER THE QUEEN'S NOSE!
IT WILL BE GLORIOUS!
OH, I'M DIZZY JUST THINKING ABOUT IT!
THAT'S JUST YOUR PERFUME.
PHILISTINE!
GOODNESS, I AM FAINT!
WHOA!
DON'T TOUCH ME! I'LL GET HIVES!
CAN'T YOU SEE I'M A DAMSEL IN DISTRESS?!
HE REALLY IS GETTING HIVES...!
YOU?! HELPLESS?!
ALL WOMEN CRAVE A PAIR OF STRONG, MANLY ARMS!
I JUST LOVE YOUR BODY!
STEADY ON THERE!
YOU MUST CAPTIVATE EVERYONE YOU MEET!
PLEASE, LET'S CHANGE THE SUBJECT!

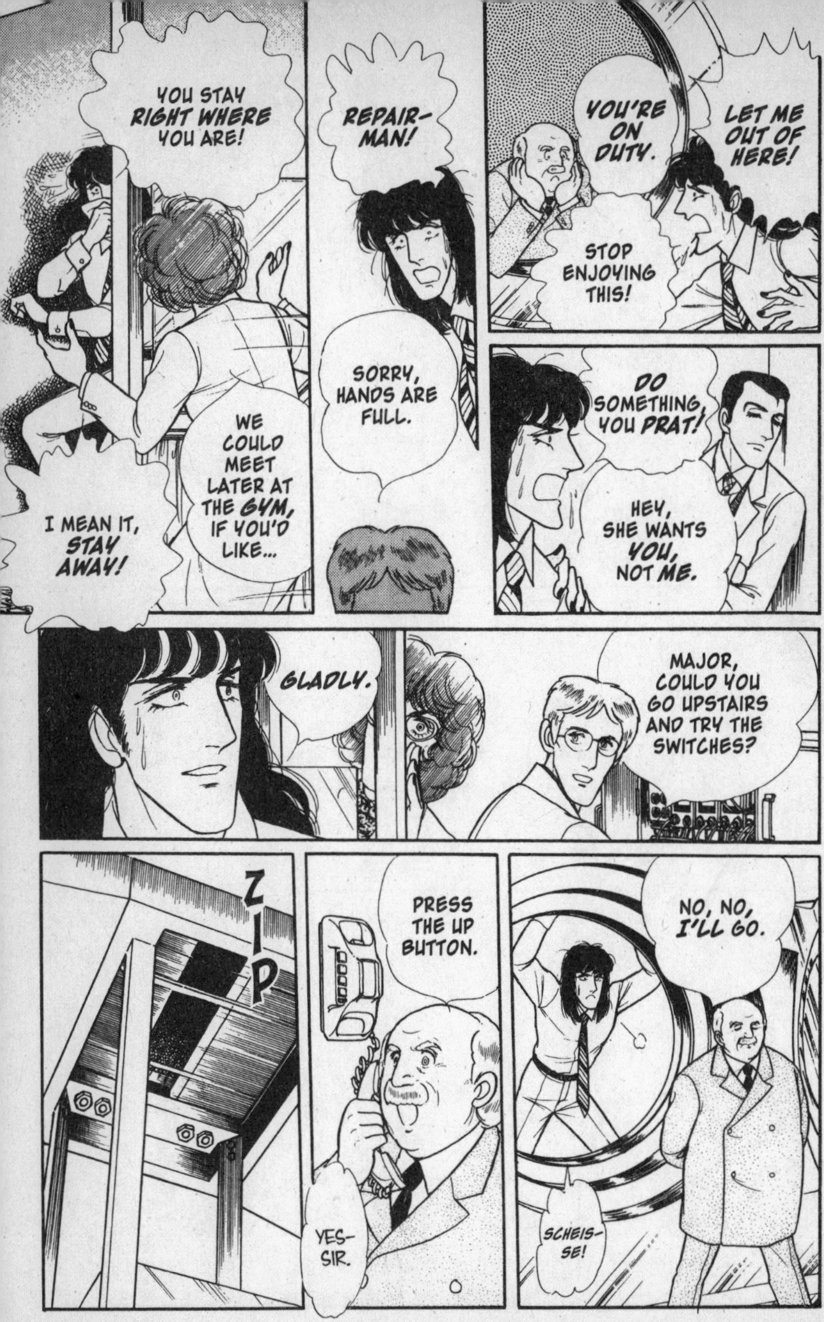
LET ME OUT OF HERE!
YOU'RE ON DUTY.
STOP ENJOYING THIS!
DO SOMETHING, YOU PRAT!
HEY, SHE WANTS YOU, NOT ME.
REPAIR-MAN!
SORRY, HANDS ARE FULL.
YOU STAY RIGHT WHERE YOU ARE!
WE COULD MEET LATER AT THE GYM, IF YOU'D LIKE...
I MEAN IT, STAY AWAY!
MAJOR, COULD YOU GO UPSTAIRS AND TRY THE SWITCHES?
GLADLY.
NO, NO, I'LL GO.
SCHEIS-SE!
PRESS THE UP BUTTON.
YES-SIR.
ZIP

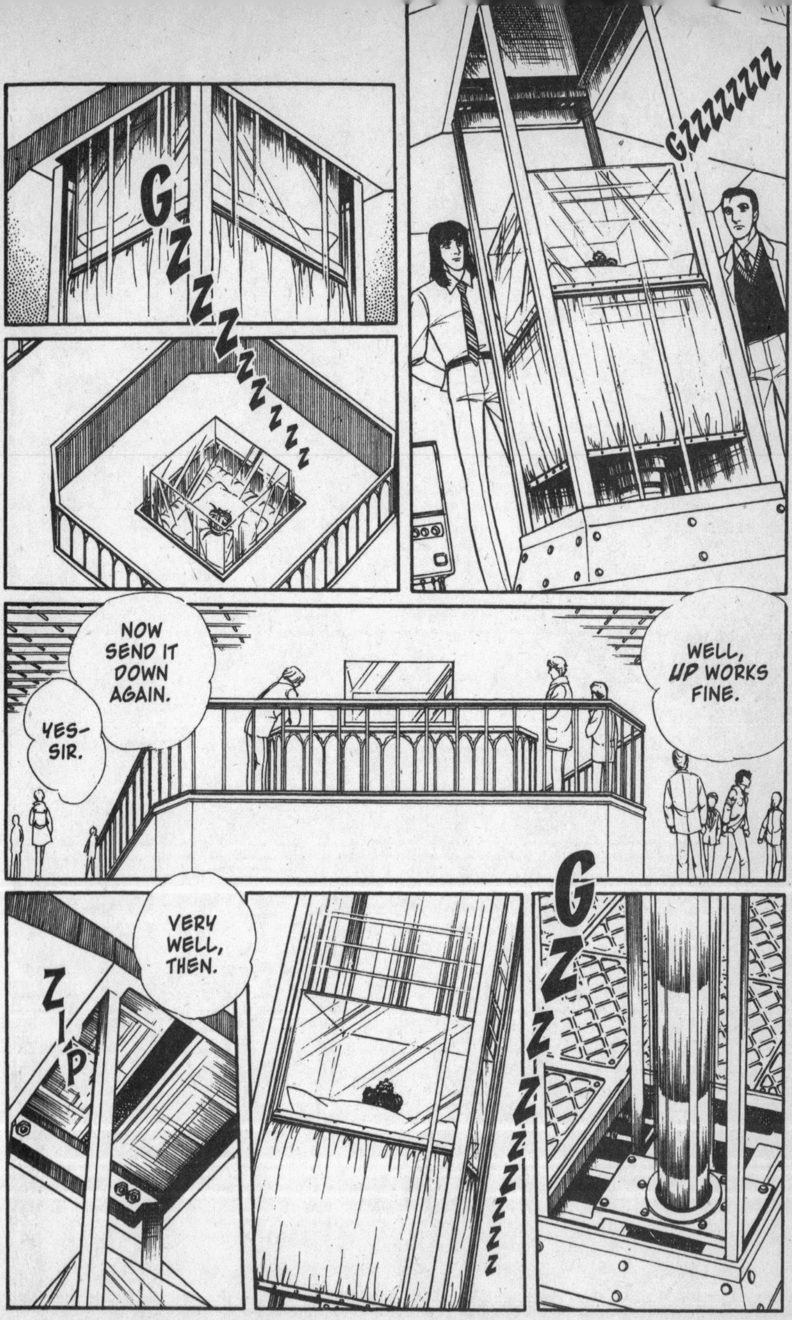
GZZZZZZZZ
GZZZZZZZZZ
WELL, UP WORKS FINE.
NOW SEND IT DOWN AGAIN.
YES-SIR.
GZZZZZZZZZ
VERY WELL, THEN.
ZIP

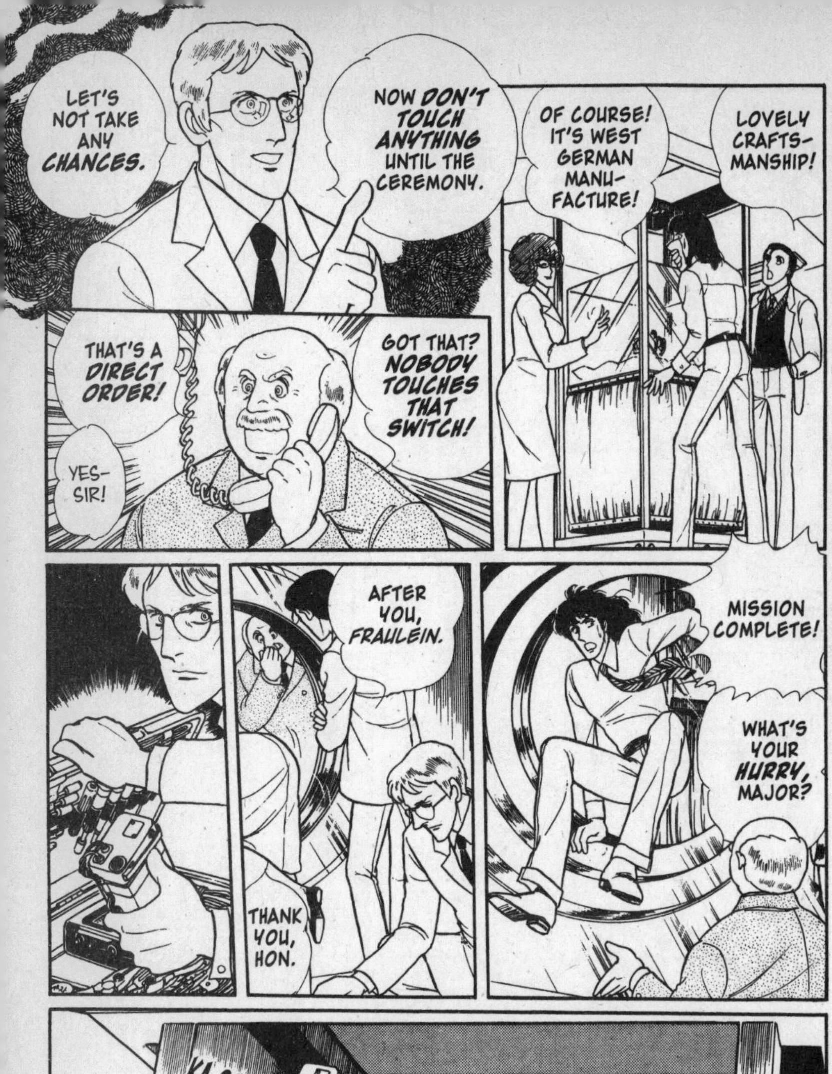
LOVELY CRAFTS-MANSHIP!
OF COURSE! IT'S WEST GERMAN MANU-FACTURE!
NOW DON'T TOUCH ANYTHING UNTIL THE CEREMONY.
LET'S NOT TAKE ANY CHANCES.
GOT THAT? NOBODY TOUCHES THAT SWITCH!
THAT'S A DIRECT ORDER!
YES-SIR!
MISSION COMPLETE!
WHAT'S YOUR HURRY, MAJOR?
AFTER YOU, FRAULEIN.
THANK YOU, HON.
KA-CHUNK

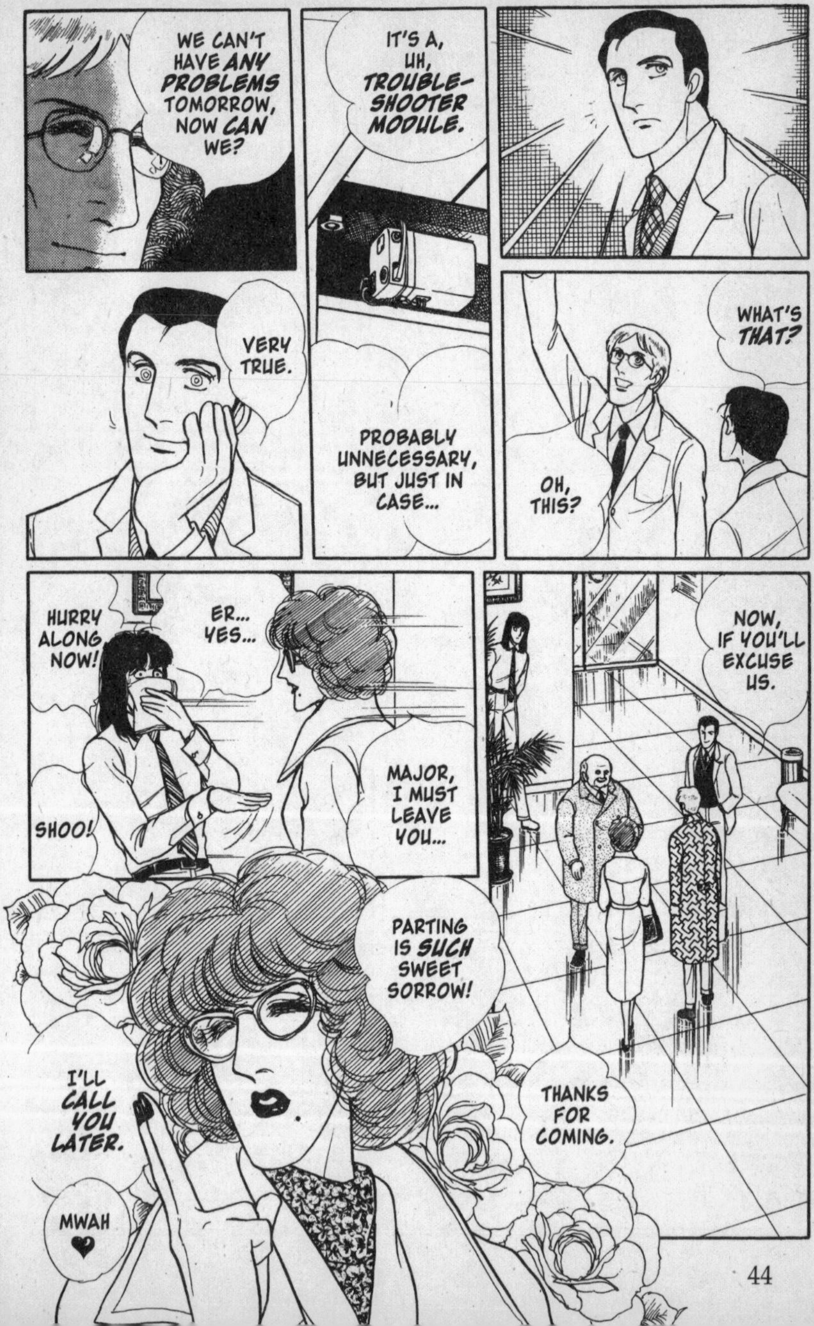
WHAT'S THAT?
OH, THIS?
IT'S A, UH, TROUBLE-SHOOTER MODULE.
PROBABLY UNNECESSARY, BUT JUST IN CASE...
WE CAN'T HAVE ANY PROBLEMS TOMORROW, NOW CAN WE?
VERY TRUE.
NOW, IF YOU'LL EXCUSE US.
THANKS FOR COMING.
MAJOR, I MUST LEAVE YOU...
ER... YES...
HURRY ALONG NOW!
SHOO!
PARTING IS SUCH SWEET SORROW!
I'LL CALL YOU LATER.
MWAH ♥

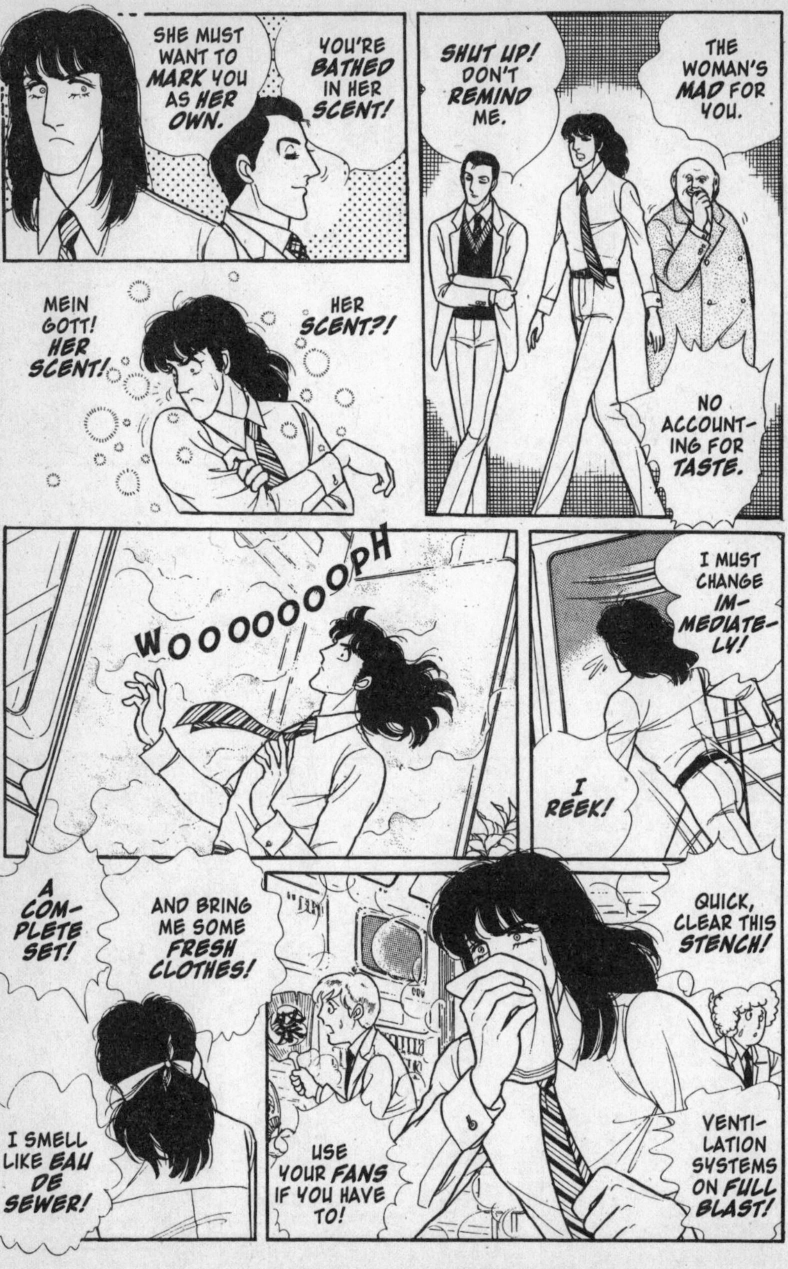
THE WOMAN'S MAD FOR YOU.
SHUT UP! DON'T REMIND ME.
NO ACCOUNTING FOR TASTE.
YOU'RE BATHED IN HER SCENT!
SHE MUST WANT TO MARK YOU AS HER OWN.
HER SCENT?!
MEIN GOTT! HER SCENT!
I MUST CHANGE IMMEDIATELY!
I REEK!
WOOOOOOOPH
QUICK, CLEAR THIS STENCH!
VENTILATION SYSTEMS ON FULL BLAST!
USE YOUR FANS IF YOU HAVE TO!
AND BRING ME SOME FRESH CLOTHES!
A COMPLETE SET!
I SMELL LIKE EAU DE SEWER!

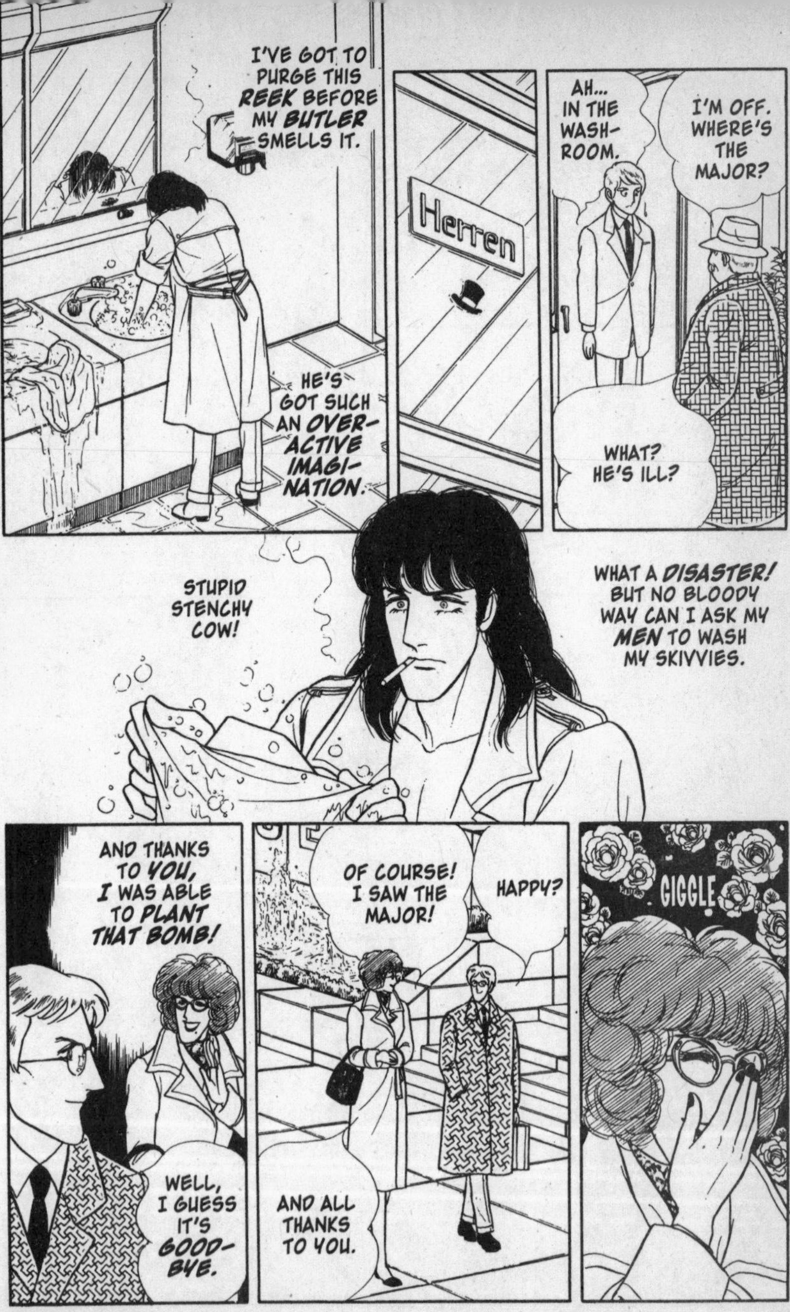

I'M OFF. WHERE'S THE MAJOR?
AH... IN THE WASH-ROOM.
WHAT? HE'S ILL?
Herren
I'VE GOT TO PURGE THIS REEK BEFORE MY BUTLER SMELLS IT.
HE'S GOT SUCH AN OVER-ACTIVE IMAGI-NATION.
WHAT A DISASTER! BUT NO BLOODY WAY CAN I ASK MY MEN TO WASH MY SKIVVIES.
STUPID STENCHY COW!
GIGGLE
HAPPY?
OF COURSE! I SAW THE MAJOR!
AND ALL THANKS TO YOU.
AND THANKS TO YOU, I WAS ABLE TO PLANT THAT BOMB!
WELL, I GUESS IT'S GOOD-BYE.

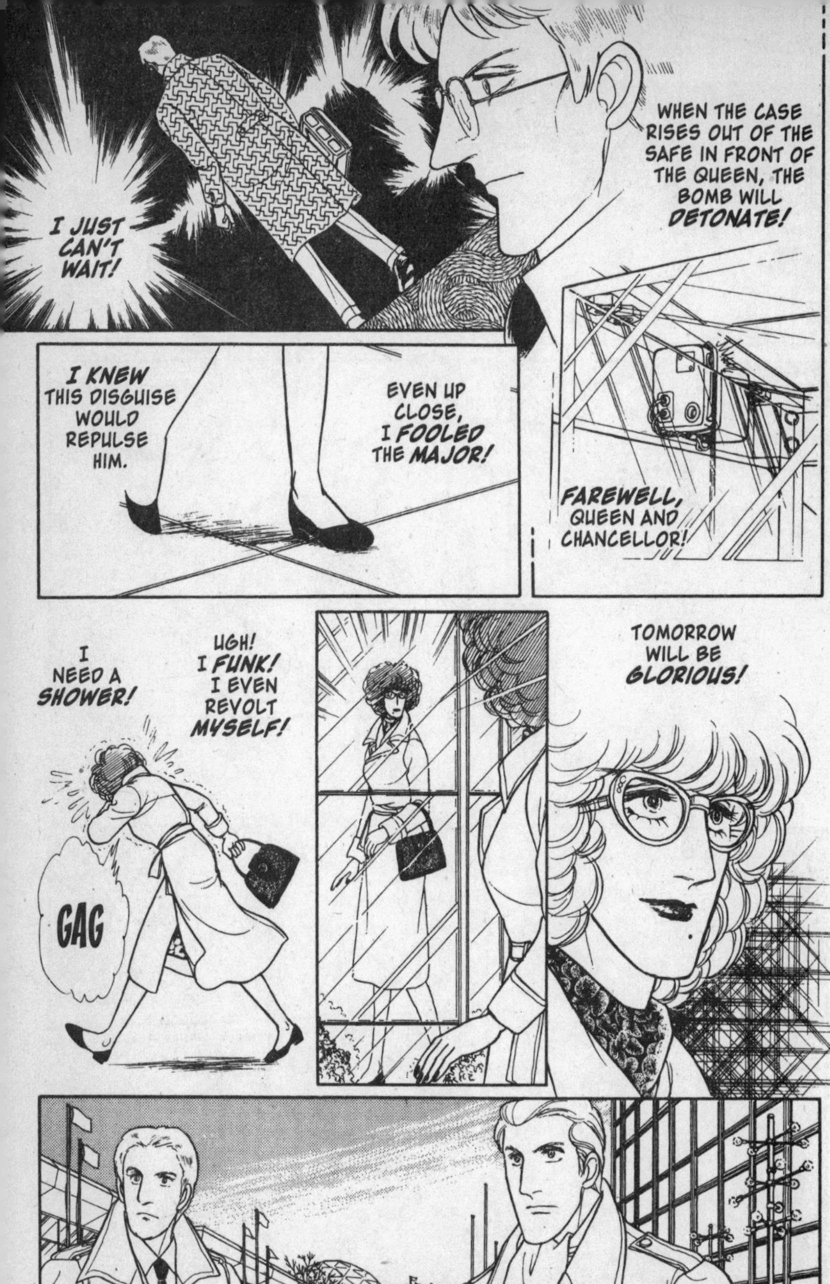
WHEN THE CASE RISES OUT OF THE SAFE IN FRONT OF THE QUEEN, THE BOMB WILL DETONATE!
I JUST CAN'T WAIT!
FAREWELL, QUEEN AND CHANCELLOR!
EVEN UP CLOSE, I FOOLED THE MAJOR!
I KNEW THIS DISGUISE WOULD REPULSE HIM.
TOMORROW WILL BE GLORIOUS!
UGH! I FUNK! I EVEN REVOLT MYSELF!
I NEED A SHOWER!
GAG

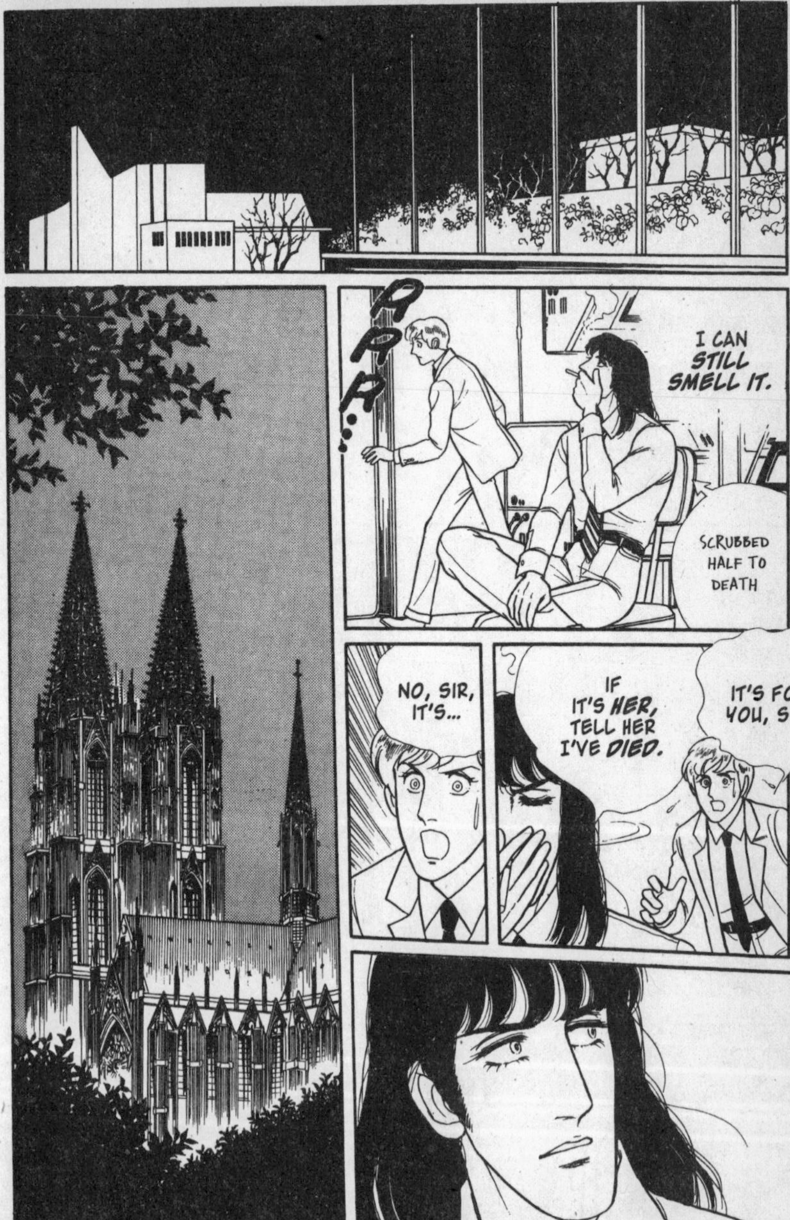
I CAN STILL SMELL IT.
SCRUBBED HALF TO DEATH
RRR...
IT'S FOR YOU, SIR.
IF IT'S HER, TELL HER I'VE DIED.
NO, SIR, IT'S...

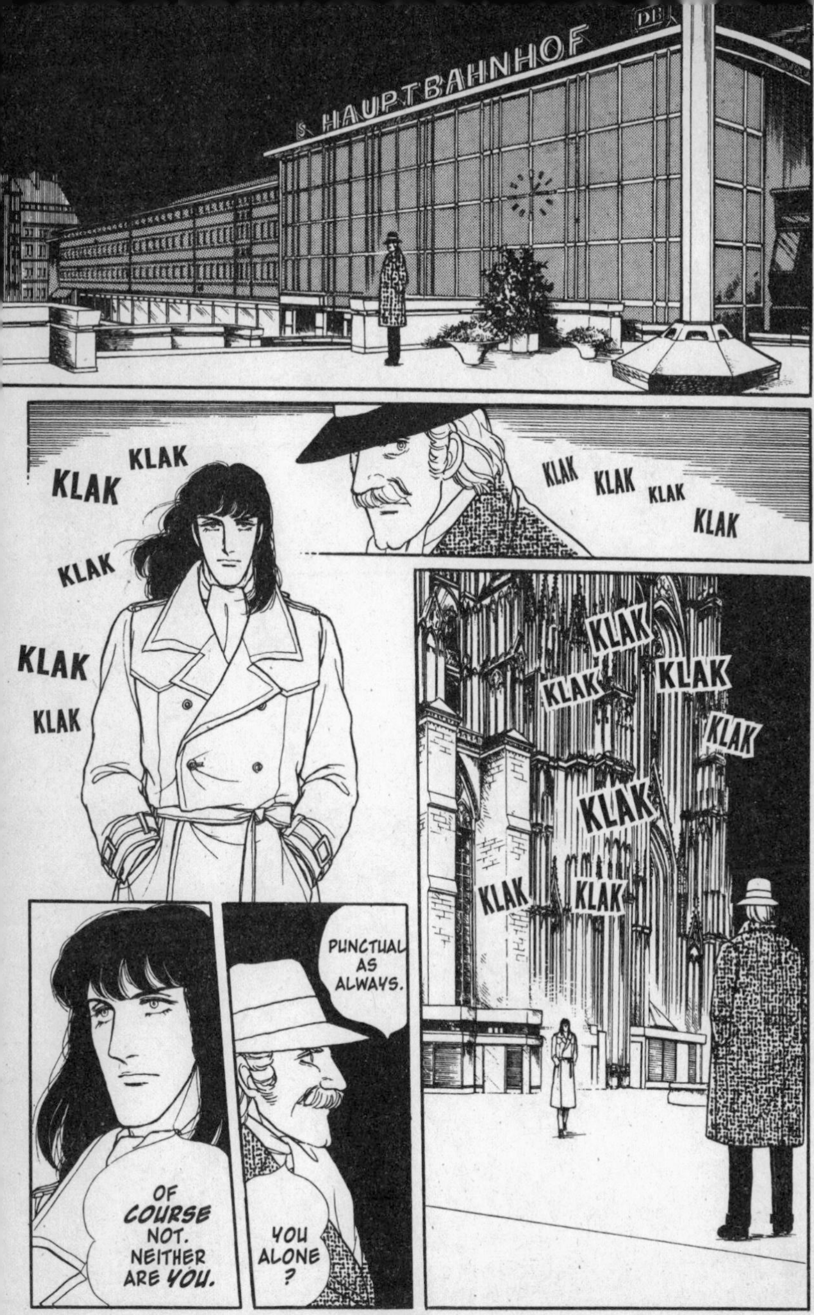
HAUPTBAHNHOF
DB
KLAK
KLAK
KLAK
KLAK
KLAK
KLAK
KLAK
KLAK
KLAK
KLAK
KLAK
KLAK
KLAK
KLAK
KLAK
KLAK
KLAK
PUNCTUAL AS ALWAYS.
YOU ALONE?
OF COURSE NOT. NEITHER ARE YOU.

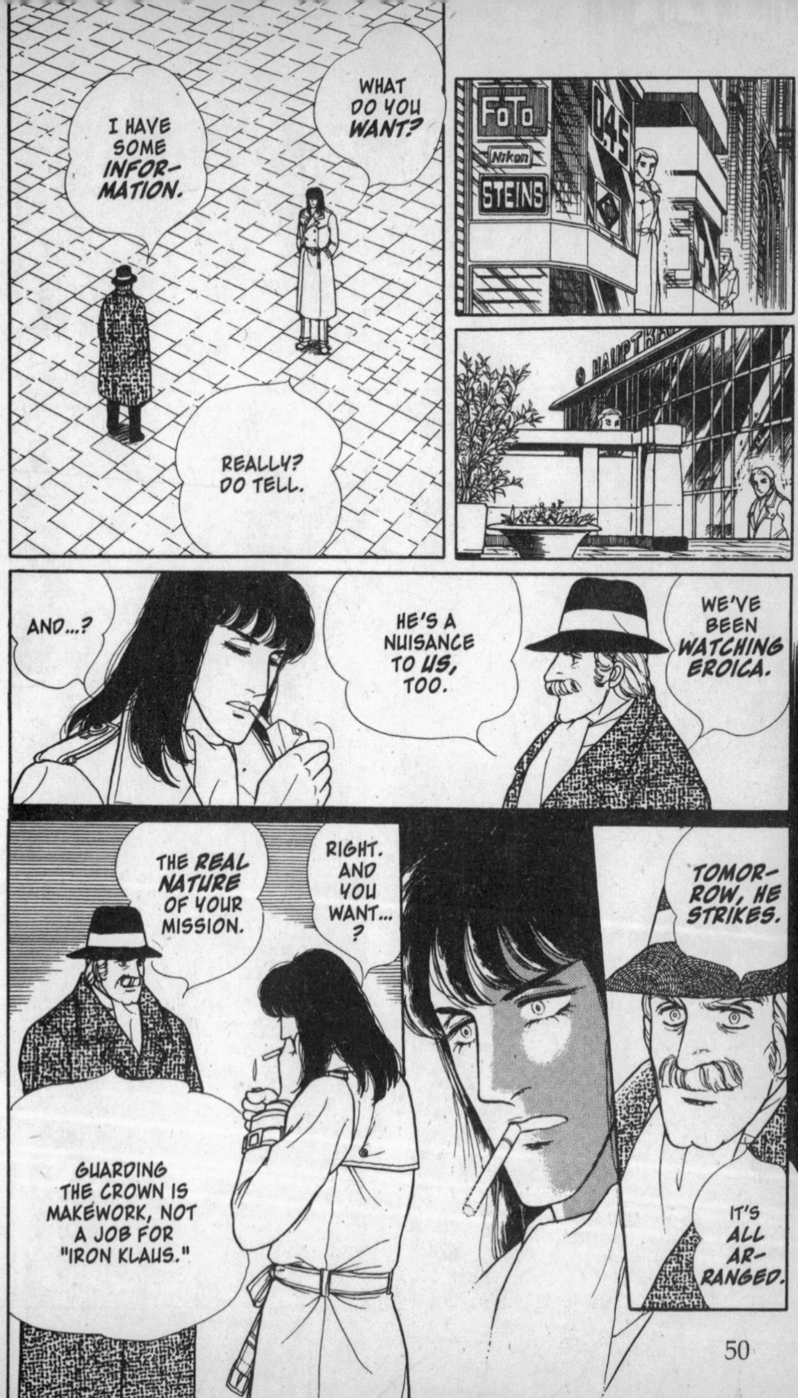
FoTo
Nikon
STEINS
045
WHAT DO YOU WANT?
I HAVE SOME INFORMATION.
REALLY? DO TELL.
WE'VE BEEN WATCHING EROICA.
HE'S A NUISANCE TO US, TOO.
AND...?
TOMORROW, HE STRIKES.
IT'S ALL ARRANGED.
RIGHT. AND YOU WANT...?
THE REAL NATURE OF YOUR MISSION.
GUARDING THE CROWN IS MAKEWORK, NOT A JOB FOR "IRON KLAUS."

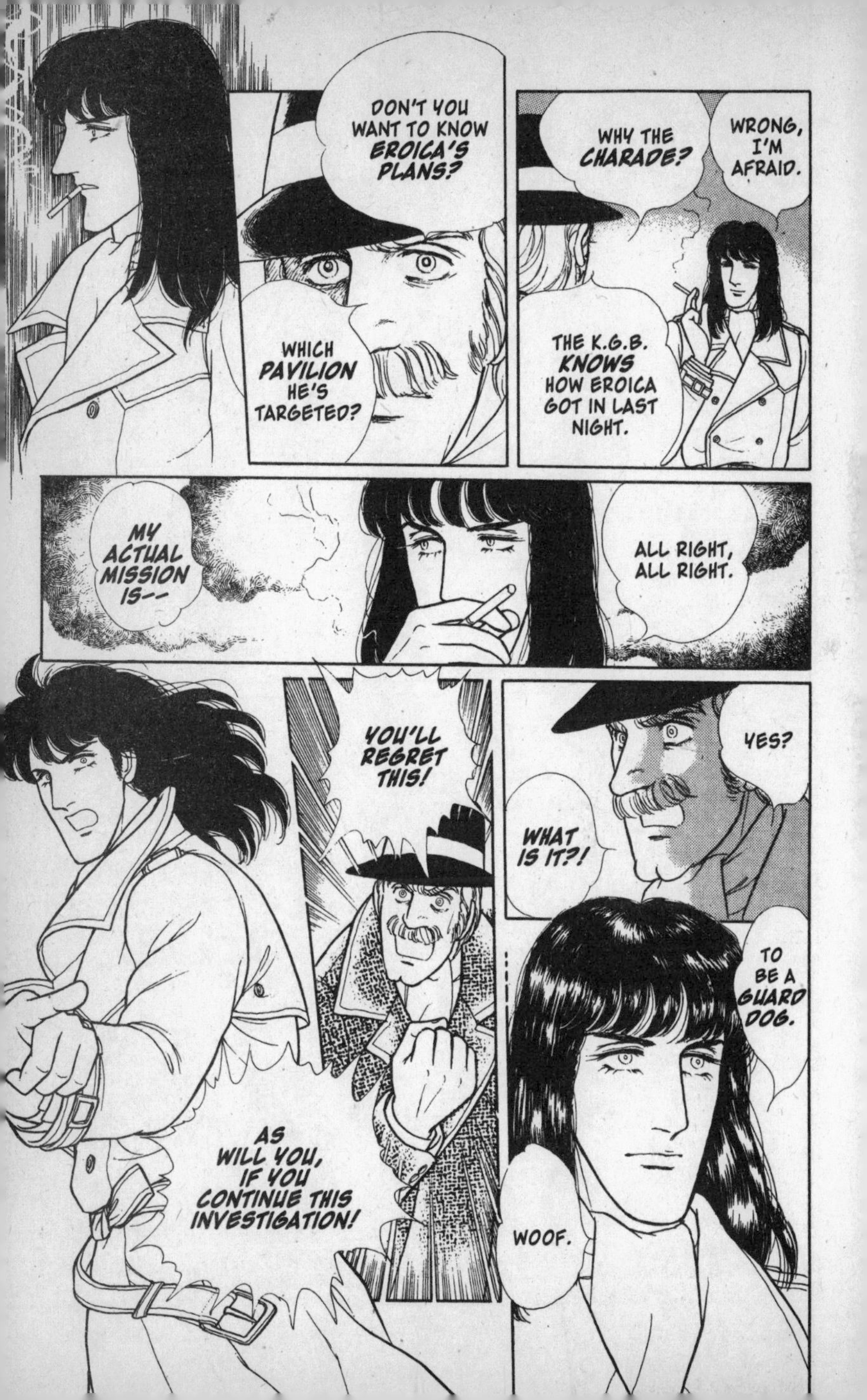
WRONG, I'M AFRAID.
WHY THE CHARADE?
THE K.G.B. KNOWS HOW EROICA GOT IN LAST NIGHT.
DON'T YOU WANT TO KNOW EROICA'S PLANS?
WHICH PAVILION HE'S TARGETED?
ALL RIGHT, ALL RIGHT.
MY ACTUAL MISSION IS--
YES?
WHAT IS IT?!
TO BE A GUARD DOG.
WOOF.
YOU'LL REGRET THIS!
AS WILL YOU, IF YOU CONTINUE THIS INVESTIGATION!

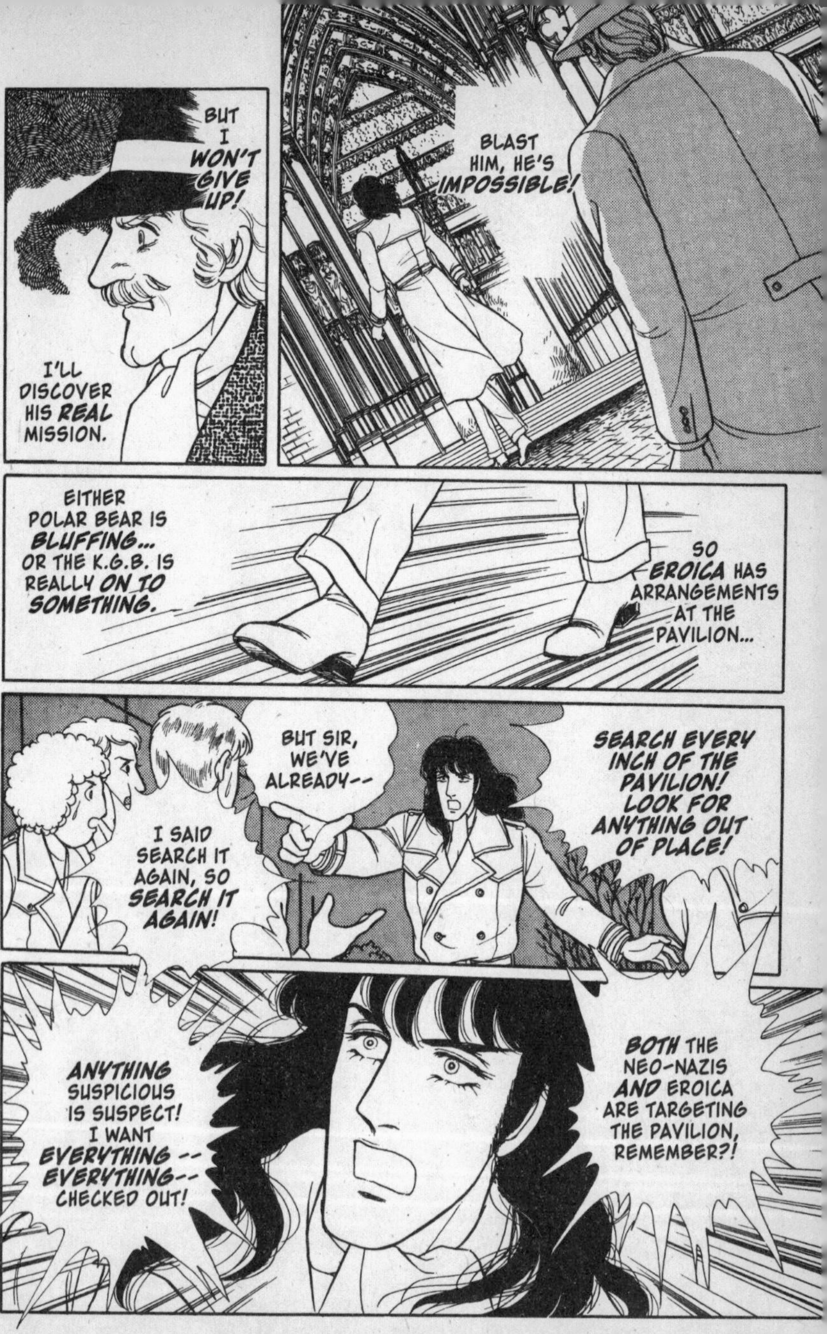
BLAST HIM, HE'S IMPOSSIBLE!
BUT I WON'T GIVE UP!
I'LL DISCOVER HIS REAL MISSION.
SO EROICA HAS ARRANGEMENTS AT THE PAVILION...
EITHER POLAR BEAR IS BLUFFING... OR THE K.G.B. IS REALLY ON TO SOMETHING.
SEARCH EVERY INCH OF THE PAVILION! LOOK FOR ANYTHING OUT OF PLACE!
BUT SIR, WE'VE ALREADY--
I SAID SEARCH IT AGAIN, SO SEARCH IT AGAIN!
BOTH THE NEO-NAZIS AND EROICA ARE TARGETING THE PAVILION, REMEMBER?!
ANYTHING SUSPICIOUS IS SUSPECT! I WANT EVERYTHING -- EVERYTHING-- CHECKED OUT!

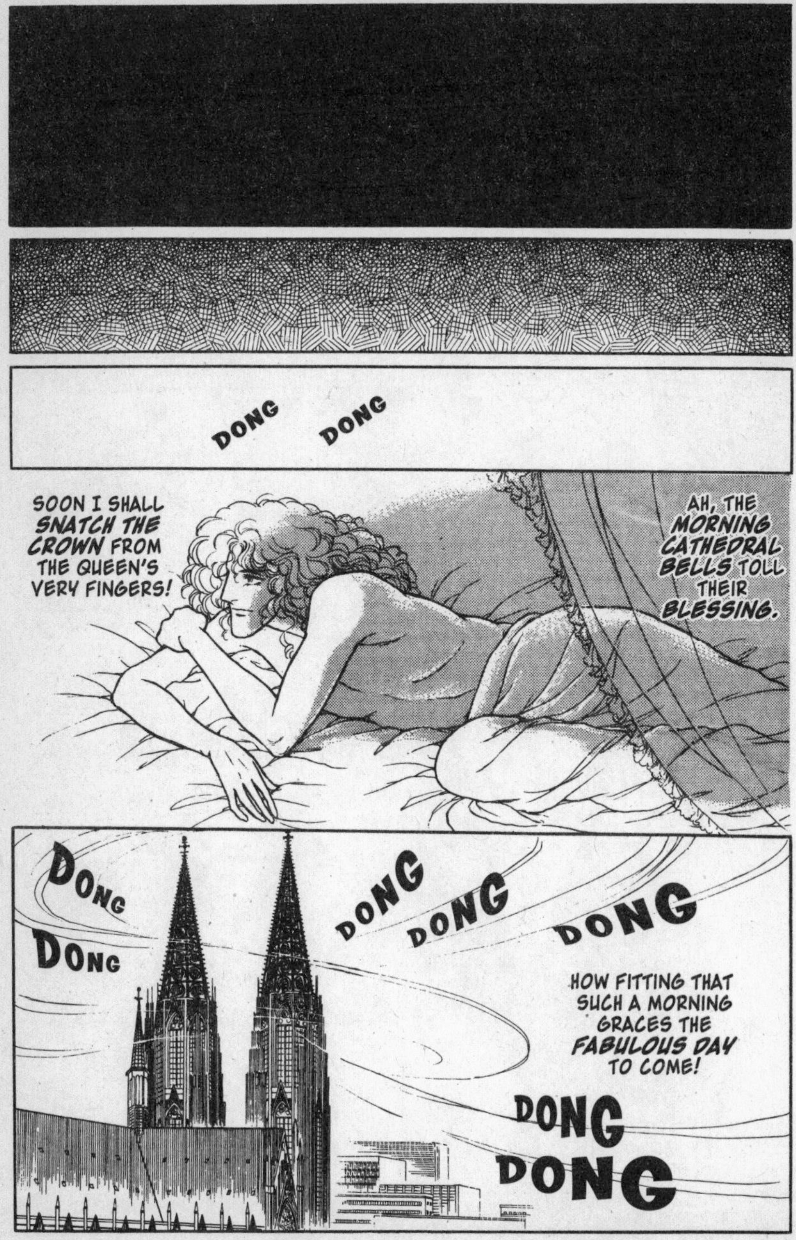
DONG
DONG
AH, THE MORNING CATHEDRAL BELLS TOLL THEIR BLESSING.
SOON I SHALL SNATCH THE CROWN FROM THE QUEEN'S VERY FINGERS!
DONG
DONG
DONG
DONG
DONG
HOW FITTING THAT SUCH A MORNING GRACES THE FABULOUS DAY TO COME!
DONG
DONG

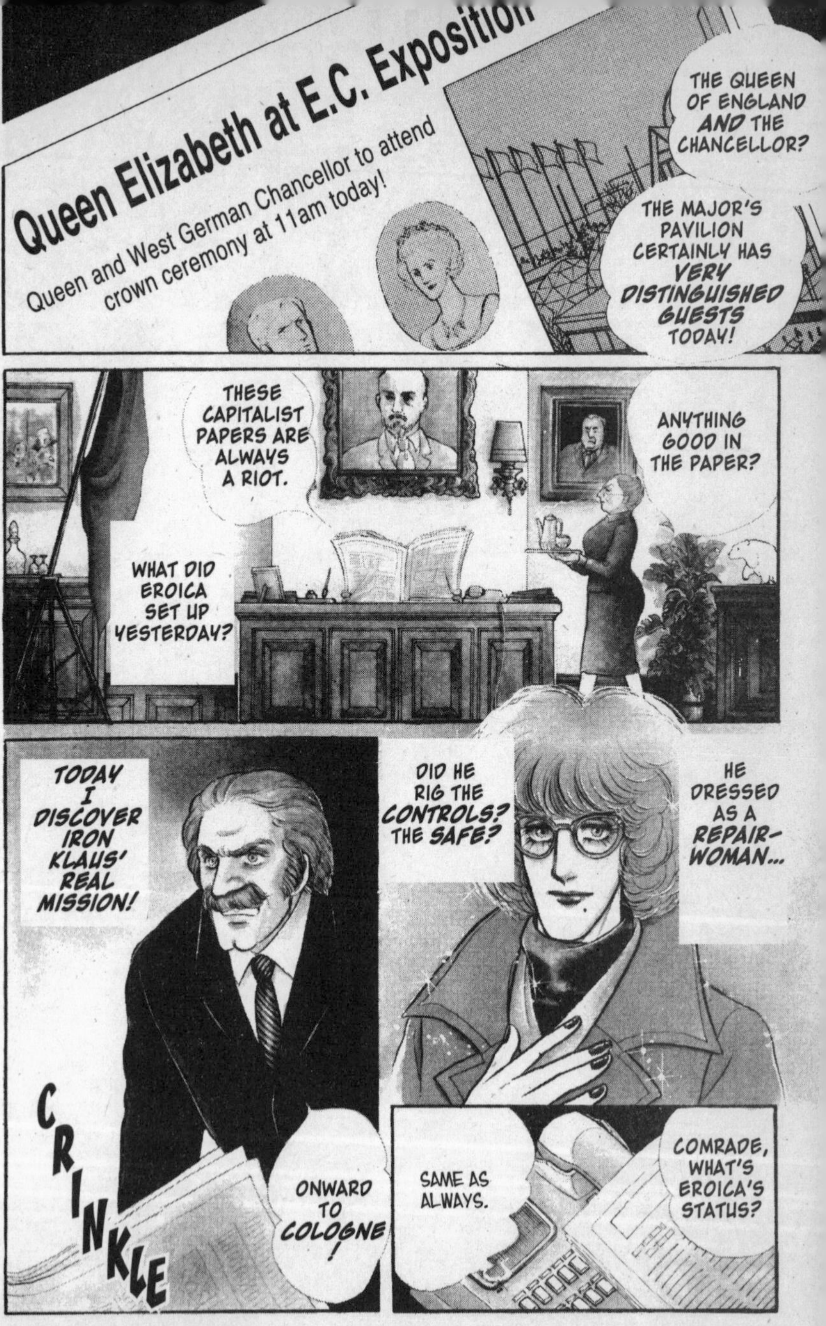
Queen Elizabeth at E.C. Exposition
Queen and West German Chancellor to attend crown ceremony at 11am today!
THE QUEEN OF ENGLAND AND THE CHANCELLOR?
THE MAJOR'S PAVILION CERTAINLY HAS VERY DISTINGUISHED GUESTS TODAY!
ANYTHING GOOD IN THE PAPER?
THESE CAPITALIST PAPERS ARE ALWAYS A RIOT.
WHAT DID EROICA SET UP YESTERDAY?
HE DRESSED AS A REPAIR-WOMAN...
DID HE RIG THE CONTROLS? THE SAFE?
COMRADE, WHAT'S EROICA'S STATUS?
SAME AS ALWAYS.
TODAY I DISCOVER IRON KLAUS' REAL MISSION!
ONWARD TO COLOGNE!
CRINKLE

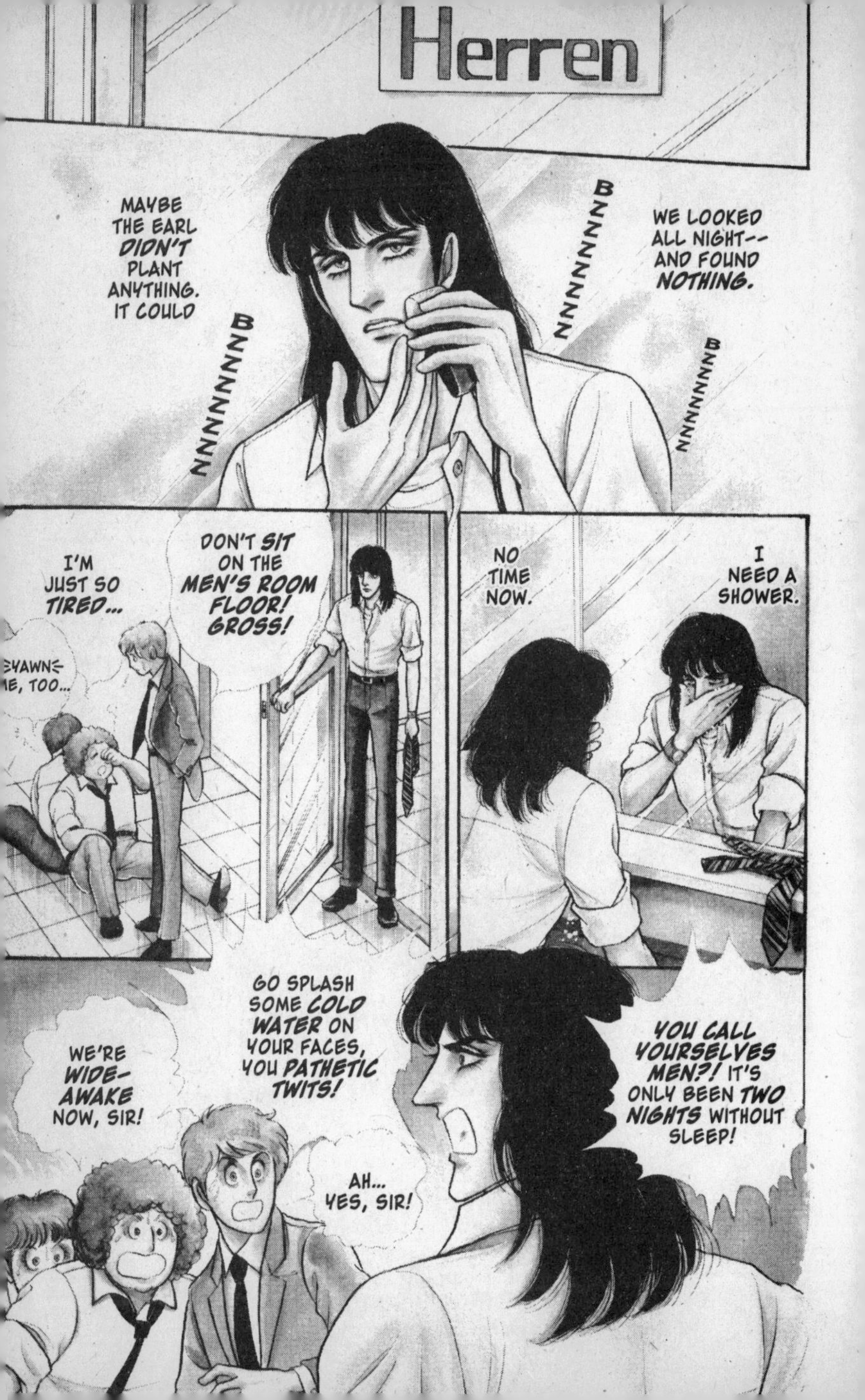
Herren
WE LOOKED ALL NIGHT-- AND FOUND NOTHING.
BZZZZZZZ
BZZZZZZZ
MAYBE THE EARL DIDN'T PLANT ANYTHING. IT COULD
BZZZZZZZZ
I NEED A SHOWER.
NO TIME NOW.
DON'T SIT ON THE MEN'S ROOM FLOOR! GROSS!
I'M JUST SO TIRED...
YAWN
E, TOO...
YOU CALL YOURSELVES MEN?! IT'S ONLY BEEN TWO NIGHTS WITHOUT SLEEP!
GO SPLASH SOME COLD WATER ON YOUR FACES, YOU PATHETIC TWITS!
AH... YES, SIR!
WE'RE WIDE-AWAKE NOW, SIR!

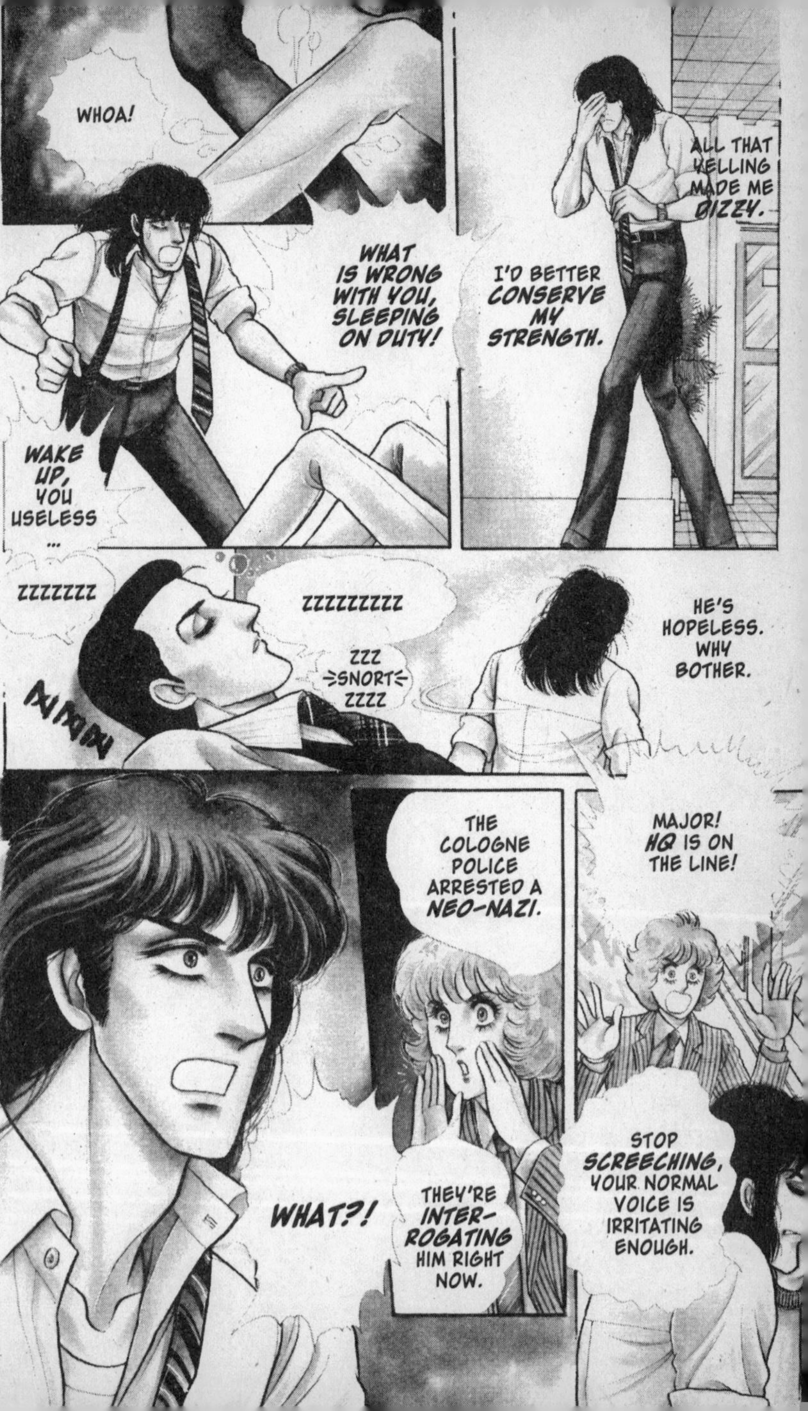
ALL THAT YELLING MADE ME DIZZY.
I'D BETTER CONSERVE MY STRENGTH.
WHOA!
WHAT IS WRONG WITH YOU, SLEEPING ON DUTY!
WAKE UP, YOU USELESS ...
HE'S HOPELESS. WHY BOTHER.
ZZZZZZZZZ
ZZZZZZZ
ZZZ ≡SNORT≡ ZZZZ
MAJOR! HQ IS ON THE LINE!
STOP SCREECHING, YOUR NORMAL VOICE IS IRRITATING ENOUGH.
THE COLOGNE POLICE ARRESTED A NEO-NAZI.
THEY'RE INTER-ROGATING HIM RIGHT NOW.
WHAT?!

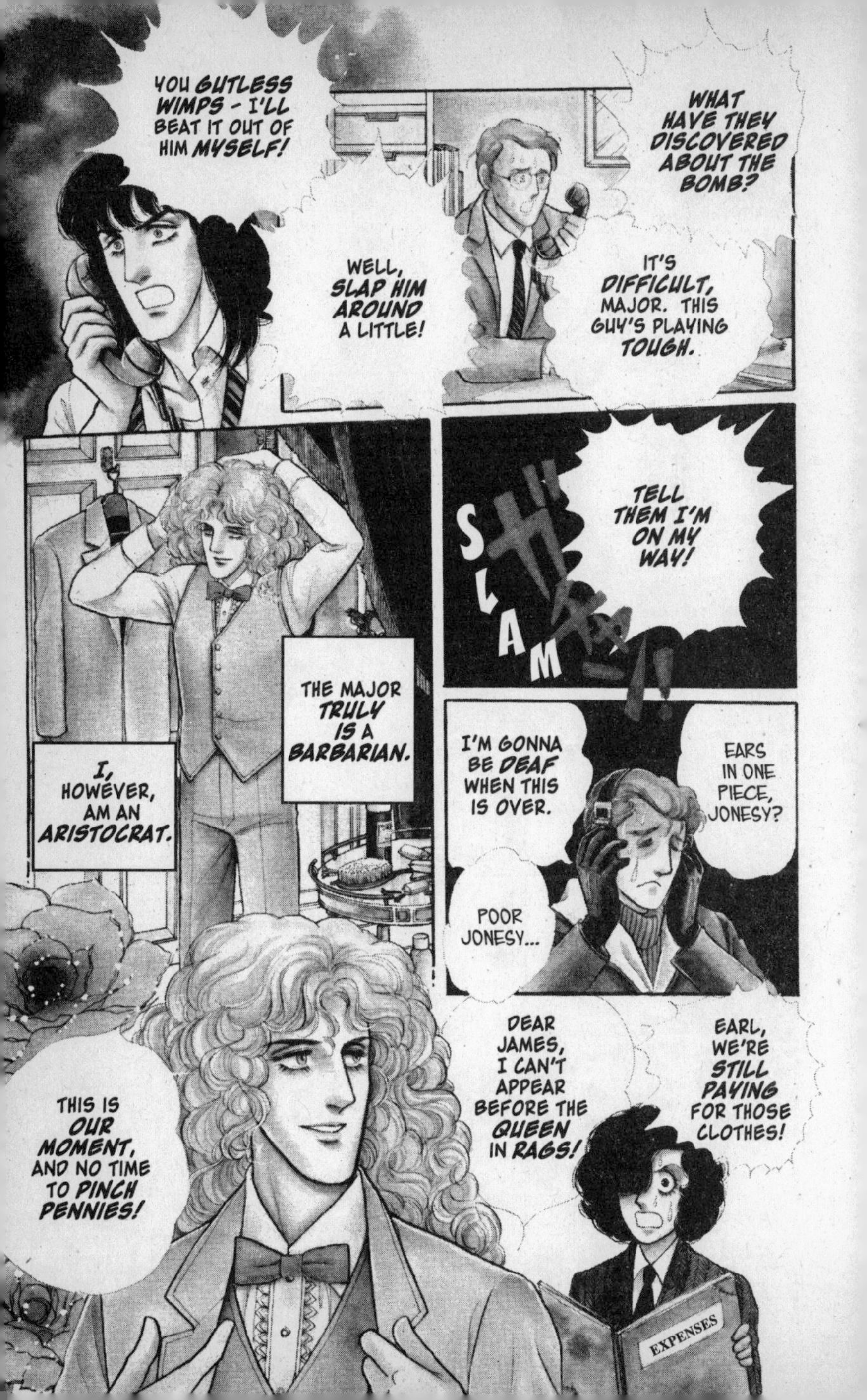
WHAT HAVE THEY DISCOVERED ABOUT THE BOMB?
IT'S DIFFICULT, MAJOR. THIS GUY'S PLAYING TOUGH.
WELL, SLAP HIM AROUND A LITTLE!
YOU GUTLESS WIMPS - I'LL BEAT IT OUT OF HIM MYSELF!
TELL THEM I'M ON MY WAY!
SLAM!
EARS IN ONE PIECE, JONESY?
I'M GONNA BE DEAF WHEN THIS IS OVER.
POOR JONESY...
THE MAJOR TRULY IS A BARBARIAN.
I, HOWEVER, AM AN ARISTOCRAT.
EARL, WE'RE STILL PAYING FOR THOSE CLOTHES!
DEAR JAMES, I CAN'T APPEAR BEFORE THE QUEEN IN RAGS!
THIS IS OUR MOMENT, AND NO TIME TO PINCH PENNIES!
EXPENSES

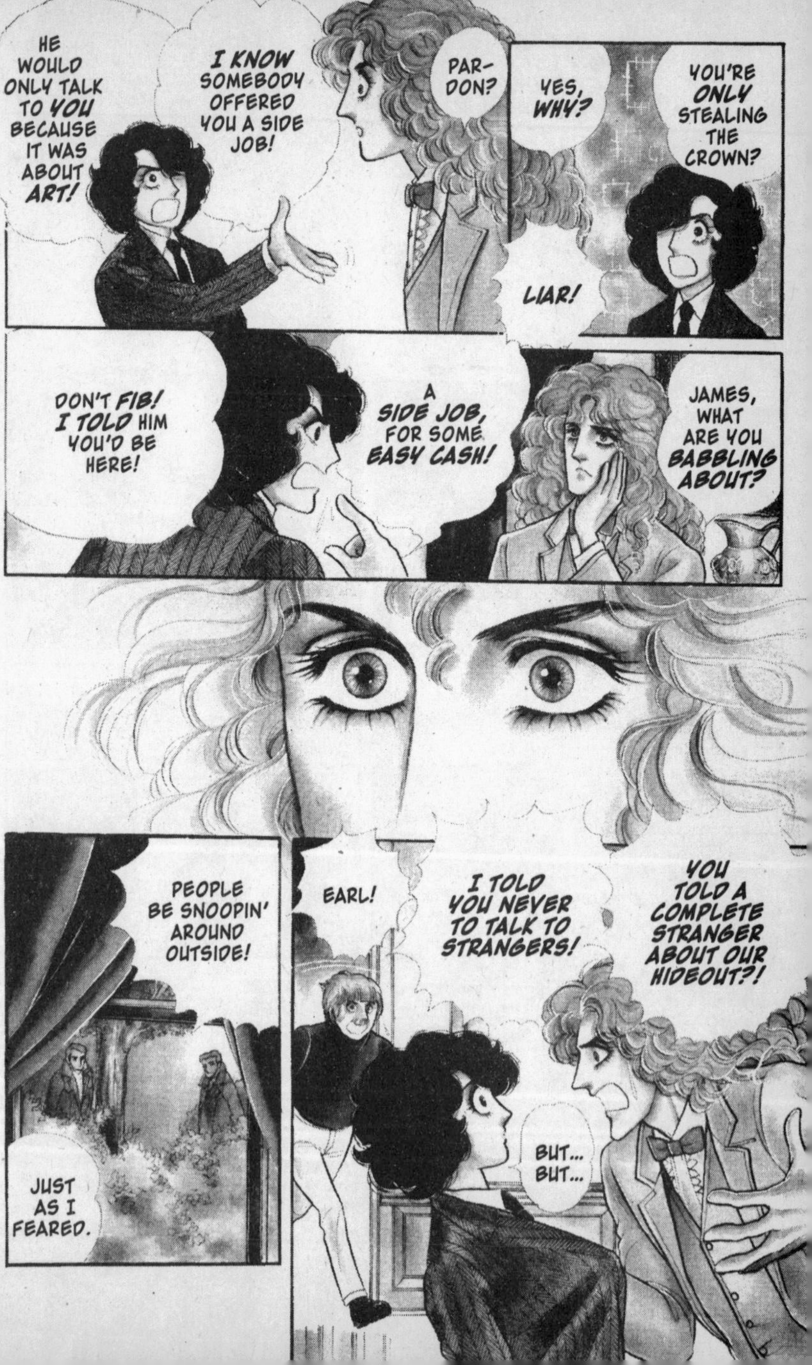
YOU'RE ONLY STEALING THE CROWN?
YES, WHY?
LIAR!
PARDON?
I KNOW SOMEBODY OFFERED YOU A SIDE JOB!
HE WOULD ONLY TALK TO YOU BECAUSE IT WAS ABOUT ART!
JAMES, WHAT ARE YOU BABBLING ABOUT?
A SIDE JOB, FOR SOME EASY CASH!
DON'T FIB! I TOLD HIM YOU'D BE HERE!
YOU TOLD A COMPLETE STRANGER ABOUT OUR HIDEOUT?!
I TOLD YOU NEVER TO TALK TO STRANGERS!
EARL!
BUT... BUT...
PEOPLE BE SNOOPIN' AROUND OUTSIDE!
JUST AS I FEARED.

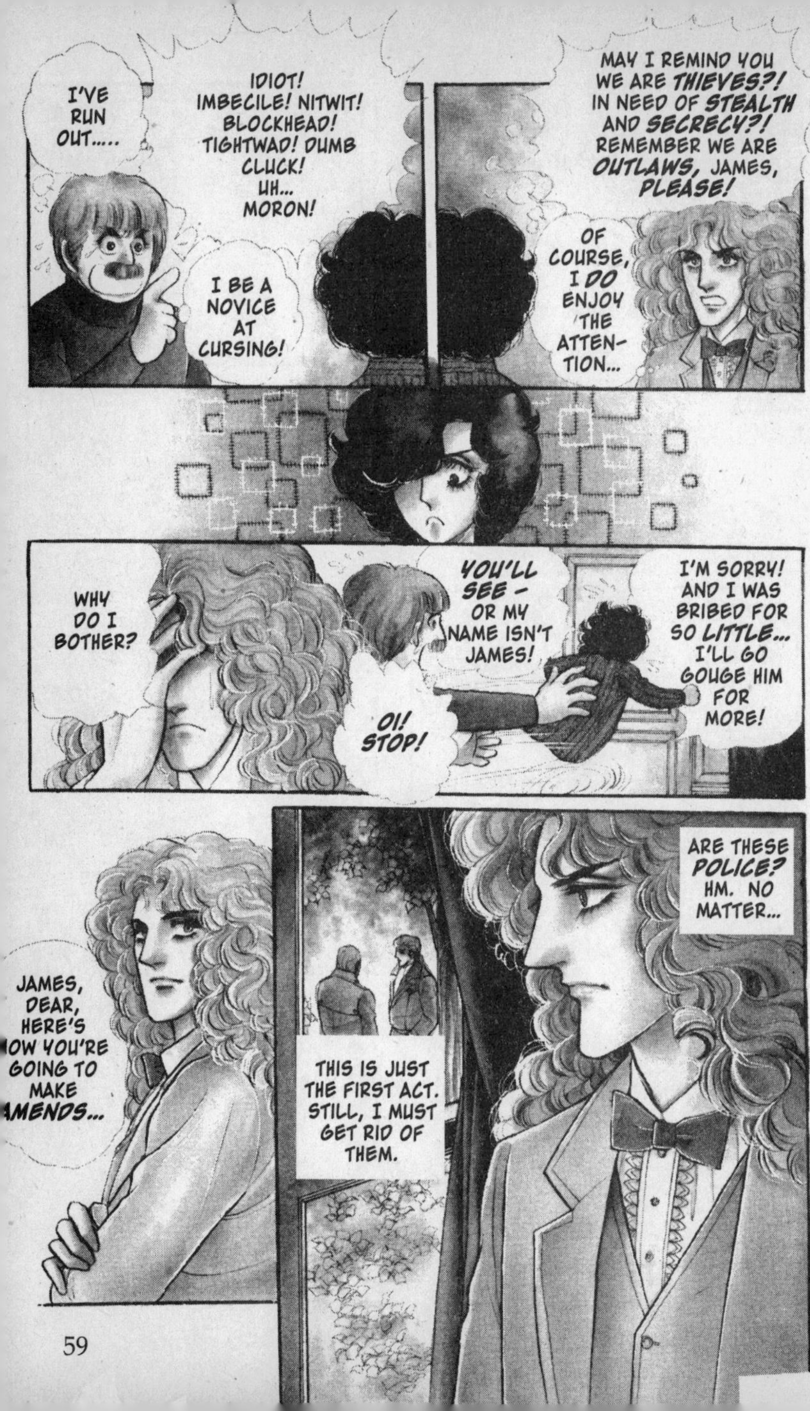

MAY I REMIND YOU WE ARE *THIEVES?!* IN NEED OF *STEALTH* AND *SECRECY?!* REMEMBER WE ARE *OUTLAWS,* JAMES, *PLEASE!*
OF COURSE, I *DO* ENJOY THE ATTENTION...
IDIOT! IMBECILE! NITWIT! BLOCKHEAD! TIGHTWAD! DUMB CLUCK! UH... MORON!
I'VE RUN OUT.....
I BE A NOVICE AT CURSING!
I'M SORRY! AND I WAS BRIBED FOR SO *LITTLE...* I'LL GO GOUGE HIM FOR MORE!
YOU'LL SEE – OR MY NAME ISN'T JAMES!
OI! STOP!
WHY DO I BOTHER?
ARE THESE *POLICE?* HM. NO MATTER...
THIS IS JUST THE FIRST ACT. STILL, I MUST GET RID OF THEM.
JAMES, DEAR, HERE'S OW YOU'RE GOING TO MAKE AMENDS...

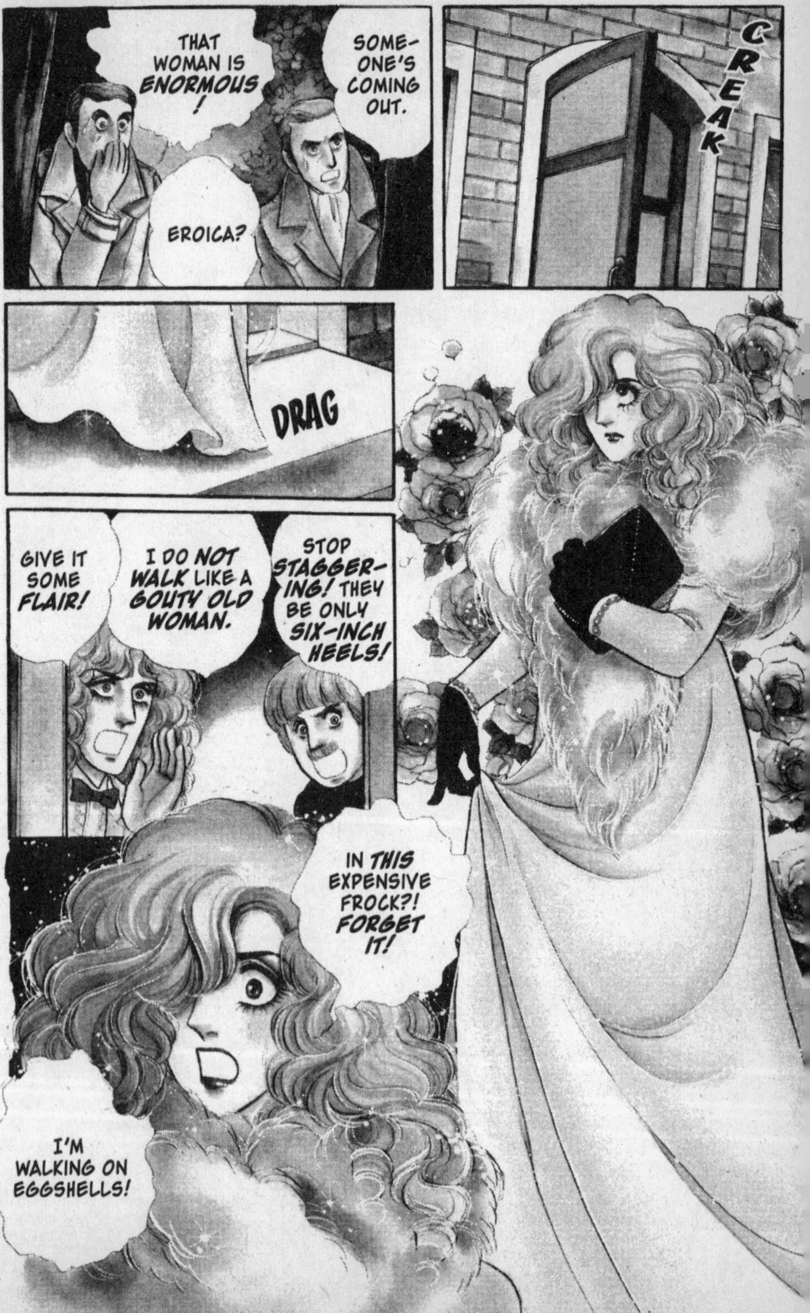
CREAK
SOME-ONE'S COMING OUT.
THAT WOMAN IS ENORMOUS!
EROICA?
DRAG
STOP STAGGERING! THEY BE ONLY SIX-INCH HEELS!
I DO NOT WALK LIKE A GOUTY OLD WOMAN.
GIVE IT SOME FLAIR!
IN THIS EXPENSIVE FROCK?! FORGET IT!
I'M WALKING ON EGGSHELLS!

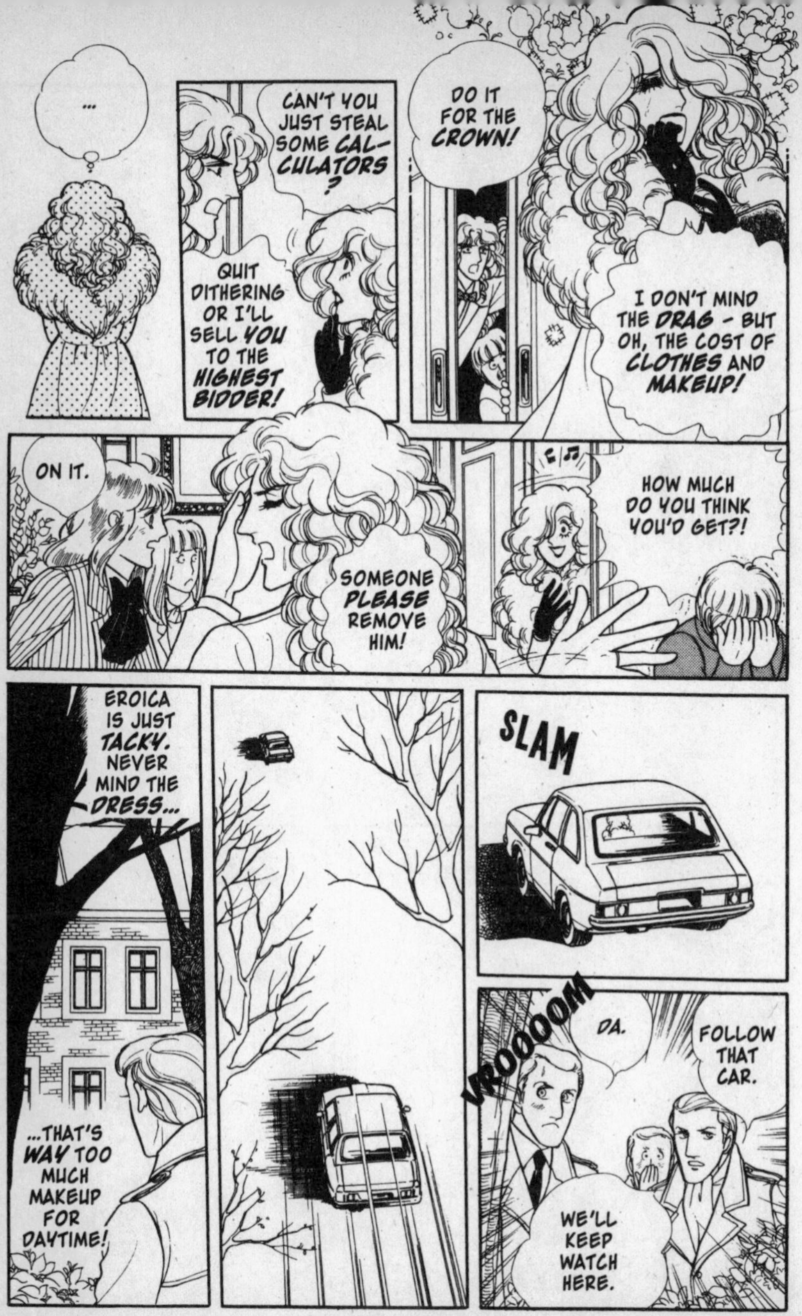
I DON'T MIND THE DRAG - BUT OH, THE COST OF CLOTHES AND MAKEUP!
DO IT FOR THE CROWN!
CAN'T YOU JUST STEAL SOME CAL-CULATORS?
QUIT DITHERING OR I'LL SELL YOU TO THE HIGHEST BIDDER!
...
HOW MUCH DO YOU THINK YOU'D GET?!
SOMEONE PLEASE REMOVE HIM!
ON IT.
SLAM
FOLLOW THAT CAR.
DA.
VROOOOM
WE'LL KEEP WATCH HERE.
ERoICA IS JUST TACKY. NEVER MIND THE DRESS...
...THAT'S WAY TOO MUCH MAKEUP FOR DAYTIME!

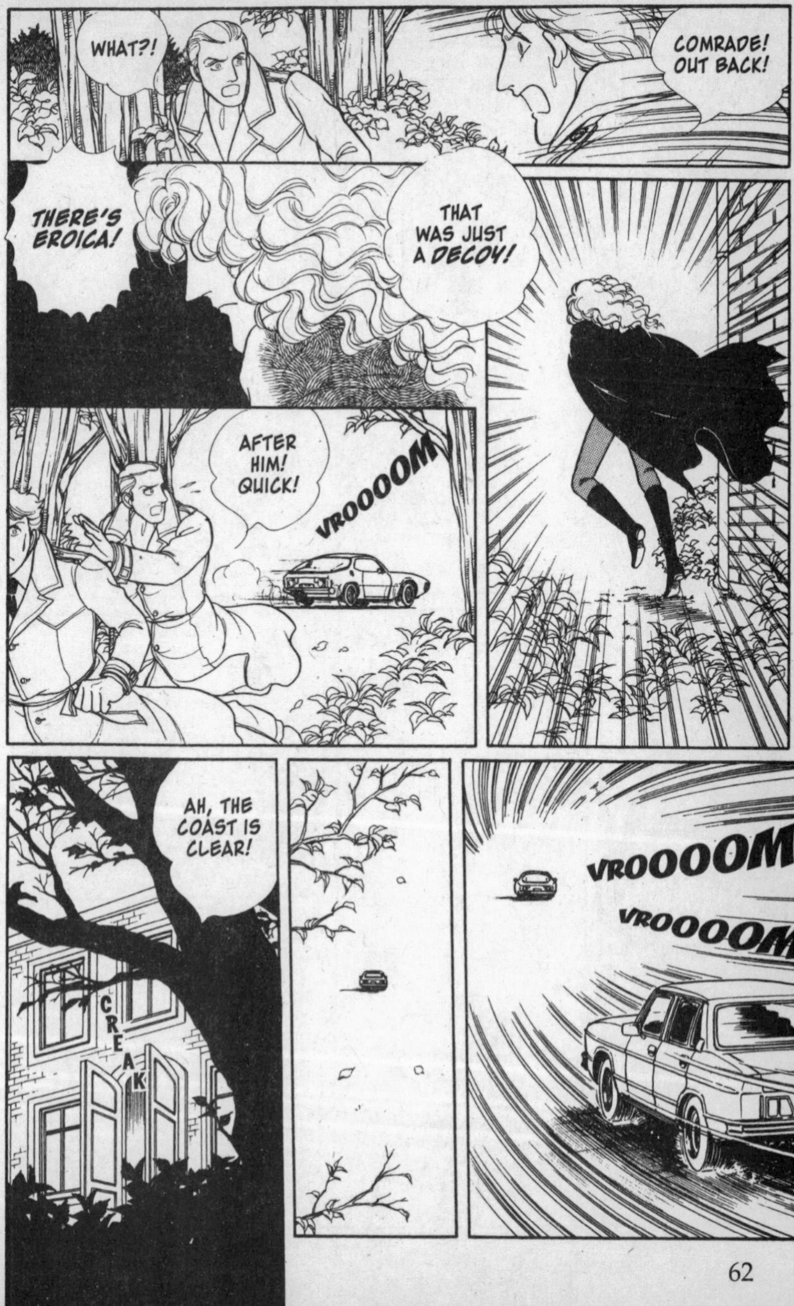
COMRADE! OUT BACK!
WHAT?!
THAT WAS JUST A *DECOY!*
THERE'S EROICA!
AFTER HIM! QUICK!
VROOOOM
VROOOOM
VROOOOM
AH, THE COAST IS CLEAR!
CREAK

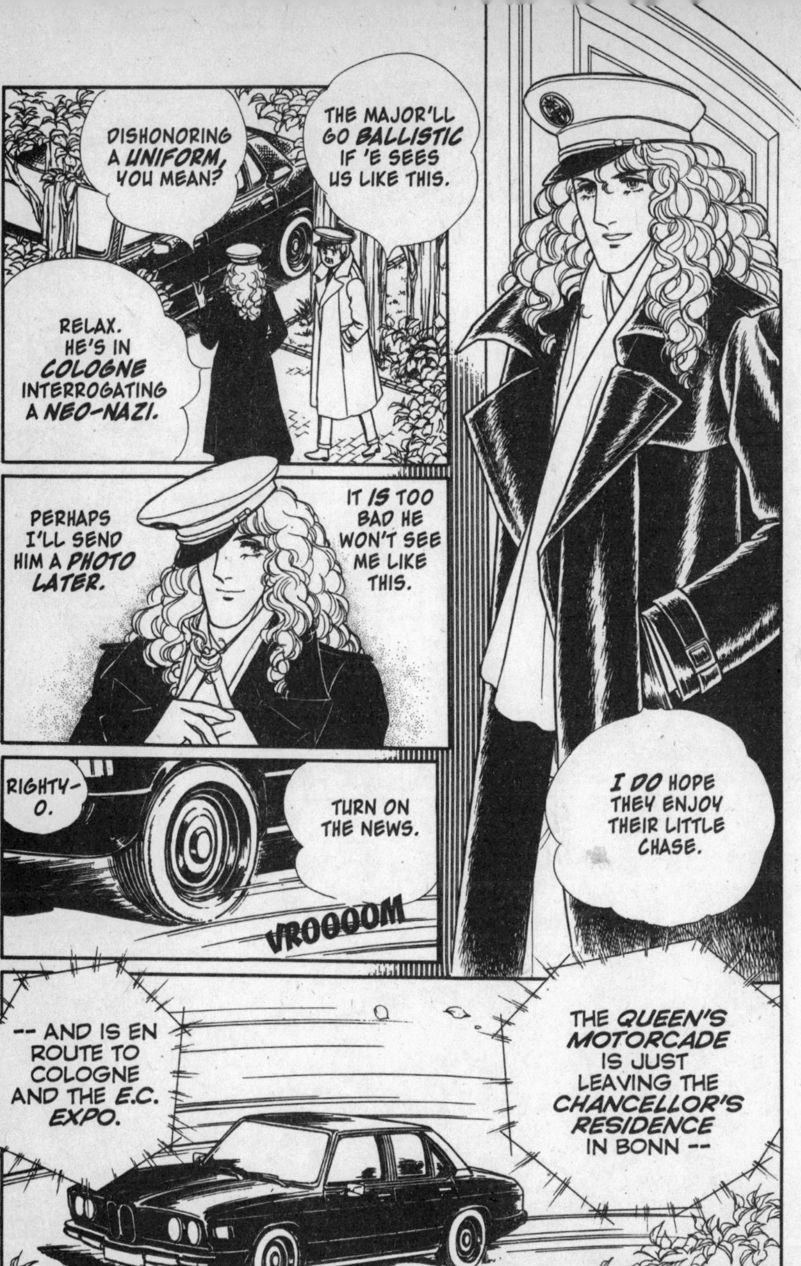
I DO HOPE THEY ENJOY THEIR LITTLE CHASE.
THE MAJOR'LL GO BALLISTIC IF 'E SEES US LIKE THIS.
DISHONORING A UNIFORM, YOU MEAN?
RELAX. HE'S IN COLOGNE INTERROGATING A NEO-NAZI.
IT IS TOO BAD HE WON'T SEE ME LIKE THIS.
PERHAPS I'LL SEND HIM A PHOTO LATER.
TURN ON THE NEWS.
RIGHTY-O.
VROOOOM
THE QUEEN'S MOTORCADE IS JUST LEAVING THE CHANCELLOR'S RESIDENCE IN BONN --
-- AND IS EN ROUTE TO COLOGNE AND THE E.C. EXPO.

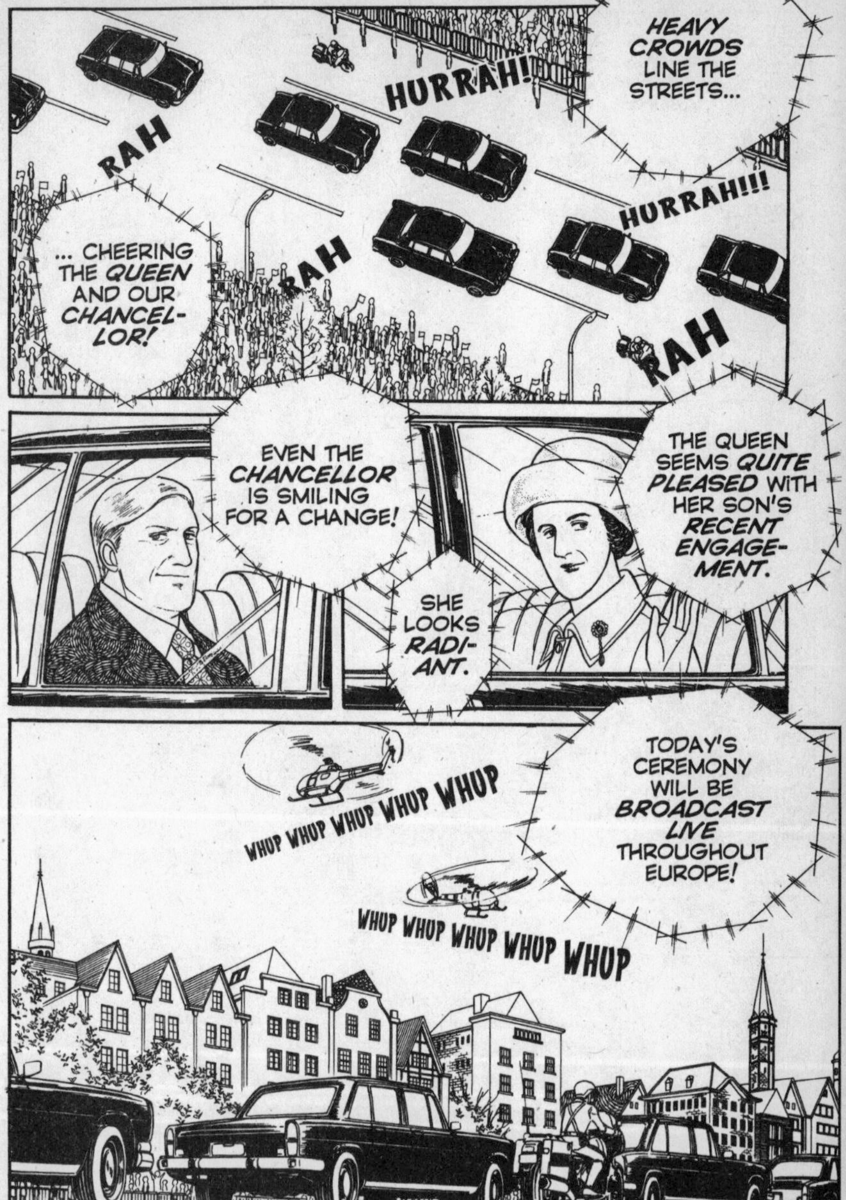
HEAVY CROWDS LINE THE STREETS...
HURRAH!
RAH
HURRAH!!!
RAH
... CHEERING THE QUEEN AND OUR CHANCEL-LOR!
RAH
THE QUEEN SEEMS QUITE PLEASED WITH HER SON'S RECENT ENGAGE-MENT.
SHE LOOKS RADI-ANT.
EVEN THE CHANCELLOR IS SMILING FOR A CHANGE!
TODAY'S CEREMONY WILL BE BROADCAST LIVE THROUGHOUT EUROPE!
WHUP WHUP WHUP WHUP
WHUP WHUP WHUP WHUP WHUP

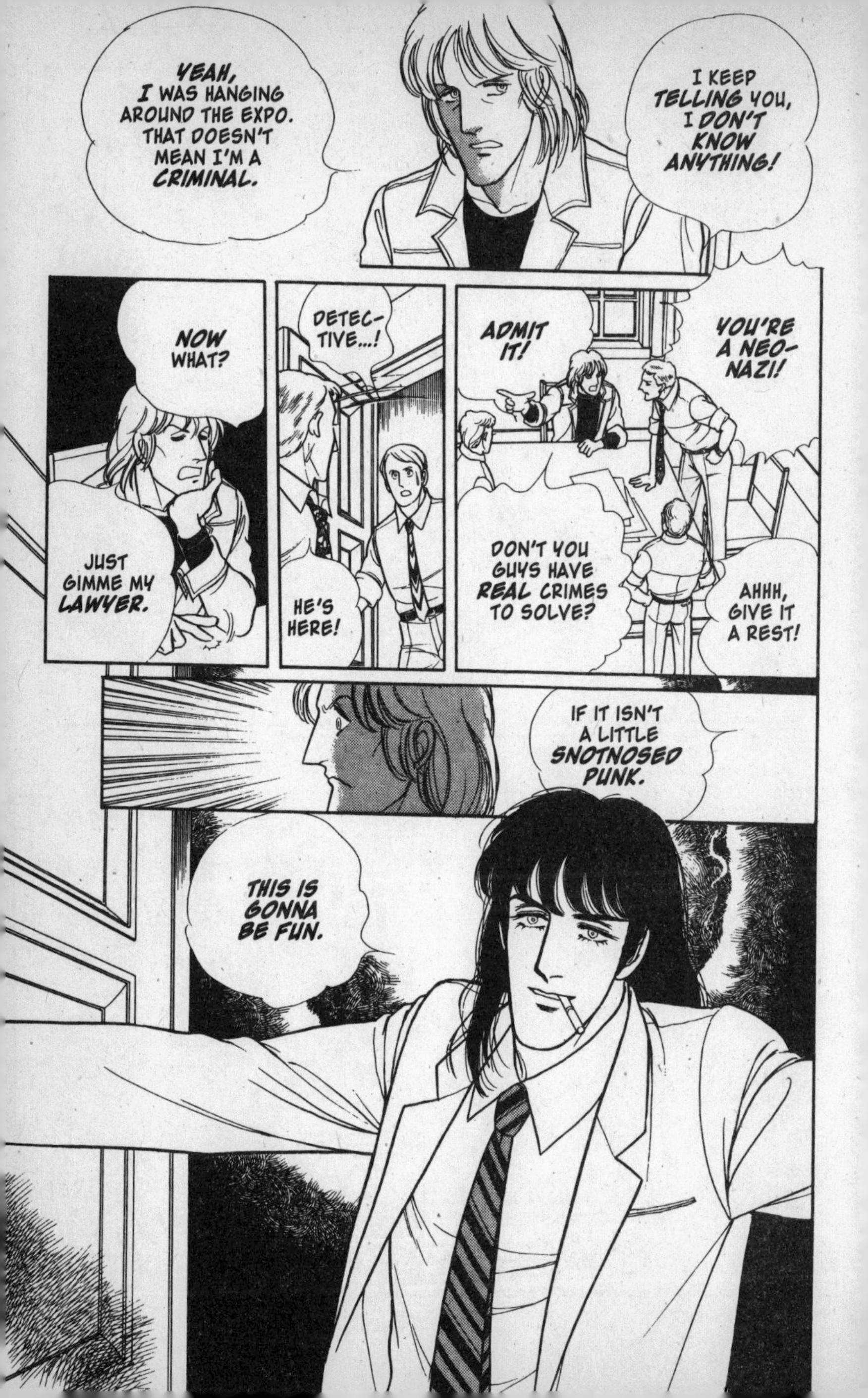
I KEEP TELLING YOU, I DON'T KNOW ANYTHING!
YEAH, I WAS HANGING AROUND THE EXPO. THAT DOESN'T MEAN I'M A CRIMINAL.
YOU'RE A NEO-NAZI!
ADMIT IT!
AHHH, GIVE IT A REST!
DON'T YOU GUYS HAVE REAL CRIMES TO SOLVE?
DETEC-TIVE...!
HE'S HERE!
NOW WHAT?
JUST GIMME MY LAWYER.
IF IT ISN'T A LITTLE SNOTNOSED PUNK.
THIS IS GONNA BE FUN.

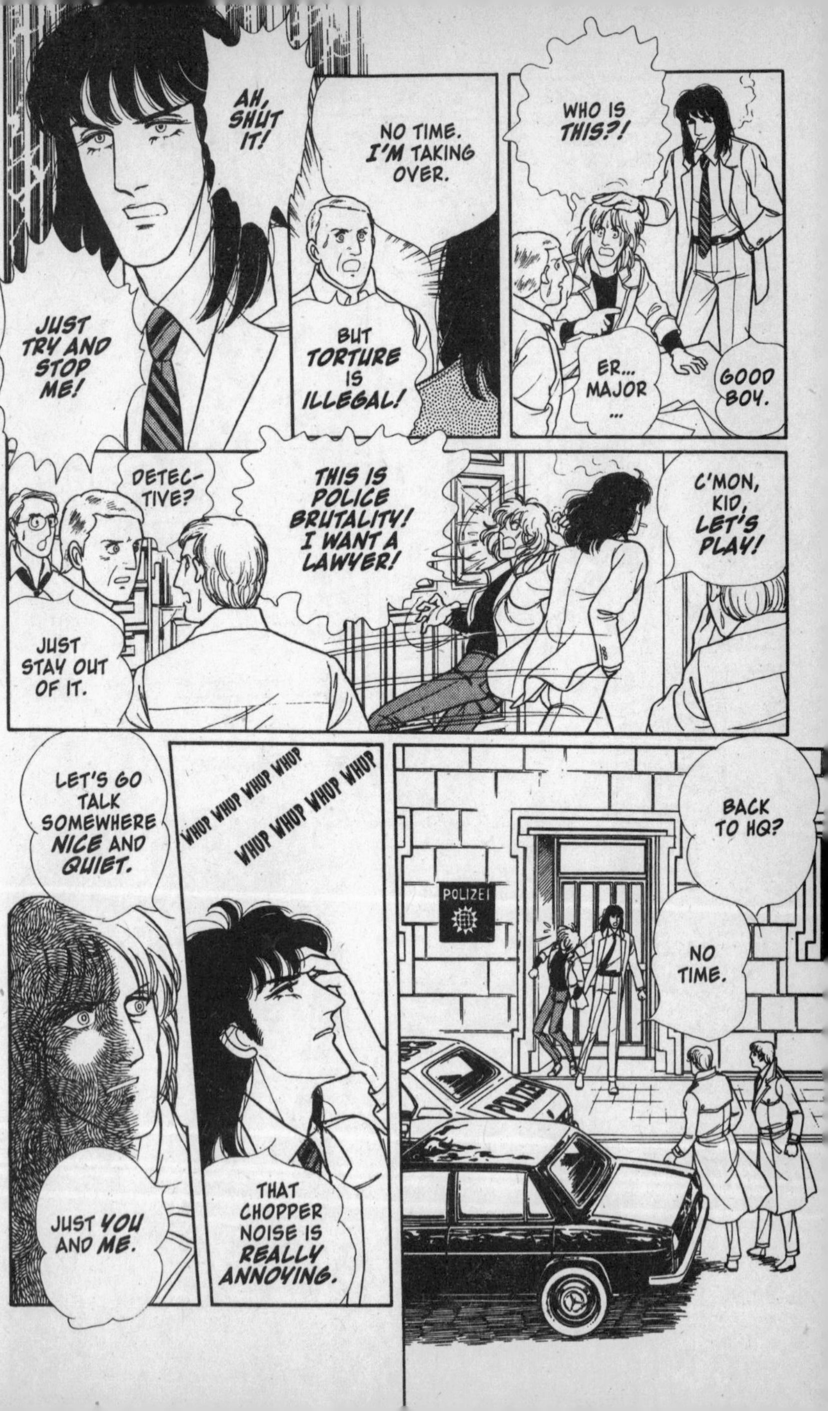
WHO IS THIS?!
ER... MAJOR ...
GOOD BOY.
NO TIME. I'M TAKING OVER.
BUT TORTURE IS ILLEGAL!
AH, SHUT IT!
JUST TRY AND STOP ME!
C'MON, KID, LET'S PLAY!
THIS IS POLICE BRUTALITY! I WANT A LAWYER!
DETECTIVE?
JUST STAY OUT OF IT.
BACK TO HQ?
NO TIME.
POLIZEI
WHOP WHOP WHOP WHOP
WHOP WHOP WHOP WHOP
LET'S GO TALK SOMEWHERE NICE AND QUIET.
THAT CHOPPER NOISE IS REALLY ANNOYING.
JUST YOU AND ME.

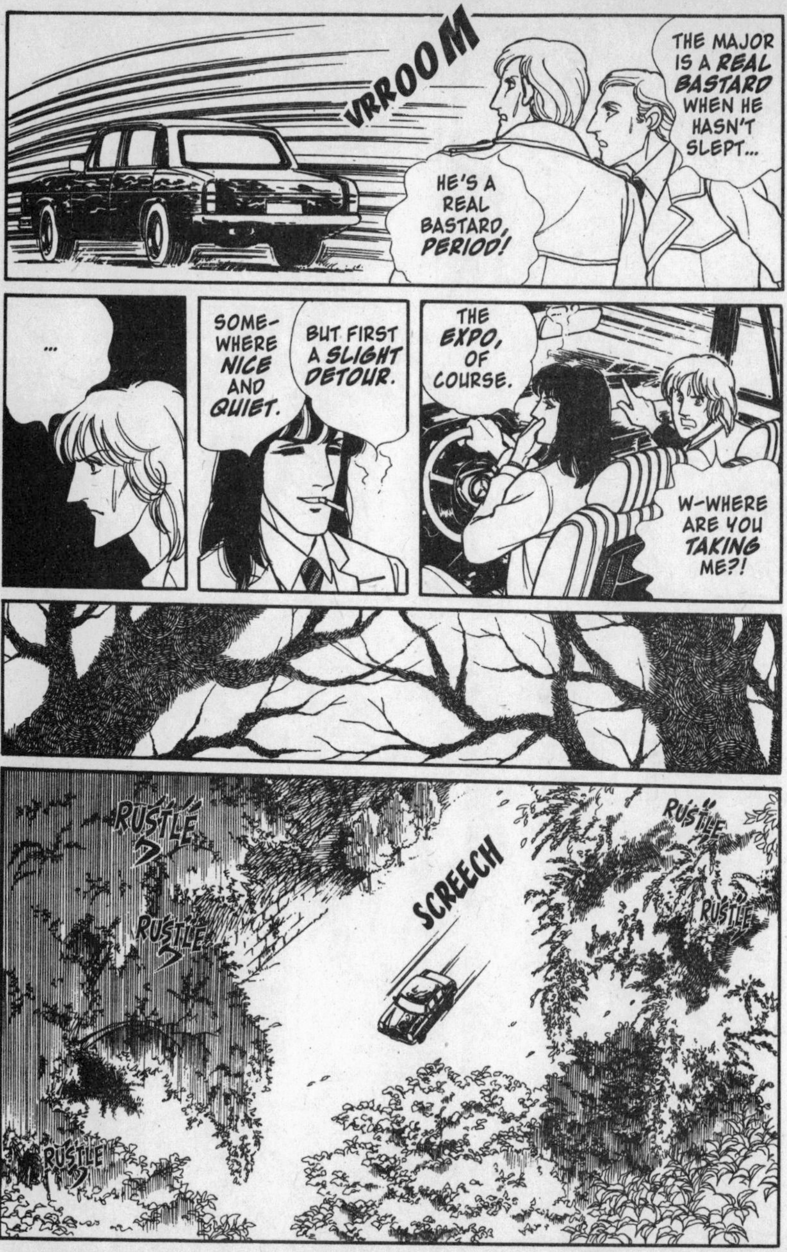
THE MAJOR IS A *REAL BASTARD* WHEN HE HASN'T SLEPT...
HE'S A REAL BASTARD, *PERIOD!*
VRROOM
W-WHERE ARE YOU *TAKING* ME?!
THE *EXPO,* OF COURSE.
BUT FIRST A *SLIGHT DETOUR.*
SOME-WHERE *NICE* AND *QUIET.*
...
RUSTLE
RUSTLE
SCREECH
RUSTLE
RUSTLE
RUSTLE

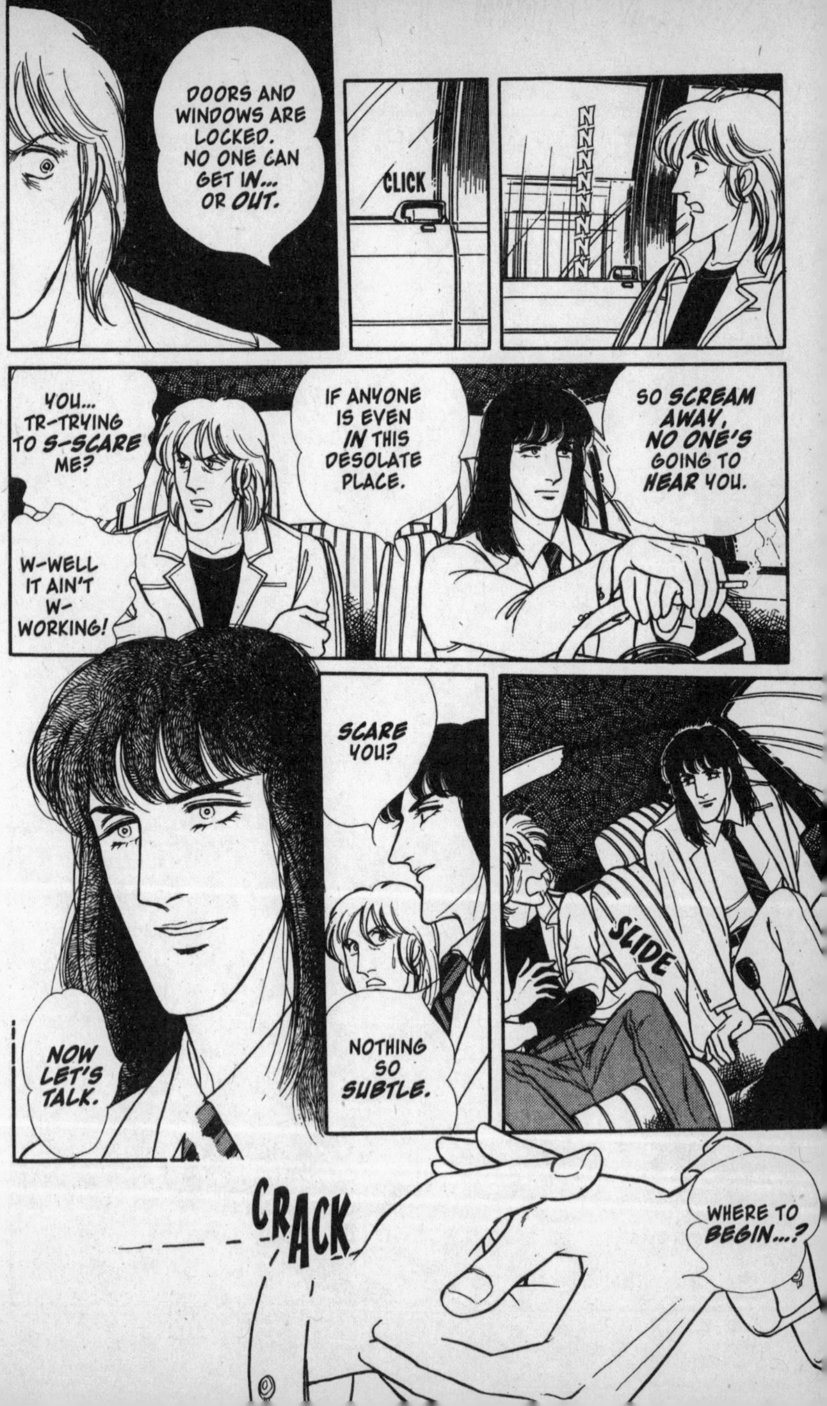
NNNNNNNNNN
CLICK
DOORS AND WINDOWS ARE LOCKED. NO ONE CAN GET IN... OR OUT.
SO SCREAM AWAY, NO ONE'S GOING TO HEAR YOU.
IF ANYONE IS EVEN IN THIS DESOLATE PLACE.
YOU... TR-TRYING TO S-SCARE ME?
W-WELL IT AIN'T W-WORKING!
SLIDE
SCARE YOU?
NOTHING SO SUBTLE.
NOW LET'S TALK.
WHERE TO BEGIN...?
CRACK

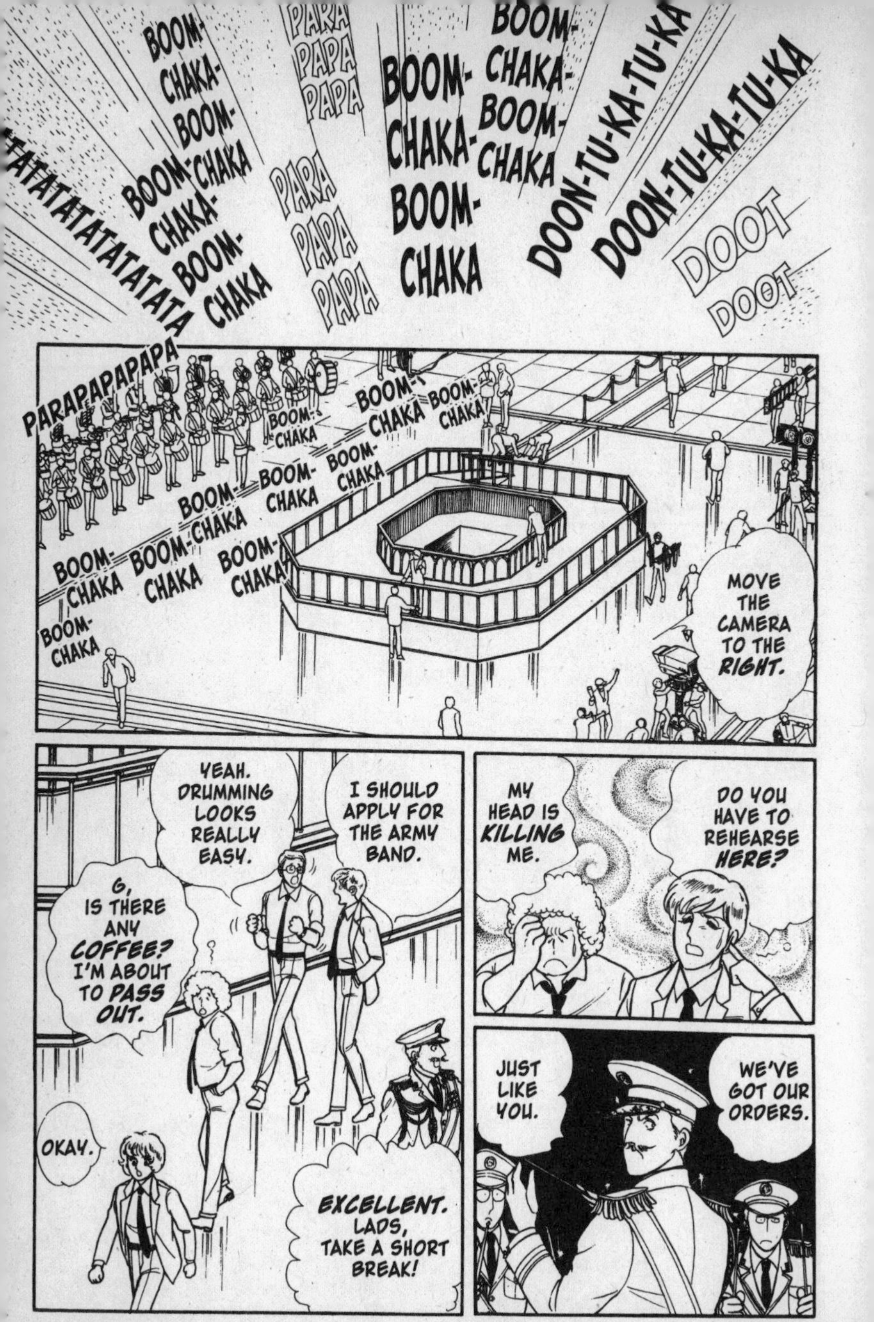
DOOT
DOOT
DOON-TU-KA-TU-KA
DOON-TU-KA-TU-KA
BOOM-CHAKA-BOOM-CHAKA
BOOM-CHAKA-BOOM-CHAKA
PARA PAPA PAPA
PARA PAPA PAPA
BOOM-CHAKA-BOOM-CHAKA
BOOM-CHAKA-BOOM-CHAKA
TATATATATATATATA
MOVE THE CAMERA TO THE RIGHT.
BOOM-CHAKA
BOOM-CHAKA
BOOM-CHAKA
BOOM-CHAKA
BOOM-CHAKA
BOOM-CHAKA
BOOM-CHAKA
BOOM-CHAKA
BOOM-CHAKA
BOOM-CHAKA
PARAPAPAPAPA
DO YOU HAVE TO REHEARSE HERE?
MY HEAD IS KILLING ME.
WE'VE GOT OUR ORDERS.
JUST LIKE YOU.
I SHOULD APPLY FOR THE ARMY BAND.
YEAH. DRUMMING LOOKS REALLY EASY.
G, IS THERE ANY COFFEE? I'M ABOUT TO PASS OUT.
EXCELLENT. LADS, TAKE A SHORT BREAK!
OKAY.

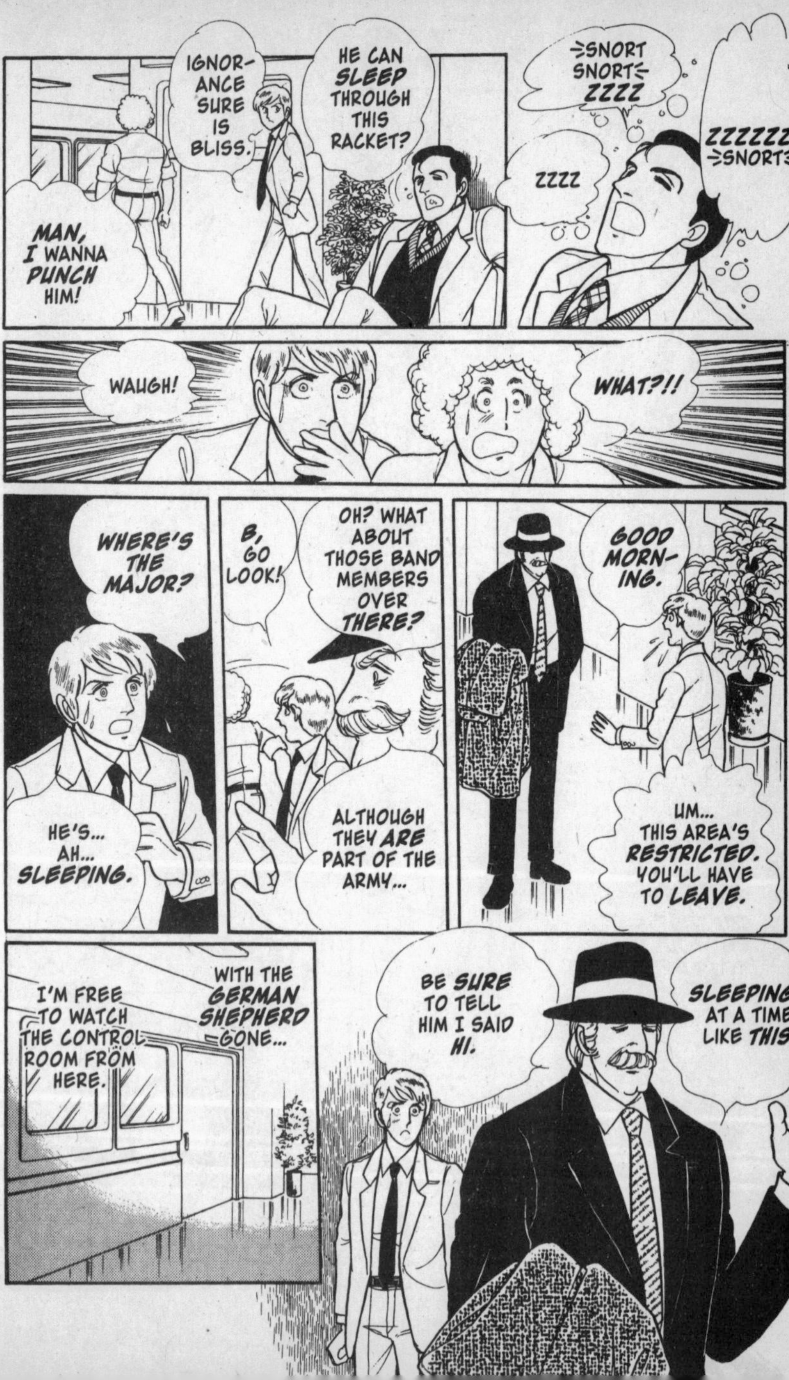
SNORT SNORT ZZZZ
ZZZZZZ SNORT
ZZZZ
HE CAN SLEEP THROUGH THIS RACKET?
IGNORANCE SURE IS BLISS.
MAN, I WANNA PUNCH HIM!
WHAT?!!
WAUGH!
GOOD MORNING.
UM... THIS AREA'S RESTRICTED. YOU'LL HAVE TO LEAVE.
OH? WHAT ABOUT THOSE BAND MEMBERS OVER THERE?
B, GO LOOK!
ALTHOUGH THEY ARE PART OF THE ARMY...
WHERE'S THE MAJOR?
HE'S... AH... SLEEPING.
SLEEPING? AT A TIME LIKE THIS?
BE SURE TO TELL HIM I SAID HI.
WITH THE GERMAN SHEPHERD GONE...
I'M FREE TO WATCH THE CONTROL ROOM FROM HERE.

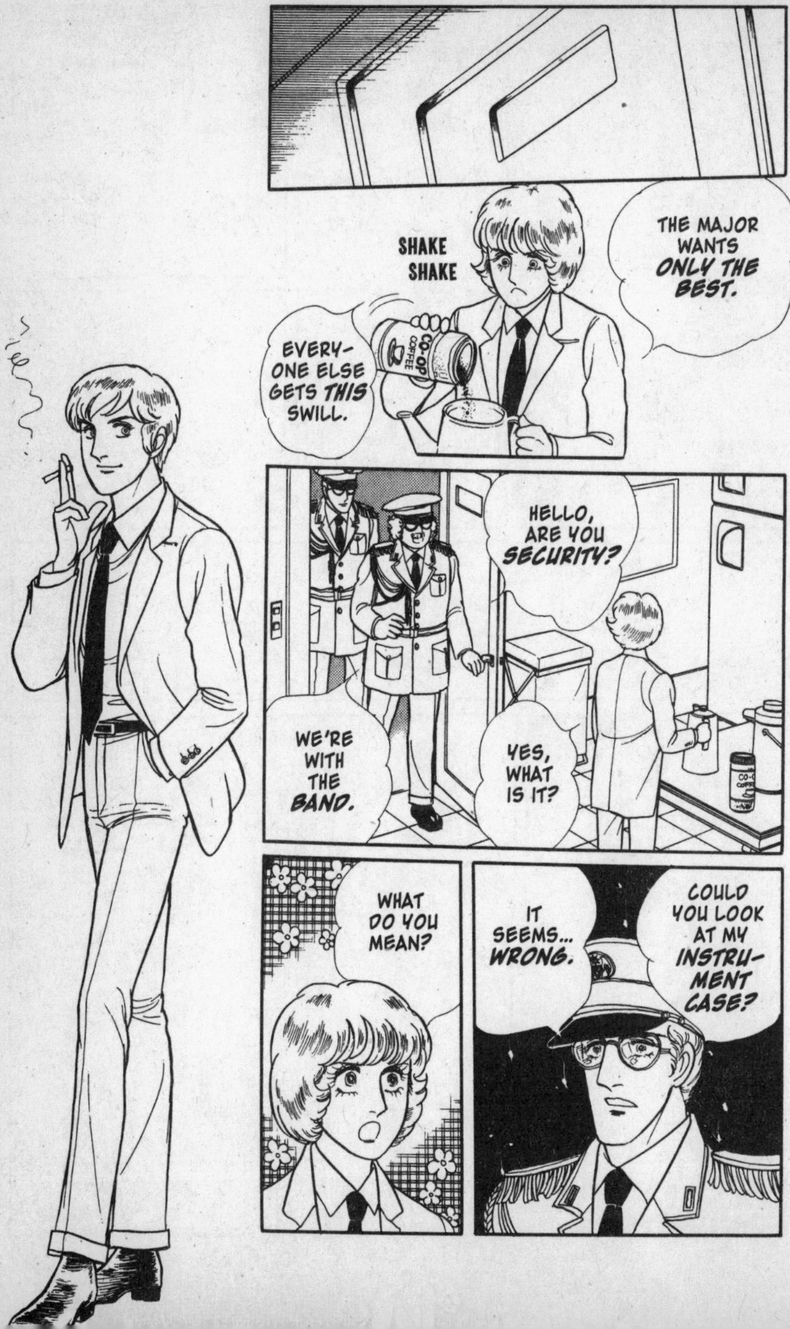
THE MAJOR WANTS ONLY THE BEST.
SHAKE SHAKE
CO-OP COFFEE
EVERY-ONE ELSE GETS THIS SWILL.
HELLO, ARE YOU SECURITY?
YES, WHAT IS IT?
WE'RE WITH THE BAND.
COULD YOU LOOK AT MY INSTRU-MENT CASE?
IT SEEMS... WRONG.
WHAT DO YOU MEAN?

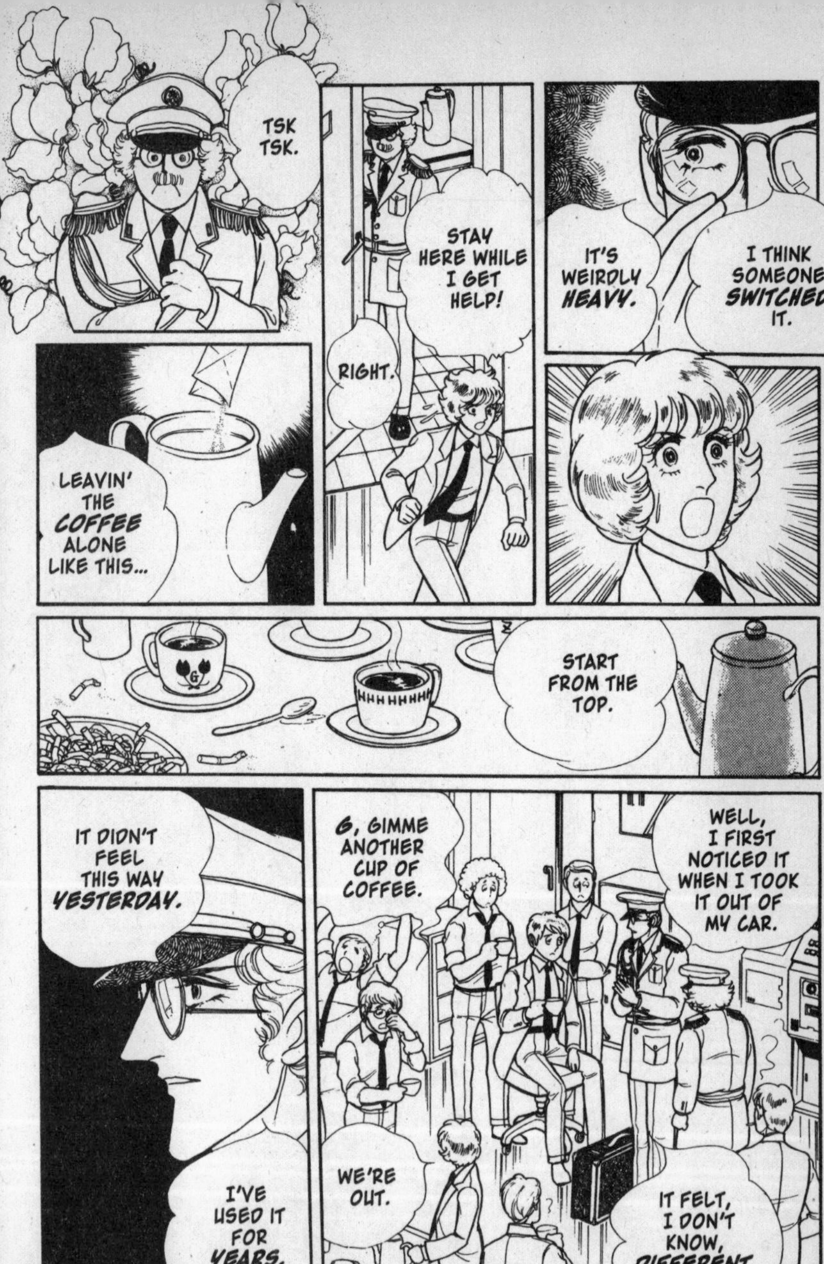
I THINK SOMEONE SWITCHED IT.
IT'S WEIRDLY HEAVY.
STAY HERE WHILE I GET HELP!
RIGHT.
TSK TSK.
LEAVIN' THE COFFEE ALONE LIKE THIS...
START FROM THE TOP.
WELL, I FIRST NOTICED IT WHEN I TOOK IT OUT OF MY CAR.
G, GIMME ANOTHER CUP OF COFFEE.
IT FELT, I DON'T KNOW, DIFFERENT.
WE'RE OUT.
IT DIDN'T FEEL THIS WAY YESTERDAY.
I'VE USED IT FOR YEARS.

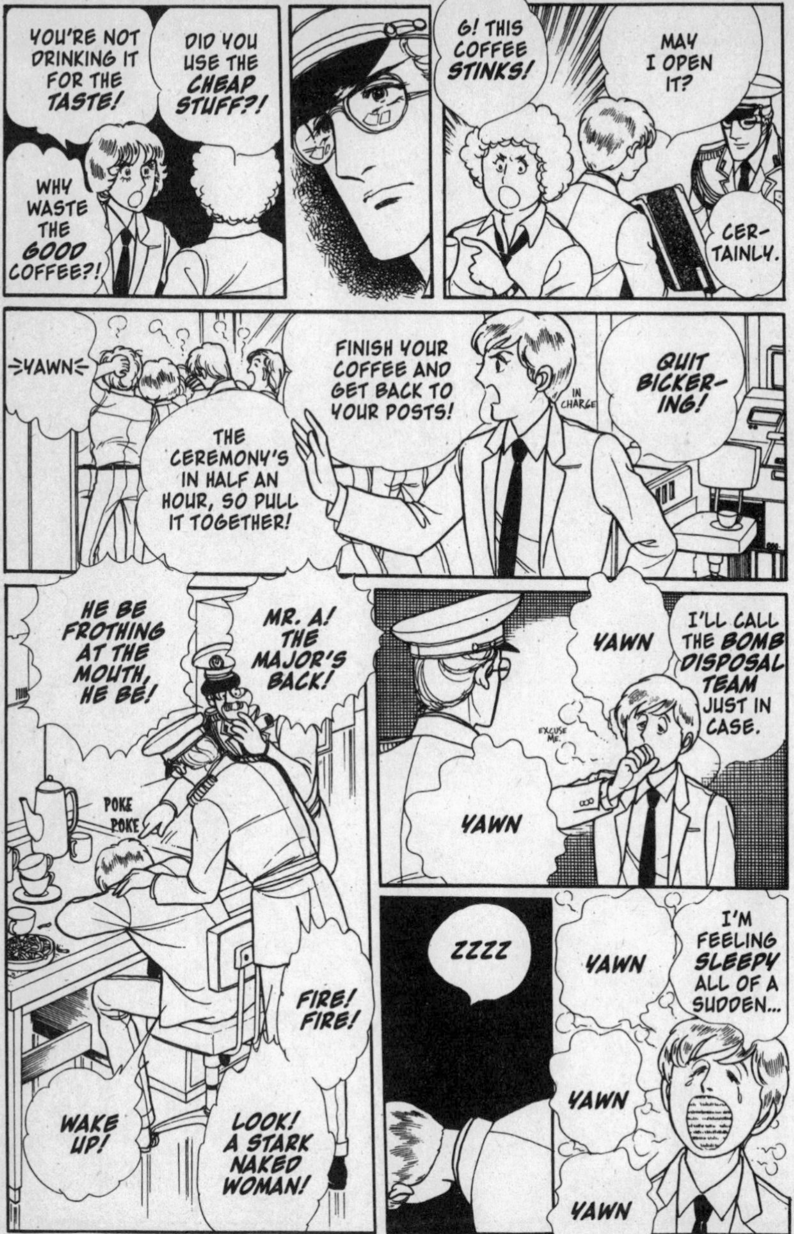
MAY I OPEN IT?
G! THIS COFFEE STINKS!
CER-TAINLY.
DID YOU USE THE CHEAP STUFF?!
YOU'RE NOT DRINKING IT FOR THE TASTE!
WHY WASTE THE GOOD COFFEE?!
QUIT BICKER-ING!
IN CHARGE
FINISH YOUR COFFEE AND GET BACK TO YOUR POSTS!
THE CEREMONY'S IN HALF AN HOUR, SO PULL IT TOGETHER!
YAWN
I'LL CALL THE BOMB DISPOSAL TEAM JUST IN CASE.
YAWN
EXCUSE ME.
YAWN
I'M FEELING SLEEPY ALL OF A SUDDEN...
YAWN
ZZZZ
YAWN
YAWN
MR. A! THE MAJOR'S BACK!
HE BE FROTHING AT THE MOUTH, HE BE!
POKE POKE
FIRE! FIRE!
LOOK! A STARK NAKED WOMAN!
WAKE UP!

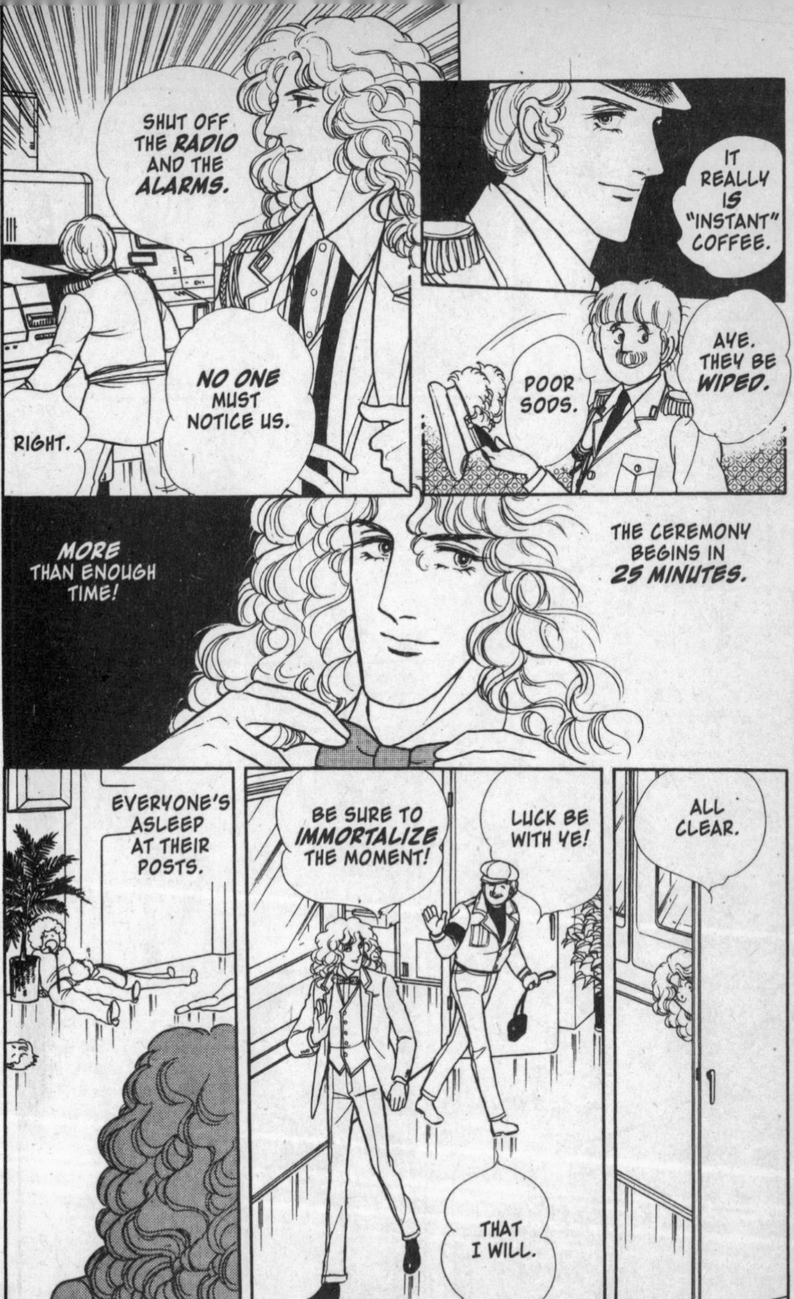
IT REALLY IS "INSTANT" COFFEE.
AYE. THEY BE WIPED.
POOR SODS.
SHUT OFF THE RADIO AND THE ALARMS.
NO ONE MUST NOTICE US.
RIGHT.
THE CEREMONY BEGINS IN 25 MINUTES.
MORE THAN ENOUGH TIME!
ALL CLEAR.
LUCK BE WITH YE!
BE SURE TO IMMORTALIZE THE MOMENT!
THAT I WILL.
EVERYONE'S ASLEEP AT THEIR POSTS.

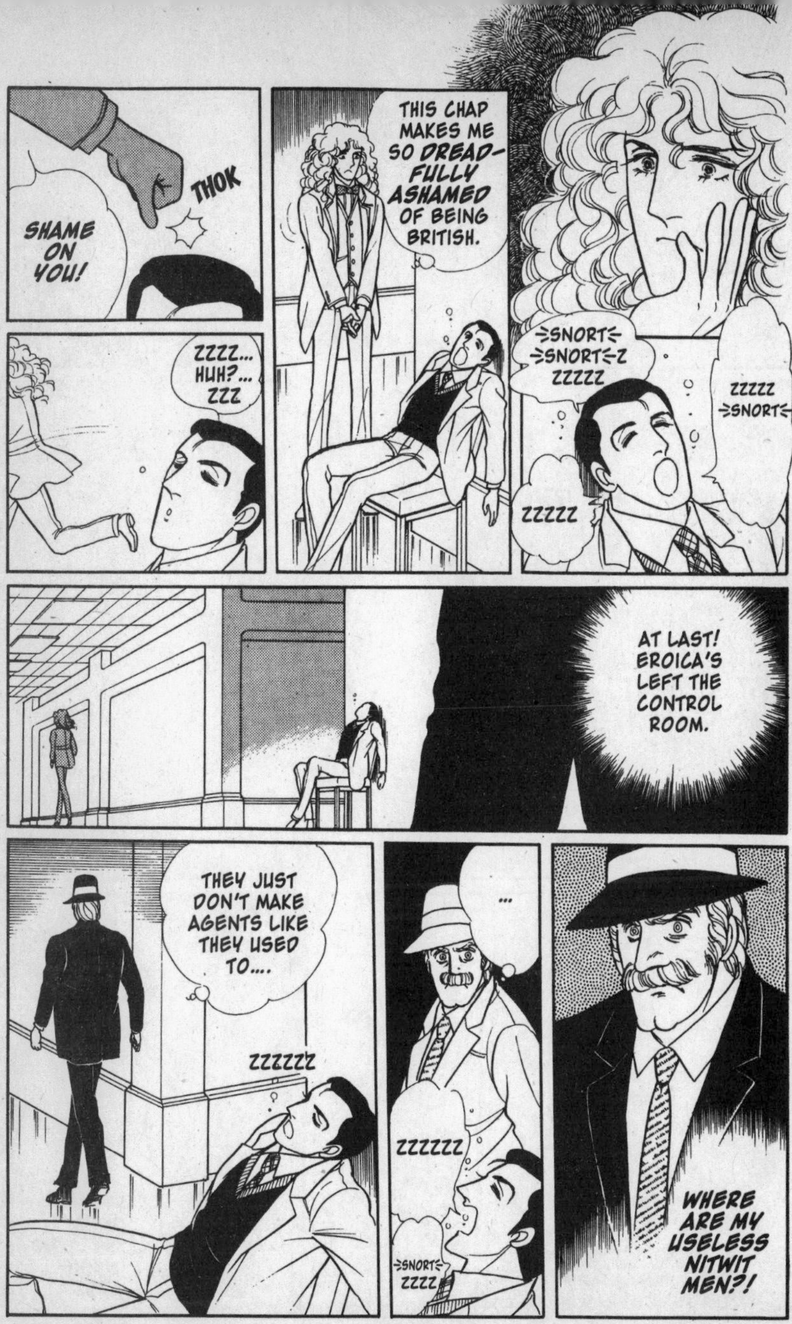

=SNORT=
=SNORT=Z
ZZZZZ
ZZZZZ
=SNORT=
ZZZZZ
THIS CHAP MAKES ME SO DREADFULLY ASHAMED OF BEING BRITISH.
THOK
SHAME ON YOU!
ZZZZ... HUH?... ZZZ
AT LAST! EROICA'S LEFT THE CONTROL ROOM.
WHERE ARE MY USELESS NITWIT MEN?!
...
ZZZZZZ
=SNORT=
ZZZZ
THEY JUST DON'T MAKE AGENTS LIKE THEY USED TO....
ZZZZZZ

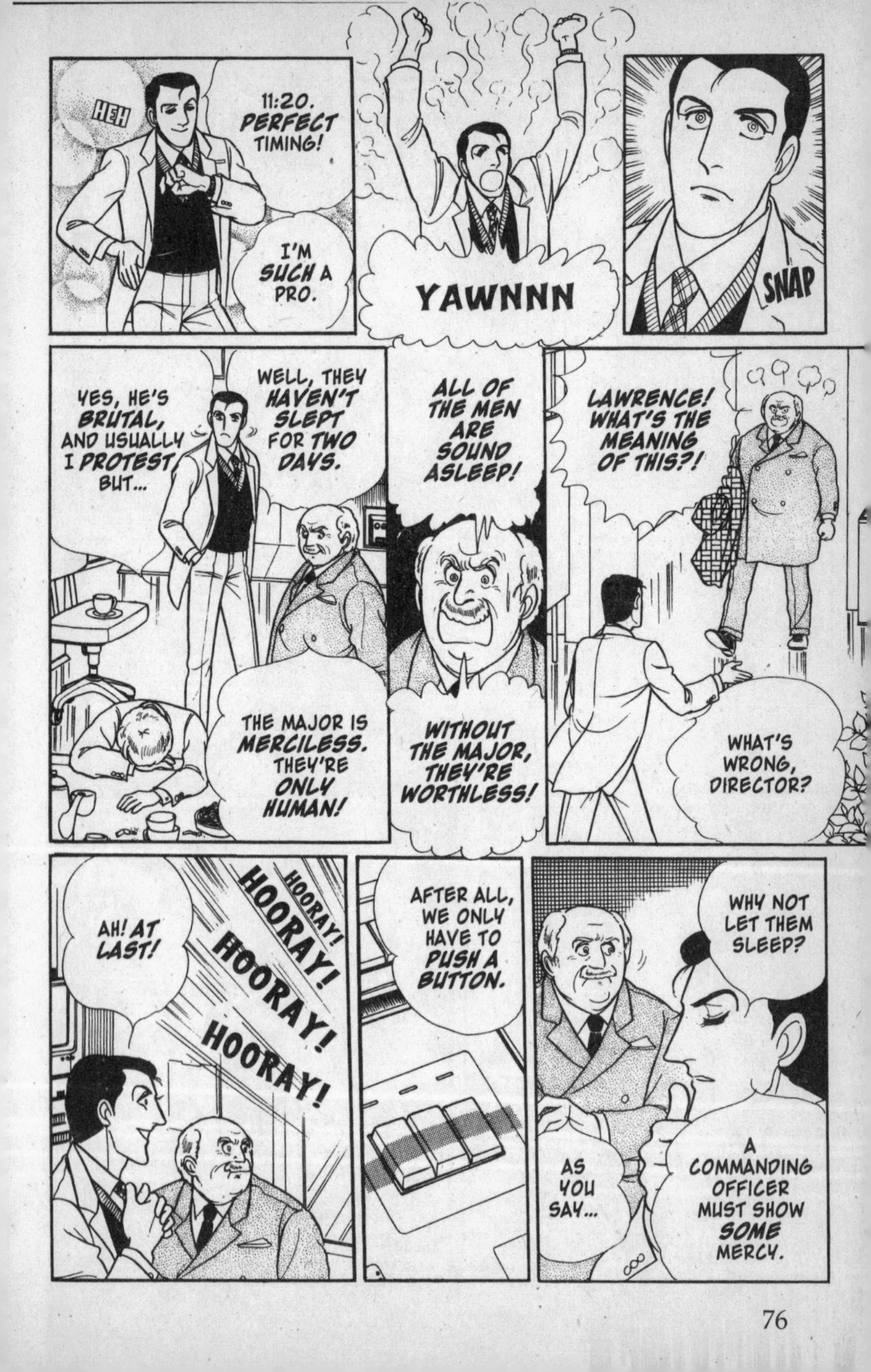
SNAP
YAWNNN
HEH
11:20. PERFECT TIMING!
I'M SUCH A PRO.
LAWRENCE! WHAT'S THE MEANING OF THIS?!
WHAT'S WRONG, DIRECTOR?
ALL OF THE MEN ARE SOUND ASLEEP!
WITHOUT THE MAJOR, THEY'RE WORTHLESS!
WELL, THEY HAVEN'T SLEPT FOR TWO DAYS.
YES, HE'S BRUTAL, AND USUALLY I PROTEST BUT...
THE MAJOR IS MERCILESS. THEY'RE ONLY HUMAN!
WHY NOT LET THEM SLEEP?
A COMMANDING OFFICER MUST SHOW SOME MERCY.
AS YOU SAY...
AFTER ALL, WE ONLY HAVE TO PUSH A BUTTON.
HOORAY!
HOORAY!
HOORAY!
HOORAY!
AH! AT LAST!

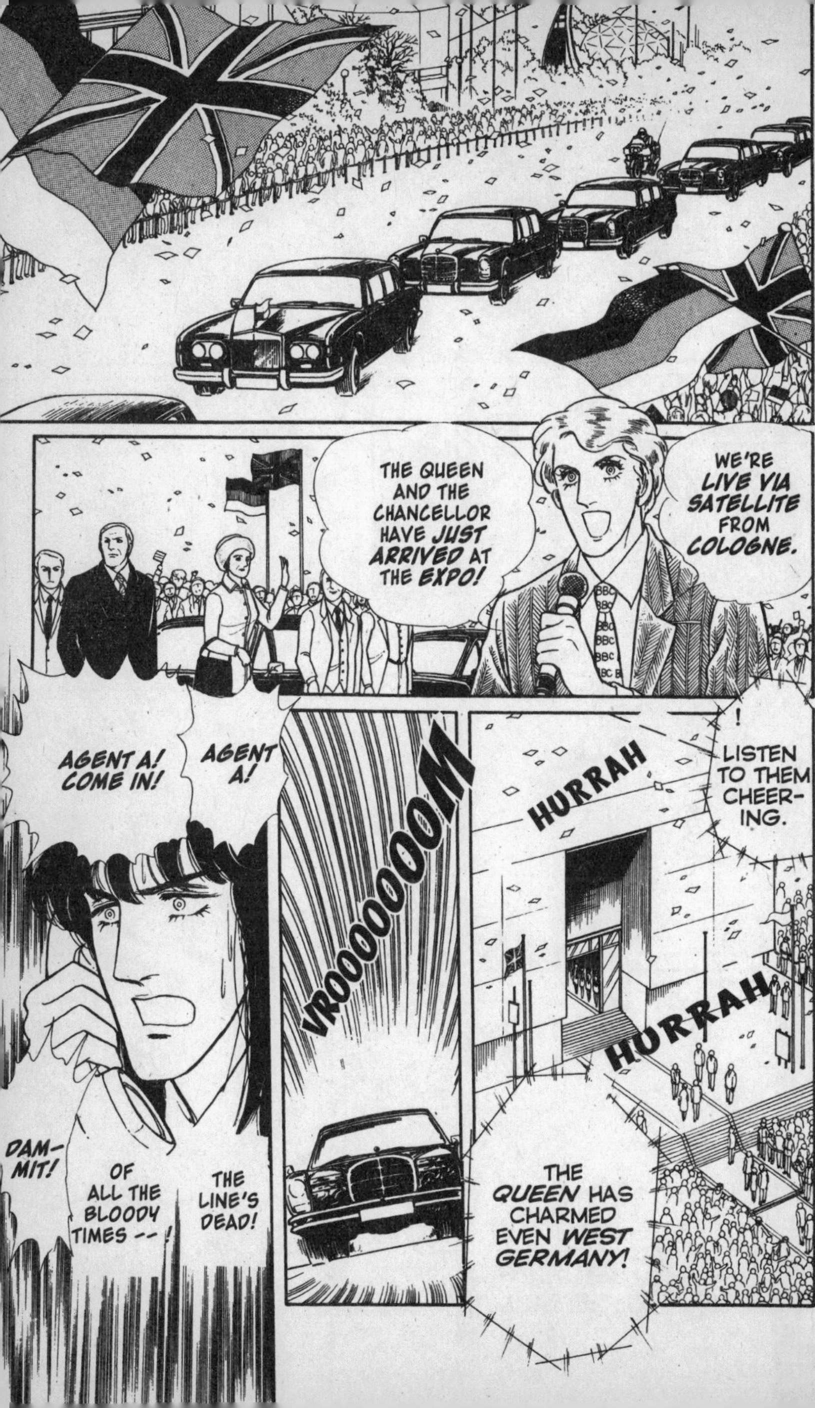
WE'RE LIVE VIA SATELLITE FROM COLOGNE.
THE QUEEN AND THE CHANCELLOR HAVE JUST ARRIVED AT THE EXPO!
!
LISTEN TO THEM CHEER-ING.
HURRAH
HURRAH
THE QUEEN HAS CHARMED EVEN WEST GERMANY!
VROOOOOOOOM
AGENT A!
AGENT A! COME IN!
THE LINE'S DEAD!
OF ALL THE BLOODY TIMES -- !
DAM-MIT!

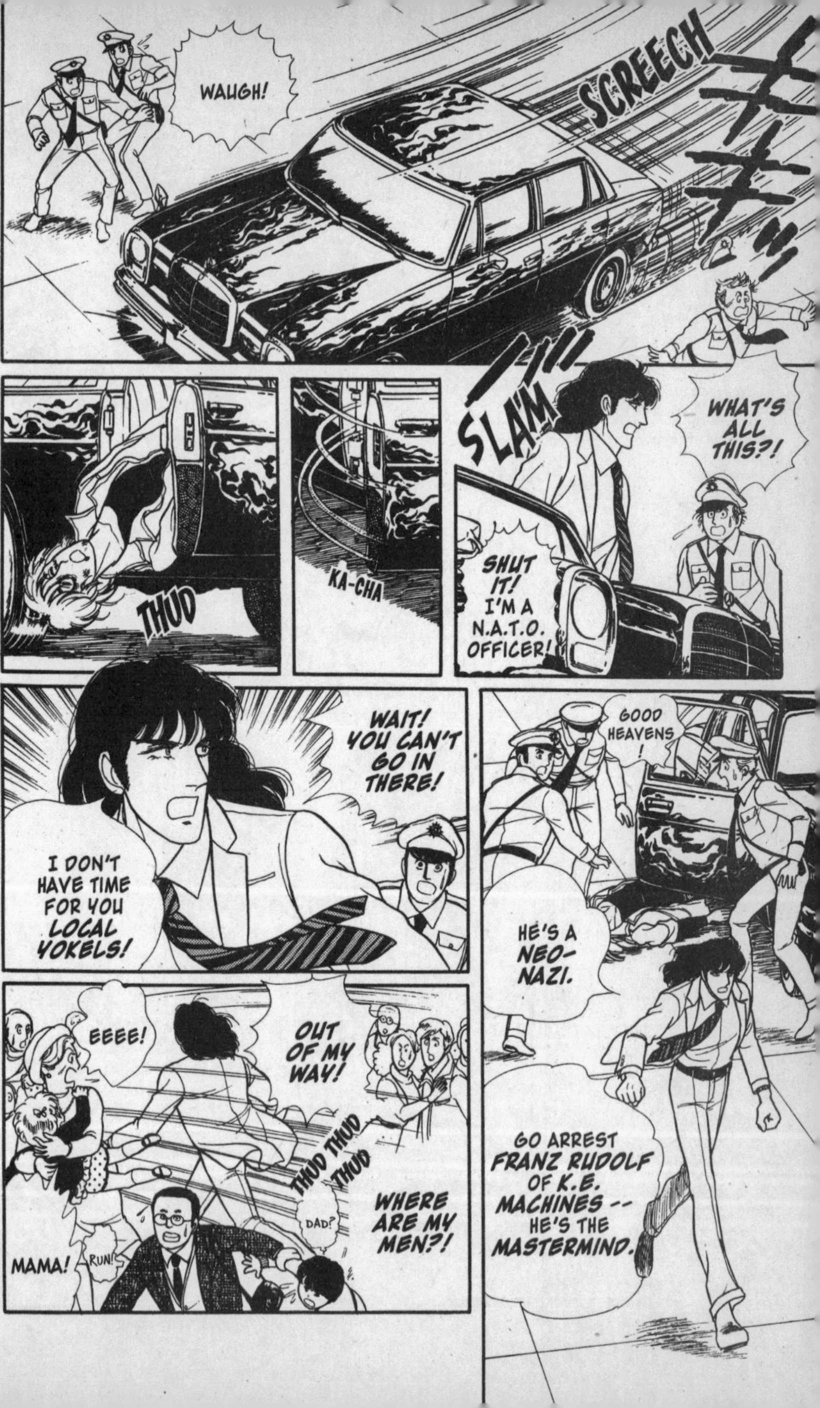
SCREECH
WAUGH!
SLAM
WHAT'S ALL THIS?!
SHUT IT! I'M A N.A.T.O. OFFICER!
KA-CHA
THUD
GOOD HEAVENS!
HE'S A NEO-NAZI.
GO ARREST FRANZ RUDOLF OF K.E. MACHINES -- HE'S THE MASTERMIND.
WAIT! YOU CAN'T GO IN THERE!
I DON'T HAVE TIME FOR YOU LOCAL YOKELS!
OUT OF MY WAY!
EEEE!
THUD THUD THUD
WHERE ARE MY MEN?!
DAD?
RUN!
MAMA!

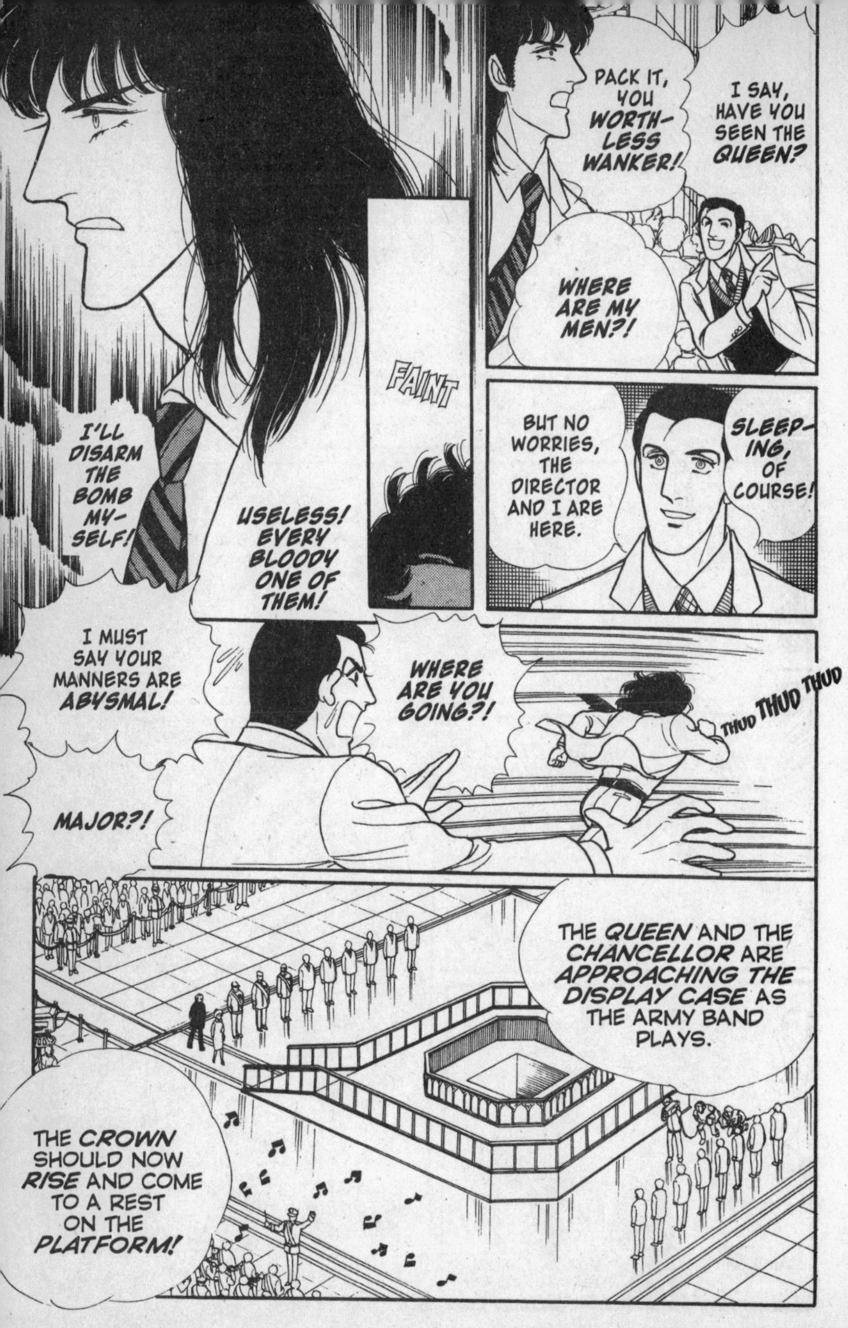
I SAY, HAVE YOU SEEN THE *QUEEN?*
PACK IT, YOU *WORTHLESS WANKER!*
WHERE ARE MY MEN?!
SLEEPING, OF COURSE!
BUT NO WORRIES, THE DIRECTOR AND I ARE HERE.
FAINT
USELESS! EVERY BLOODY ONE OF THEM!
I'LL DISARM THE BOMB MYSELF!
THUD THUD THUD
WHERE ARE YOU GOING?!
I MUST SAY YOUR MANNERS ARE *ABYSMAL!*
MAJOR?!
THE *QUEEN* AND THE *CHANCELLOR* ARE *APPROACHING THE DISPLAY CASE* AS THE ARMY BAND PLAYS.
THE *CROWN* SHOULD NOW *RISE* AND COME TO A REST ON THE *PLATFORM!*

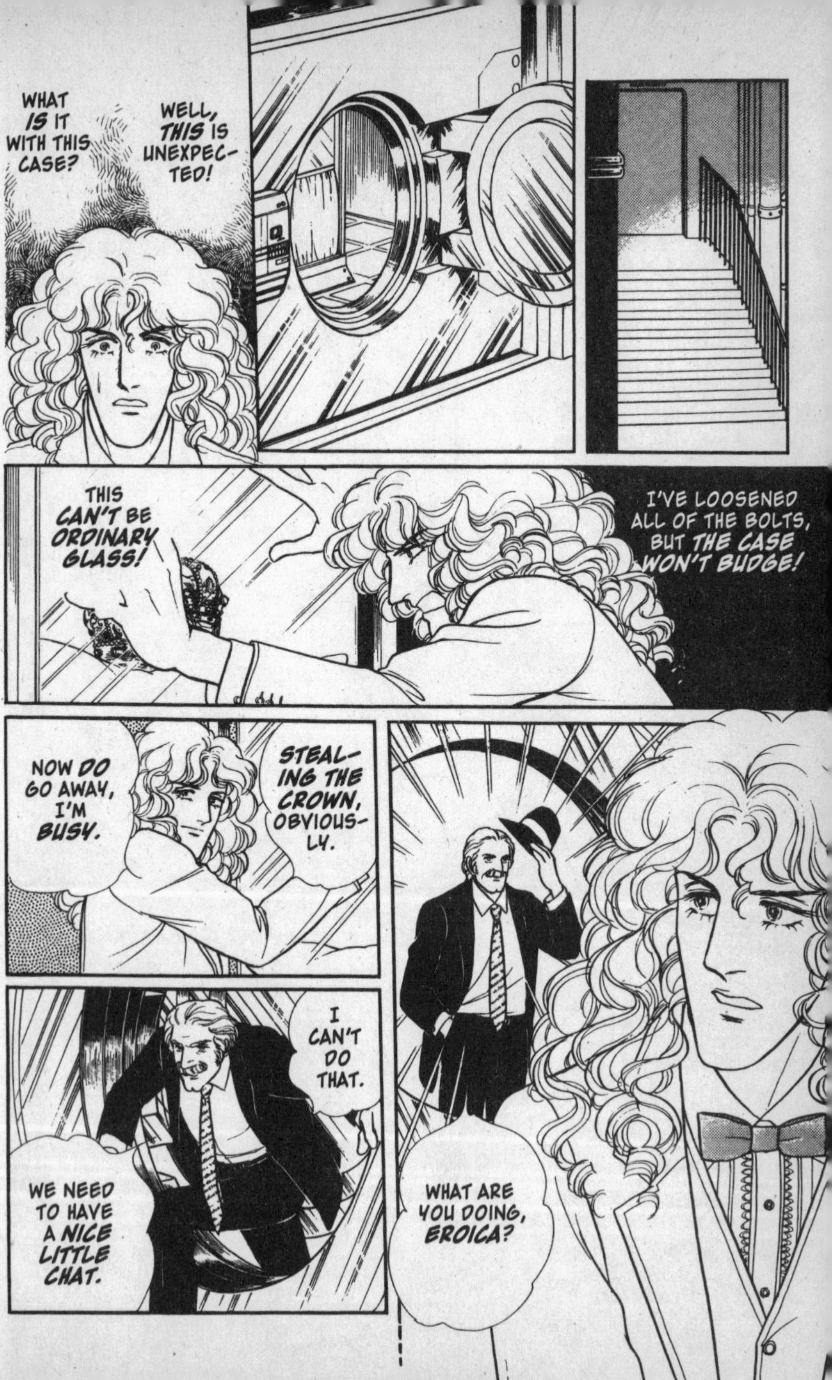
WELL, THIS IS UNEXPECTED!
WHAT IS IT WITH THIS CASE?
I'VE LOOSENED ALL OF THE BOLTS, BUT THE CASE WON'T BUDGE!
THIS CAN'T BE ORDINARY GLASS!
WHAT ARE YOU DOING, EROICA?
STEALING THE CROWN, OBVIOUSLY.
NOW DO GO AWAY, I'M BUSY.
I CAN'T DO THAT.
WE NEED TO HAVE A NICE LITTLE CHAT.

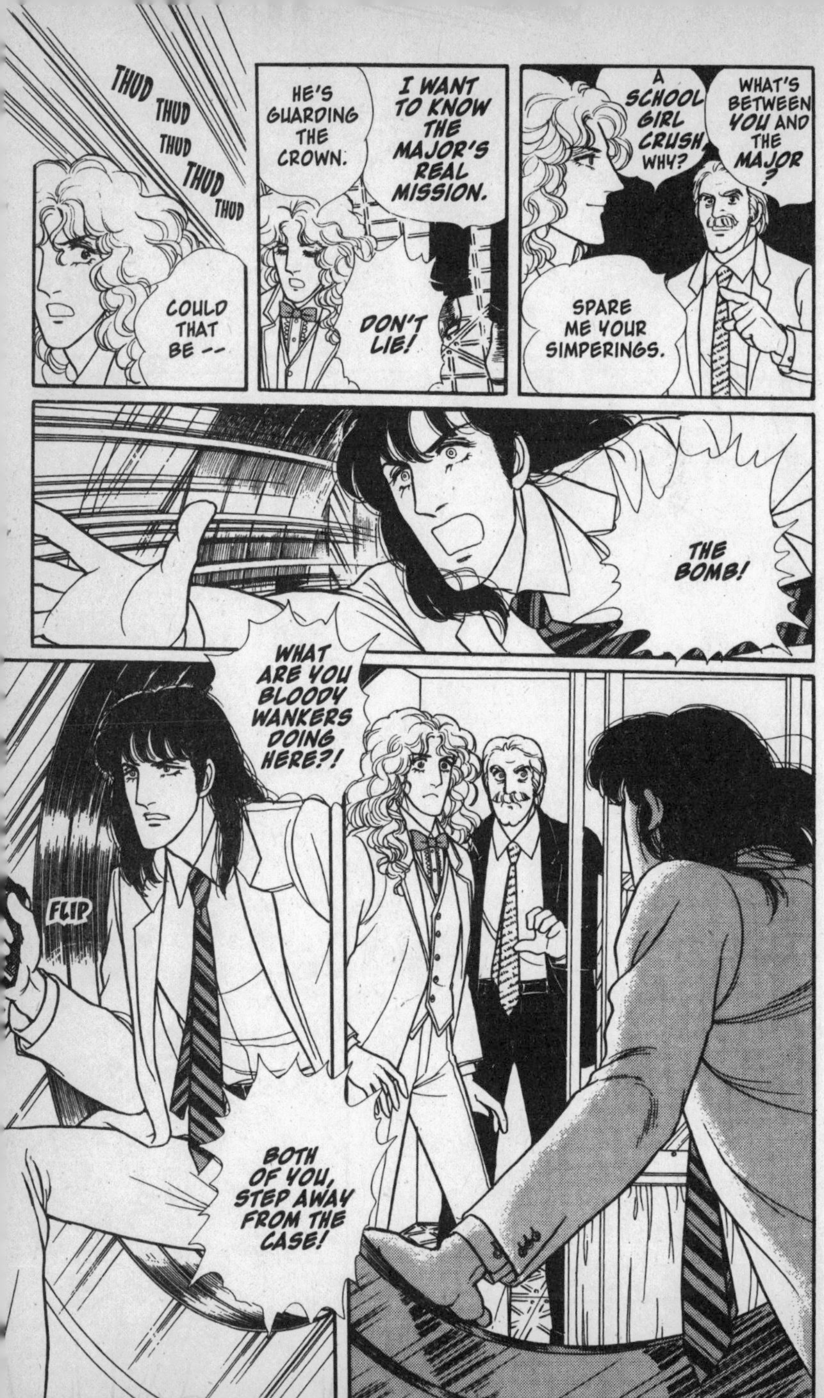
WHAT'S BETWEEN YOU AND THE MAJOR?
A SCHOOL GIRL CRUSH. WHY?
SPARE ME YOUR SIMPERINGS.
I WANT TO KNOW THE MAJOR'S REAL MISSION.
HE'S GUARDING THE CROWN.
DON'T LIE!
THUD THUD THUD THUD THUD
COULD THAT BE --
THE BOMB!
WHAT ARE YOU BLOODY WANKERS DOING HERE?!
FLIP
BOTH OF YOU, STEP AWAY FROM THE CASE!

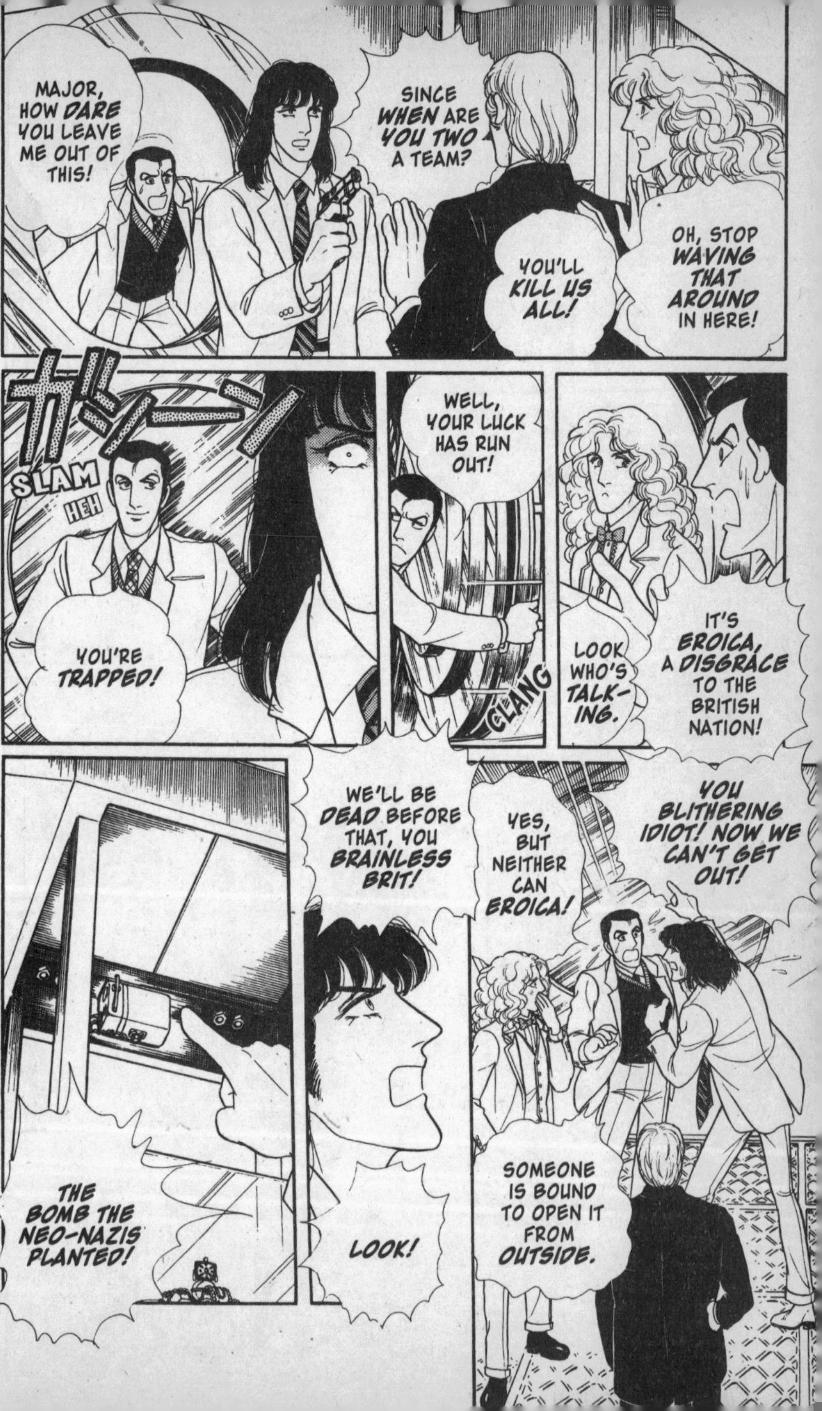
OH, STOP WAVING THAT AROUND IN HERE!
YOU'LL KILL US ALL!
SINCE WHEN ARE YOU TWO A TEAM?
MAJOR, HOW DARE YOU LEAVE ME OUT OF THIS!
IT'S EROICA, A DISGRACE TO THE BRITISH NATION!
LOOK WHO'S TALKING.
WELL, YOUR LUCK HAS RUN OUT!
CLANG
SLAM
HEH
YOU'RE TRAPPED!
YOU BLITHERING IDIOT! NOW WE CAN'T GET OUT!
YES, BUT NEITHER CAN EROICA!
SOMEONE IS BOUND TO OPEN IT FROM OUTSIDE.
WE'LL BE DEAD BEFORE THAT, YOU BRAINLESS BRIT!
LOOK!
THE BOMB THE NEO-NAZIS PLANTED!

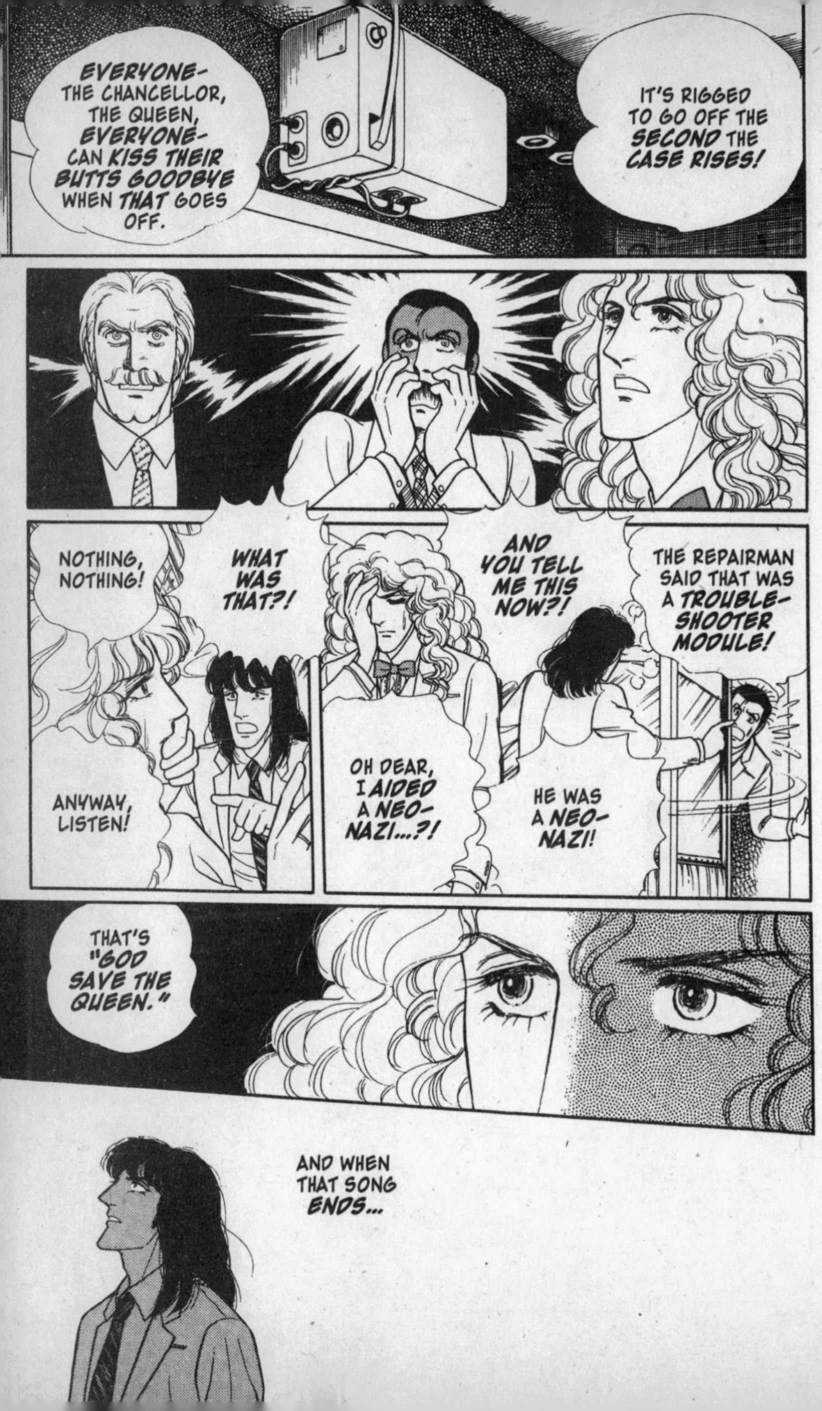
IT'S RIGGED TO GO OFF THE SECOND THE CASE RISES!
EVERYONE- THE CHANCELLOR, THE QUEEN, EVERYONE- CAN KISS THEIR BUTTS GOODBYE WHEN THAT GOES OFF.
THE REPAIRMAN SAID THAT WAS A TROUBLE-SHOOTER MODULE!
AND YOU TELL ME THIS NOW?!
HE WAS A NEO-NAZI!
OH DEAR, I AIDED A NEO-NAZI...?!
WHAT WAS THAT?!
NOTHING, NOTHING!
ANYWAY, LISTEN!
THAT'S "GOD SAVE THE QUEEN."
AND WHEN THAT SONG ENDS...

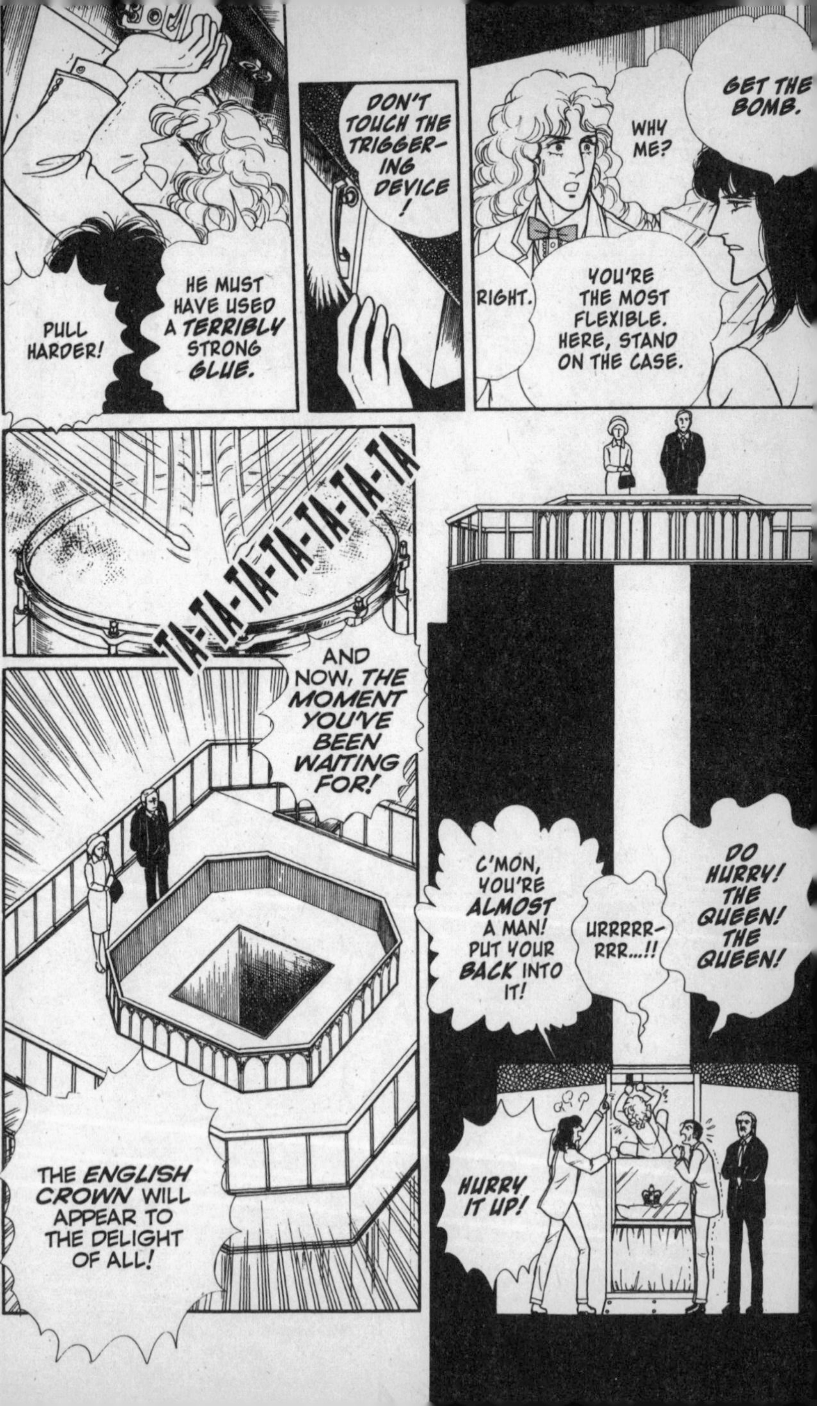
GET THE BOMB.
WHY ME?
YOU'RE THE MOST FLEXIBLE. HERE, STAND ON THE CASE.
RIGHT.
DON'T TOUCH THE TRIGGERING DEVICE!
HE MUST HAVE USED A TERRIBLY STRONG GLUE.
PULL HARDER!
DO HURRY! THE QUEEN! THE QUEEN!
URRRRR-RRR...!!
C'MON, YOU'RE ALMOST A MAN! PUT YOUR BACK INTO IT!
HURRY IT UP!
TA-TA-TA-TA-TA-TA-TA-TA
AND NOW, THE MOMENT YOU'VE BEEN WAITING FOR!
THE ENGLISH CROWN WILL APPEAR TO THE DELIGHT OF ALL!

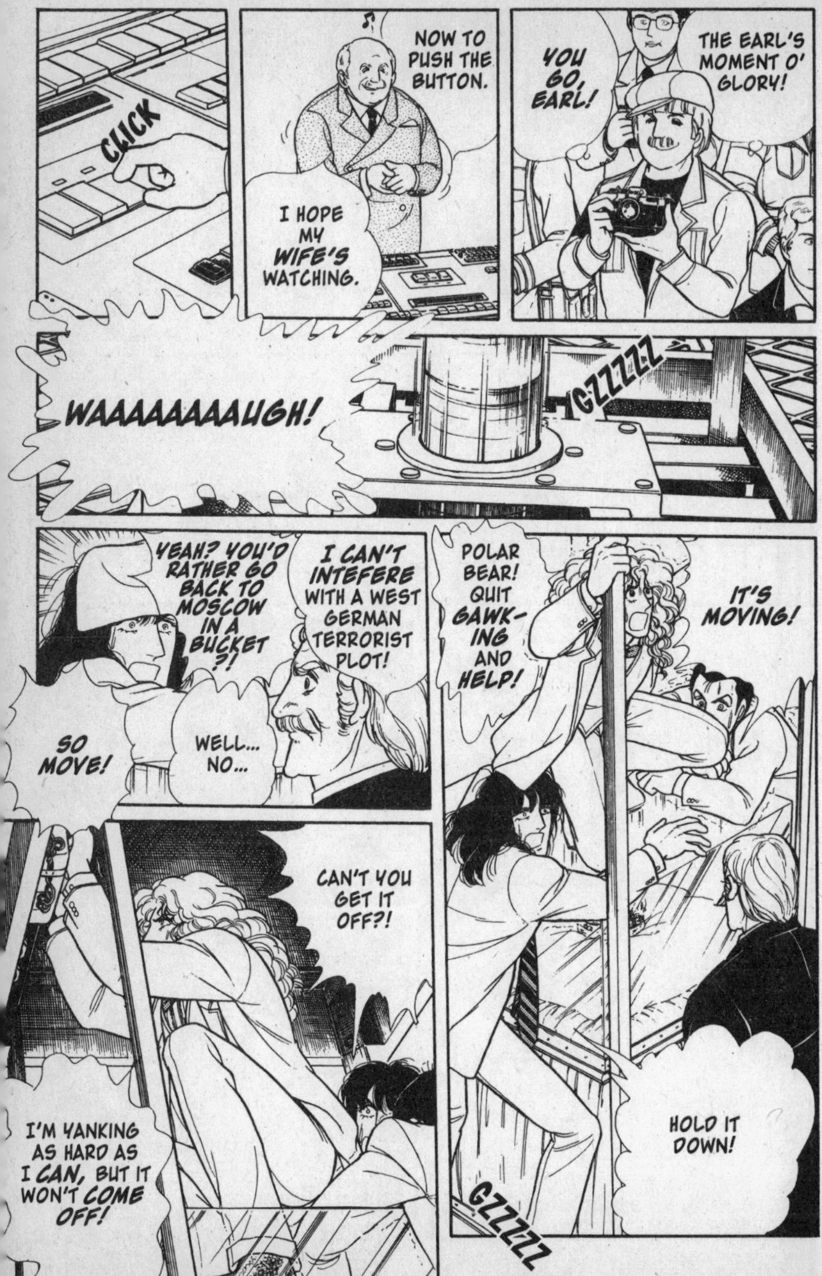
THE EARL'S MOMENT O' GLORY!
YOU GO, EARL!
NOW TO PUSH THE BUTTON.
I HOPE MY WIFE'S WATCHING.
CLICK
GZZZZZ
WAAAAAAAAUGH!
IT'S MOVING!
POLAR BEAR! QUIT GAWKING AND HELP!
HOLD IT DOWN!
GZZZZZ
I CAN'T INTEFERE WITH A WEST GERMAN TERRORIST PLOT!
YEAH? YOU'D RATHER GO BACK TO MOSCOW IN A BUCKET?!
WELL... NO...
SO MOVE!
CAN'T YOU GET IT OFF?!
I'M YANKING AS HARD AS I CAN, BUT IT WON'T COME OFF!

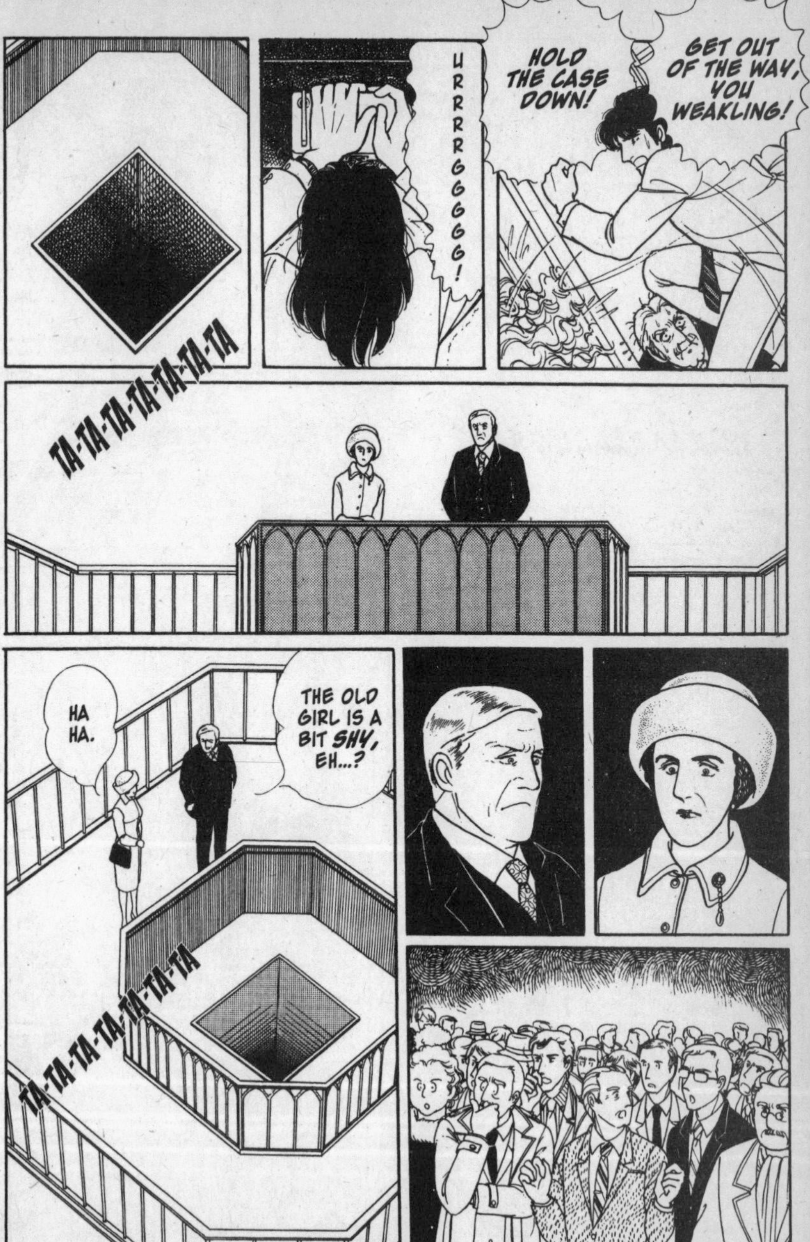
GET OUT OF THE WAY, YOU WEAKLING!
HOLD THE CASE DOWN!
URRRRGGGGG!
TA-TA-TA-TA-TA-TA-TA
THE OLD GIRL IS A BIT SHY, EH...?
HA HA.
TA-TA-TA-TA-TA-TA-TA

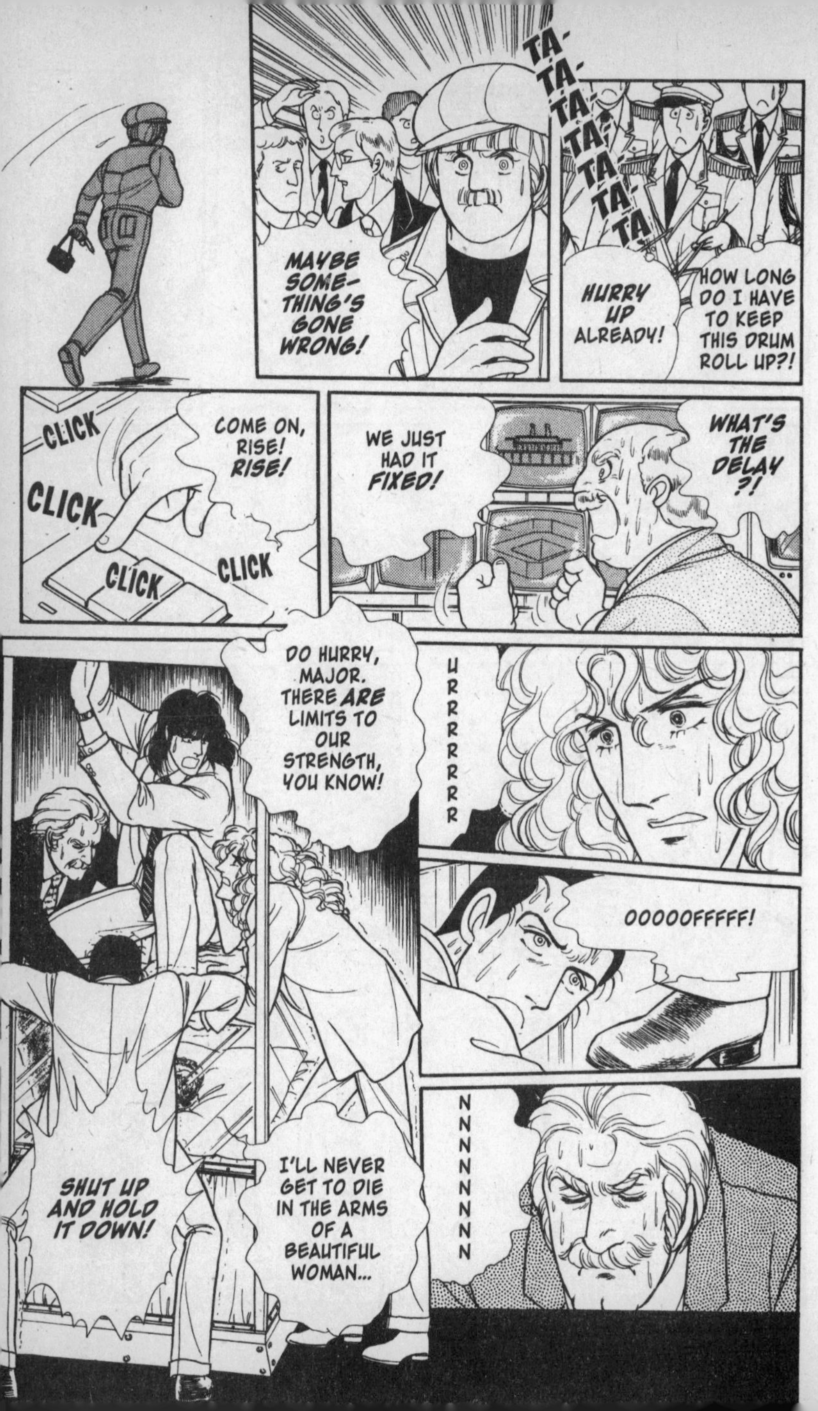
TA-TA-TA-TA-TA-TA-TA-TA
HOW LONG DO I HAVE TO KEEP THIS DRUM ROLL UP?!
HURRY UP ALREADY!
MAYBE SOME-THING'S GONE WRONG!
WHAT'S THE DELAY?!
WE JUST HAD IT FIXED!
COME ON, RISE! RISE!
CLICK
CLICK
CLICK
CLICK
URRRRRRRR
OOOOOFFFFF!
NNNNNNNNNN
DO HURRY, MAJOR. THERE ARE LIMITS TO OUR STRENGTH, YOU KNOW!
I'LL NEVER GET TO DIE IN THE ARMS OF A BEAUTIFUL WOMAN...
SHUT UP AND HOLD IT DOWN!

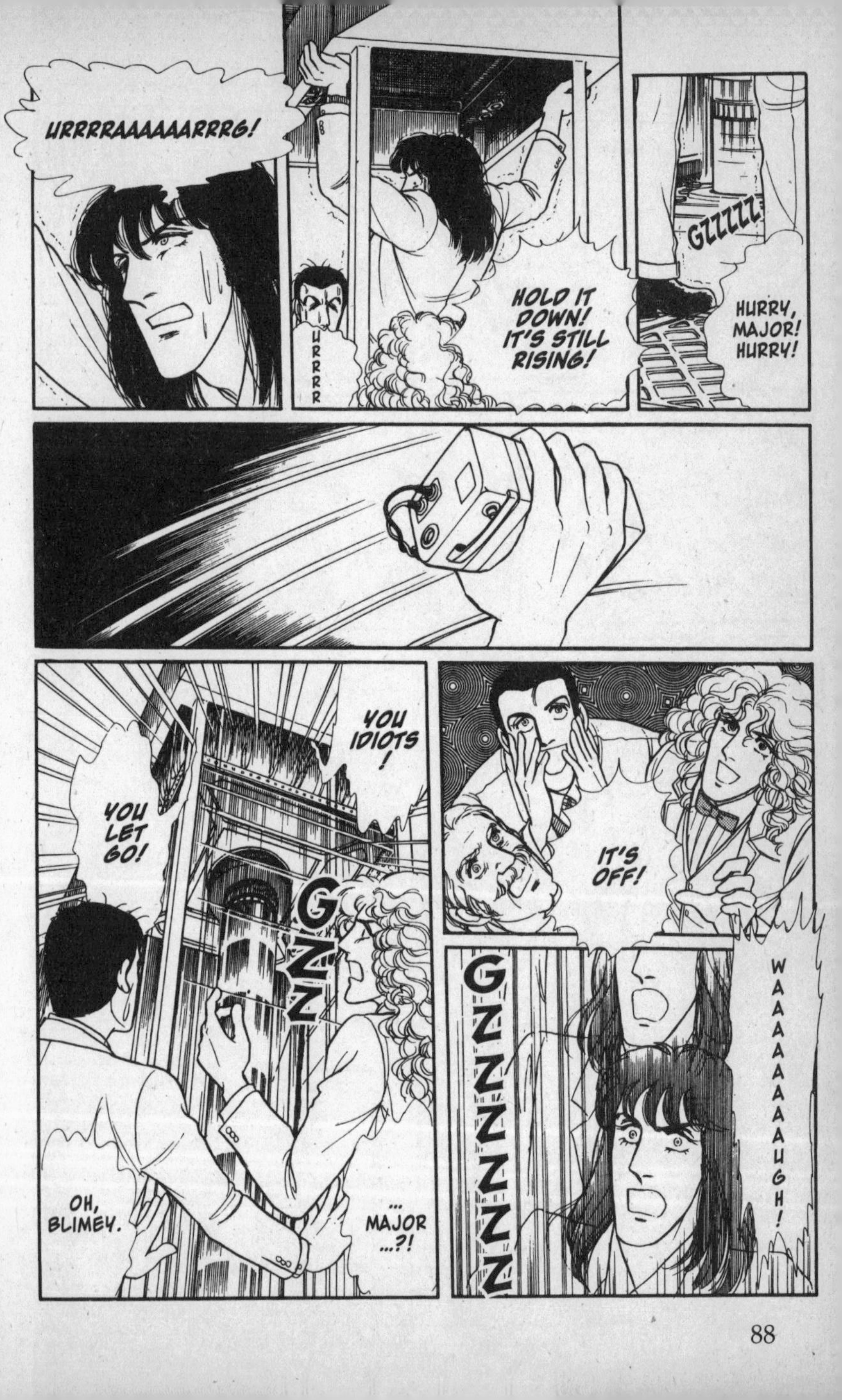
GZZZZZ
HURRY, MAJOR! HURRY!
HOLD IT DOWN! IT'S STILL RISING!
URRRR
URRRRAAAAAAARRRG!
IT'S OFF!
GZZZZZZZ
WAAAAAAAAAAUGH!
YOU IDIOTS!
YOU LET GO!
GZZ
...MAJOR...?!
OH, BLIMEY.

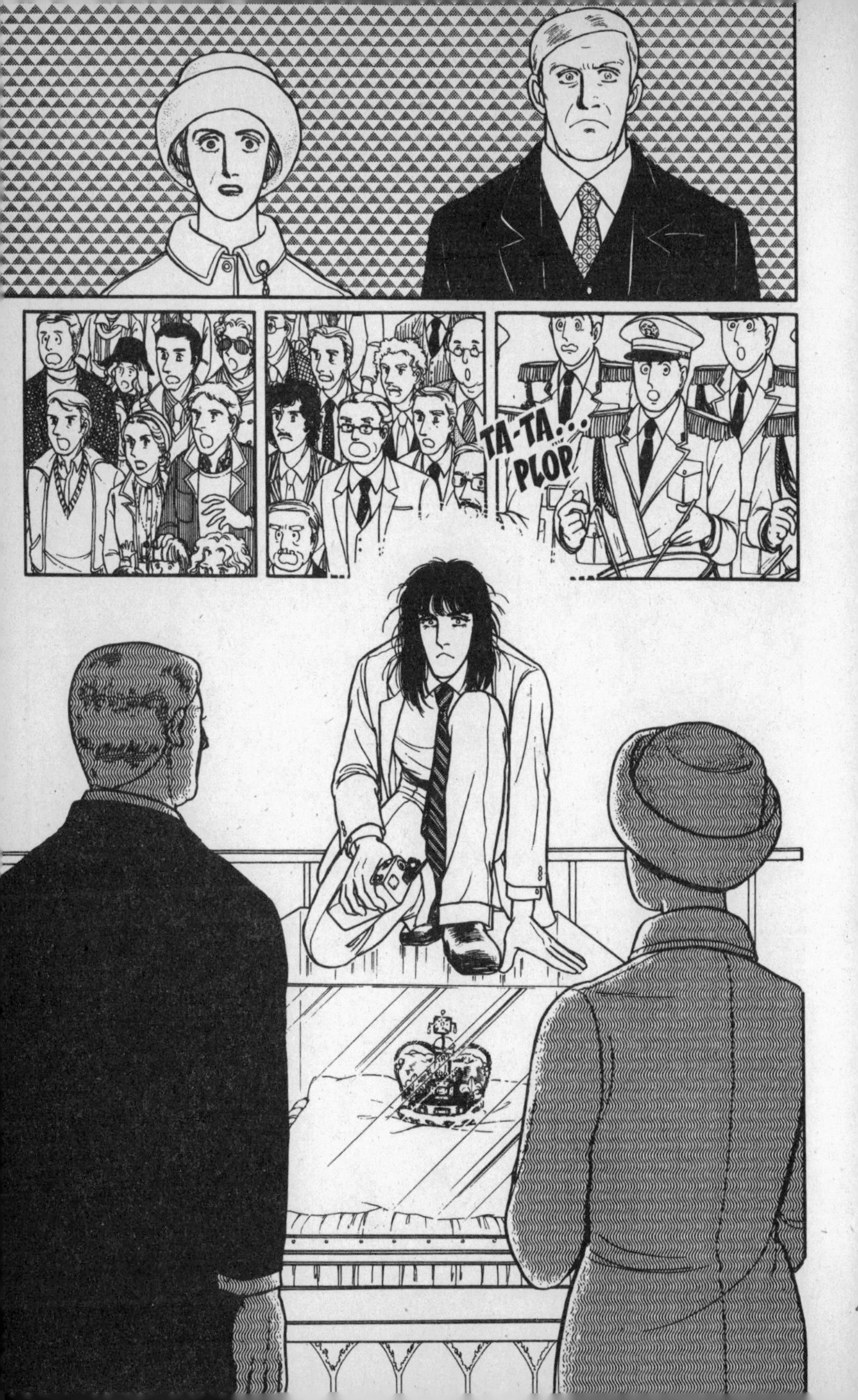
TA-TA!...
PLOP

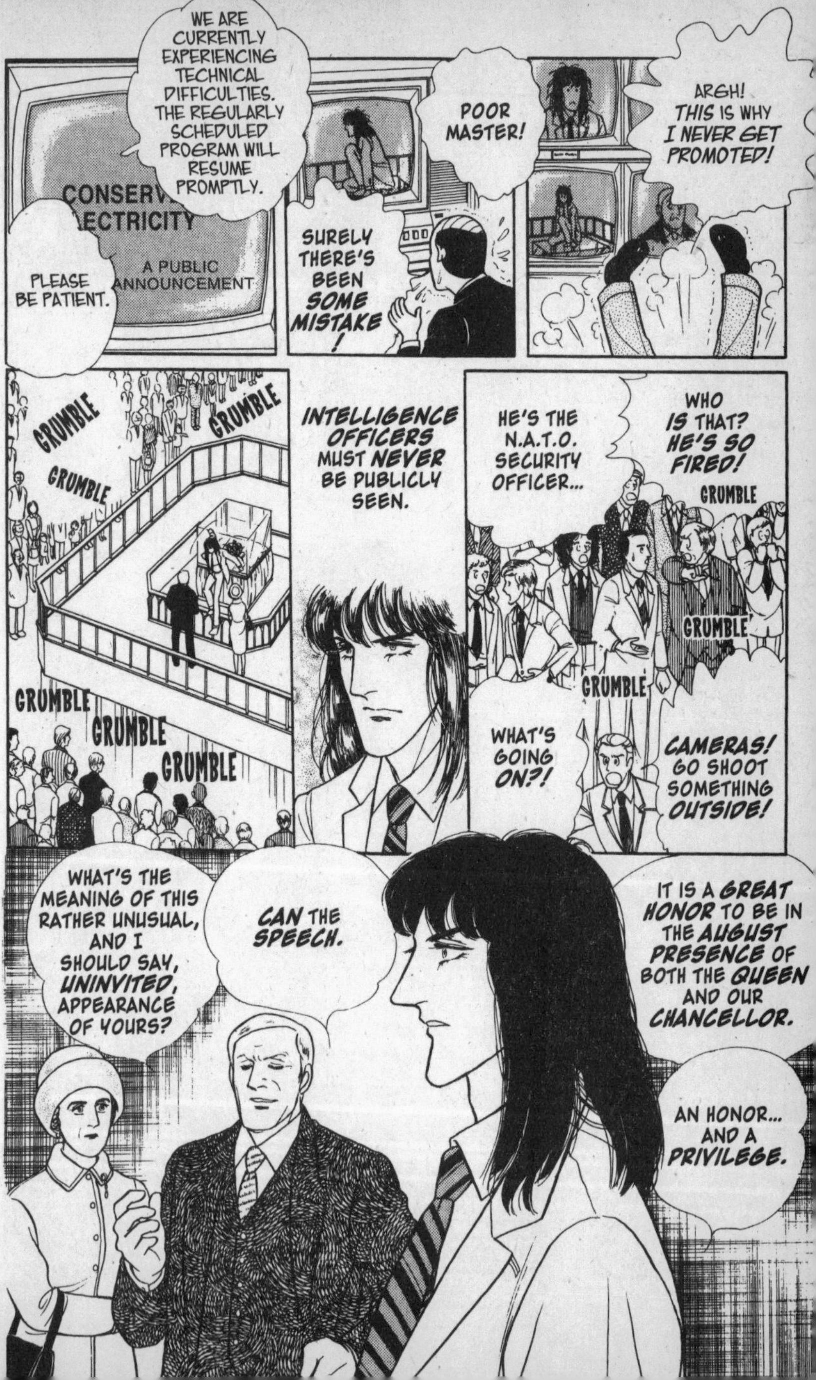

ARGH! THIS IS WHY I NEVER GET PROMOTED!
POOR MASTER!
SURELY THERE'S BEEN SOME MISTAKE!
WE ARE CURRENTLY EXPERIENCING TECHNICAL DIFFICULTIES. THE REGULARLY SCHEDULED PROGRAM WILL RESUME PROMPTLY.
CONSERV
ECTRICITY
A PUBLIC ANNOUNCEMENT
PLEASE BE PATIENT.
WHO IS THAT? HE'S SO FIRED!
HE'S THE N.A.T.O. SECURITY OFFICER...
GRUMBLE
GRUMBLE
GRUMBLE
CAMERAS! GO SHOOT SOMETHING OUTSIDE!
WHAT'S GOING ON?!
INTELLIGENCE OFFICERS MUST NEVER BE PUBLICLY SEEN.
GRUMBLE
GRUMBLE
GRUMBLE
GRUMBLE
GRUMBLE
GRUMBLE
IT IS A GREAT HONOR TO BE IN THE AUGUST PRESENCE OF BOTH THE QUEEN AND OUR CHANCELLOR.
CAN THE SPEECH.
WHAT'S THE MEANING OF THIS RATHER UNUSUAL, AND I SHOULD SAY, UNINVITED, APPEARANCE OF YOURS?
AN HONOR... AND A PRIVILEGE.

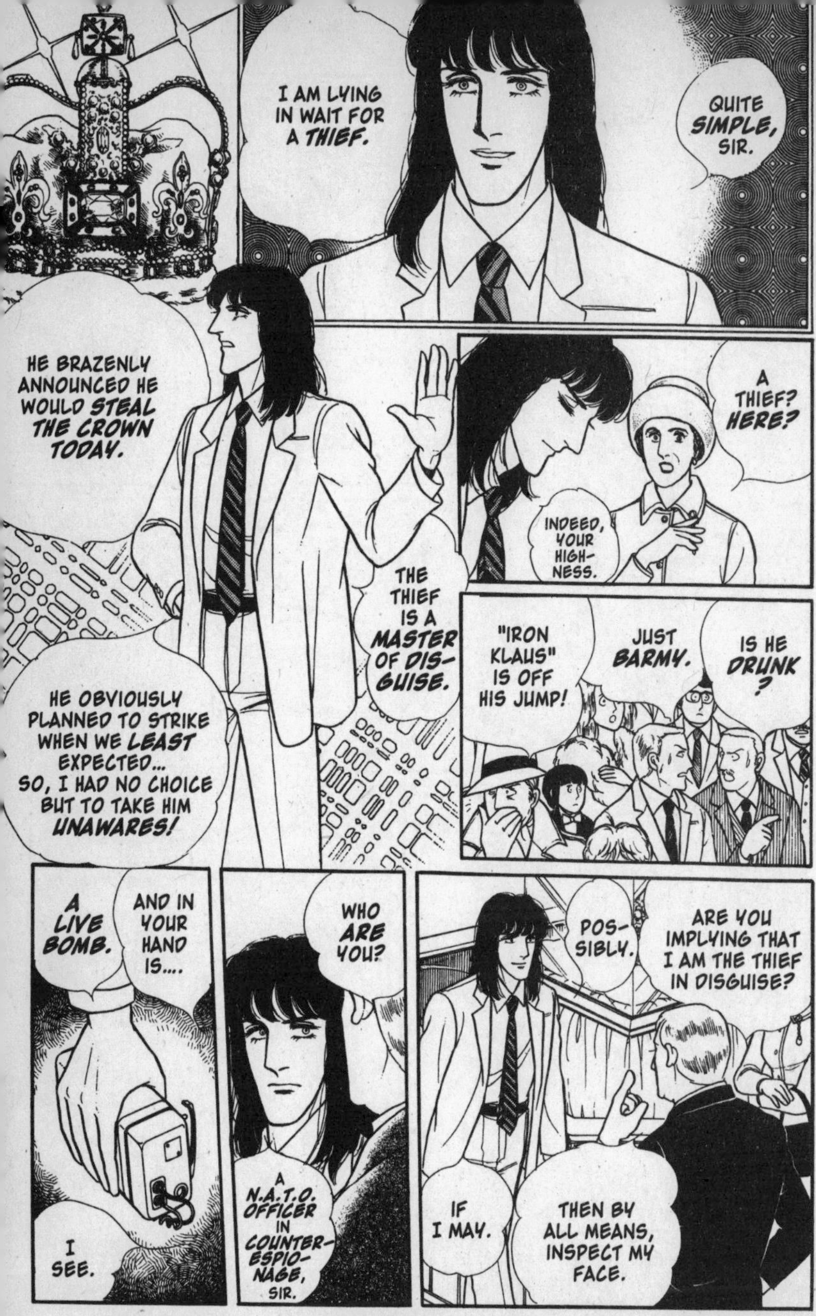
QUITE SIMPLE, SIR.
I AM LYING IN WAIT FOR A THIEF.
A THIEF? HERE?
INDEED, YOUR HIGH- NESS.
IS HE DRUNK?
JUST BARMY.
"IRON KLAUS" IS OFF HIS JUMP!
HE BRAZENLY ANNOUNCED HE WOULD STEAL THE CROWN TODAY.
THE THIEF IS A MASTER OF DIS- GUISE.
HE OBVIOUSLY PLANNED TO STRIKE WHEN WE LEAST EXPECTED... SO, I HAD NO CHOICE BUT TO TAKE HIM UNAWARES!
ARE YOU IMPLYING THAT I AM THE THIEF IN DISGUISE?
POS- SIBLY.
THEN BY ALL MEANS, INSPECT MY FACE.
IF I MAY.
WHO ARE YOU?
A N.A.T.O. OFFICER IN COUNTER- ESPIO- NAGE, SIR.
AND IN YOUR HAND IS....
A LIVE BOMB.
I SEE.

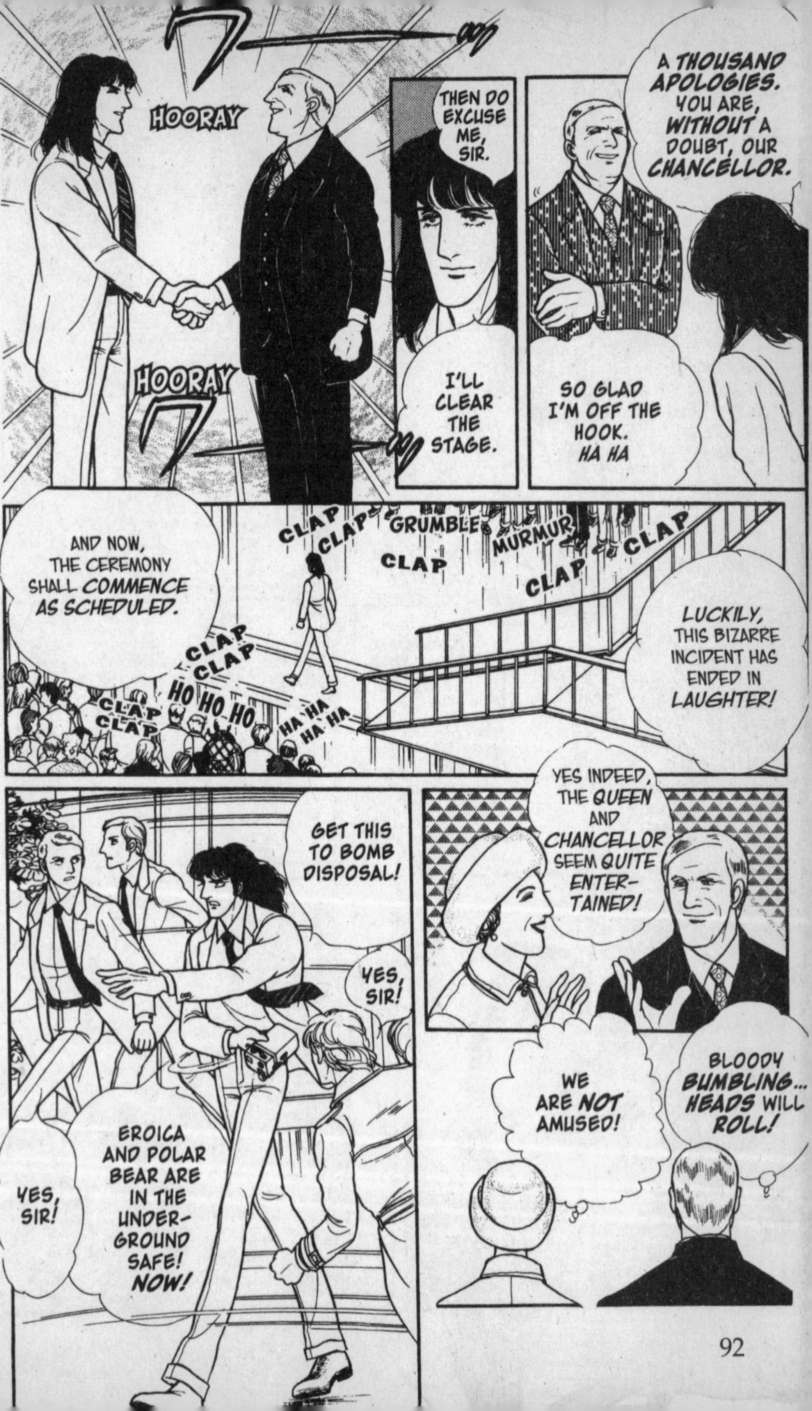
A THOUSAND APOLOGIES. YOU ARE, WITHOUT A DOUBT, OUR CHANCELLOR.
SO GLAD I'M OFF THE HOOK. HA HA
THEN DO EXCUSE ME, SIR.
I'LL CLEAR THE STAGE.
HOORAY
HOORAY
LUCKILY, THIS BIZARRE INCIDENT HAS ENDED IN LAUGHTER!
CLAP CLAP
CLAP
MURMUR
GRUMBLE
CLAP
CLAP
CLAP
AND NOW, THE CEREMONY SHALL COMMENCE AS SCHEDULED.
HA HA HA HA
HO HO HO
CLAP CLAP
CLAP CLAP
YES INDEED, THE QUEEN AND CHANCELLOR SEEM QUITE ENTER-TAINED!
BLOODY BUMBLING... HEADS WILL ROLL!
WE ARE NOT AMUSED!
GET THIS TO BOMB DISPOSAL!
YES, SIR!
EROICA AND POLAR BEAR ARE IN THE UNDER-GROUND SAFE! NOW!
YES, SIR!

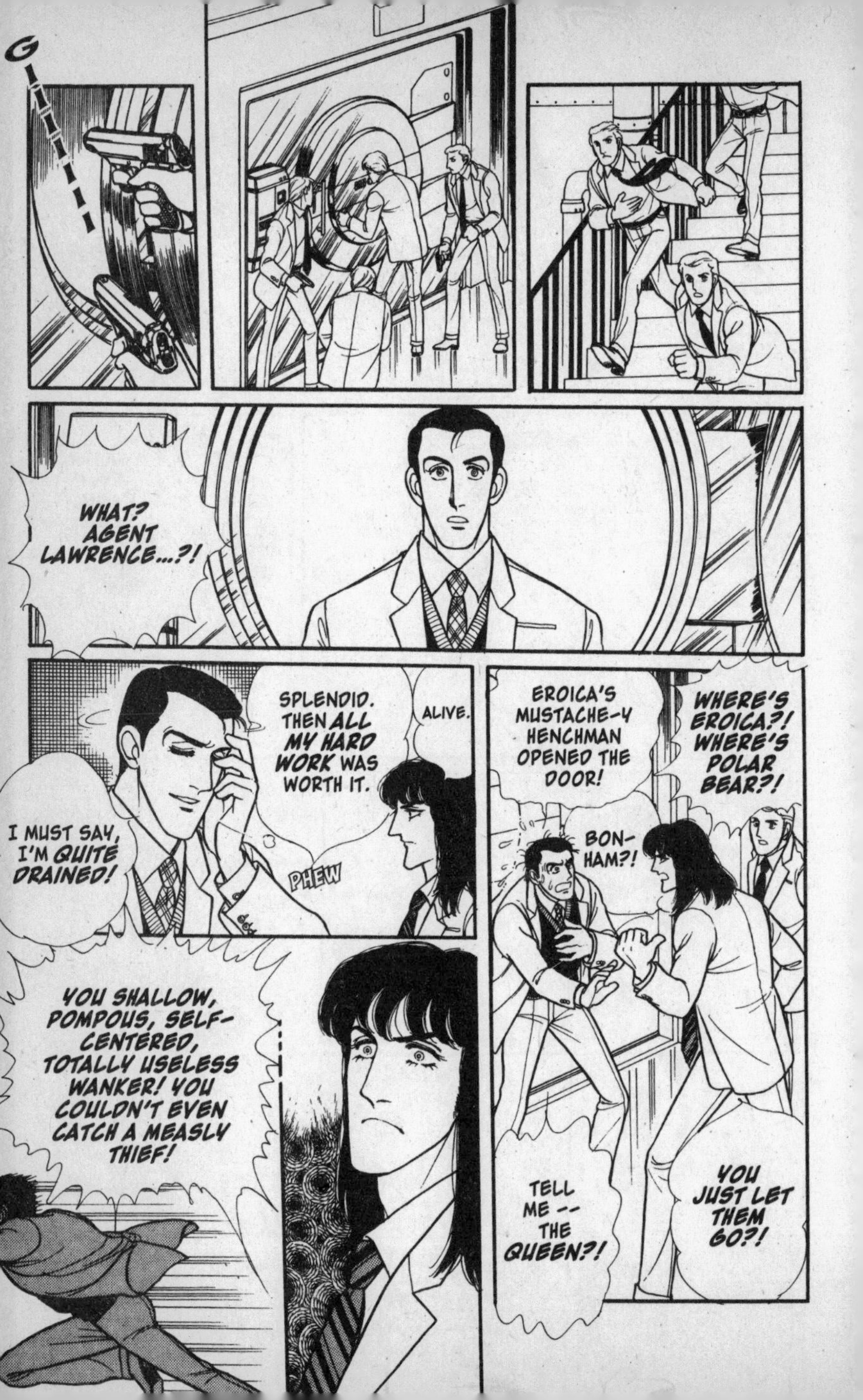
G
WHAT? AGENT LAWRENCE...?!
WHERE'S EROICA?! WHERE'S POLAR BEAR?!
EROICA'S MUSTACHE-Y HENCHMAN OPENED THE DOOR!
BON-HAM?!
YOU JUST LET THEM GO?!
TELL ME -- THE QUEEN?!
ALIVE.
SPLENDID. THEN ALL MY HARD WORK WAS WORTH IT.
PHEW
I MUST SAY, I'M QUITE DRAINED!
YOU SHALLOW, POMPOUS, SELF-CENTERED, TOTALLY USELESS WANKER! YOU COULDN'T EVEN CATCH A MEASLY THIEF!

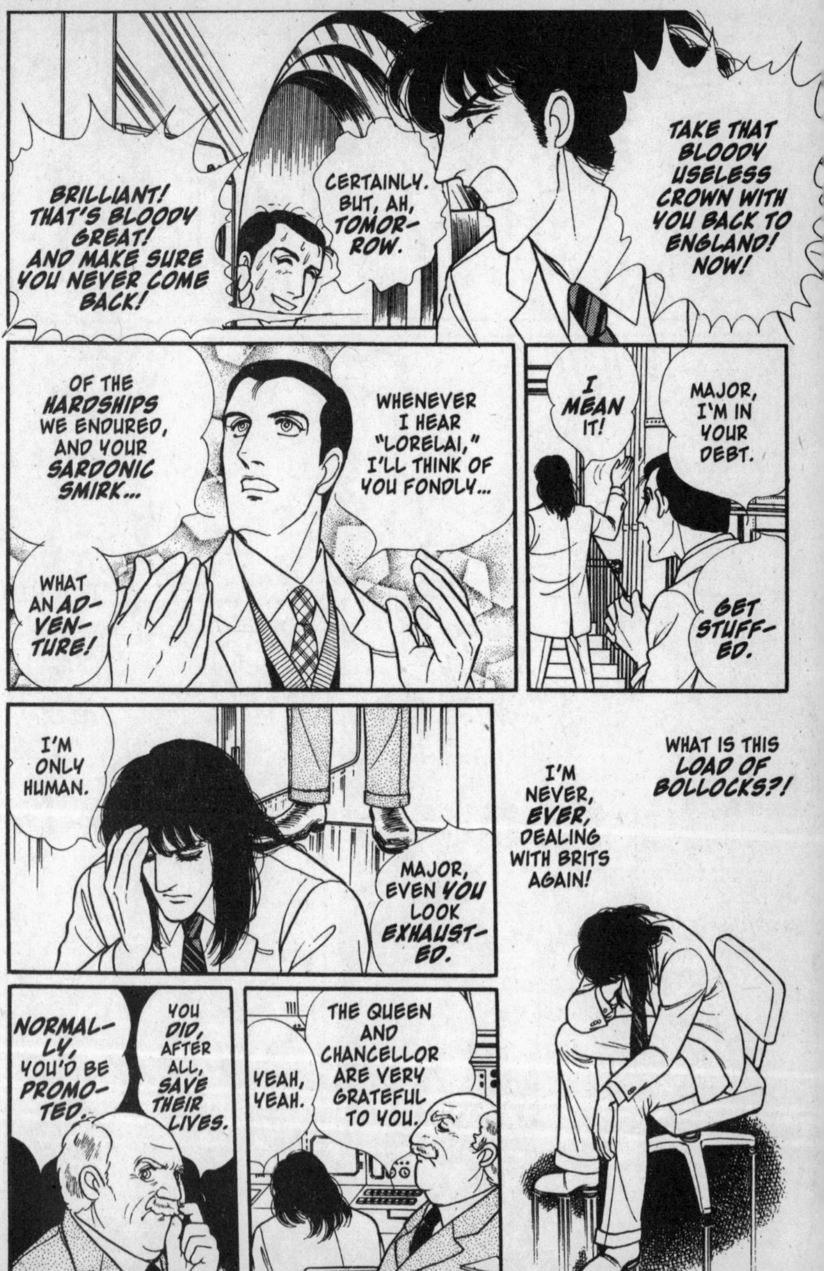
TAKE THAT BLOODY USELESS CROWN WITH YOU BACK TO ENGLAND! NOW!
CERTAINLY. BUT, AH, TOMORROW.
BRILLIANT! THAT'S BLOODY GREAT! AND MAKE SURE YOU NEVER COME BACK!
MAJOR, I'M IN YOUR DEBT.
I MEAN IT!
GET STUFFED.
WHENEVER I HEAR "LORELAI," I'LL THINK OF YOU FONDLY...
OF THE HARDSHIPS WE ENDURED, AND YOUR SARDONIC SMIRK...
WHAT AN ADVENTURE!
WHAT IS THIS LOAD OF BOLLOCKS?!
I'M NEVER, EVER, DEALING WITH BRITS AGAIN!
MAJOR, EVEN YOU LOOK EXHAUSTED.
I'M ONLY HUMAN.
THE QUEEN AND CHANCELLOR ARE VERY GRATEFUL TO YOU.
YEAH, YEAH.
YOU DID, AFTER ALL, SAVE THEIR LIVES.
NORMALLY, YOU'D BE PROMOTED..

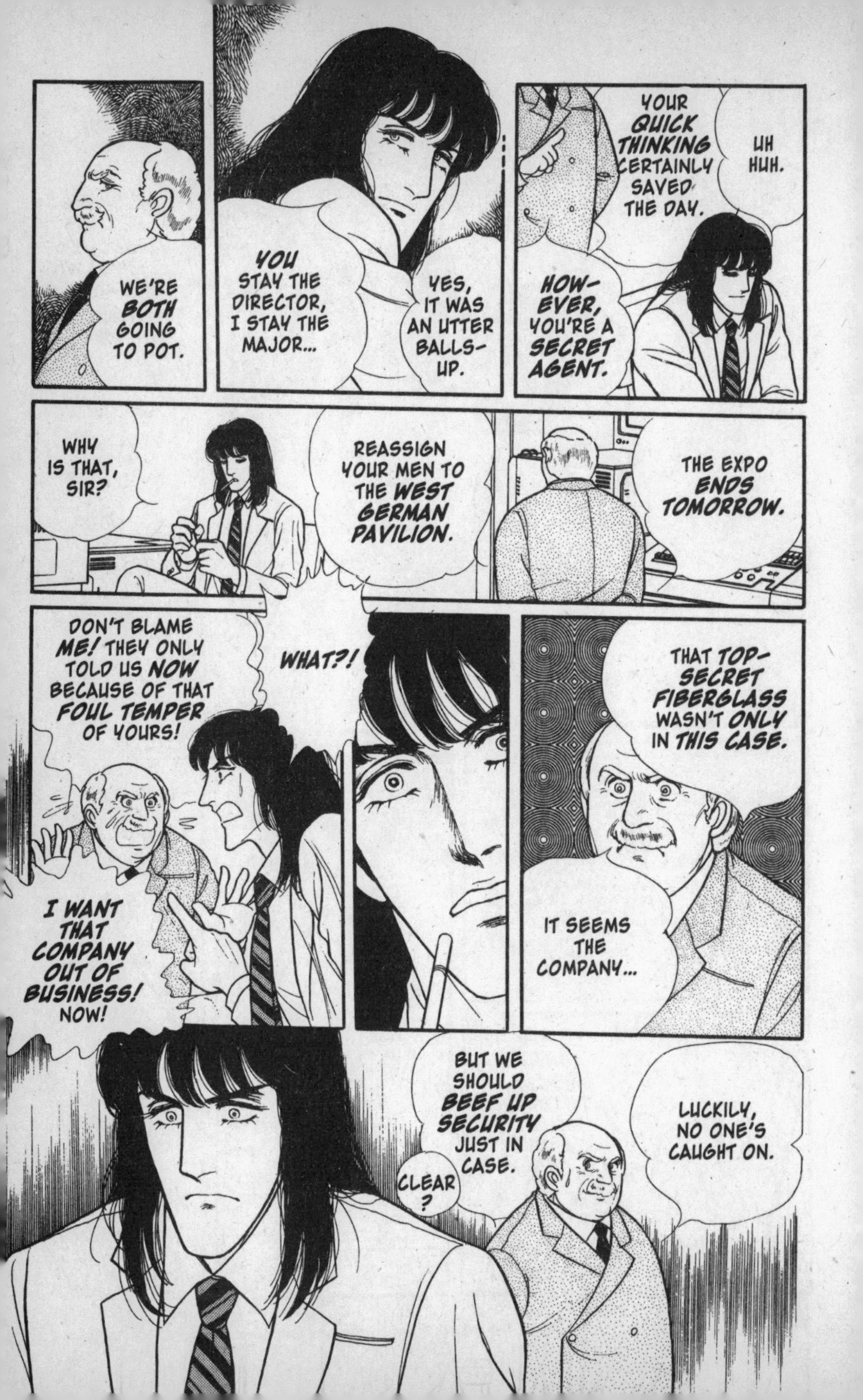
YOUR QUICK THINKING CERTAINLY SAVED THE DAY.
UH HUH.
HOW-EVER, YOU'RE A SECRET AGENT.
YES, IT WAS AN UTTER BALLS-UP.
YOU STAY THE DIRECTOR, I STAY THE MAJOR...
WE'RE BOTH GOING TO POT.
THE EXPO ENDS TOMORROW.
REASSIGN YOUR MEN TO THE WEST GERMAN PAVILION.
WHY IS THAT, SIR?
THAT TOP-SECRET FIBERGLASS WASN'T ONLY IN THIS CASE.
IT SEEMS THE COMPANY...
WHAT?!
I WANT THAT COMPANY OUT OF BUSINESS! NOW!
DON'T BLAME ME! THEY ONLY TOLD US NOW BECAUSE OF THAT FOUL TEMPER OF YOURS!
LUCKILY, NO ONE'S CAUGHT ON.
BUT WE SHOULD BEEF UP SECURITY JUST IN CASE.
CLEAR?

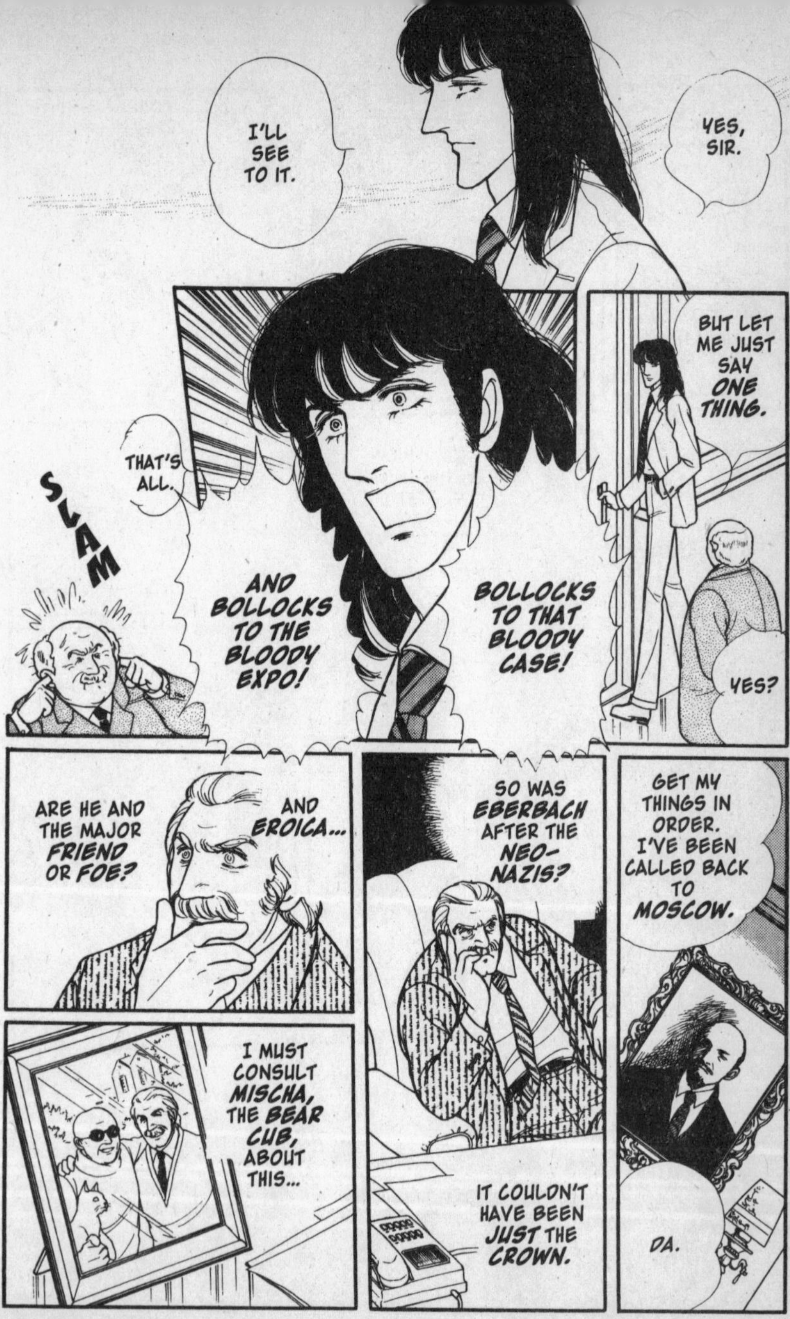
YES, SIR.
I'LL SEE TO IT.
BUT LET ME JUST SAY ONE THING.
YES?
BOLLOCKS TO THAT BLOODY CASE!
AND BOLLOCKS TO THE BLOODY EXPO!
THAT'S ALL.
SLAM
GET MY THINGS IN ORDER. I'VE BEEN CALLED BACK TO MOSCOW.
DA.
SO WAS EBERBACH AFTER THE NEO-NAZIS?
IT COULDN'T HAVE BEEN JUST THE CROWN.
AND EROICA...
ARE HE AND THE MAJOR FRIEND OR FOE?
I MUST CONSULT MISCHA, THE BEAR CUB, ABOUT THIS...

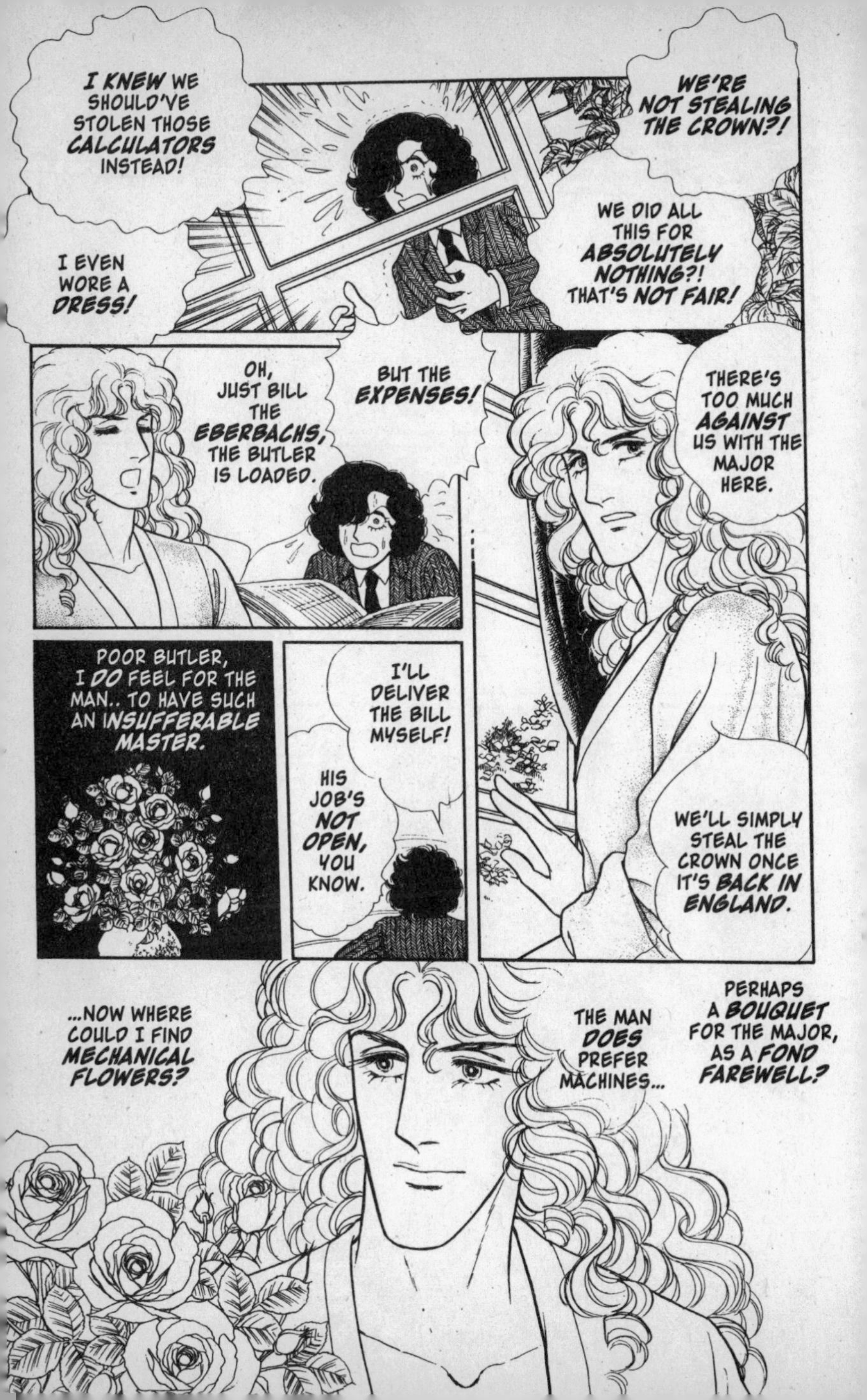
WE'RE NOT STEALING THE CROWN?!
WE DID ALL THIS FOR ABSOLUTELY NOTHING?! THAT'S NOT FAIR!
I KNEW WE SHOULD'VE STOLEN THOSE CALCULATORS INSTEAD!
I EVEN WORE A DRESS!
THERE'S TOO MUCH AGAINST US WITH THE MAJOR HERE.
WE'LL SIMPLY STEAL THE CROWN ONCE IT'S BACK IN ENGLAND.
BUT THE EXPENSES!
OH, JUST BILL THE EBERBACHS, THE BUTLER IS LOADED.
I'LL DELIVER THE BILL MYSELF!
HIS JOB'S NOT OPEN, YOU KNOW.
POOR BUTLER, I DO FEEL FOR THE MAN.. TO HAVE SUCH AN INSUFFERABLE MASTER.
PERHAPS A BOUQUET FOR THE MAJOR, AS A FOND FAREWELL?
THE MAN DOES PREFER MACHINES...
...NOW WHERE COULD I FIND MECHANICAL FLOWERS?

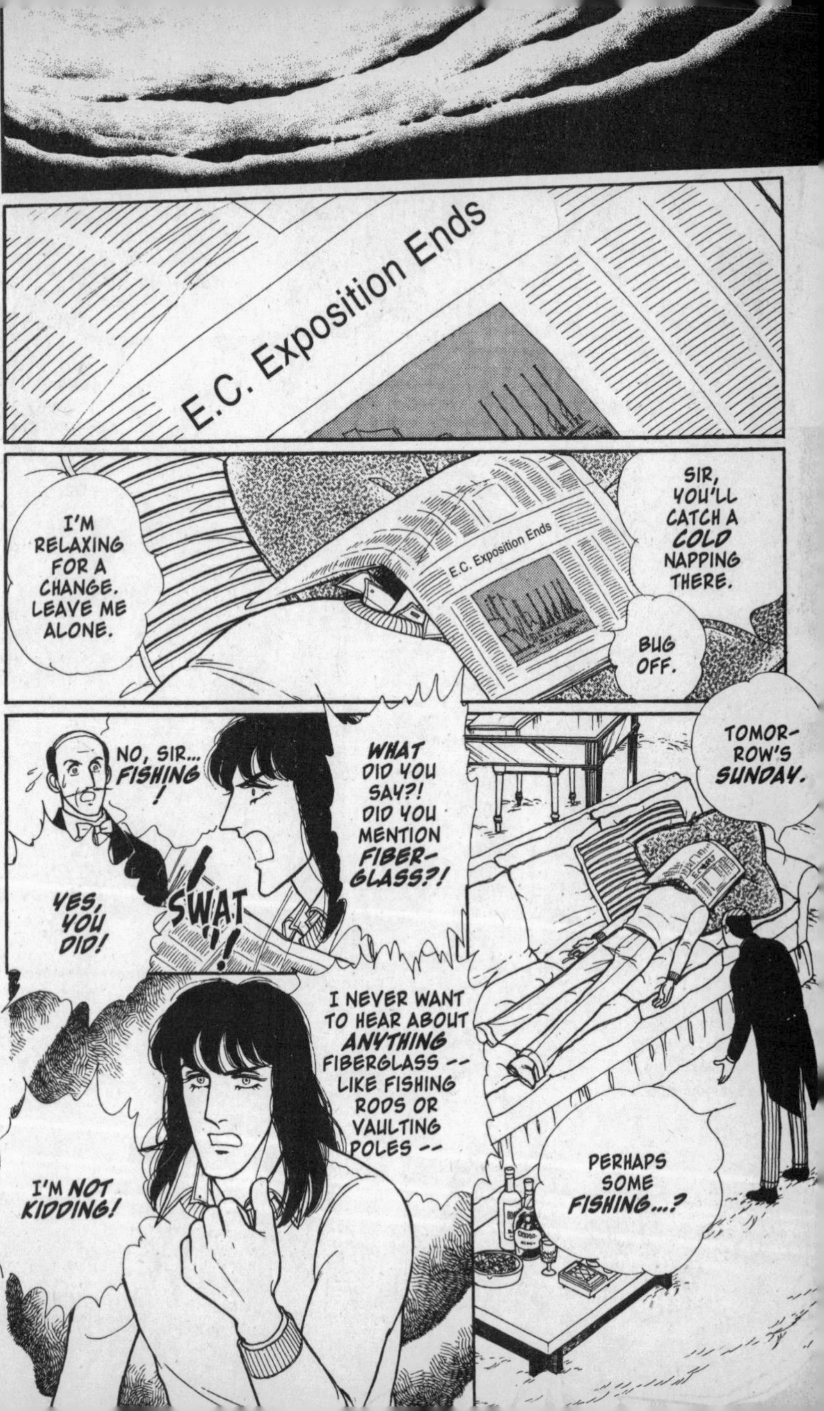
E.C. Exposition Ends
SIR, YOU'LL CATCH A COLD NAPPING THERE.
E.C. Exposition Ends
BUG OFF.
I'M RELAXING FOR A CHANGE. LEAVE ME ALONE.
TOMORROW'S SUNDAY.
PERHAPS SOME FISHING...?
WHAT DID YOU SAY?! DID YOU MENTION FIBERGLASS?!
NO, SIR... FISHING!
SWAT!!
YES, YOU DID!
I NEVER WANT TO HEAR ABOUT ANYTHING FIBERGLASS -- LIKE FISHING RODS OR VAULTING POLES --
I'M NOT KIDDING!

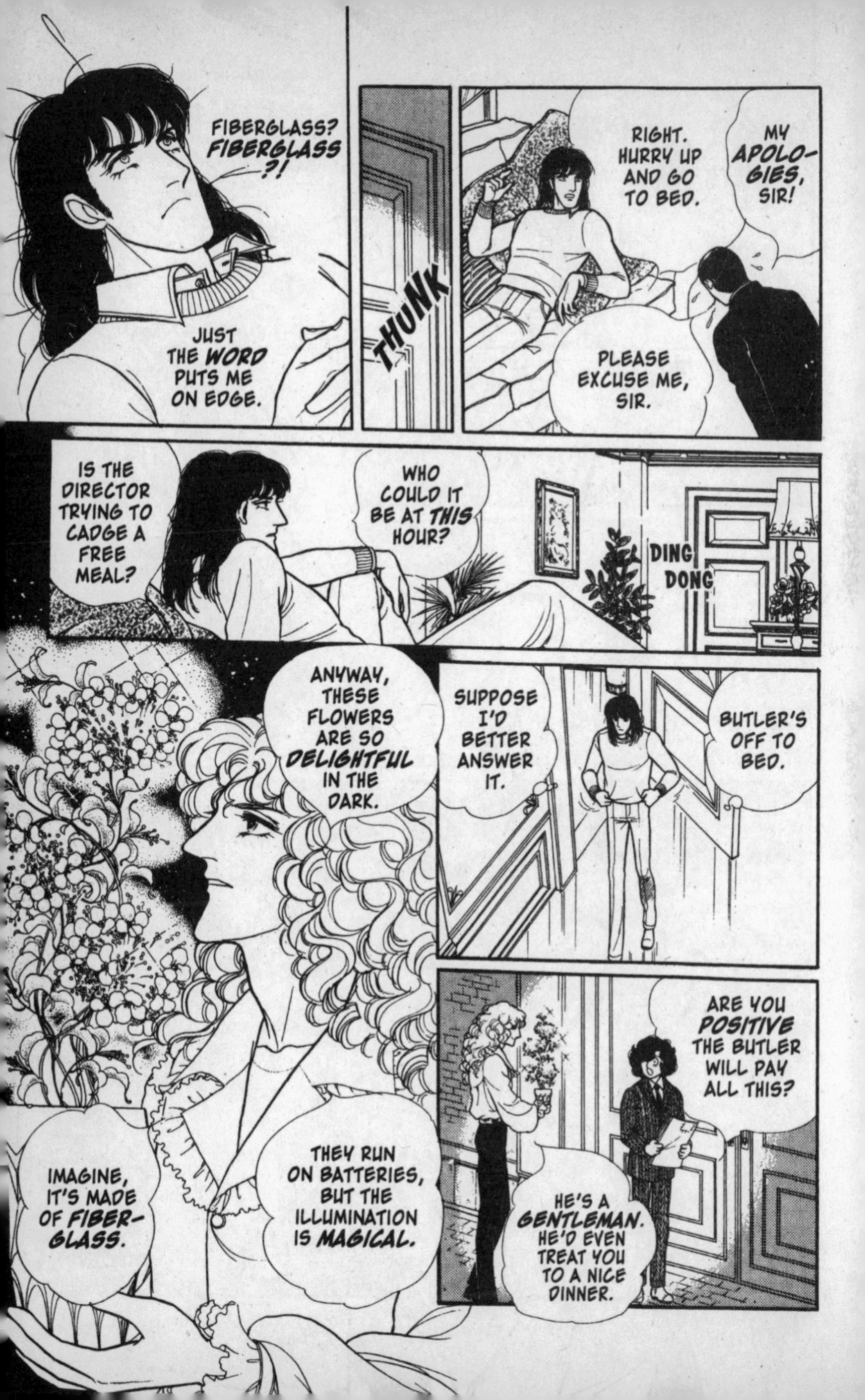
MY APOLOGIES, SIR!
RIGHT. HURRY UP AND GO TO BED.
PLEASE EXCUSE ME, SIR.
THUNK
FIBERGLASS? FIBERGLASS?!
JUST THE WORD PUTS ME ON EDGE.
DING DONG
WHO COULD IT BE AT THIS HOUR?
IS THE DIRECTOR TRYING TO CADGE A FREE MEAL?
BUTLER'S OFF TO BED.
SUPPOSE I'D BETTER ANSWER IT.
ARE YOU POSITIVE THE BUTLER WILL PAY ALL THIS?
HE'S A GENTLEMAN. HE'D EVEN TREAT YOU TO A NICE DINNER.
ANYWAY, THESE FLOWERS ARE SO DELIGHTFUL IN THE DARK.
THEY RUN ON BATTERIES, BUT THE ILLUMINATION IS MAGICAL.
IMAGINE, IT'S MADE OF FIBERGLASS.

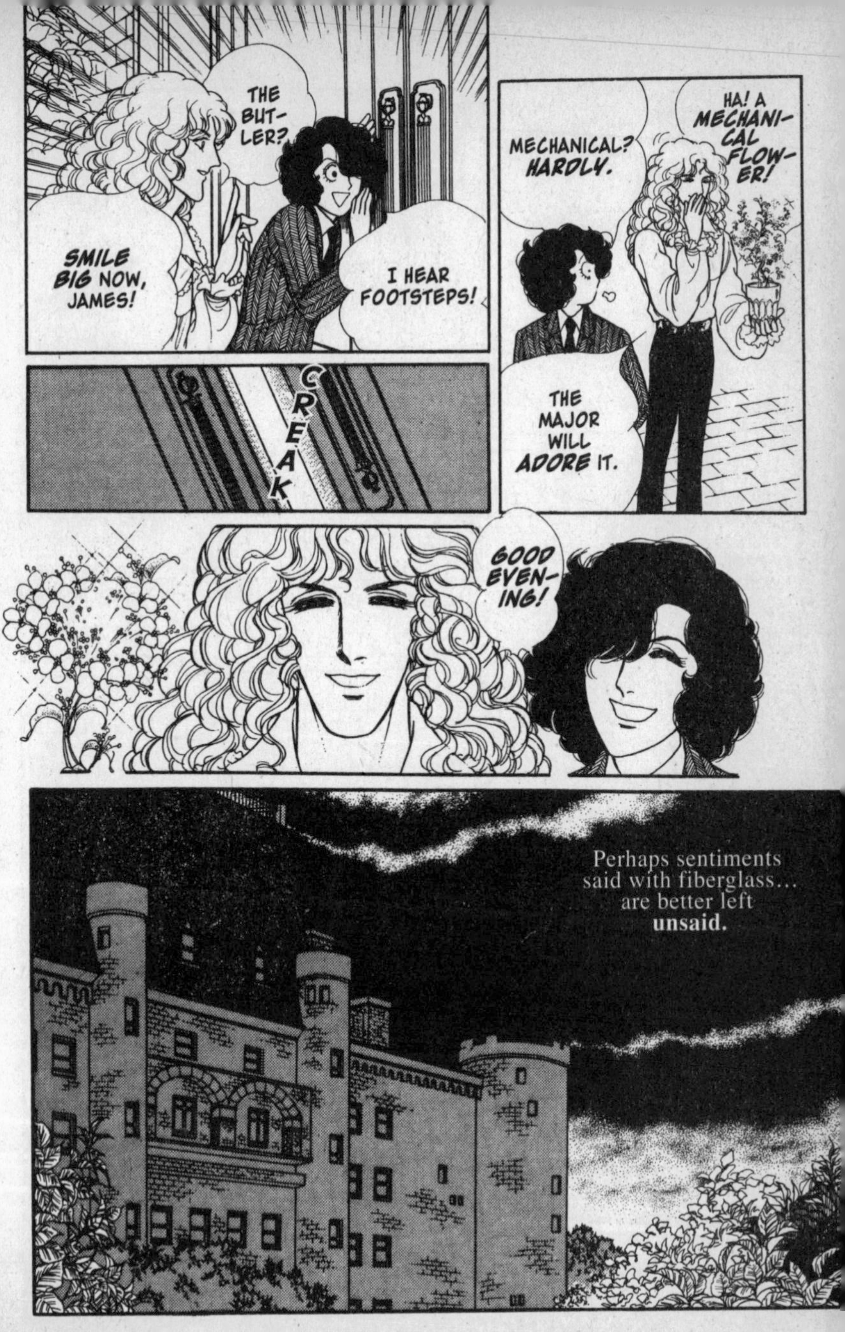

HA! A MECHANICAL FLOWER!
MECHANICAL? HARDLY.
THE MAJOR WILL ADORE IT.
I HEAR FOOTSTEPS!
THE BUTLER?
SMILE BIG NOW, JAMES!
CREAK
GOOD EVENING!
Perhaps sentiments said with fiberglass… are better left unsaid.

From
Eroica
With Love
(Side Story)

Midnight
Collector

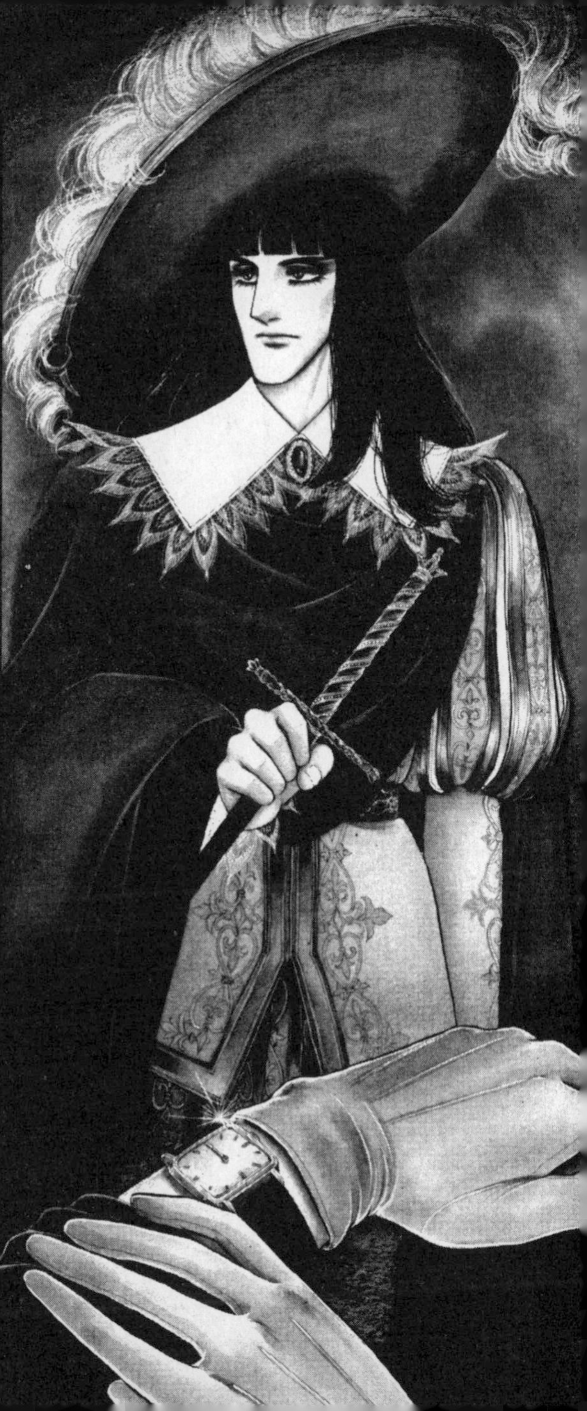

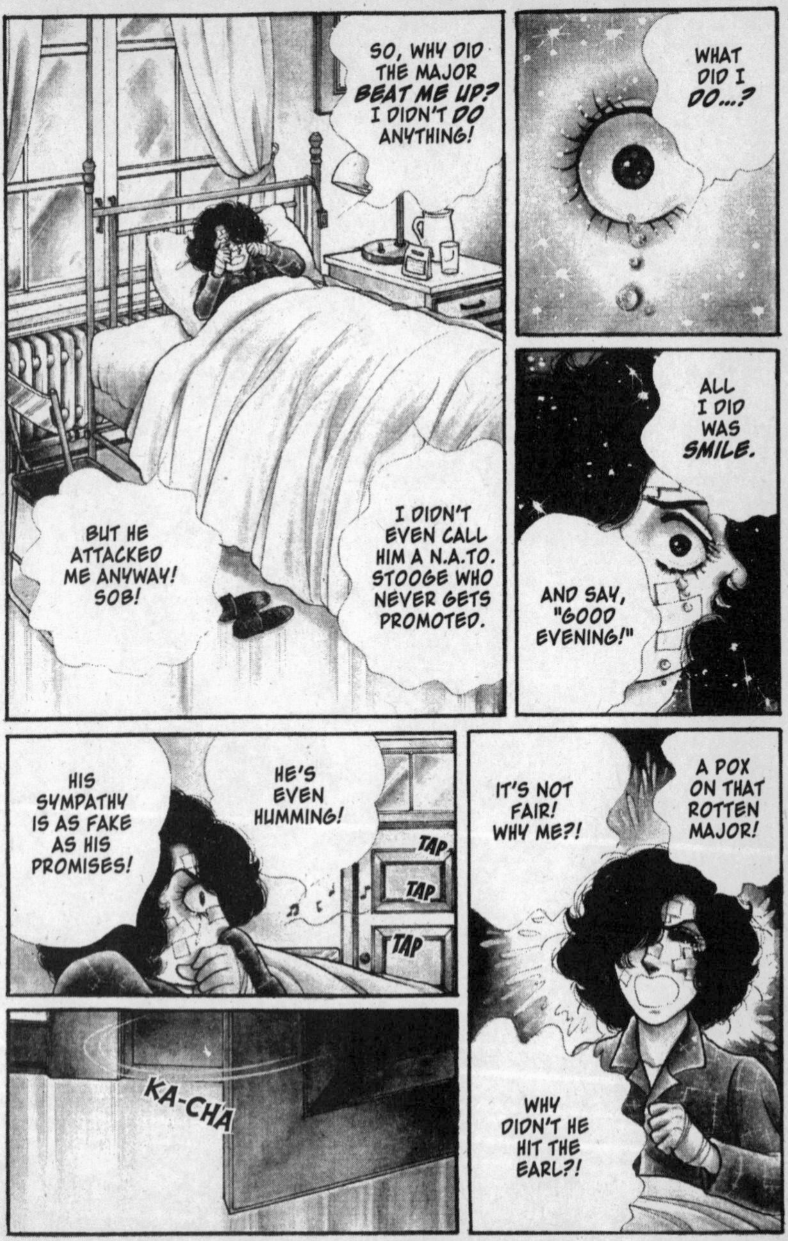
WHAT DID I DO...?
ALL I DID WAS SMILE.
AND SAY, "GOOD EVENING!"
SO, WHY DID THE MAJOR BEAT ME UP? I DIDN'T DO ANYTHING!
I DIDN'T EVEN CALL HIM A N.A.TO. STOOGE WHO NEVER GETS PROMOTED.
BUT HE ATTACKED ME ANYWAY! SOB!
A POX ON THAT ROTTEN MAJOR!
IT'S NOT FAIR! WHY ME?!
WHY DIDN'T HE HIT THE EARL?!
HE'S EVEN HUMMING!
HIS SYMPATHY IS AS FAKE AS HIS PROMISES!
TAP
TAP
TAP
KA-CHA

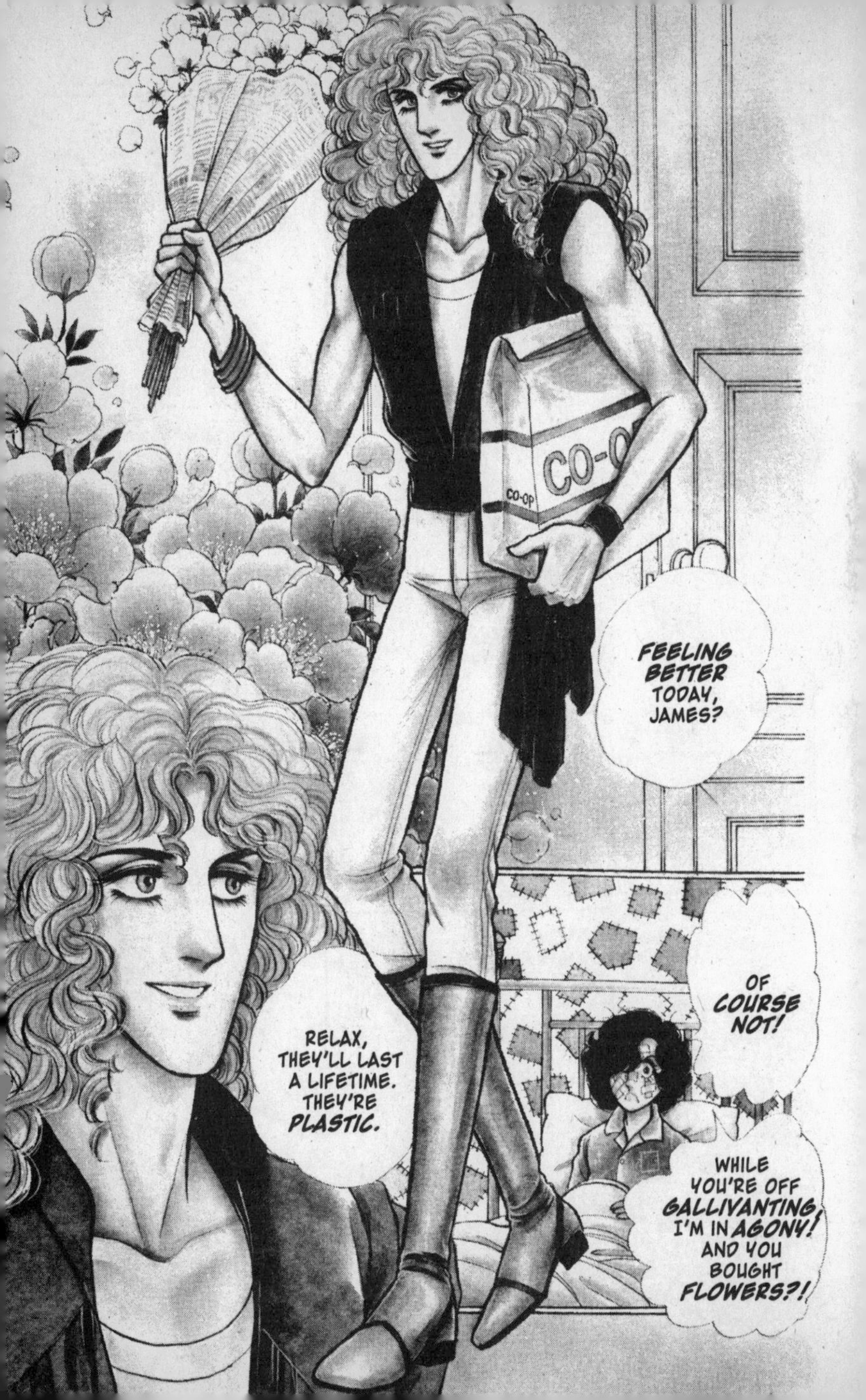
CO-OP
CO-OP
FEELING BETTER TODAY, JAMES?
OF COURSE NOT!
WHILE YOU'RE OFF GALLIVANTING I'M IN AGONY! AND YOU BOUGHT FLOWERS?!
RELAX, THEY'LL LAST A LIFETIME. THEY'RE PLASTIC.

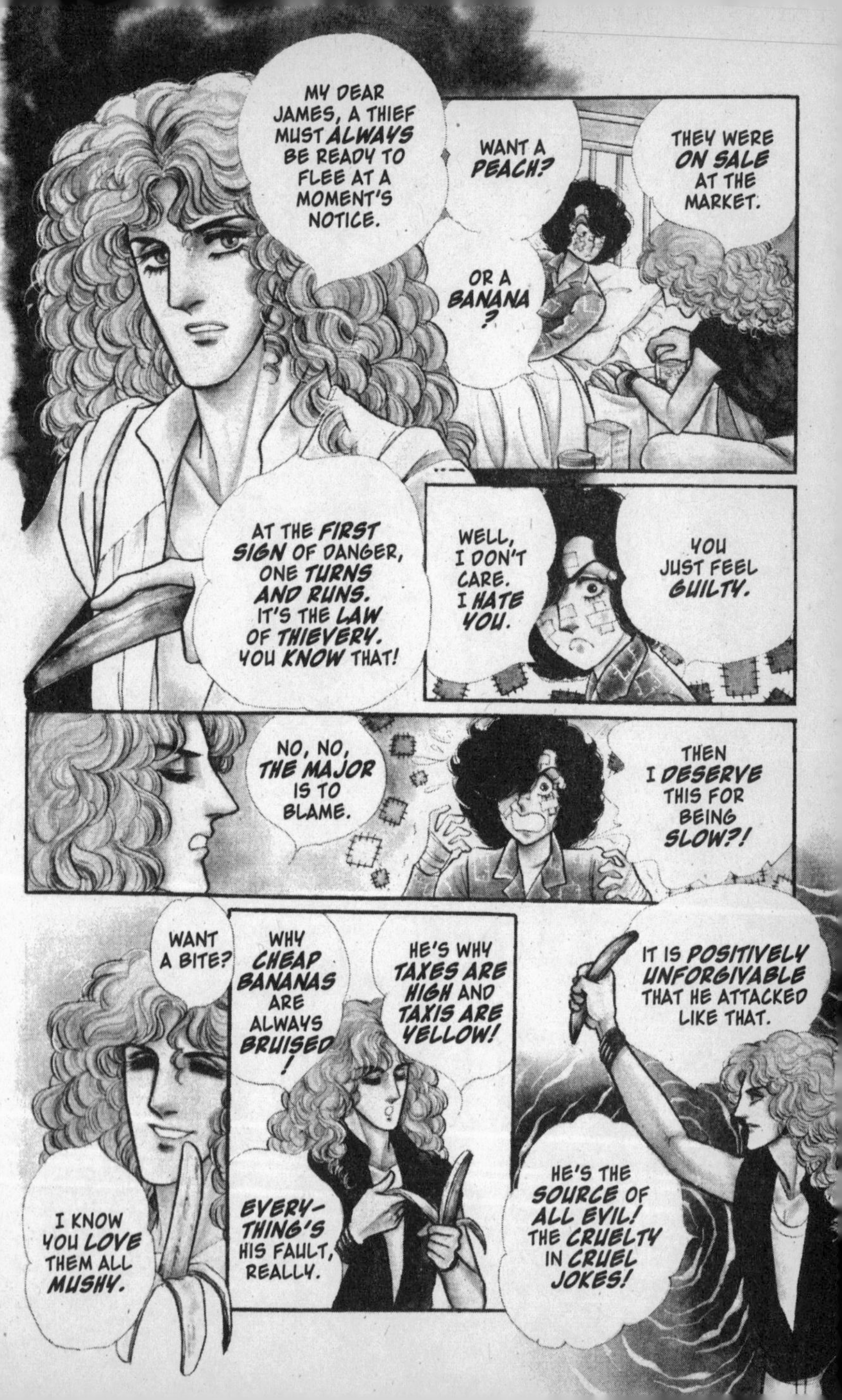
THEY WERE ON SALE AT THE MARKET.
WANT A PEACH?
OR A BANANA?
YOU JUST FEEL GUILTY.
WELL, I DON'T CARE. I HATE YOU.
MY DEAR JAMES, A THIEF MUST ALWAYS BE READY TO FLEE AT A MOMENT'S NOTICE.
AT THE FIRST SIGN OF DANGER, ONE TURNS AND RUNS. IT'S THE LAW OF THIEVERY. YOU KNOW THAT!
THEN I DESERVE THIS FOR BEING SLOW?!
NO, NO, THE MAJOR IS TO BLAME.
IT IS POSITIVELY UNFORGIVABLE THAT HE ATTACKED LIKE THAT.
HE'S THE SOURCE OF ALL EVIL! THE CRUELTY IN CRUEL JOKES!
HE'S WHY TAXES ARE HIGH AND TAXIS ARE YELLOW!
WHY CHEAP BANANAS ARE ALWAYS BRUISED!
EVERYTHING'S HIS FAULT, REALLY.
WANT A BITE?
I KNOW YOU LOVE THEM ALL MUSHY.

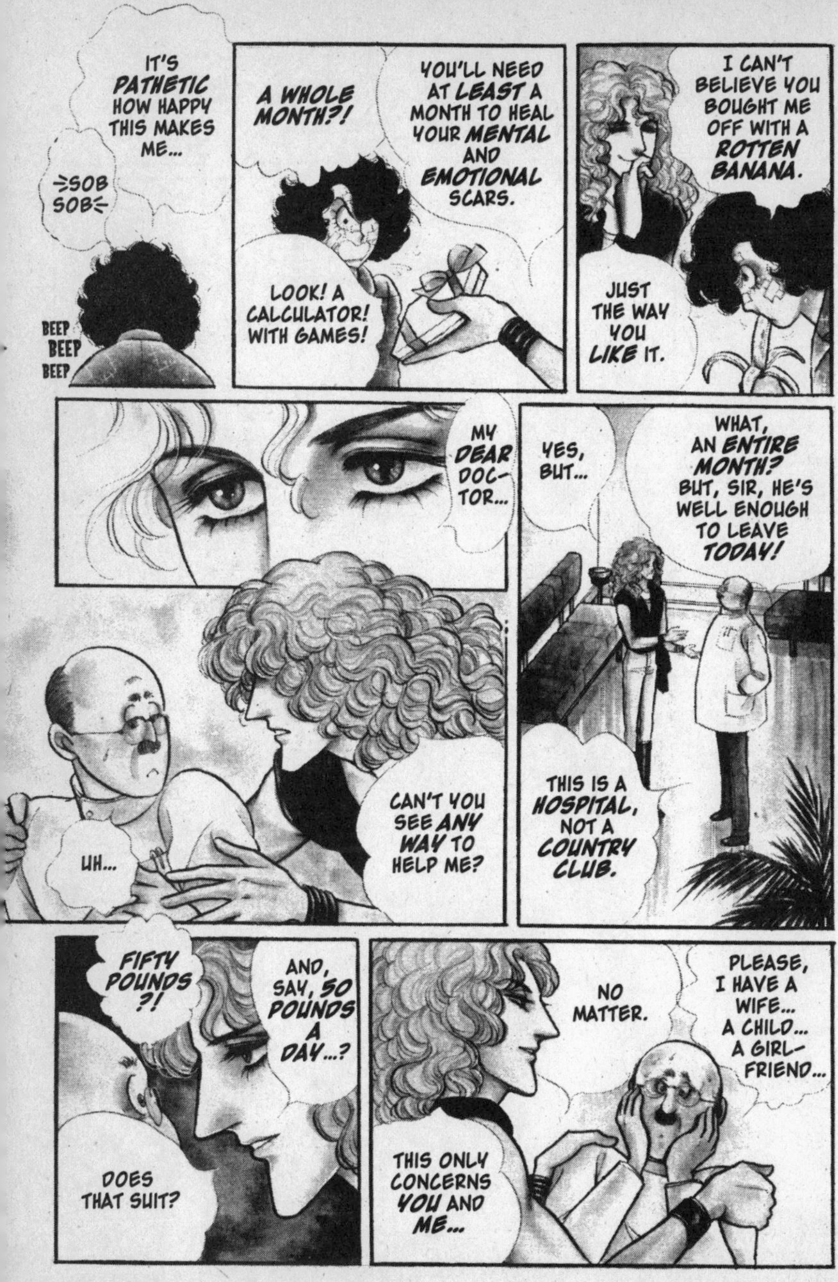
I CAN'T BELIEVE YOU BOUGHT ME OFF WITH A ROTTEN BANANA.
JUST THE WAY YOU LIKE IT.
YOU'LL NEED AT LEAST A MONTH TO HEAL YOUR MENTAL AND EMOTIONAL SCARS.
A WHOLE MONTH?!
LOOK! A CALCULATOR! WITH GAMES!
IT'S PATHETIC HOW HAPPY THIS MAKES ME...
≥SOB SOB≤
BEEP BEEP BEEP
WHAT, AN ENTIRE MONTH? BUT, SIR, HE'S WELL ENOUGH TO LEAVE TODAY!
YES, BUT...
THIS IS A HOSPITAL, NOT A COUNTRY CLUB.
MY DEAR DOC- TOR...
CAN'T YOU SEE ANY WAY TO HELP ME?
UH...
PLEASE, I HAVE A WIFE... A CHILD... A GIRL- FRIEND...
NO MATTER.
THIS ONLY CONCERNS YOU AND ME...
AND, SAY, 50 POUNDS A DAY...?
FIFTY POUNDS ?!
DOES THAT SUIT?

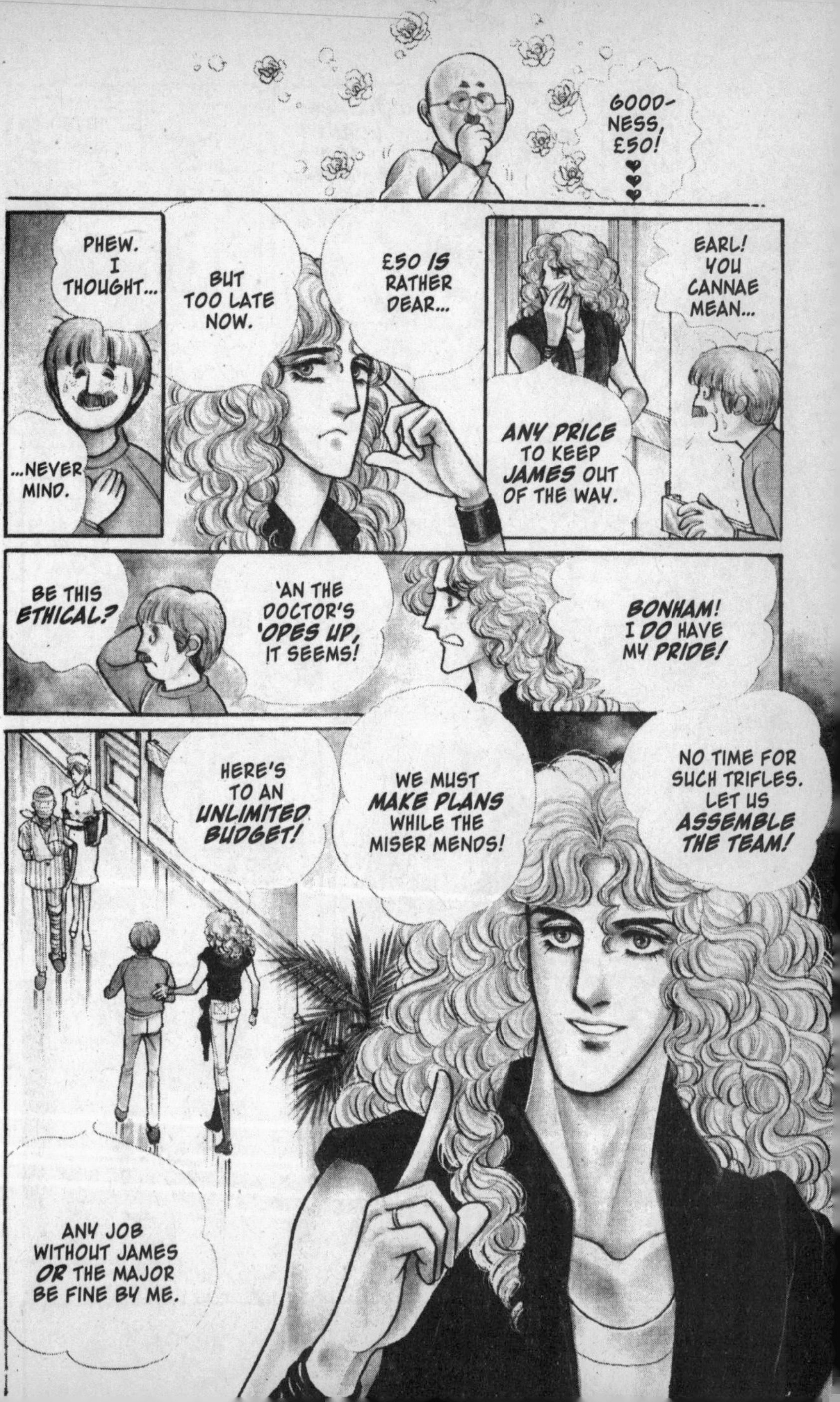
GOODNESS, £50!
EARL! YOU CANNAE MEAN...
ANY PRICE TO KEEP JAMES OUT OF THE WAY.
£50 IS RATHER DEAR...
BUT TOO LATE NOW.
PHEW. I THOUGHT...
...NEVER MIND.
BONHAM! I DO HAVE MY PRIDE!
'AN THE DOCTOR'S 'OPES UP, IT SEEMS!
BE THIS ETHICAL?
NO TIME FOR SUCH TRIFLES. LET US ASSEMBLE THE TEAM!
WE MUST MAKE PLANS WHILE THE MISER MENDS!
HERE'S TO AN UNLIMITED BUDGET!
ANY JOB WITHOUT JAMES OR THE MAJOR BE FINE BY ME.

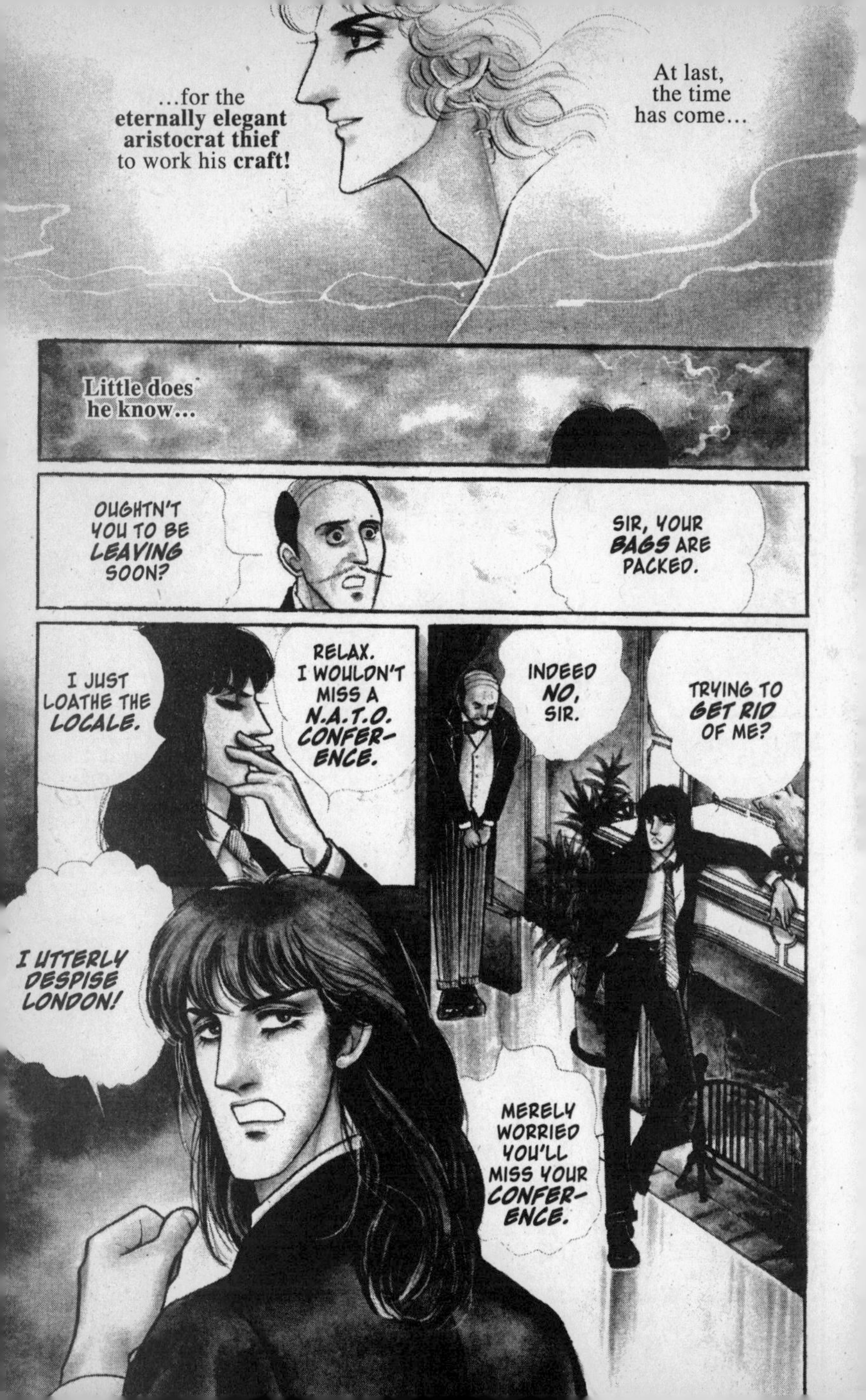
At last, the time has come…
…for the eternally elegant aristocrat thief to work his craft!
Little does he know…
SIR, YOUR BAGS ARE PACKED.
OUGHTN'T YOU TO BE LEAVING SOON?
TRYING TO GET RID OF ME?
INDEED NO, SIR.
MERELY WORRIED YOU'LL MISS YOUR CONFER-ENCE.
RELAX. I WOULDN'T MISS A N.A.T.O. CONFER-ENCE.
I JUST LOATHE THE LOCALE.
I UTTERLY DESPISE LONDON!

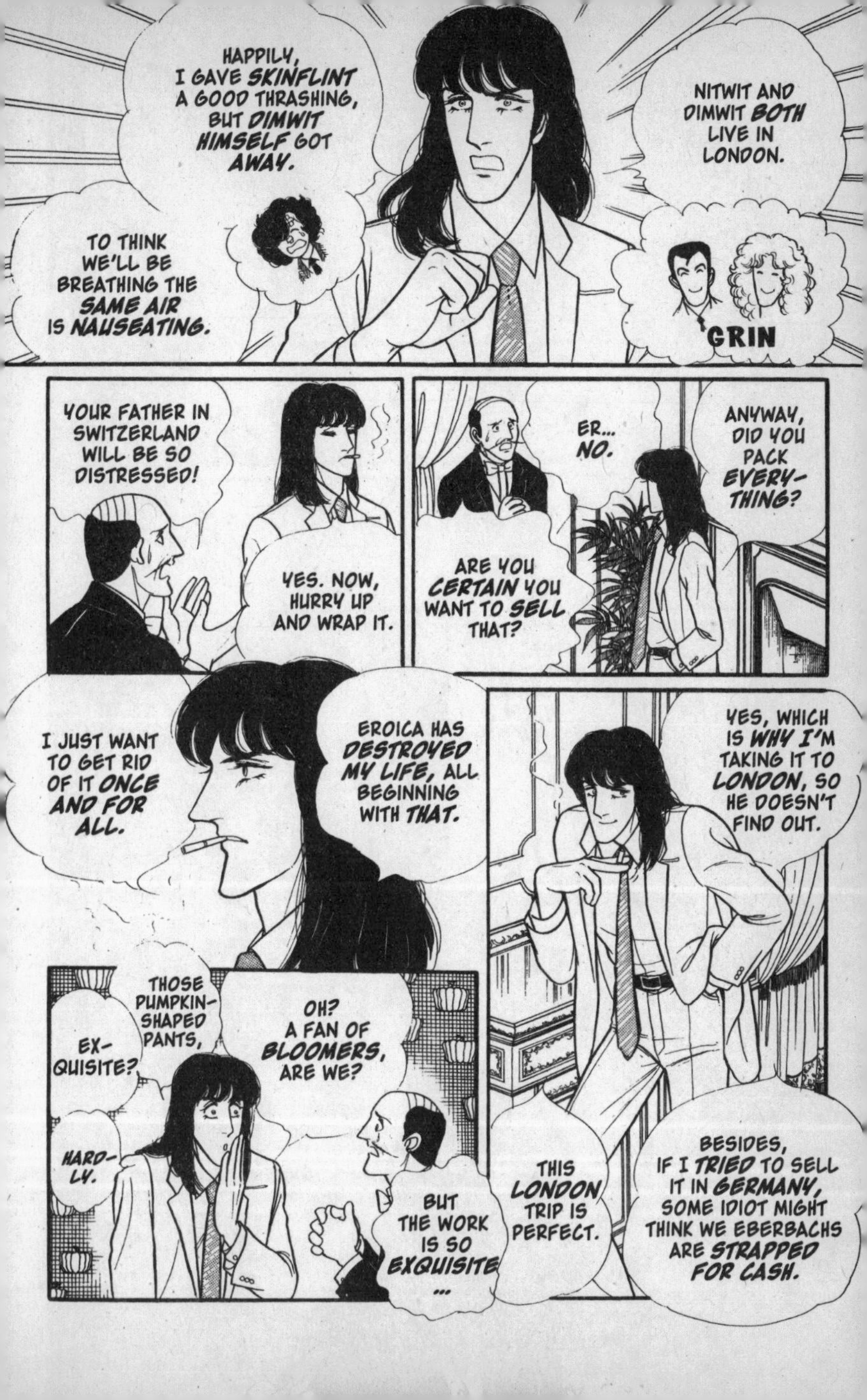

HAPPILY, I GAVE SKINFLINT A GOOD THRASHING, BUT DIMWIT HIMSELF GOT AWAY.
NITWIT AND DIMWIT BOTH LIVE IN LONDON.
GRIN
TO THINK WE'LL BE BREATHING THE SAME AIR IS NAUSEATING.
ANYWAY, DID YOU PACK EVERY-THING?
ER... NO.
ARE YOU CERTAIN YOU WANT TO SELL THAT?
YOUR FATHER IN SWITZERLAND WILL BE SO DISTRESSED!
YES. NOW, HURRY UP AND WRAP IT.
YES, WHICH IS WHY I'M TAKING IT TO LONDON, SO HE DOESN'T FIND OUT.
BESIDES, IF I TRIED TO SELL IT IN GERMANY, SOME IDIOT MIGHT THINK WE EBERBACHS ARE STRAPPED FOR CASH.
THIS LONDON TRIP IS PERFECT.
EROICA HAS DESTROYED MY LIFE, ALL BEGINNING WITH THAT.
I JUST WANT TO GET RID OF IT ONCE AND FOR ALL.
BUT THE WORK IS SO EXQUISITE...
EX-QUISITE?
THOSE PUMPKIN-SHAPED PANTS,
OH? A FAN OF BLOOMERS, ARE WE?
HARD-LY.

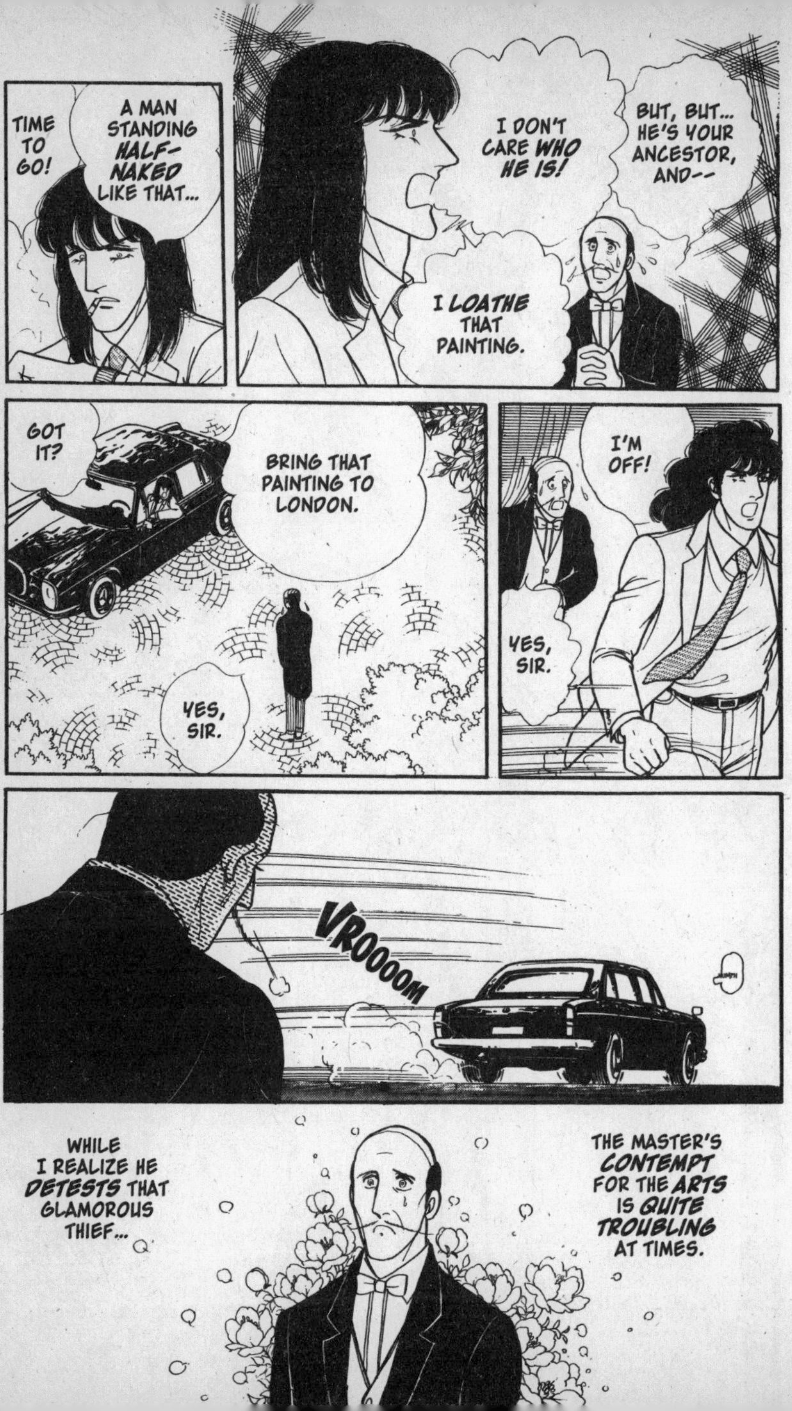
BUT, BUT... HE'S YOUR ANCESTOR, AND--
I DON'T CARE *WHO* HE IS!
I *LOATHE* THAT PAINTING.
A MAN STANDING *HALF-NAKED* LIKE THAT...
TIME TO GO!
I'M OFF!
YES, SIR.
BRING THAT PAINTING TO LONDON.
GOT IT?
YES, SIR.
VROOOOM
WHILE I REALIZE HE *DETESTS* THAT GLAMOROUS THIEF...
THE MASTER'S *CONTEMPT* FOR THE *ARTS* IS *QUITE TROUBLING* AT TIMES.

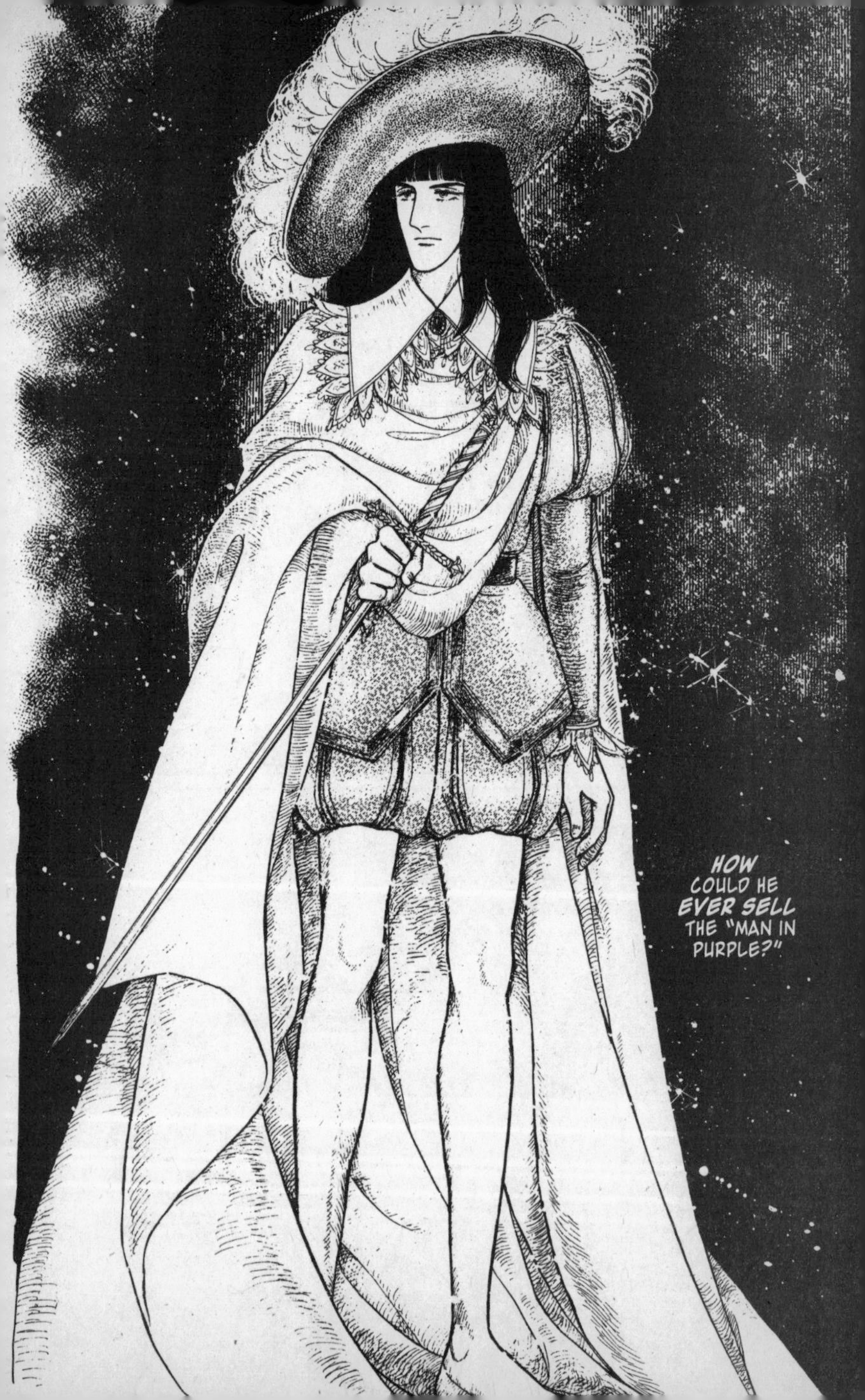
HOW COULD HE EVER SELL THE "MAN IN PURPLE?"

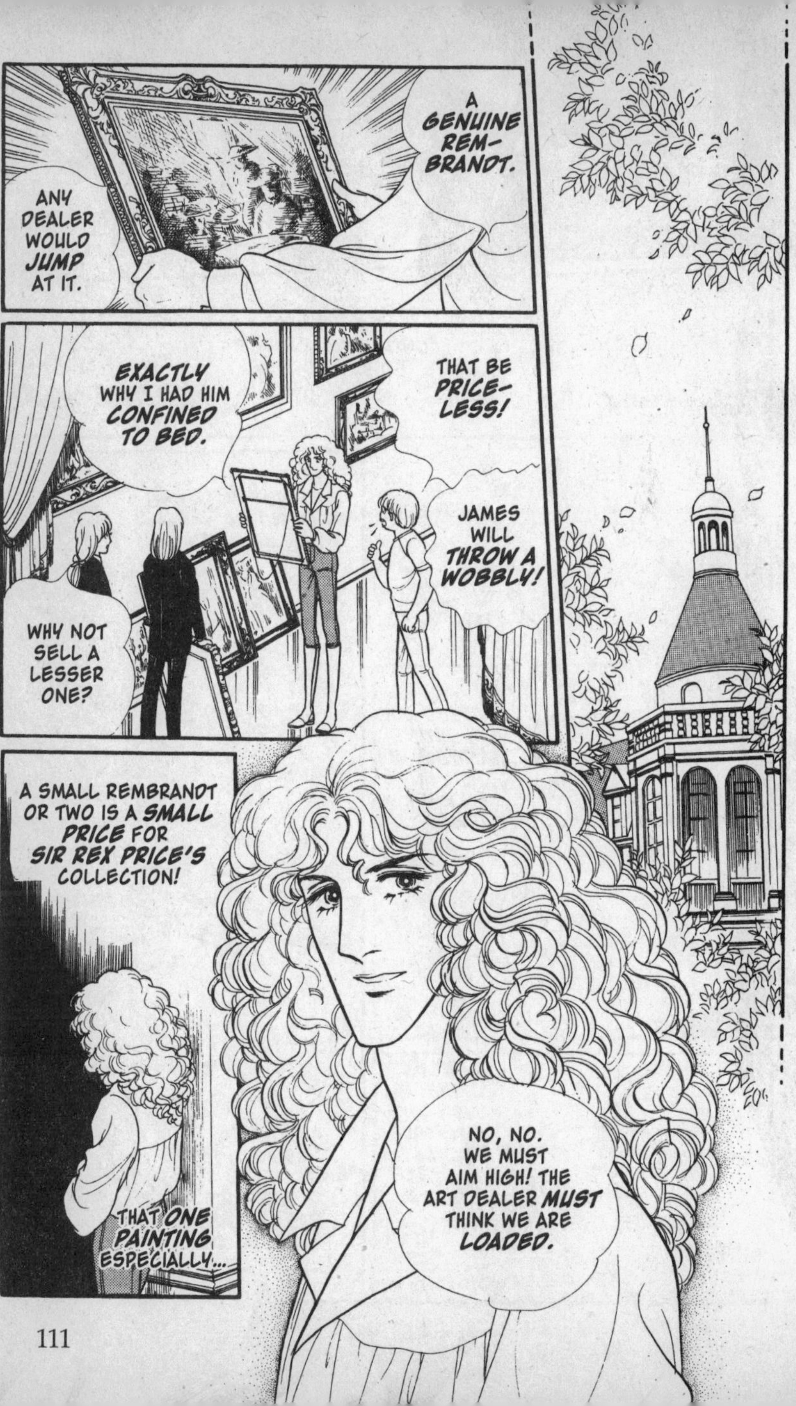
A GENUINE REMBRANDT.
ANY DEALER WOULD JUMP AT IT.
THAT BE PRICELESS!
EXACTLY WHY I HAD HIM CONFINED TO BED.
JAMES WILL THROW A WOBBLY!
WHY NOT SELL A LESSER ONE?
NO, NO. WE MUST AIM HIGH! THE ART DEALER MUST THINK WE ARE LOADED.
A SMALL REMBRANDT OR TWO IS A SMALL PRICE FOR SIR REX PRICE'S COLLECTION!
THAT ONE PAINTING ESPECIALLY...

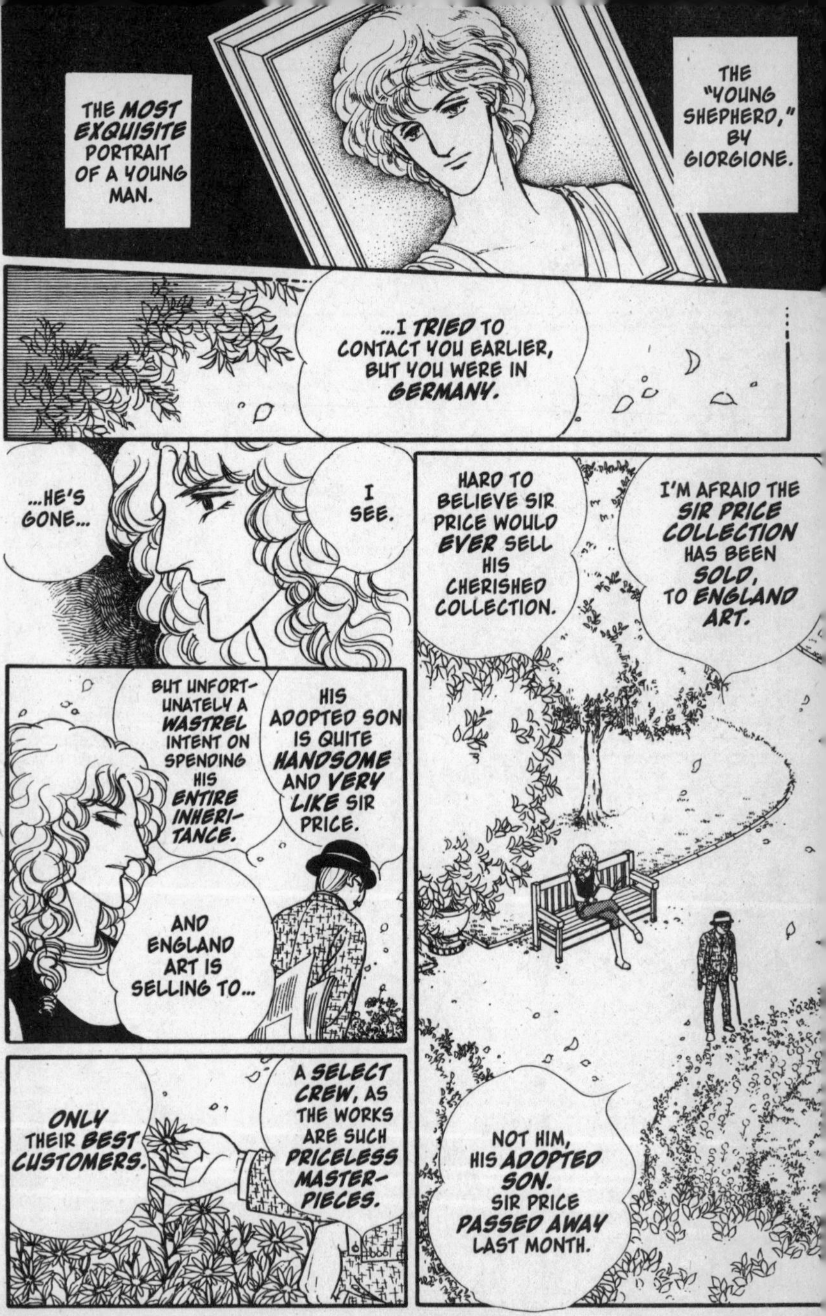
THE "YOUNG SHEPHERD," BY GIORGIONE.
THE MOST EXQUISITE PORTRAIT OF A YOUNG MAN.
...I TRIED TO CONTACT YOU EARLIER, BUT YOU WERE IN GERMANY.
I'M AFRAID THE SIR PRICE COLLECTION HAS BEEN SOLD, TO ENGLAND ART.
HARD TO BELIEVE SIR PRICE WOULD EVER SELL HIS CHERISHED COLLECTION.
NOT HIM, HIS ADOPTED SON. SIR PRICE PASSED AWAY LAST MONTH.
I SEE.
...HE'S GONE...
HIS ADOPTED SON IS QUITE HANDSOME AND VERY LIKE SIR PRICE.
BUT UNFORTUNATELY A WASTREL INTENT ON SPENDING HIS ENTIRE INHERITANCE.
AND ENGLAND ART IS SELLING TO...
A SELECT CREW, AS THE WORKS ARE SUCH PRICELESS MASTERPIECES.
ONLY THEIR BEST CUSTOMERS.

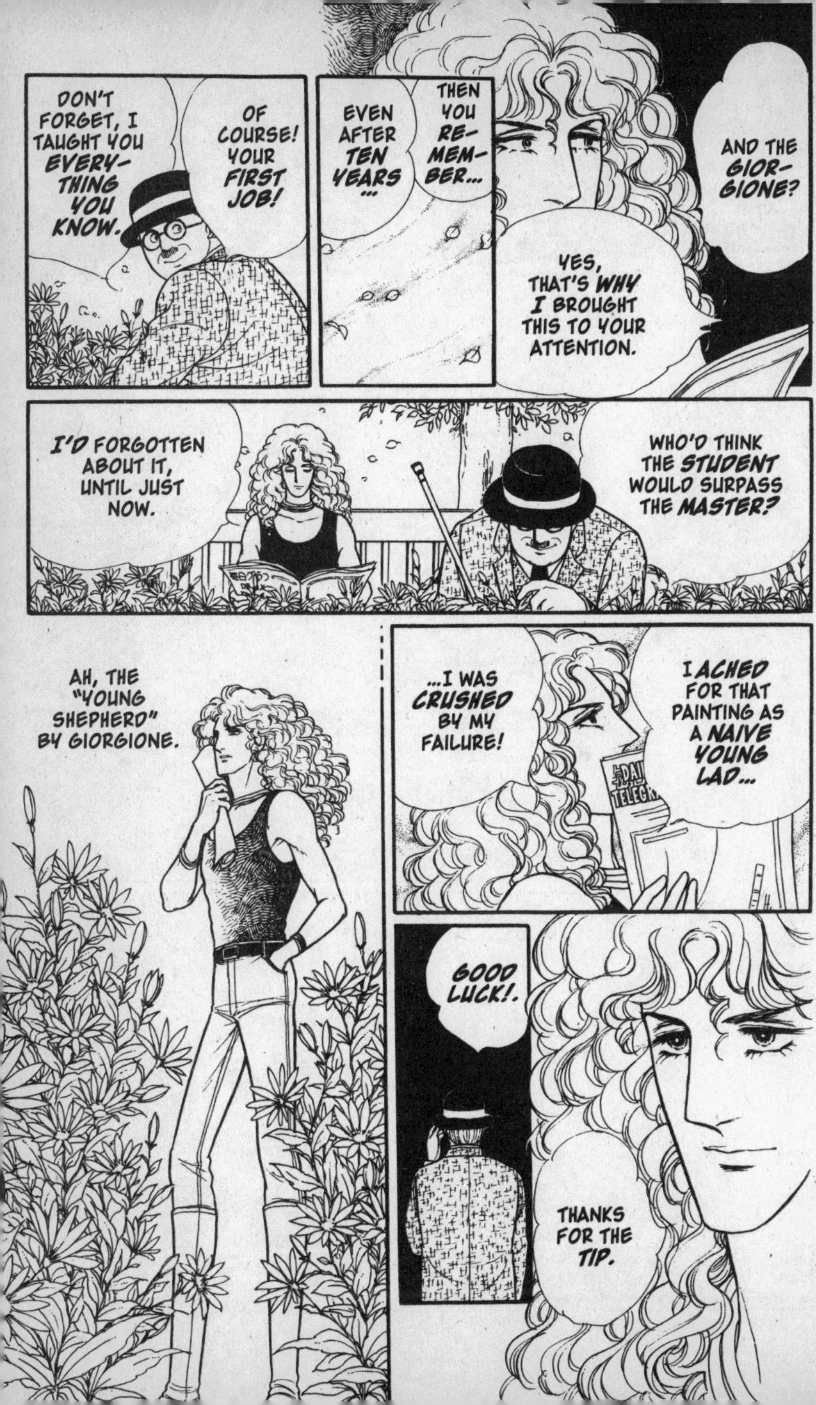
AND THE GIORGIONE?
YES, THAT'S WHY I BROUGHT THIS TO YOUR ATTENTION.
THEN YOU RE-MEMBER...
EVEN AFTER TEN YEARS...
OF COURSE! YOUR FIRST JOB!
DON'T FORGET, I TAUGHT YOU EVERY-THING YOU KNOW.
WHO'D THINK THE STUDENT WOULD SURPASS THE MASTER?
I'D FORGOTTEN ABOUT IT, UNTIL JUST NOW.
I ACHED FOR THAT PAINTING AS A NAIVE YOUNG LAD...
...I WAS CRUSHED BY MY FAILURE!
THANKS FOR THE TIP.
GOOD LUCK!.
AH, THE "YOUNG SHEPHERD" BY GIORGIONE.

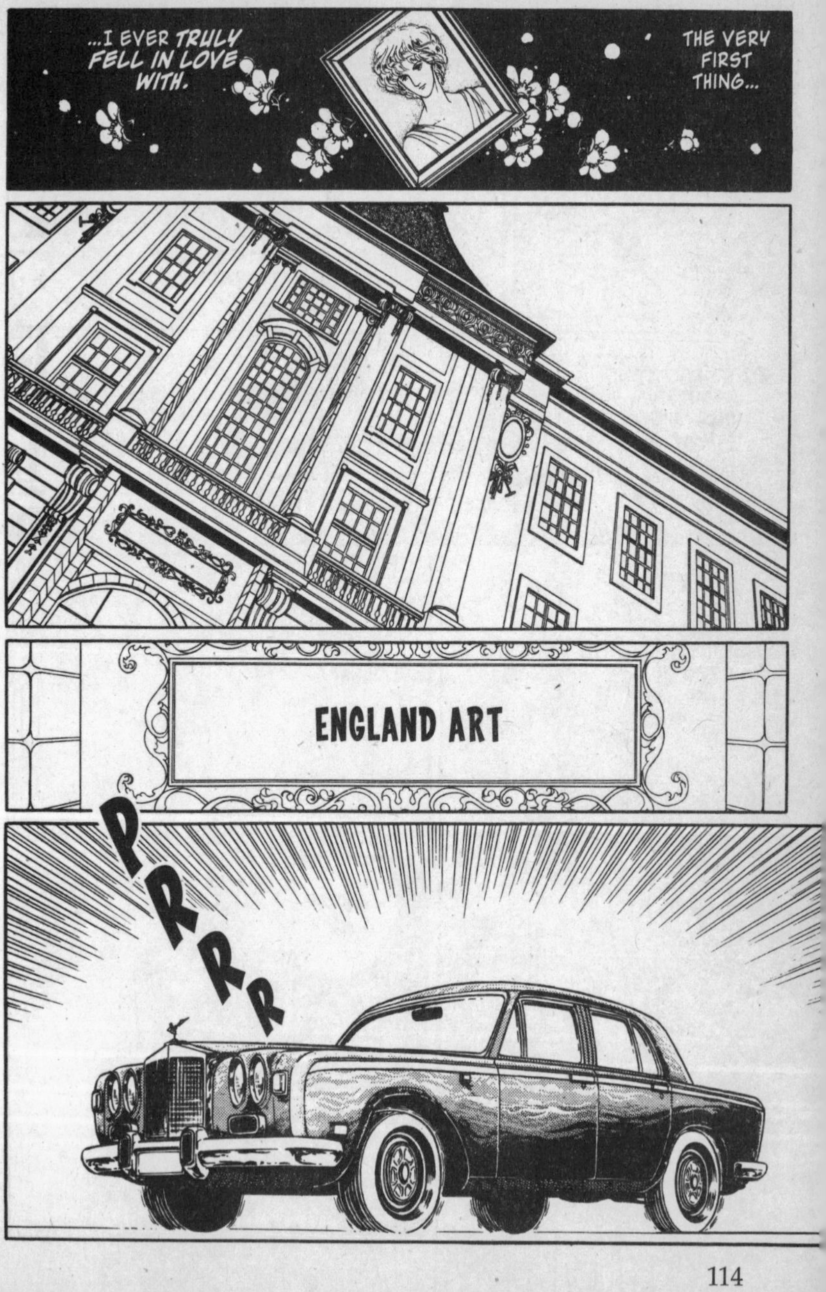
THE VERY FIRST THING...
...I EVER TRULY FELL IN LOVE WITH.
ENGLAND ART
PRRR

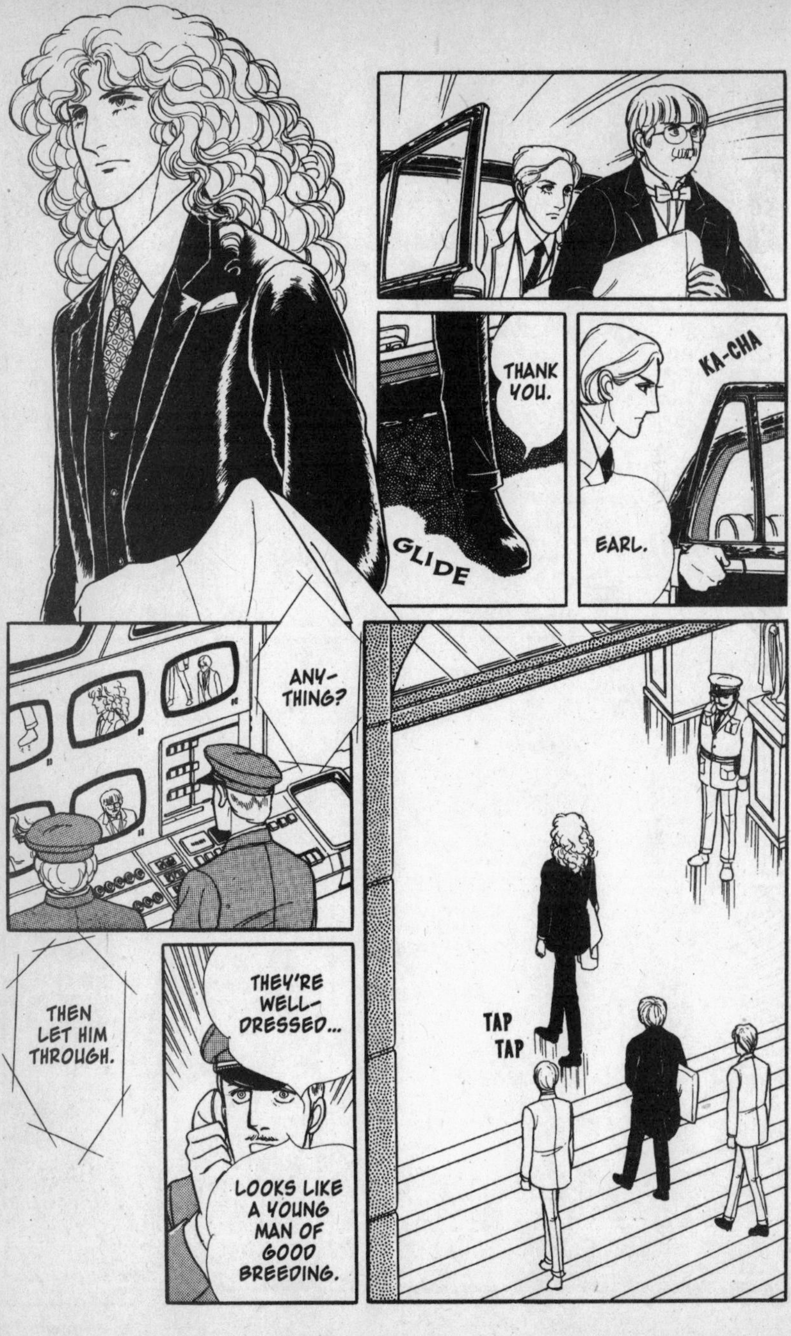
KA-CHA
EARL.
THANK YOU.
GLIDE
TAP TAP
ANY-THING?
THEY'RE WELL-DRESSED...
LOOKS LIKE A YOUNG MAN OF GOOD BREEDING.
THEN LET HIM THROUGH.

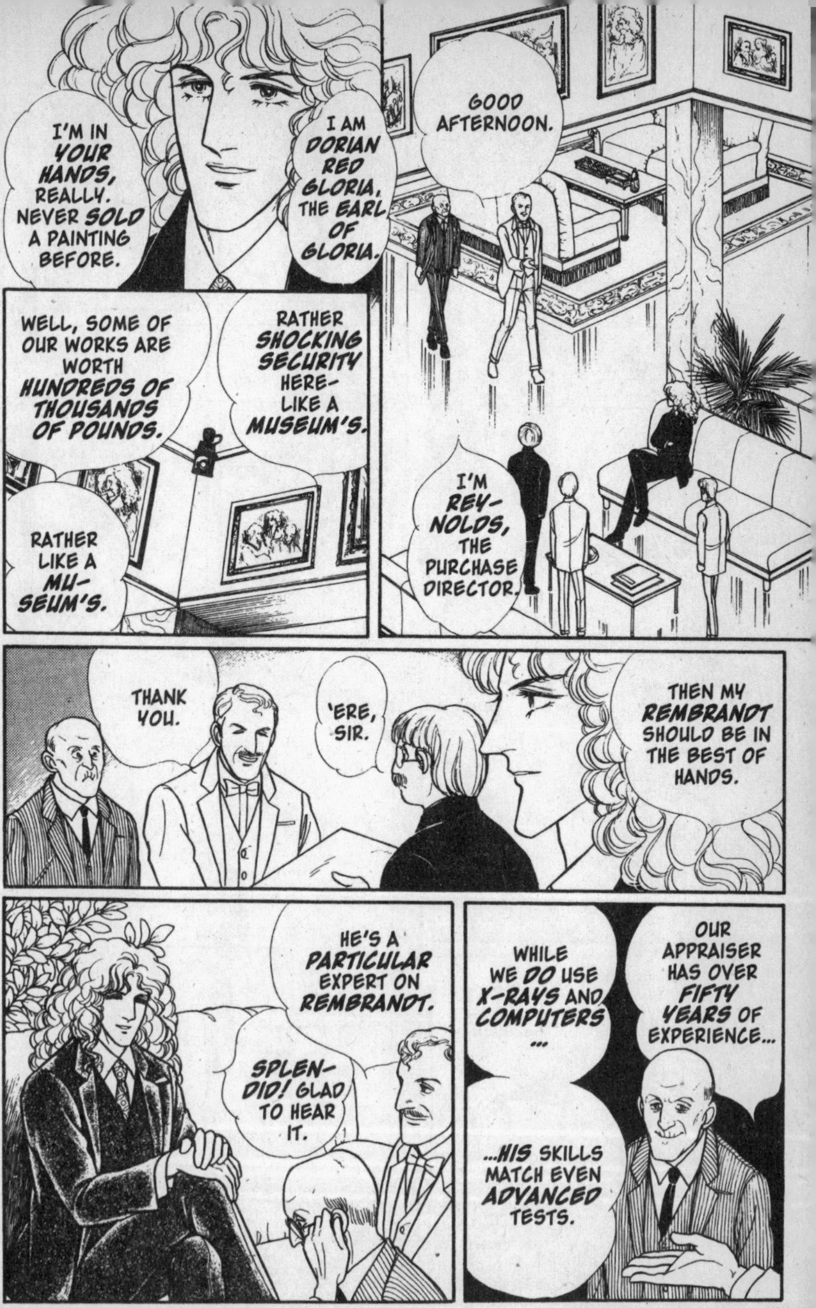
GOOD AFTERNOON.
I'M REYNOLDS, THE PURCHASE DIRECTOR.
I AM DORIAN RED GLORIA, THE EARL OF GLORIA.
I'M IN YOUR HANDS, REALLY. NEVER SOLD A PAINTING BEFORE.
RATHER SHOCKING SECURITY HERE- LIKE A MUSEUM'S.
WELL, SOME OF OUR WORKS ARE WORTH HUNDREDS OF THOUSANDS OF POUNDS.
RATHER LIKE A MU-SEUM'S.
THEN MY REMBRANDT SHOULD BE IN THE BEST OF HANDS.
'ERE, SIR.
THANK YOU.
OUR APPRAISER HAS OVER FIFTY YEARS OF EXPERIENCE...
WHILE WE DO USE X-RAYS AND COMPUTERS ...
...HIS SKILLS MATCH EVEN ADVANCED TESTS.
HE'S A PARTICULAR EXPERT ON REMBRANDT.
SPLEN-DID! GLAD TO HEAR IT.

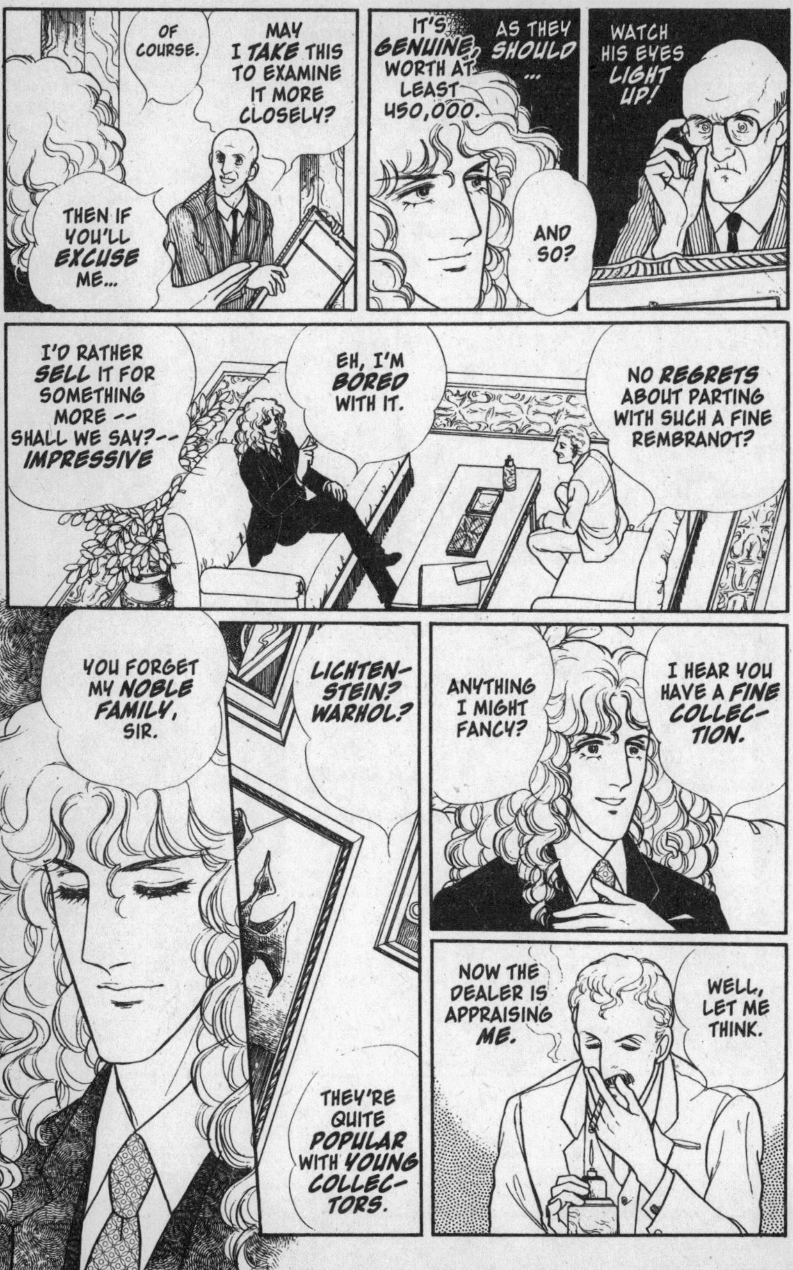
WATCH HIS EYES LIGHT UP!
AS THEY SHOULD ...
IT'S GENUINE, WORTH AT LEAST 450,000.
AND SO?
MAY I TAKE THIS TO EXAMINE IT MORE CLOSELY?
OF COURSE.
THEN IF YOU'LL EXCUSE ME...
NO REGRETS ABOUT PARTING WITH SUCH A FINE REMBRANDT?
EH, I'M BORED WITH IT.
I'D RATHER SELL IT FOR SOMETHING MORE -- SHALL WE SAY?-- IMPRESSIVE
I HEAR YOU HAVE A FINE COLLECTION.
ANYTHING I MIGHT FANCY?
WELL, LET ME THINK.
NOW THE DEALER IS APPRAISING ME.
LICHTENSTEIN? WARHOL?
THEY'RE QUITE POPULAR WITH YOUNG COLLECTORS.
YOU FORGET MY NOBLE FAMILY, SIR.

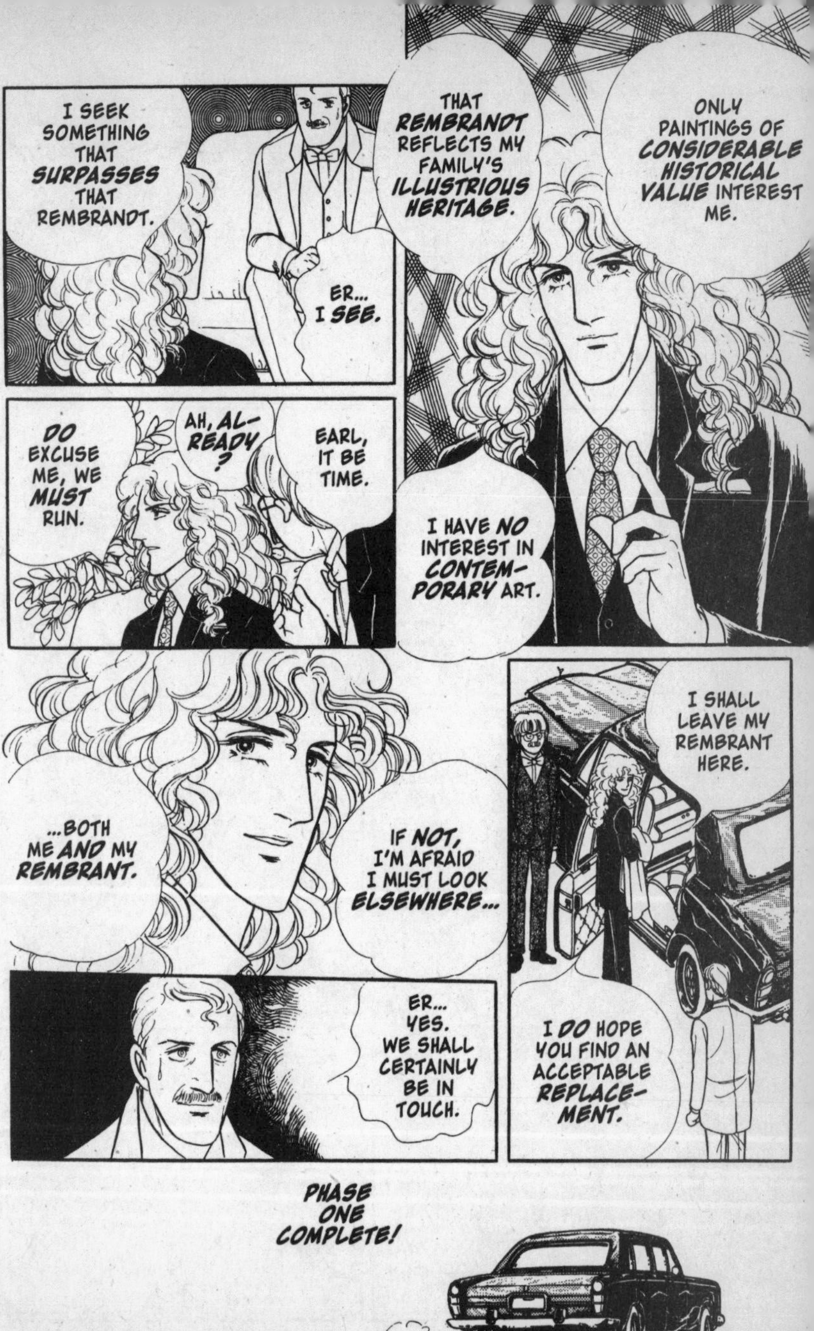

ONLY PAINTINGS OF CONSIDERABLE HISTORICAL VALUE INTEREST ME.
THAT REMBRANDT REFLECTS MY FAMILY'S ILLUSTRIOUS HERITAGE.
I HAVE NO INTEREST IN CONTEMPORARY ART.
I SEEK SOMETHING THAT SURPASSES THAT REMBRANDT.
ER... I SEE.
EARL, IT BE TIME.
AH, ALREADY?
DO EXCUSE ME, WE MUST RUN.
I SHALL LEAVE MY REMBRANT HERE.
I DO HOPE YOU FIND AN ACCEPTABLE REPLACEMENT.
IF NOT, I'M AFRAID I MUST LOOK ELSEWHERE...
...BOTH ME AND MY REMBRANT.
ER... YES. WE SHALL CERTAINLY BE IN TOUCH.
PHASE ONE COMPLETE!

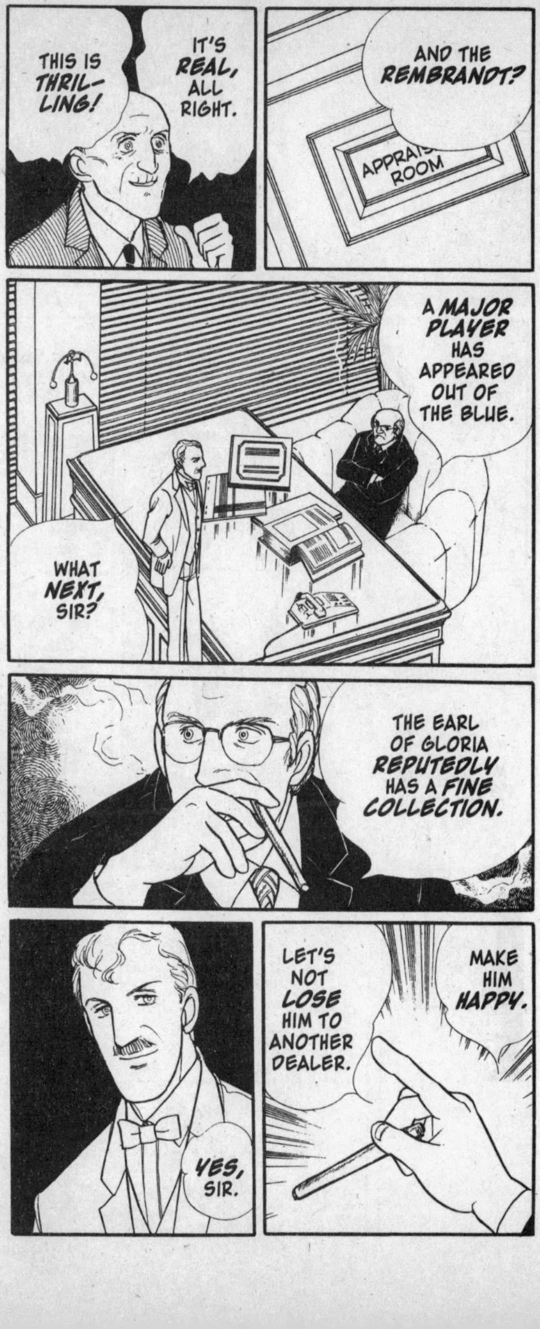
AND THE REMBRANDT?
IT'S REAL, ALL RIGHT.
THIS IS THRILLING!
A MAJOR PLAYER HAS APPEARED OUT OF THE BLUE.
WHAT NEXT, SIR?
THE EARL OF GLORIA REPUTEDLY HAS A FINE COLLECTION.
MAKE HIM HAPPY.
LET'S NOT LOSE HIM TO ANOTHER DEALER.
YES, SIR.
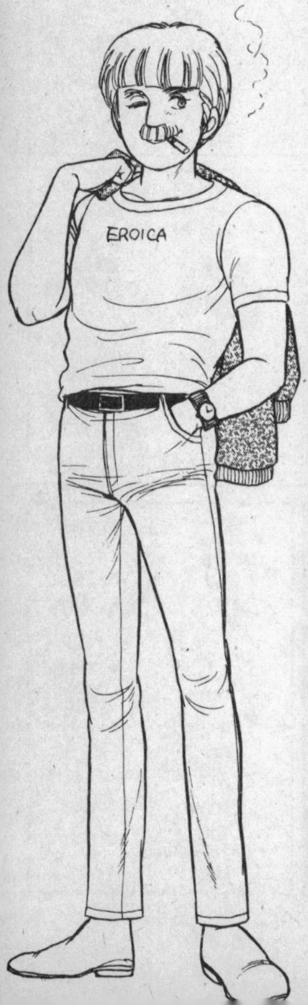
EROICA

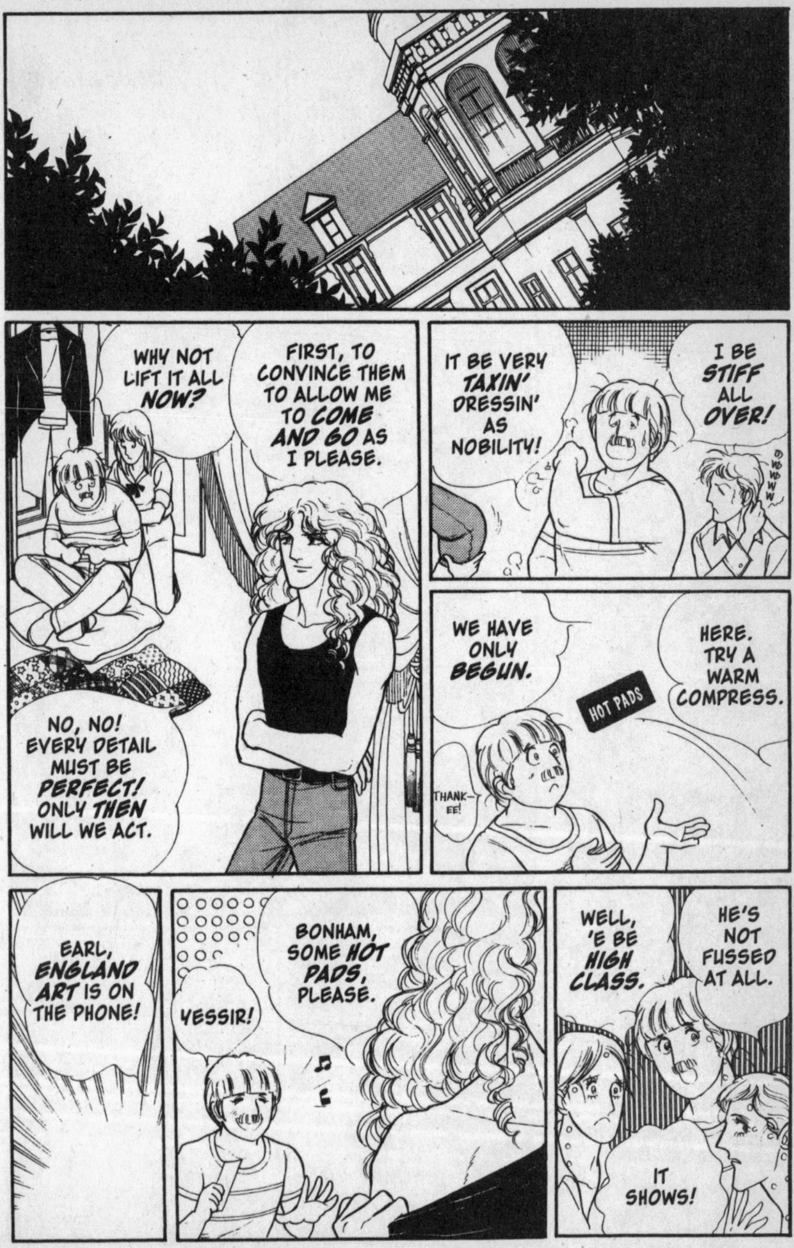
FIRST, TO CONVINCE THEM TO ALLOW ME TO COME AND GO AS I PLEASE.
WHY NOT LIFT IT ALL NOW?
NO, NO! EVERY DETAIL MUST BE PERFECT! ONLY THEN WILL WE ACT.
I BE STIFF ALL OVER!
IT BE VERY TAXIN' DRESSIN' AS NOBILITY!
HERE. TRY A WARM COMPRESS.
HOT PADS
WE HAVE ONLY BEGUN.
THANK-EE!
HE'S NOT FUSSED AT ALL.
WELL, 'E BE HIGH CLASS.
IT SHOWS!
BONHAM, SOME HOT PADS, PLEASE.
YESSIR!
EARL, ENGLAND ART IS ON THE PHONE!

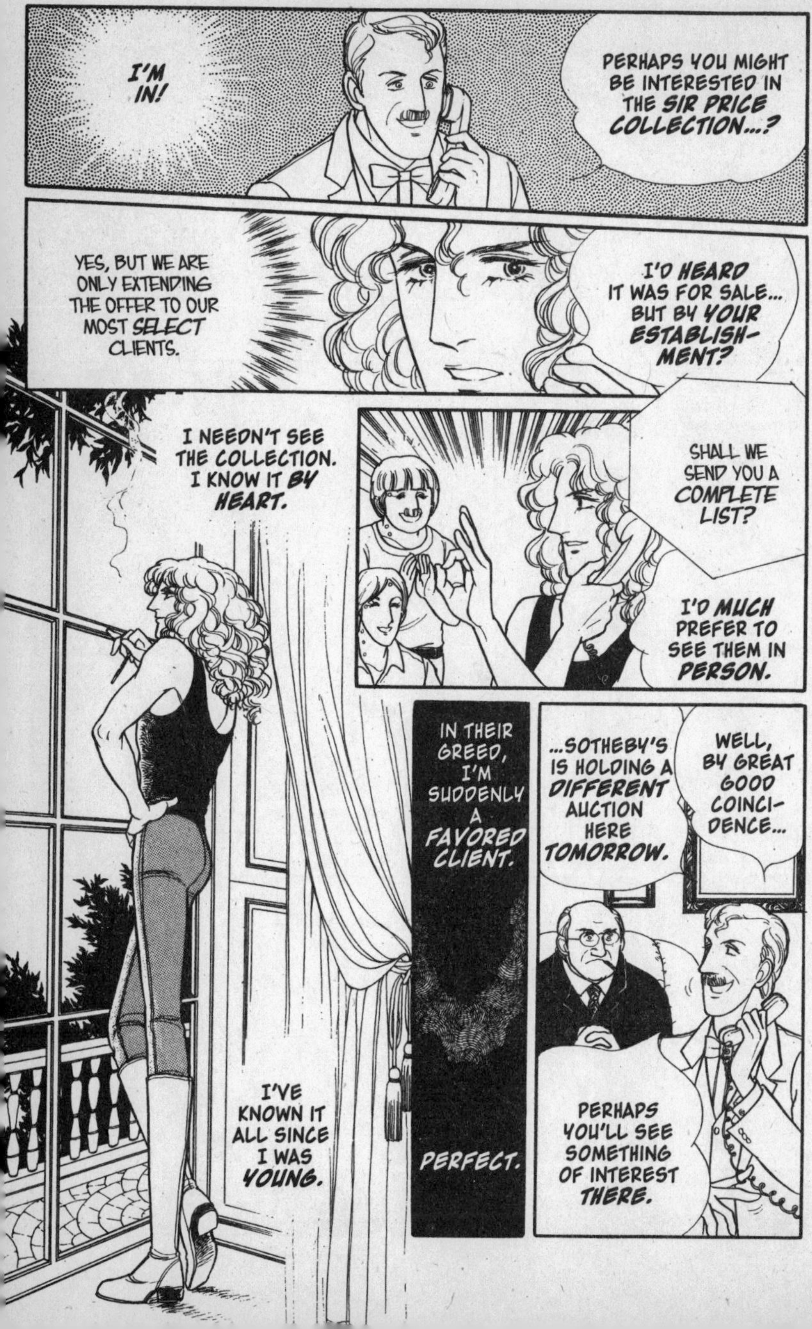
PERHAPS YOU MIGHT BE INTERESTED IN THE SIR PRICE COLLECTION...?
I'M IN!
I'D HEARD IT WAS FOR SALE... BUT BY YOUR ESTABLISHMENT?
YES, BUT WE ARE ONLY EXTENDING THE OFFER TO OUR MOST SELECT CLIENTS.
SHALL WE SEND YOU A COMPLETE LIST?
I'D MUCH PREFER TO SEE THEM IN PERSON.
WELL, BY GREAT GOOD COINCIDENCE...
...SOTHEBY'S IS HOLDING A DIFFERENT AUCTION HERE TOMORROW.
PERHAPS YOU'LL SEE SOMETHING OF INTEREST THERE.
IN THEIR GREED, I'M SUDDENLY A FAVORED CLIENT.
PERFECT.
I NEEDN'T SEE THE COLLECTION. I KNOW IT BY HEART.
I'VE KNOWN IT ALL SINCE I WAS YOUNG.

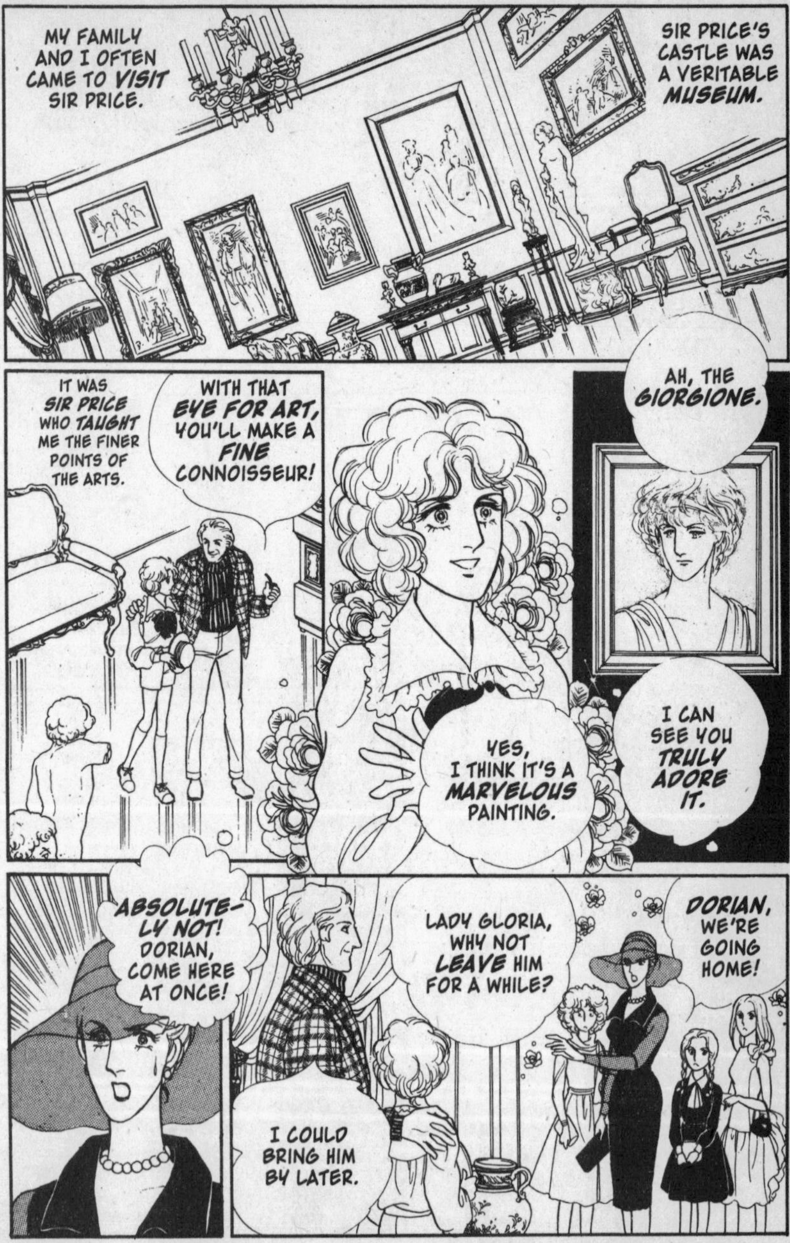
SIR PRICE'S CASTLE WAS A VERITABLE MUSEUM.
MY FAMILY AND I OFTEN CAME TO VISIT SIR PRICE.
AH, THE GIORGIONE.
YES, I THINK IT'S A MARVELOUS PAINTING.
I CAN SEE YOU TRULY ADORE IT.
IT WAS SIR PRICE WHO TAUGHT ME THE FINER POINTS OF THE ARTS.
WITH THAT EYE FOR ART, YOU'LL MAKE A FINE CONNOISSEUR!
DORIAN, WE'RE GOING HOME!
LADY GLORIA, WHY NOT LEAVE HIM FOR A WHILE?
I COULD BRING HIM BY LATER.
ABSOLUTELY NOT! DORIAN, COME HERE AT ONCE!

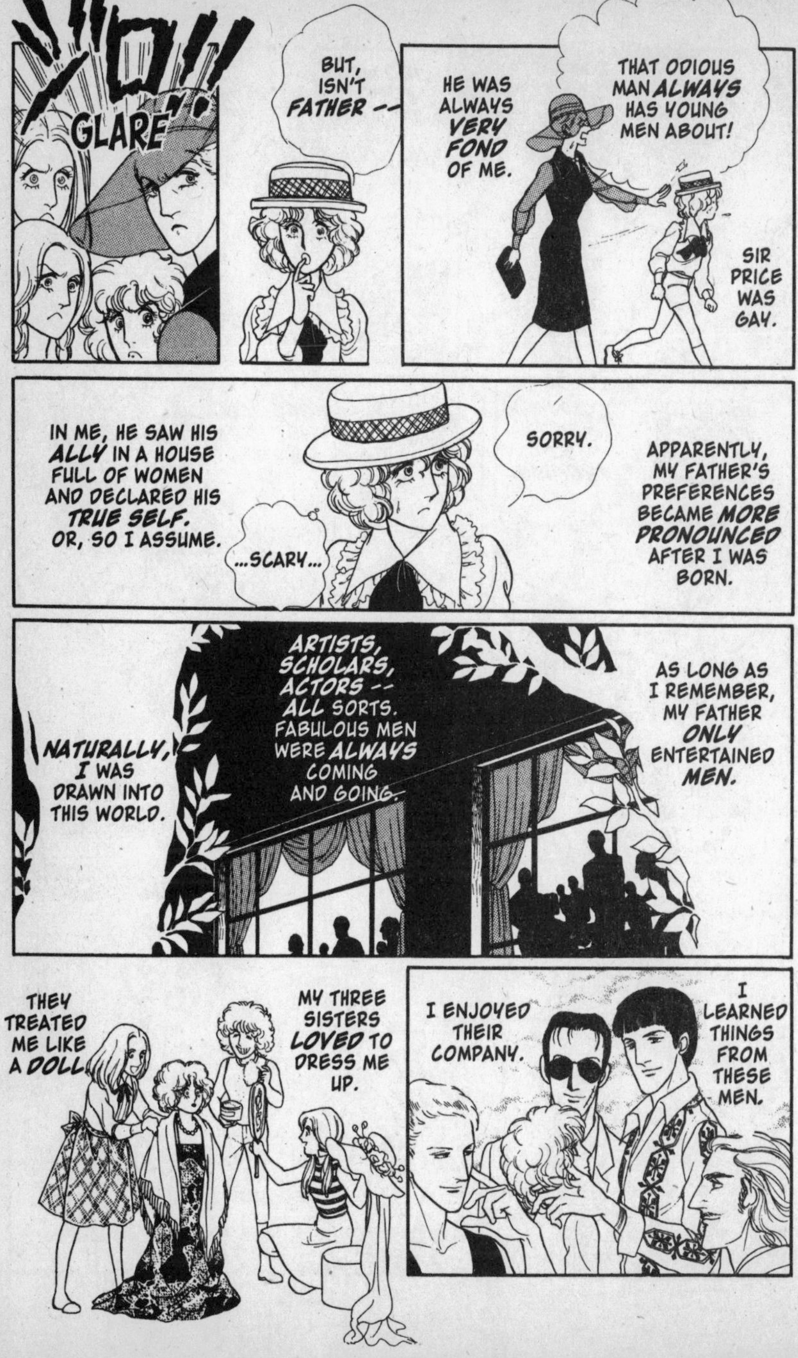
THAT ODIOUS MAN ALWAYS HAS YOUNG MEN ABOUT!
HE WAS ALWAYS VERY FOND OF ME.
SIR PRICE WAS GAY.
BUT, ISN'T FATHER --
GLARE
APPARENTLY, MY FATHER'S PREFERENCES BECAME MORE PRONOUNCED AFTER I WAS BORN.
SORRY.
IN ME, HE SAW HIS ALLY IN A HOUSE FULL OF WOMEN AND DECLARED HIS TRUE SELF. OR, SO I ASSUME.
...SCARY...
AS LONG AS I REMEMBER, MY FATHER ONLY ENTERTAINED MEN.
ARTISTS, SCHOLARS, ACTORS -- ALL SORTS. FABULOUS MEN WERE ALWAYS COMING AND GOING.
NATURALLY, I WAS DRAWN INTO THIS WORLD.
I LEARNED THINGS FROM THESE MEN.
I ENJOYED THEIR COMPANY.
MY THREE SISTERS LOVED TO DRESS ME UP.
THEY TREATED ME LIKE A DOLL.

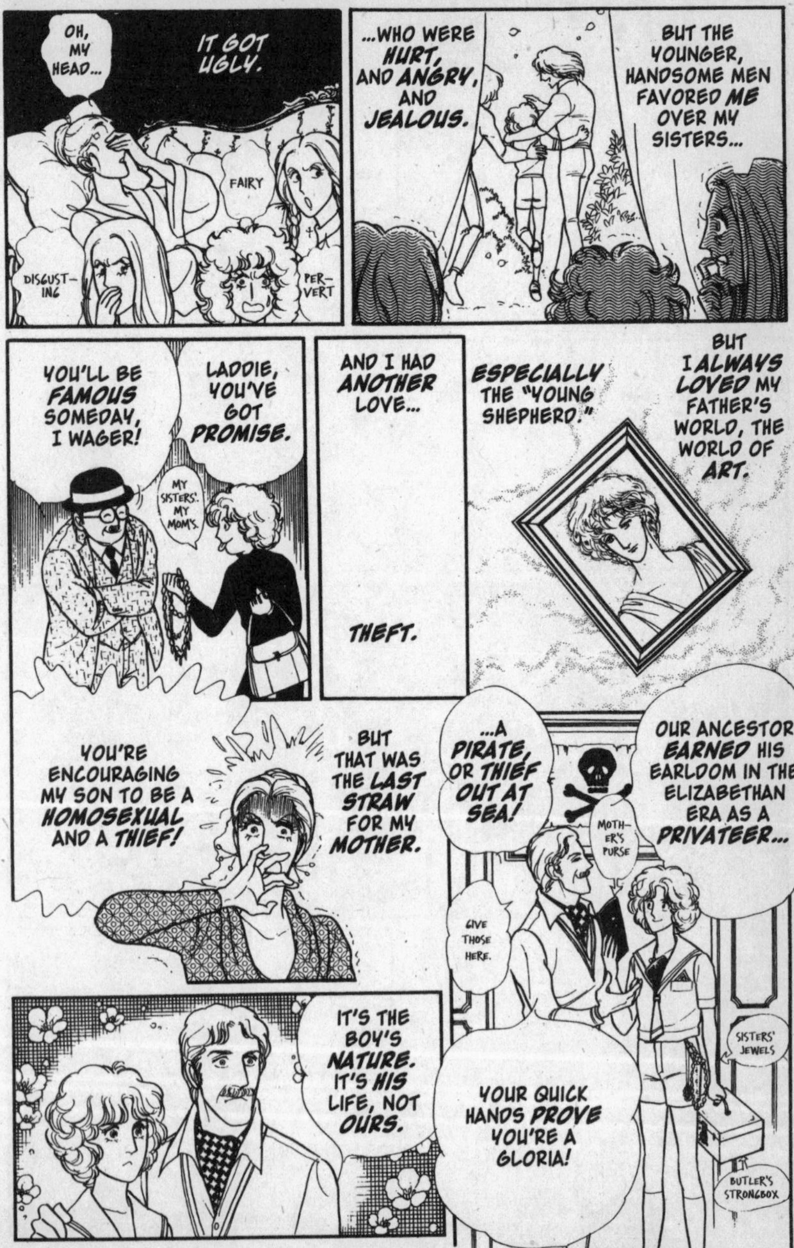
BUT THE YOUNGER, HANDSOME MEN FAVORED ME OVER MY SISTERS...
...WHO WERE HURT, AND ANGRY, AND JEALOUS.
IT GOT UGLY.
OH, MY HEAD...
FAIRY
PER-VERT
DISGUST-ING
BUT I ALWAYS LOVED MY FATHER'S WORLD, THE WORLD OF ART.
ESPECIALLY THE "YOUNG SHEPHERD."
AND I HAD ANOTHER LOVE...
THEFT.
LADDIE, YOU'VE GOT PROMISE.
YOU'LL BE FAMOUS SOMEDAY, I WAGER!
MY SISTERS'. MY MOM'S.
OUR ANCESTOR EARNED HIS EARLDOM IN THE ELIZABETHAN ERA AS A PRIVATEER...
...A PIRATE, OR THIEF OUT AT SEA!
MOTHER'S PURSE
GIVE THOSE HERE.
SISTERS' JEWELS
YOUR QUICK HANDS PROVE YOU'RE A GLORIA!
BUTLER'S STRONGBOX
BUT THAT WAS THE LAST STRAW FOR MY MOTHER.
YOU'RE ENCOURAGING MY SON TO BE A HOMOSEXUAL AND A THIEF!
IT'S THE BOY'S NATURE. IT'S HIS LIFE, NOT OURS.

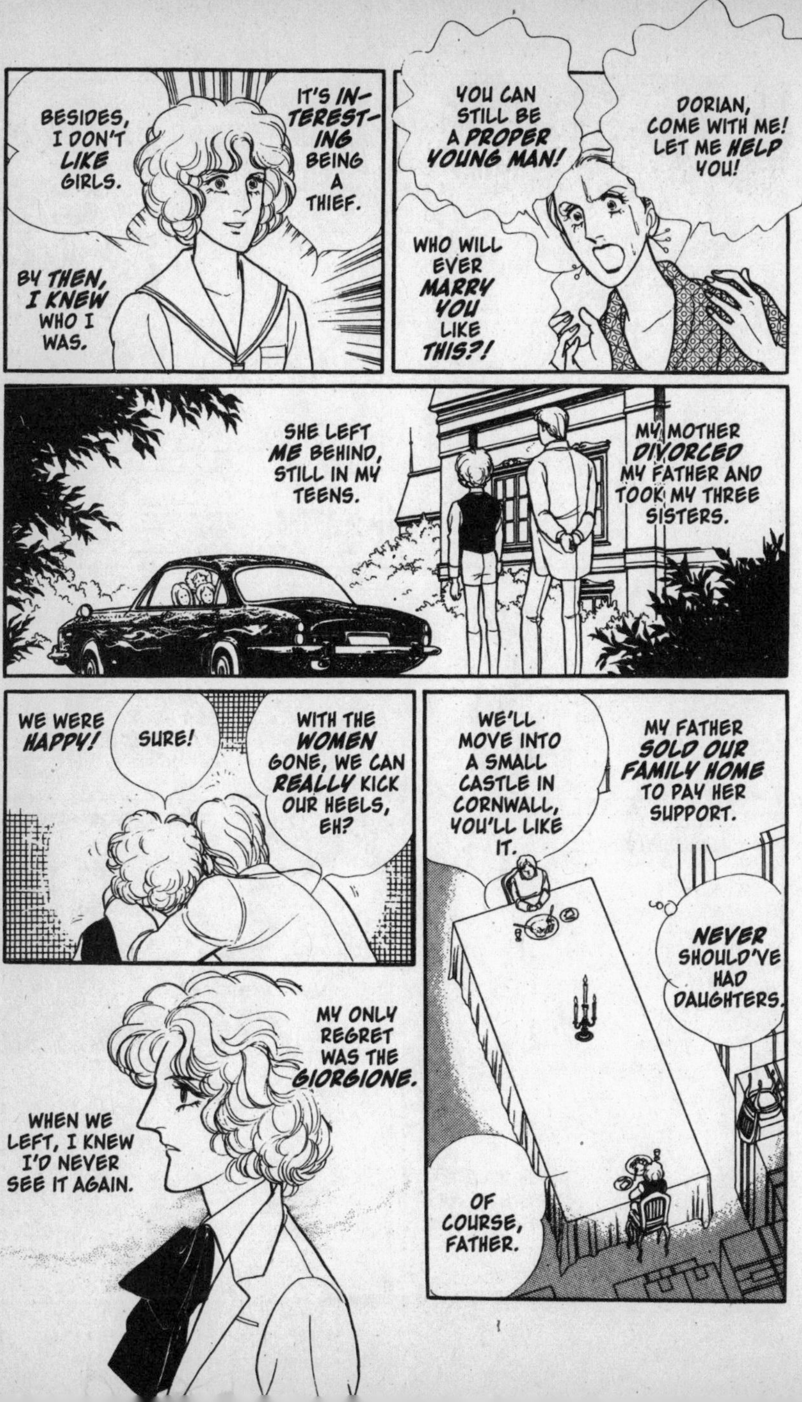
DORIAN, COME WITH ME! LET ME HELP YOU!
YOU CAN STILL BE A PROPER YOUNG MAN!
WHO WILL EVER MARRY YOU LIKE THIS?!
IT'S INTERESTING BEING A THIEF.
BESIDES, I DON'T LIKE GIRLS.
BY THEN, I KNEW WHO I WAS.
MY MOTHER DIVORCED MY FATHER AND TOOK MY THREE SISTERS.
SHE LEFT ME BEHIND, STILL IN MY TEENS.
MY FATHER SOLD OUR FAMILY HOME TO PAY HER SUPPORT.
WE'LL MOVE INTO A SMALL CASTLE IN CORNWALL, YOU'LL LIKE IT.
NEVER SHOULD'VE HAD DAUGHTERS.
OF COURSE, FATHER.
WITH THE WOMEN GONE, WE CAN REALLY KICK OUR HEELS, EH?
SURE!
WE WERE HAPPY!
MY ONLY REGRET WAS THE GIORGIONE.
WHEN WE LEFT, I KNEW I'D NEVER SEE IT AGAIN.

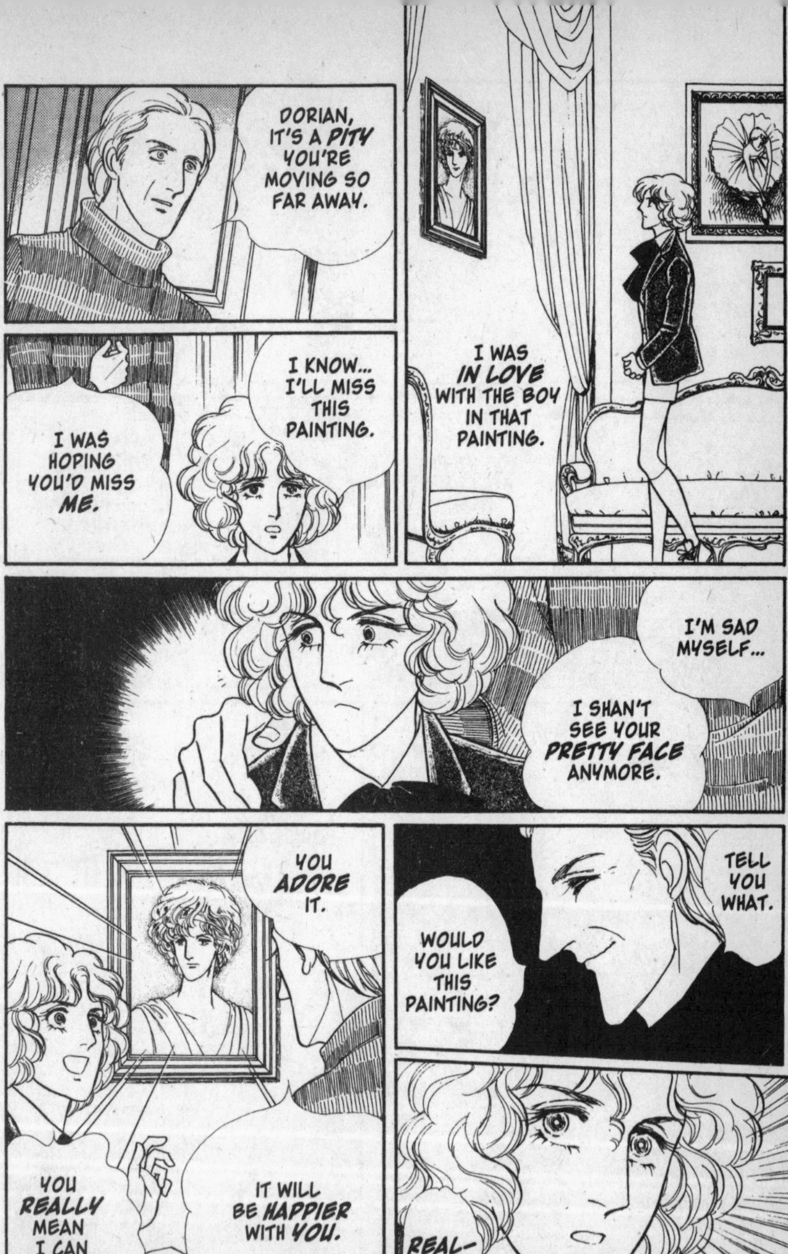
I WAS IN LOVE WITH THE BOY IN THAT PAINTING.
DORIAN, IT'S A PITY YOU'RE MOVING SO FAR AWAY.
I KNOW... I'LL MISS THIS PAINTING.
I WAS HOPING YOU'D MISS ME.
I'M SAD MYSELF...
I SHAN'T SEE YOUR PRETTY FACE ANYMORE.
TELL YOU WHAT.
WOULD YOU LIKE THIS PAINTING?
REAL-LY?
YOU ADORE IT.
IT WILL BE HAPPIER WITH YOU.
YOU REALLY MEAN I CAN HAVE IT?

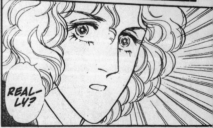

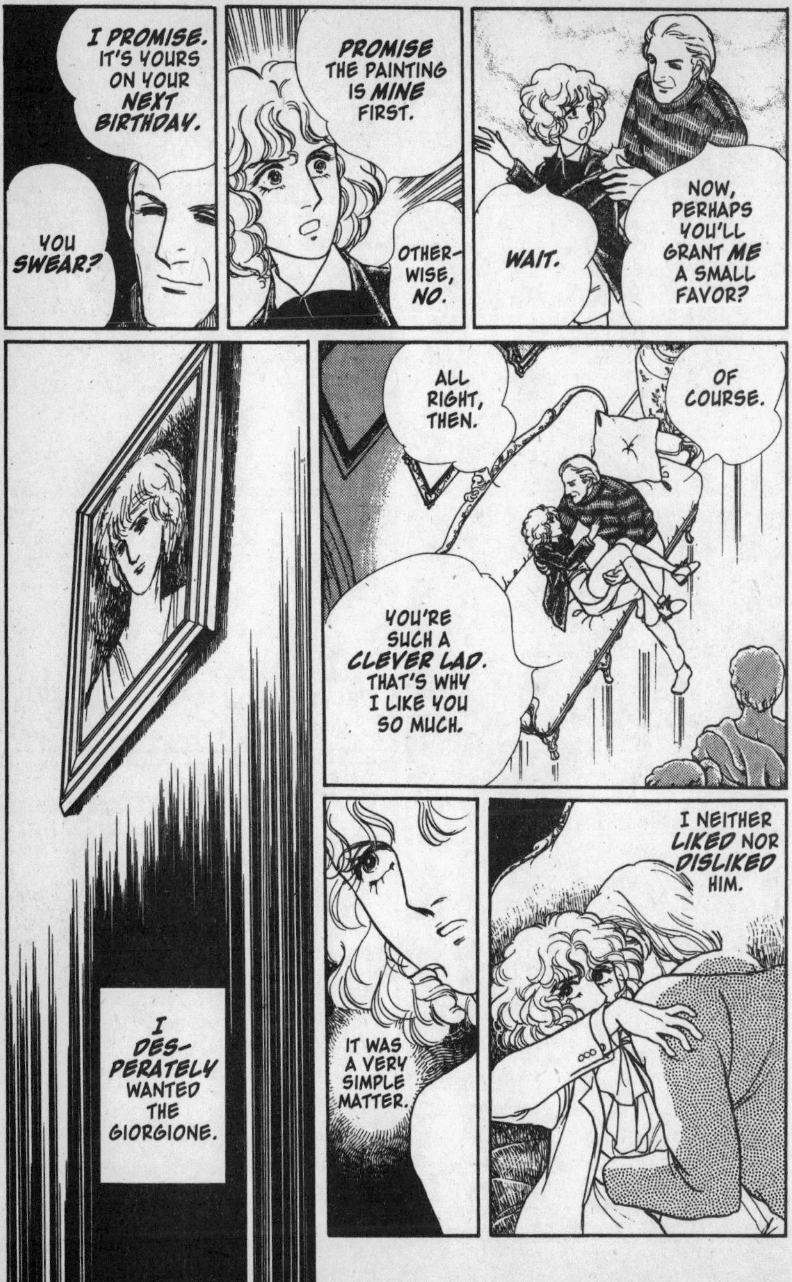
NOW, PERHAPS YOU'LL GRANT ME A SMALL FAVOR?
WAIT.
PROMISE THE PAINTING IS MINE FIRST.
OTHER-WISE, NO.
I PROMISE. IT'S YOURS ON YOUR NEXT BIRTHDAY.
YOU SWEAR?
OF COURSE.
ALL RIGHT, THEN.
YOU'RE SUCH A CLEVER LAD. THAT'S WHY I LIKE YOU SO MUCH.
I NEITHER LIKED NOR DISLIKED HIM.
IT WAS A VERY SIMPLE MATTER.
I DES-PERATELY WANTED THE GIORGIONE.

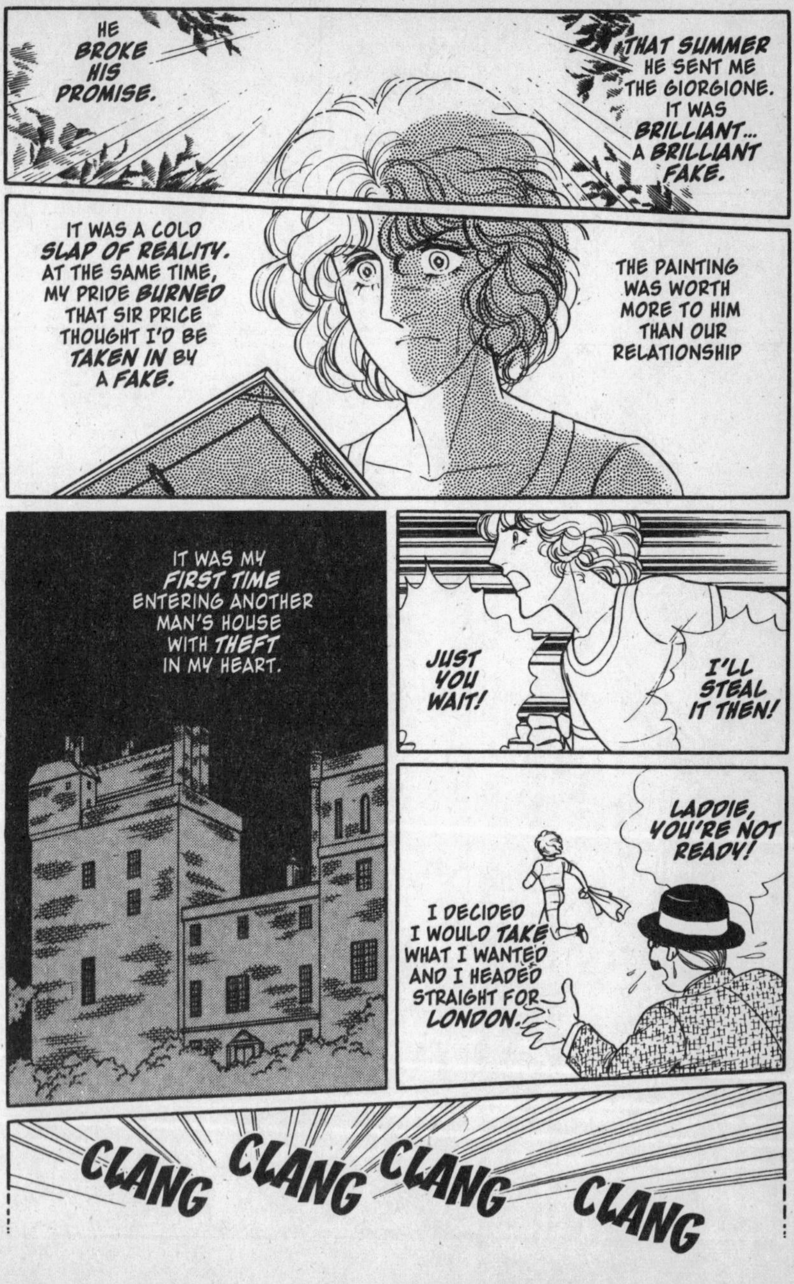
THAT SUMMER HE SENT ME THE GIORGIONE. IT WAS BRILLIANT... A BRILLIANT FAKE.
HE BROKE HIS PROMISE.
THE PAINTING WAS WORTH MORE TO HIM THAN OUR RELATIONSHIP
IT WAS A COLD SLAP OF REALITY. AT THE SAME TIME, MY PRIDE BURNED THAT SIR PRICE THOUGHT I'D BE TAKEN IN BY A FAKE.
I'LL STEAL IT THEN!
JUST YOU WAIT!
LADDIE, YOU'RE NOT READY!
I DECIDED I WOULD TAKE WHAT I WANTED AND I HEADED STRAIGHT FOR LONDON.
IT WAS MY FIRST TIME ENTERING ANOTHER MAN'S HOUSE WITH THEFT IN MY HEART.
CLANG CLANG CLANG CLANG

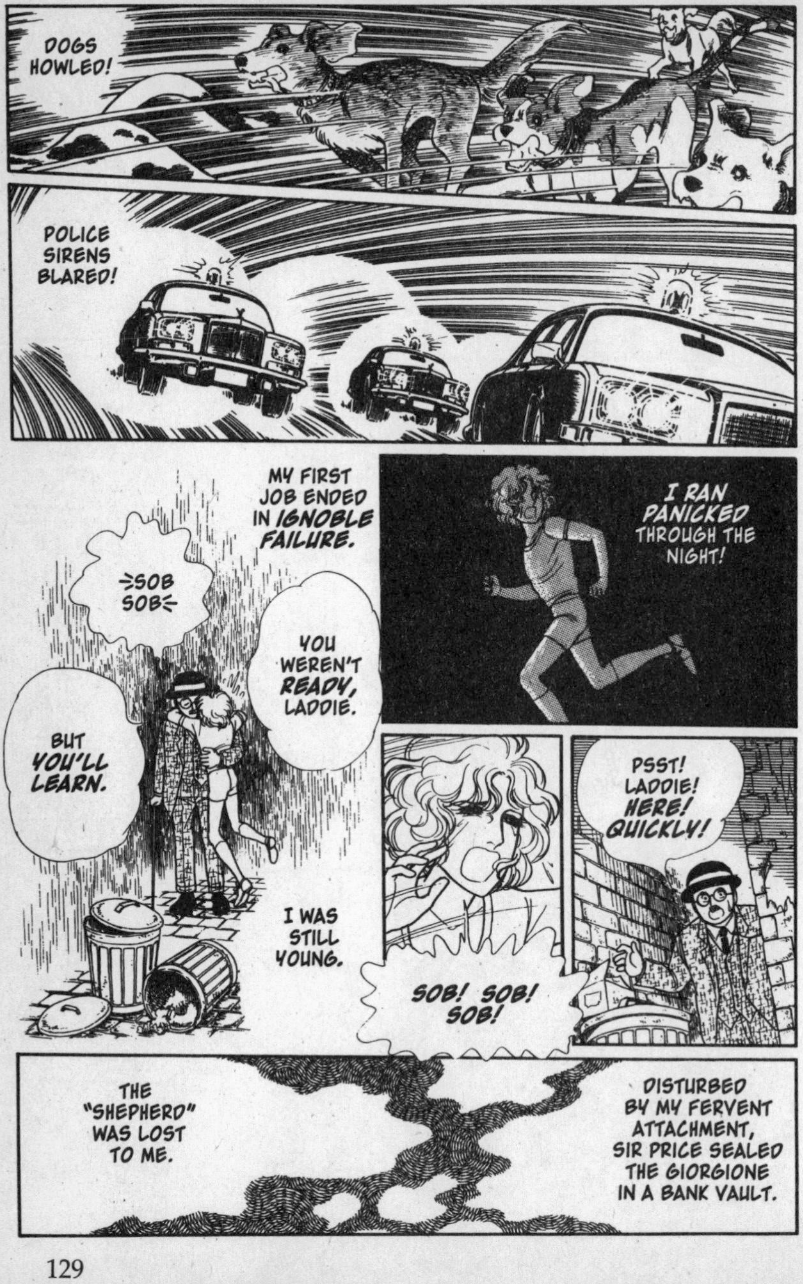
DOGS HOWLED!
POLICE SIRENS BLARED!
I RAN PANICKED THROUGH THE NIGHT!
PSST! LADDIE! HERE! QUICKLY!
SOB! SOB! SOB!
MY FIRST JOB ENDED IN IGNOBLE FAILURE.
SOB SOB
YOU WEREN'T READY, LADDIE.
BUT YOU'LL LEARN.
I WAS STILL YOUNG.
DISTURBED BY MY FERVENT ATTACHMENT, SIR PRICE SEALED THE GIORGIONE IN A BANK VAULT.
THE "SHEPHERD" WAS LOST TO ME.

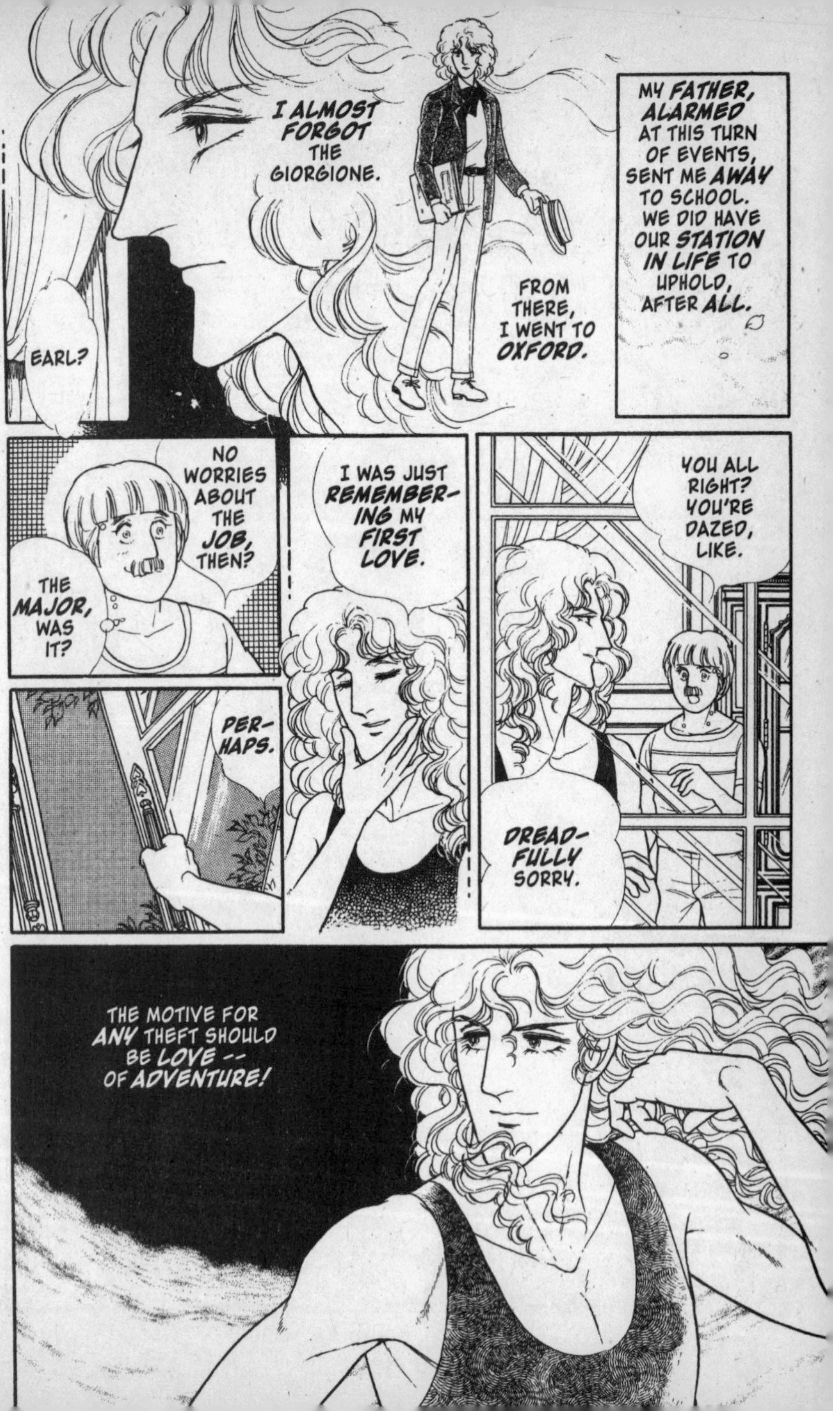
MY FATHER, ALARMED AT THIS TURN OF EVENTS, SENT ME AWAY TO SCHOOL. WE DID HAVE OUR STATION IN LIFE TO UPHOLD, AFTER ALL.
FROM THERE, I WENT TO OXFORD.
I ALMOST FORGOT THE GIORGIONE.
EARL?
YOU ALL RIGHT? YOU'RE DAZED, LIKE.
DREAD-FULLY SORRY.
I WAS JUST REMEMBER-ING MY FIRST LOVE.
NO WORRIES ABOUT THE JOB, THEN?
THE MAJOR, WAS IT?
PER-HAPS.
THE MOTIVE FOR ANY THEFT SHOULD BE LOVE -- OF ADVENTURE!

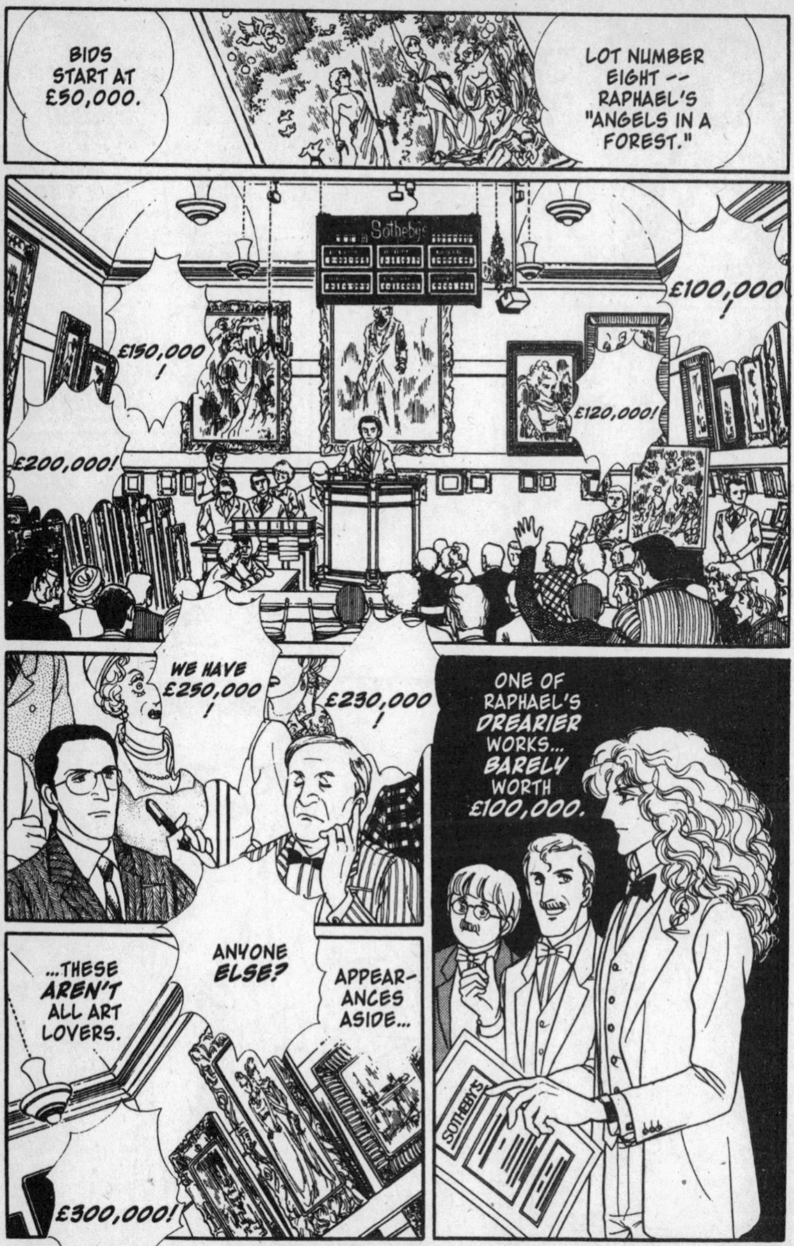
LOT NUMBER EIGHT -- RAPHAEL'S "ANGELS IN A FOREST."
BIDS START AT £50,000.
£100,000!
£120,000!
£150,000!
£200,000!
ONE OF RAPHAEL'S DREARIER WORKS... BARELY WORTH £100,000.
£230,000!
WE HAVE £250,000!
APPEARANCES ASIDE...
ANYONE ELSE?
...THESE AREN'T ALL ART LOVERS.
£300,000!

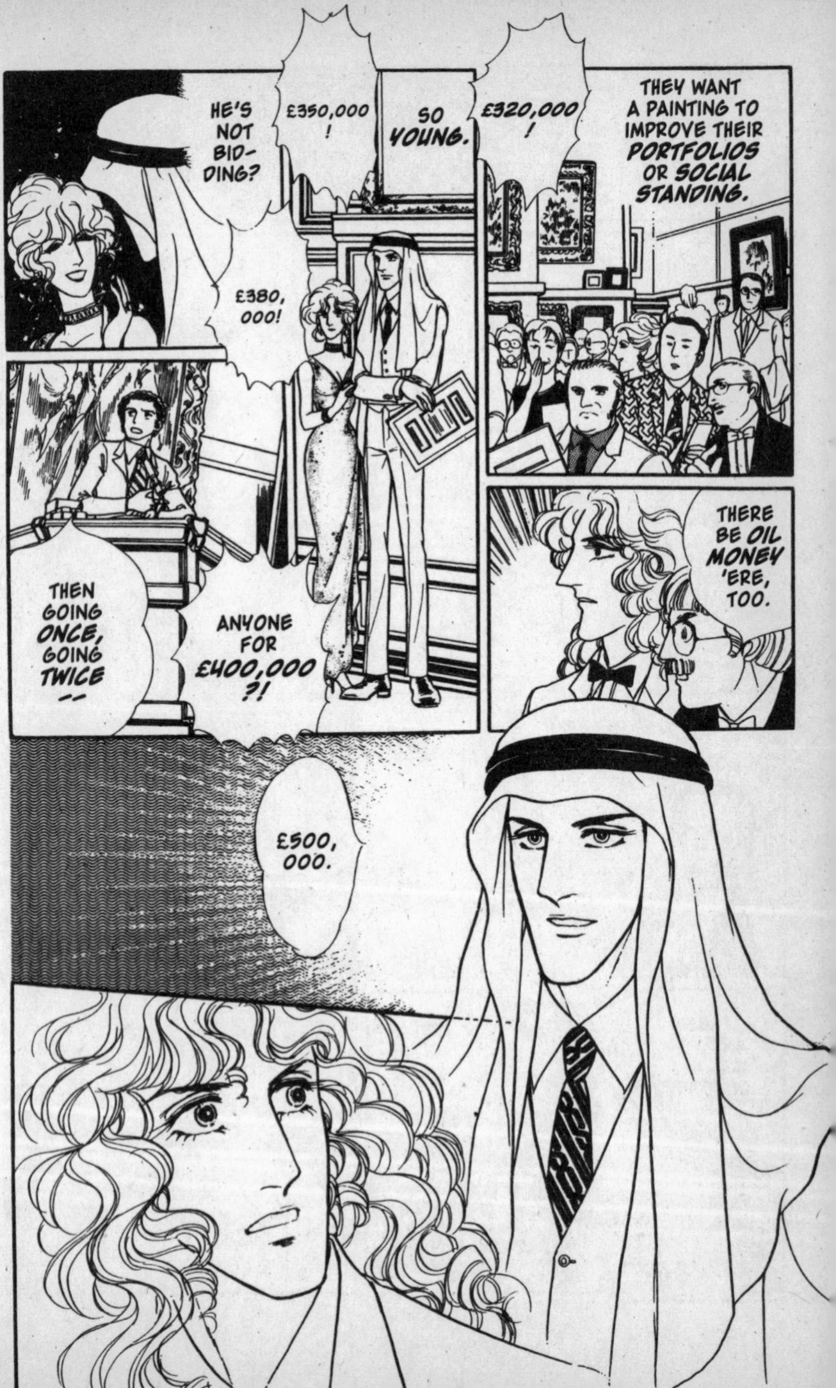
£320,000!
THEY WANT A PAINTING TO IMPROVE THEIR PORTFOLIOS OR SOCIAL STANDING.
THERE BE OIL MONEY 'ERE, TOO.
SO YOUNG.
£350,000!
£380,000!
ANYONE FOR £400,000?!
HE'S NOT BID-DING?
THEN GOING ONCE, GOING TWICE --
£500,000.

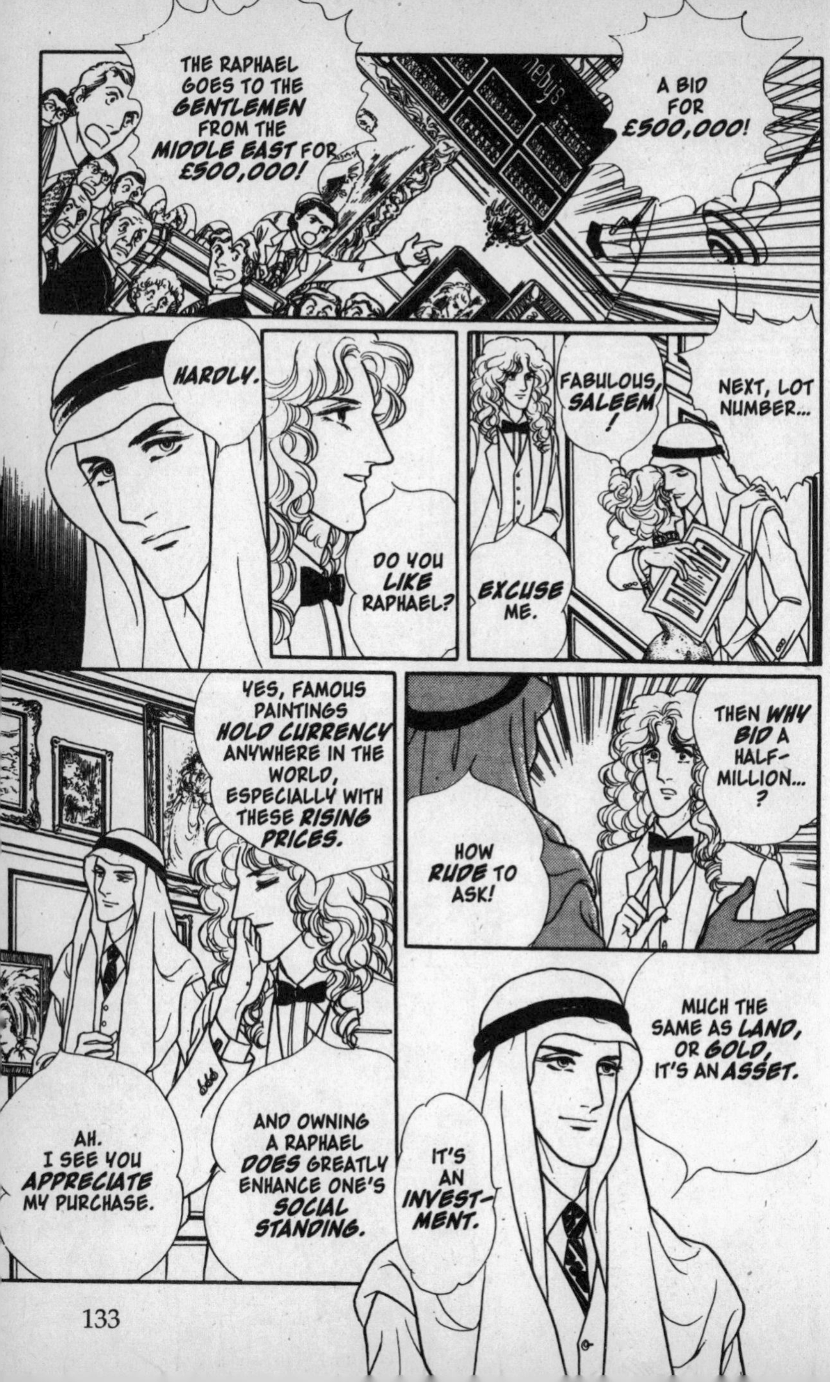
A BID FOR £500,000!
THE RAPHAEL GOES TO THE GENTLEMEN FROM THE MIDDLE EAST FOR £500,000!
NEXT, LOT NUMBER...
FABULOUS, SALEEM!
EXCUSE ME.
DO YOU LIKE RAPHAEL?
HARDLY.
THEN WHY BID A HALF-MILLION...?
HOW RUDE TO ASK!
MUCH THE SAME AS LAND, OR GOLD, IT'S AN ASSET.
IT'S AN INVESTMENT.
YES, FAMOUS PAINTINGS HOLD CURRENCY ANYWHERE IN THE WORLD, ESPECIALLY WITH THESE RISING PRICES.
AND OWNING A RAPHAEL DOES GREATLY ENHANCE ONE'S SOCIAL STANDING.
AH. I SEE YOU APPRECIATE MY PURCHASE.

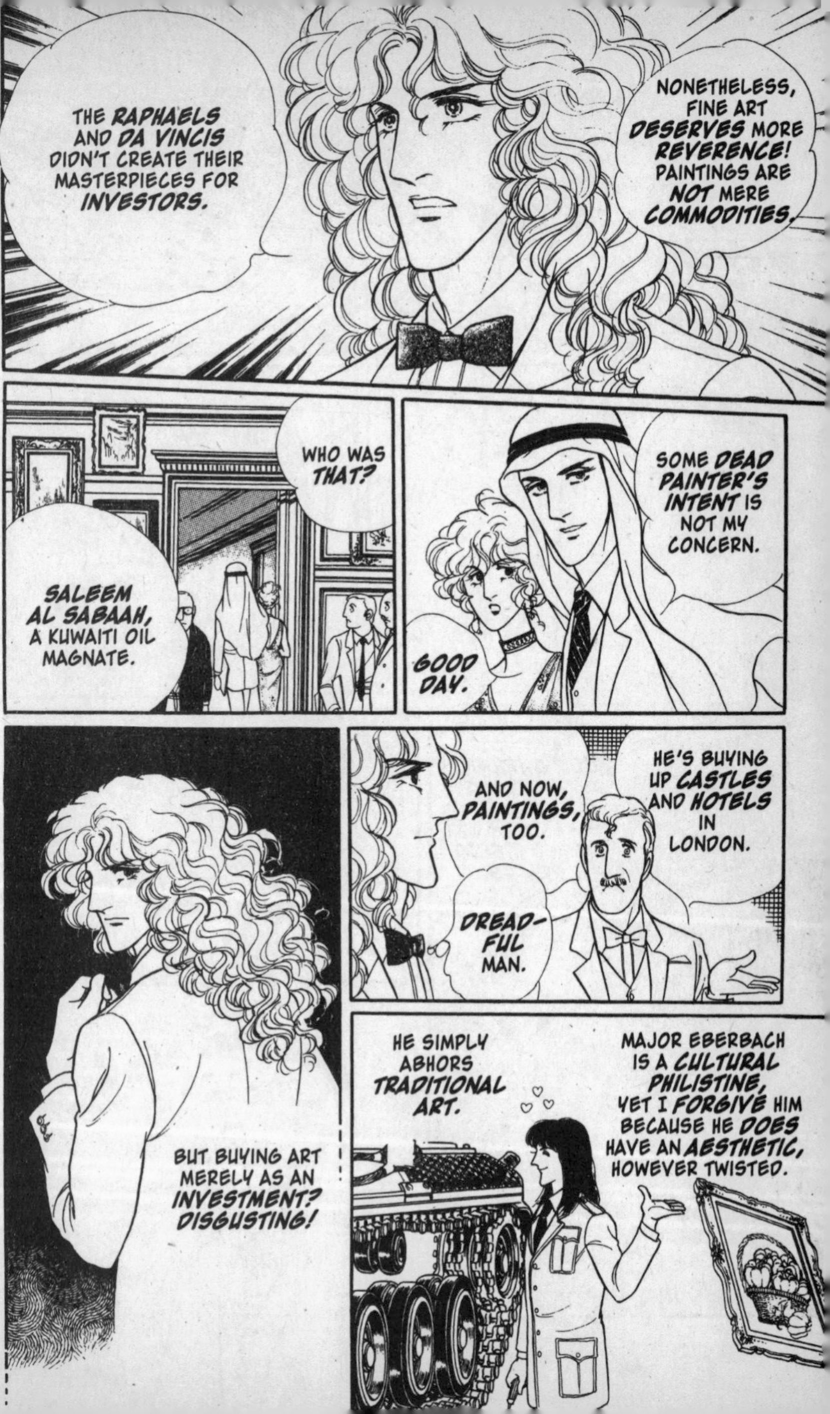
NONETHELESS, FINE ART DESERVES MORE REVERENCE! PAINTINGS ARE NOT MERE COMMODITIES.
THE RAPHAELS AND DA VINCIS DIDN'T CREATE THEIR MASTERPIECES FOR INVESTORS.
SOME DEAD PAINTER'S INTENT IS NOT MY CONCERN.
GOOD DAY.
WHO WAS THAT?
SALEEM AL SABAAH, A KUWAITI OIL MAGNATE.
HE'S BUYING UP CASTLES AND HOTELS IN LONDON.
AND NOW, PAINTINGS, TOO.
DREAD-FUL MAN.
MAJOR EBERBACH IS A CULTURAL PHILISTINE, YET I FORGIVE HIM BECAUSE HE DOES HAVE AN AESTHETIC, HOWEVER TWISTED.
HE SIMPLY ABHORS TRADITIONAL ART.
BUT BUYING ART MERELY AS AN INVESTMENT? DISGUSTING!

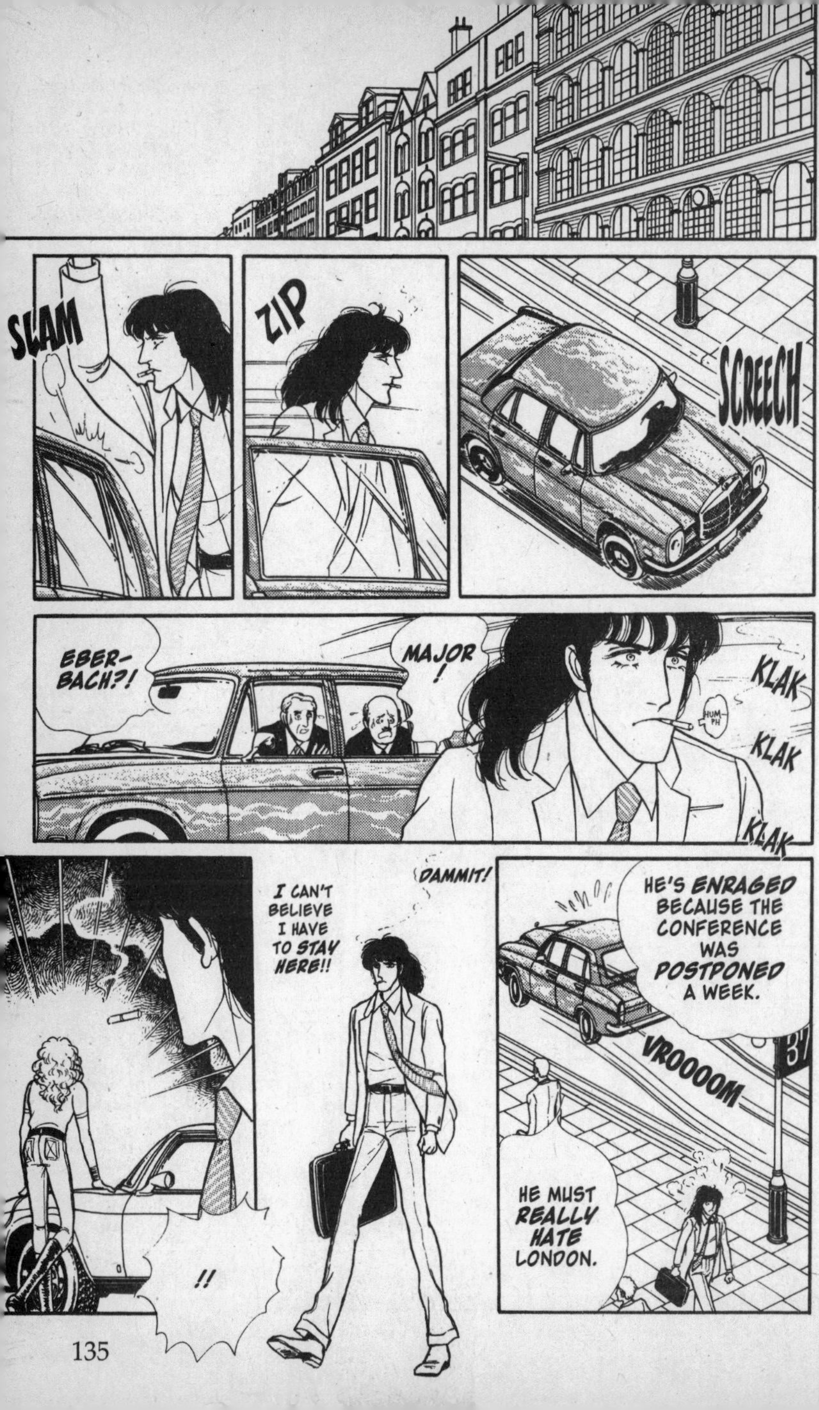
SCREECH
ZIP
SLAM
KLAK
KLAK
KLAK
HUMPH
MAJOR!
EBER-BACH?!
HE'S ENRAGED BECAUSE THE CONFERENCE WAS POSTPONED A WEEK.
VROOOOM
HE MUST REALLY HATE LONDON.
DAMMIT!
I CAN'T BELIEVE I HAVE TO STAY HERE!!
!!

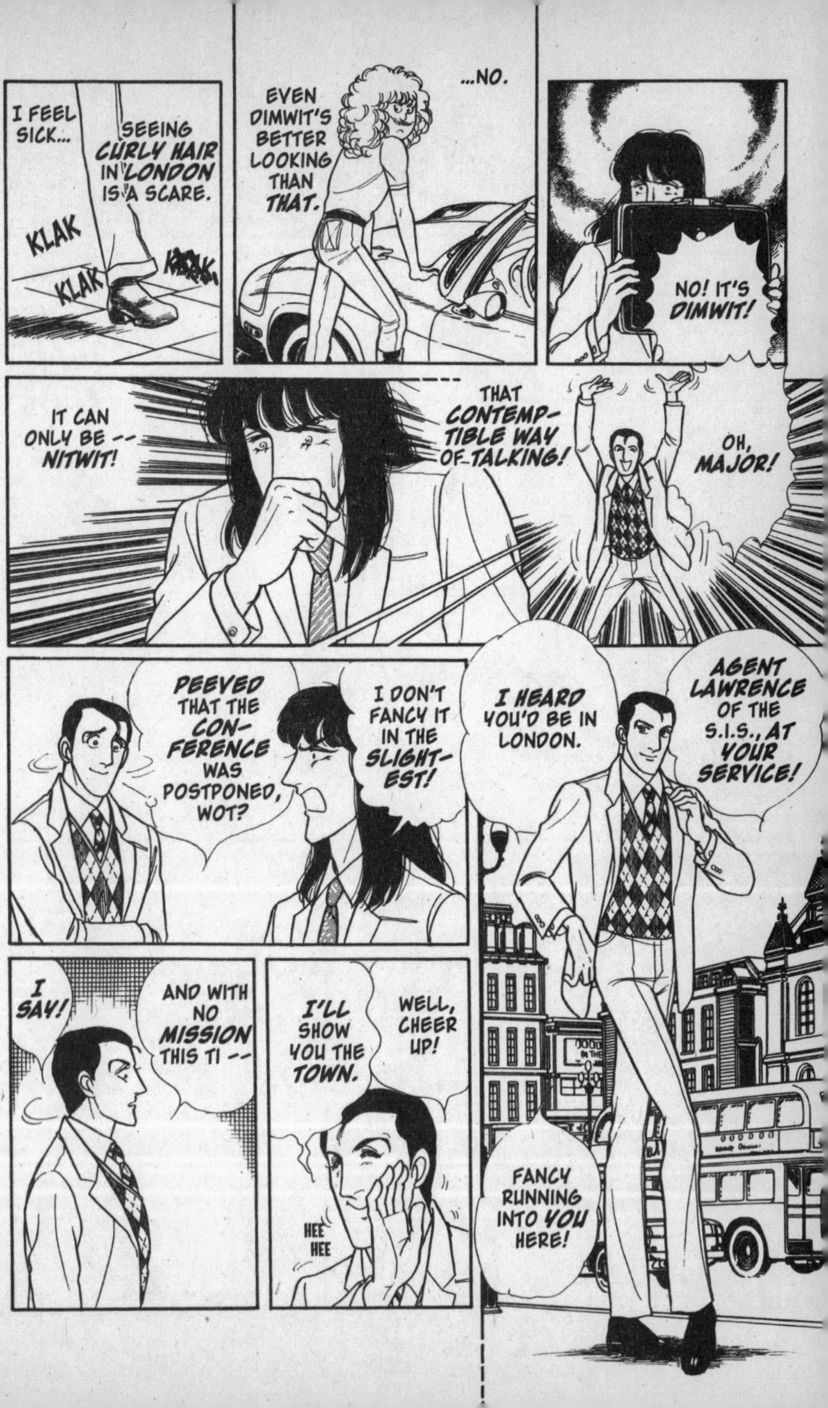

NO! IT'S DIMWIT!
...NO.
EVEN DIMWIT'S BETTER LOOKING THAN THAT.
I FEEL SICK...
SEEING CURLY HAIR IN LONDON IS A SCARE.
KLAK
KLAK
OH, MAJOR!
THAT CONTEMPTIBLE WAY OF TALKING!
IT CAN ONLY BE -- NITWIT!
AGENT LAWRENCE OF THE S.I.S., AT YOUR SERVICE!
I HEARD YOU'D BE IN LONDON.
FANCY RUNNING INTO YOU HERE!
I DON'T FANCY IT IN THE SLIGHTEST!
PEEVED THAT THE CONFERENCE WAS POSTPONED, WOT?
WELL, CHEER UP!
I'LL SHOW YOU THE TOWN.
HEE HEE
AND WITH NO MISSION THIS TI --
I SAY!

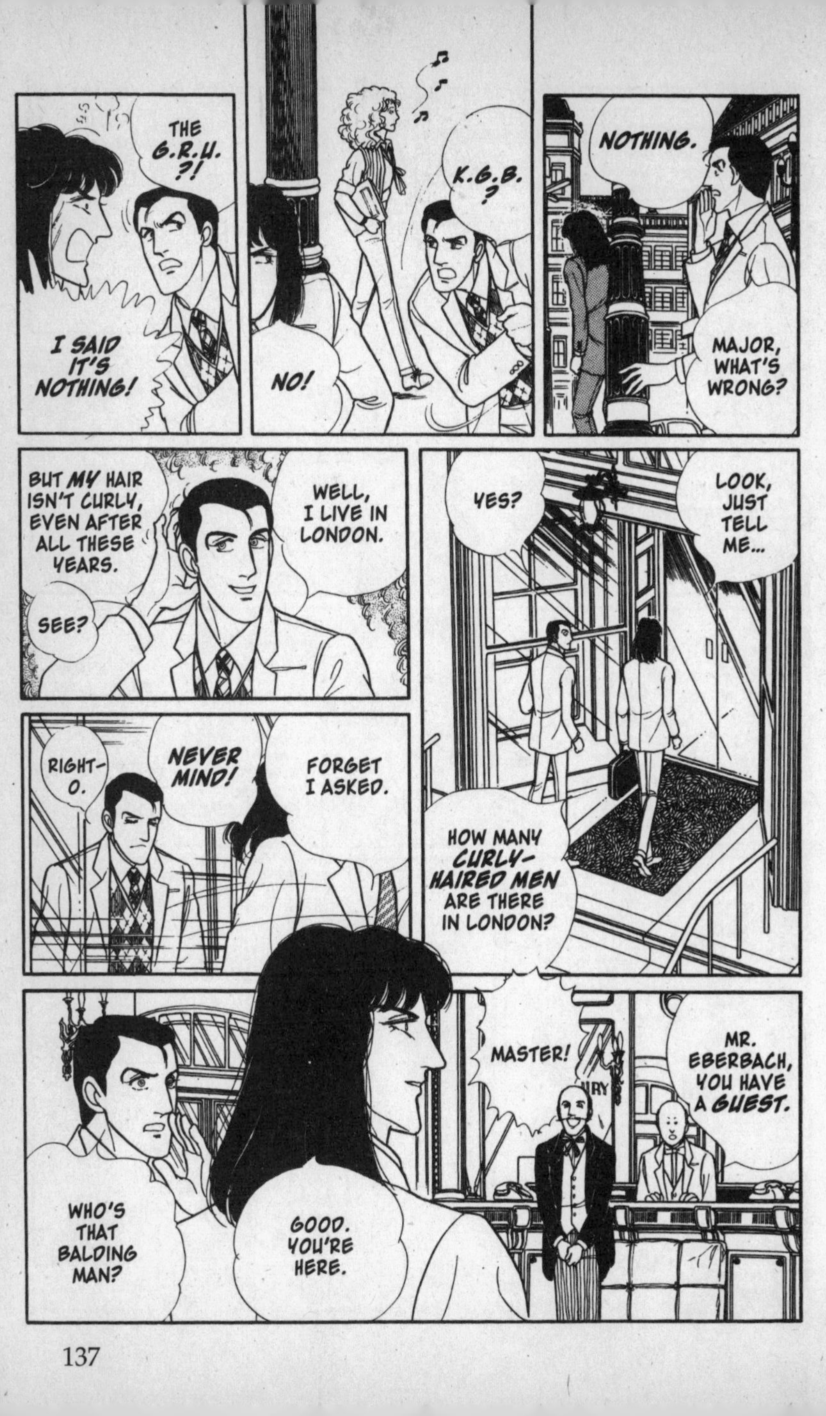
NOTHING.
MAJOR, WHAT'S WRONG?
K.G.B.?
NO!
THE G.R.U.?!
I SAID IT'S NOTHING!
LOOK, JUST TELL ME...
YES?
HOW MANY CURLY-HAIRED MEN ARE THERE IN LONDON?
WELL, I LIVE IN LONDON.
BUT MY HAIR ISN'T CURLY, EVEN AFTER ALL THESE YEARS.
SEE?
FORGET I ASKED.
NEVER MIND!
RIGHT-O.
MR. EBERBACH, YOU HAVE A GUEST.
MASTER!
GOOD. YOU'RE HERE.
WHO'S THAT BALDING MAN?

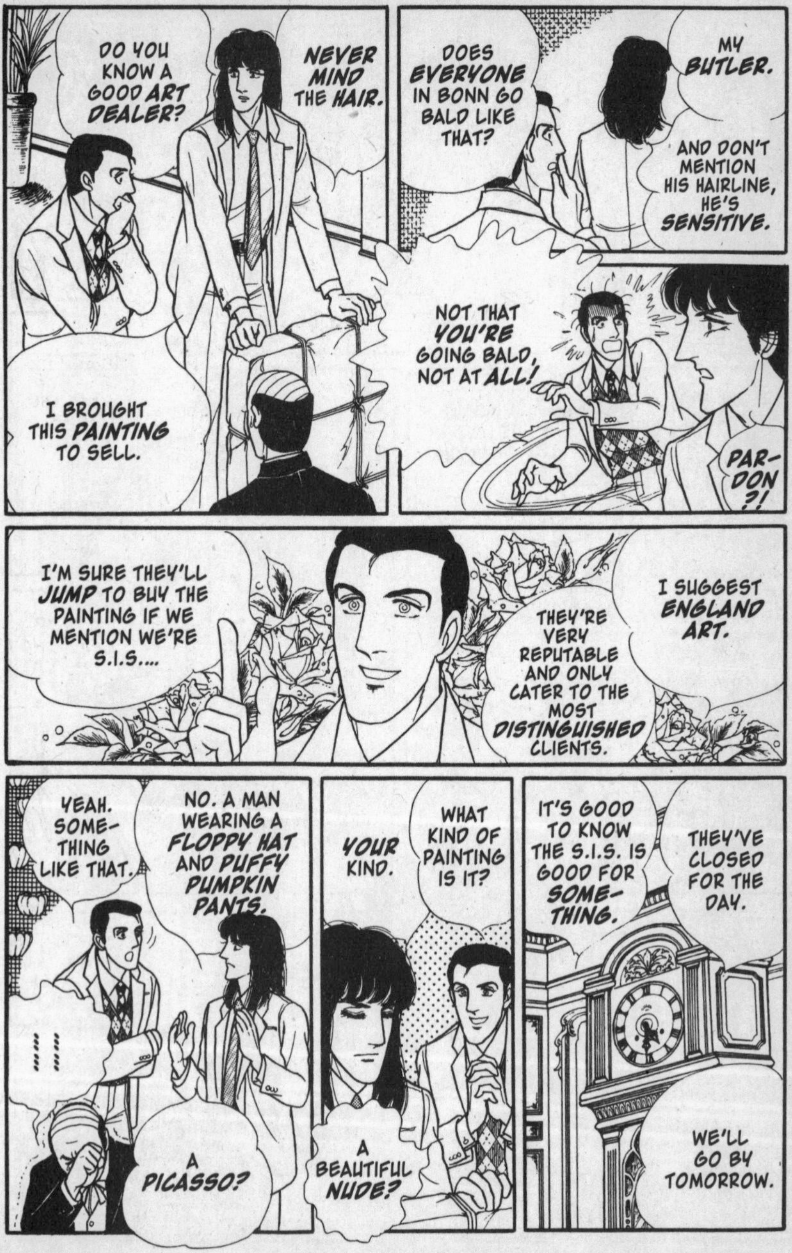
MY BUTLER.
DOES EVERYONE IN BONN GO BALD LIKE THAT?
AND DON'T MENTION HIS HAIRLINE, HE'S SENSITIVE.
NOT THAT YOU'RE GOING BALD, NOT AT ALL!
PAR-DON?!
NEVER MIND THE HAIR.
DO YOU KNOW A GOOD ART DEALER?
I BROUGHT THIS PAINTING TO SELL.
I SUGGEST ENGLAND ART.
THEY'RE VERY REPUTABLE AND ONLY CATER TO THE MOST DISTINGUISHED CLIENTS.
I'M SURE THEY'LL JUMP TO BUY THE PAINTING IF WE MENTION WE'RE S.I.S....
THEY'VE CLOSED FOR THE DAY.
IT'S GOOD TO KNOW THE S.I.S. IS GOOD FOR SOME-THING.
WE'LL GO BY TOMORROW.
WHAT KIND OF PAINTING IS IT?
YOUR KIND.
A BEAUTIFUL NUDE?
NO. A MAN WEARING A FLOPPY HAT AND PUFFY PUMPKIN PANTS.
YEAH. SOME-THING LIKE THAT.
......
A PICASSO?

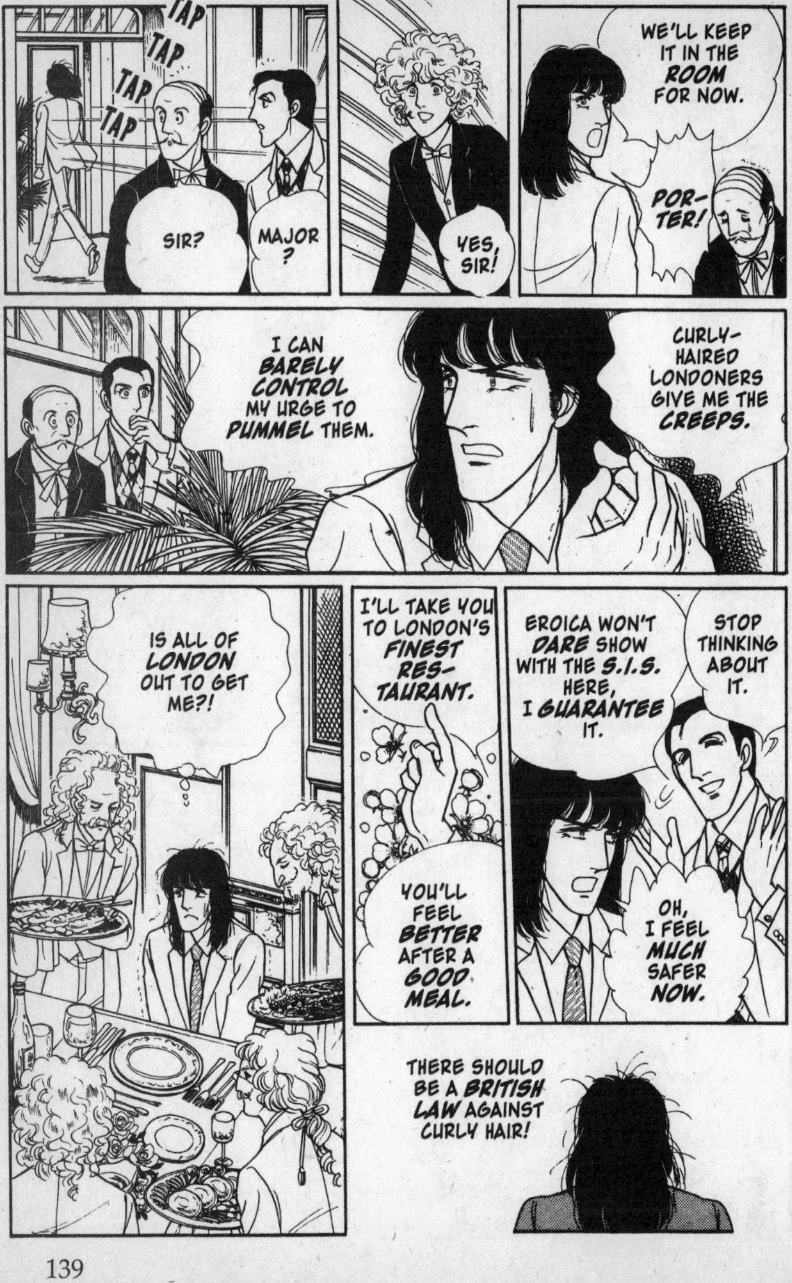
WE'LL KEEP IT IN THE ROOM FOR NOW.
POR-TER!
YES, SIR!
TAP TAP TAP TAP
MAJOR?
SIR?
CURLY-HAIRED LONDONERS GIVE ME THE CREEPS.
I CAN BARELY CONTROL MY URGE TO PUMMEL THEM.
STOP THINKING ABOUT IT.
EROICA WON'T DARE SHOW WITH THE S.I.S. HERE, I GUARANTEE IT.
OH, I FEEL MUCH SAFER NOW.
I'LL TAKE YOU TO LONDON'S FINEST RES-TAURANT.
YOU'LL FEEL BETTER AFTER A GOOD MEAL.
THERE SHOULD BE A BRITISH LAW AGAINST CURLY HAIR!
IS ALL OF LONDON OUT TO GET ME?!

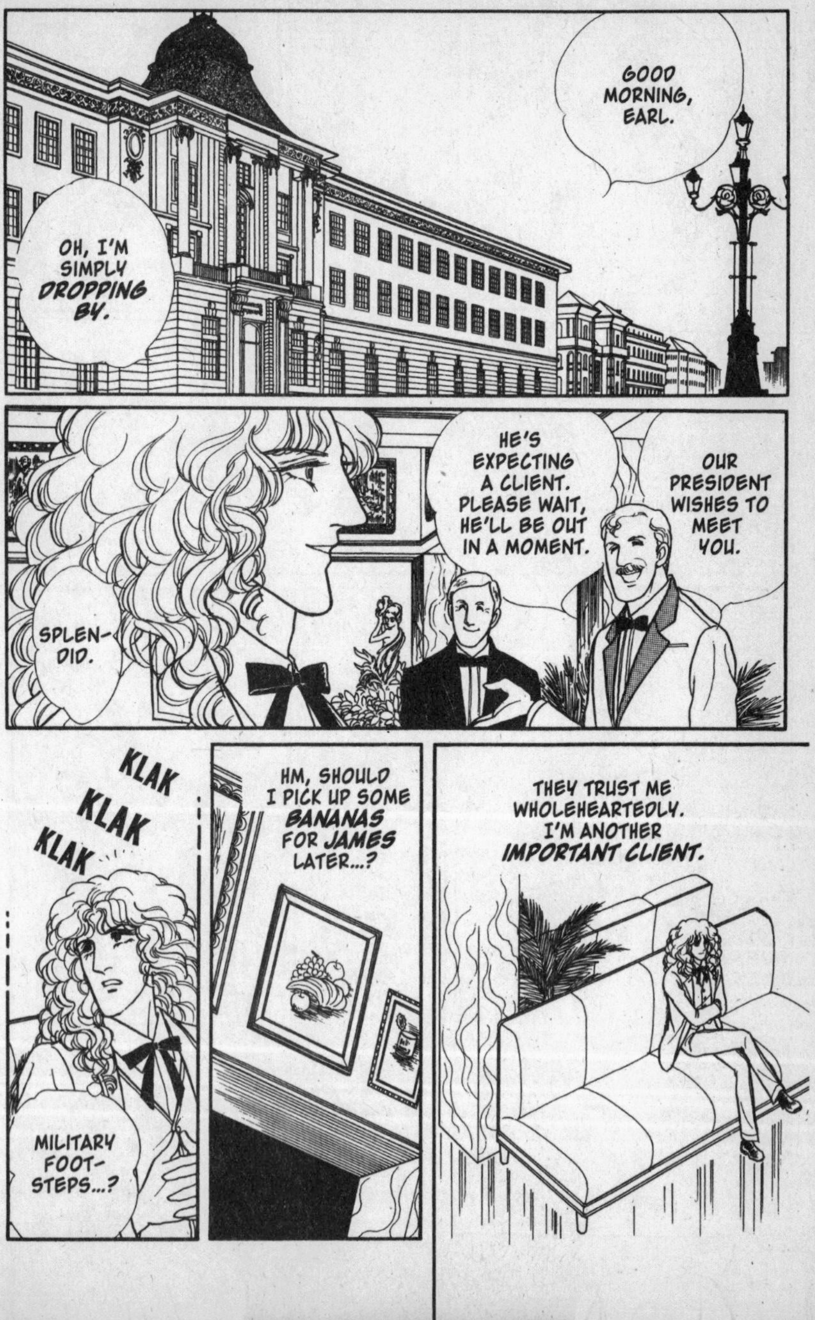
GOOD MORNING, EARL.
OH, I'M SIMPLY DROPPING BY.
OUR PRESIDENT WISHES TO MEET YOU.
HE'S EXPECTING A CLIENT. PLEASE WAIT, HE'LL BE OUT IN A MOMENT.
SPLEN-DID.
THEY TRUST ME WHOLEHEARTEDLY. I'M ANOTHER IMPORTANT CLIENT.
HM, SHOULD I PICK UP SOME BANANAS FOR JAMES LATER...?
KLAK
KLAK
KLAK
MILITARY FOOT-STEPS...?

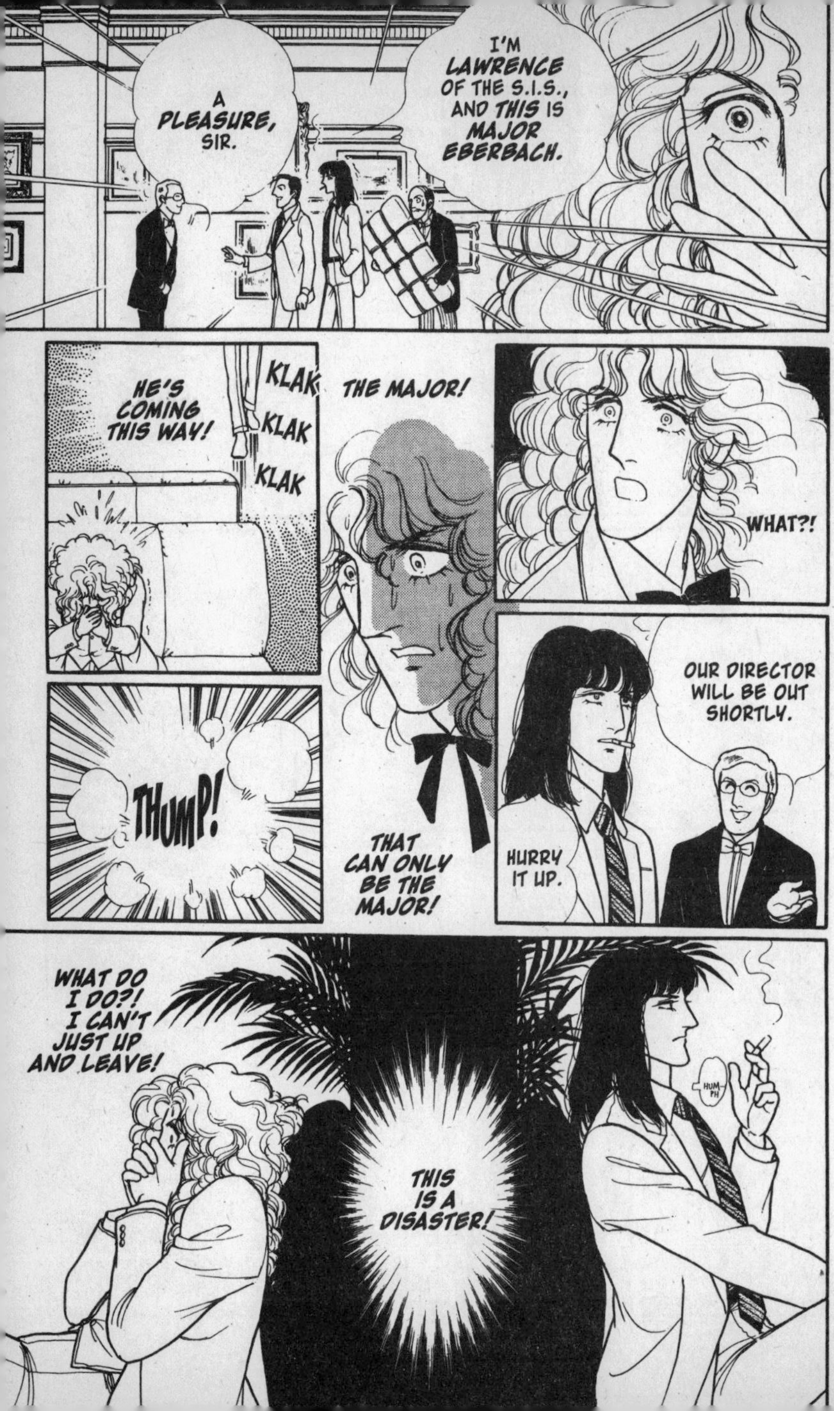
I'M LAWRENCE OF THE S.I.S., AND THIS IS MAJOR EBERBACH.
A PLEASURE, SIR.
WHAT?!
OUR DIRECTOR WILL BE OUT SHORTLY.
HURRY IT UP.
THE MAJOR!
THAT CAN ONLY BE THE MAJOR!
HE'S COMING THIS WAY!
KLAK
KLAK
KLAK
THUMP!
HUMPH
WHAT DO I DO?! I CAN'T JUST UP AND LEAVE!
THIS IS A DISASTER!

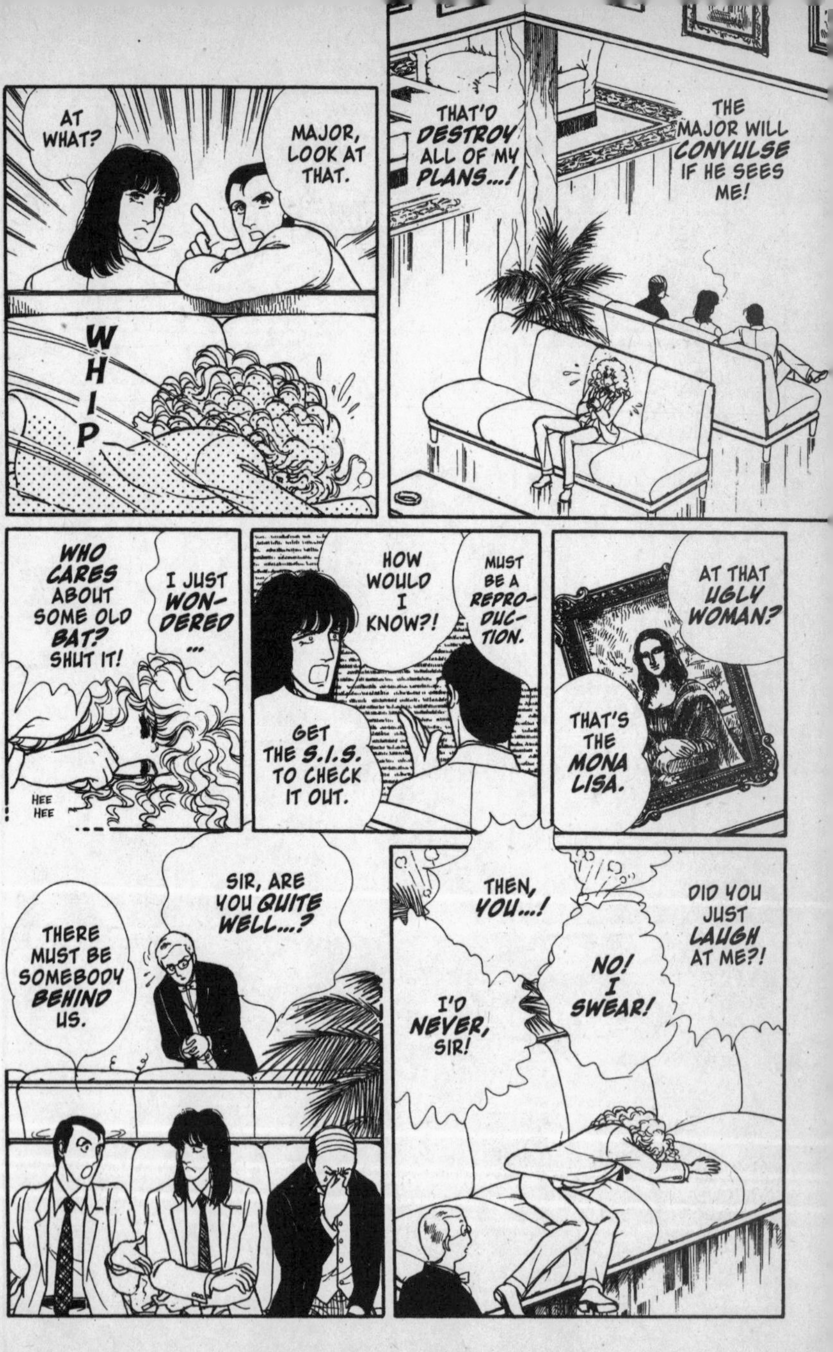
THE MAJOR WILL CONVULSE IF HE SEES ME!
THAT'D DESTROY ALL OF MY PLANS...!
MAJOR, LOOK AT THAT.
AT WHAT?
WHIP
AT THAT UGLY WOMAN?
THAT'S THE MONA LISA.
MUST BE A REPRODUCTION.
HOW WOULD I KNOW?!
GET THE S.I.S. TO CHECK IT OUT.
I JUST WONDERED...
WHO CARES ABOUT SOME OLD BAT? SHUT IT!
HEE HEE
DID YOU JUST LAUGH AT ME?!
THEN, YOU...!
NO! I SWEAR!
I'D NEVER, SIR!
SIR, ARE YOU QUITE WELL...?
THERE MUST BE SOMEBODY BEHIND US.

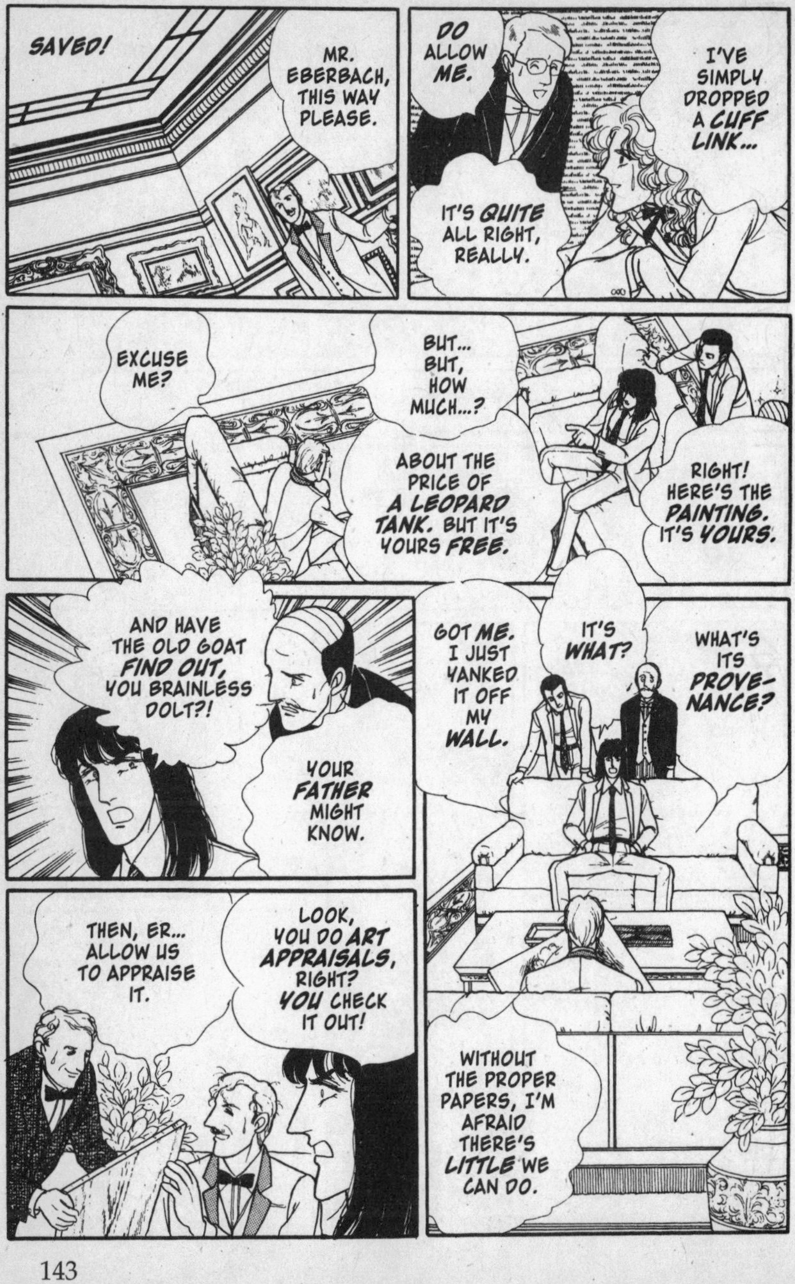
I'VE SIMPLY DROPPED A CUFF LINK...
DO ALLOW ME.
IT'S QUITE ALL RIGHT, REALLY.
MR. EBERBACH, THIS WAY PLEASE.
SAVED!
RIGHT! HERE'S THE PAINTING. IT'S YOURS.
BUT... BUT, HOW MUCH...?
ABOUT THE PRICE OF A LEOPARD TANK. BUT IT'S YOURS FREE.
EXCUSE ME?
WHAT'S ITS PROVENANCE?
IT'S WHAT?
GOT ME. I JUST YANKED IT OFF MY WALL.
WITHOUT THE PROPER PAPERS, I'M AFRAID THERE'S LITTLE WE CAN DO.
YOUR FATHER MIGHT KNOW.
AND HAVE THE OLD GOAT FIND OUT, YOU BRAINLESS DOLT?!
LOOK, YOU DO ART APPRAISALS, RIGHT? YOU CHECK IT OUT!
THEN, ER... ALLOW US TO APPRAISE IT.

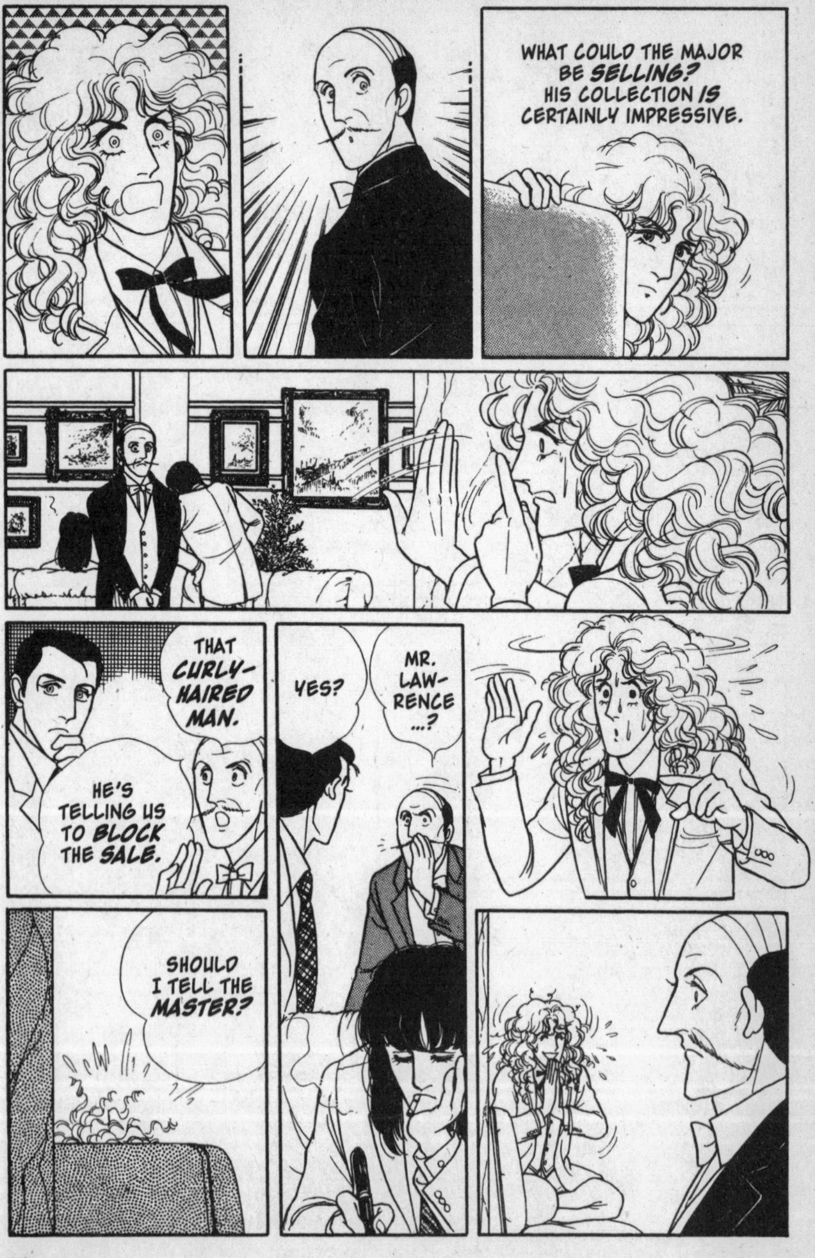
WHAT COULD THE MAJOR BE *SELLING?* HIS COLLECTION *IS* CERTAINLY IMPRESSIVE.
MR. LAWRENCE ...?
YES?
THAT *CURLY-HAIRED MAN.*
HE'S TELLING US TO *BLOCK* THE *SALE.*
SHOULD I TELL THE *MASTER?*

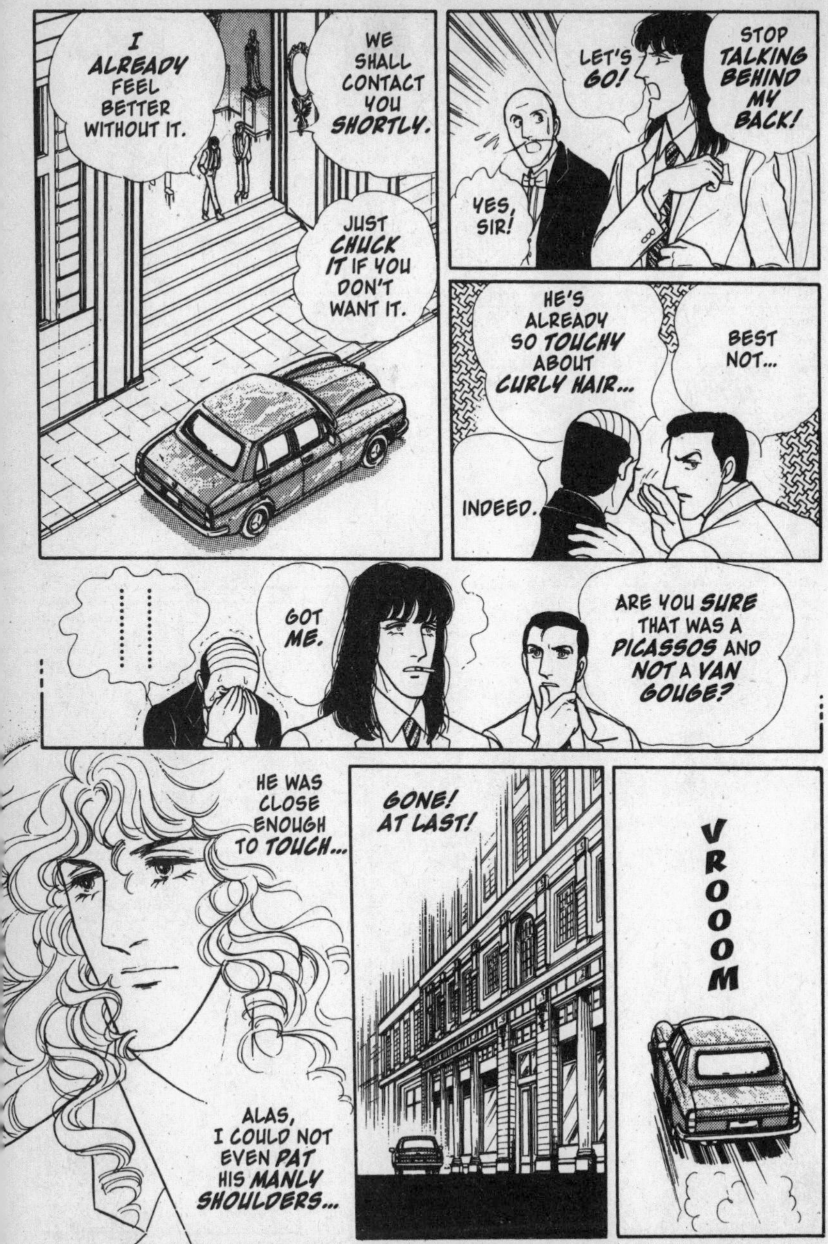
STOP TALKING BEHIND MY BACK!
LET'S GO!
YES, SIR!
BEST NOT...
HE'S ALREADY SO TOUCHY ABOUT CURLY HAIR...
INDEED.
WE SHALL CONTACT YOU SHORTLY.
I ALREADY FEEL BETTER WITHOUT IT.
JUST CHUCK IT IF YOU DON'T WANT IT.
ARE YOU SURE THAT WAS A PICASSOS AND NOT A VAN GOUGE?
GOT ME.
......
VROOOM
GONE! AT LAST!
HE WAS CLOSE ENOUGH TO TOUCH...
ALAS, I COULD NOT EVEN PAT HIS MANLY SHOULDERS...

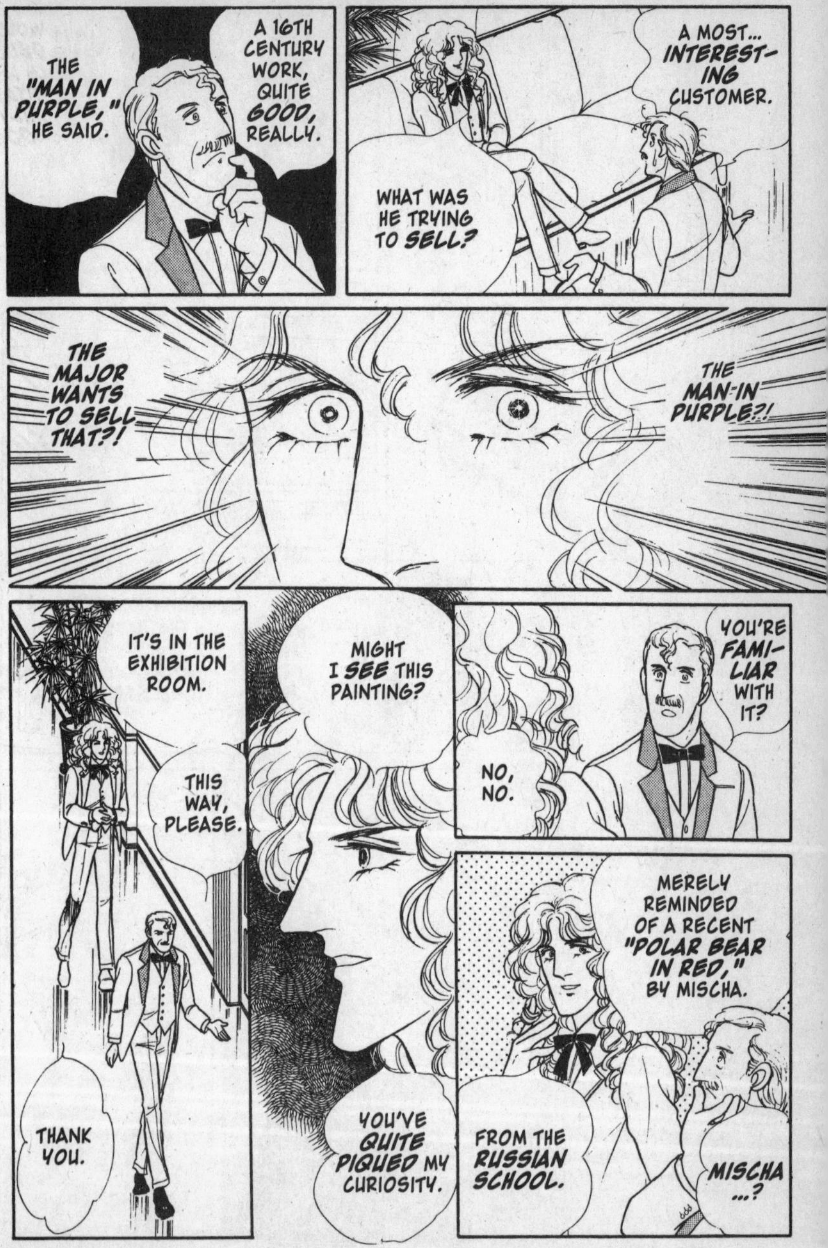
A MOST... INTERESTING CUSTOMER.
WHAT WAS HE TRYING TO SELL?
A 16TH CENTURY WORK, QUITE GOOD, REALLY.
THE "MAN IN PURPLE," HE SAID.
THE MAN-IN PURPLE?!
THE MAJOR WANTS TO SELL THAT?!
YOU'RE FAMILIAR WITH IT?
NO, NO.
MERELY REMINDED OF A RECENT "POLAR BEAR IN RED," BY MISCHA.
FROM THE RUSSIAN SCHOOL.
MISCHA ...?
MIGHT I SEE THIS PAINTING?
YOU'VE QUITE PIQUED MY CURIOSITY.
IT'S IN THE EXHIBITION ROOM.
THIS WAY, PLEASE.
THANK YOU.

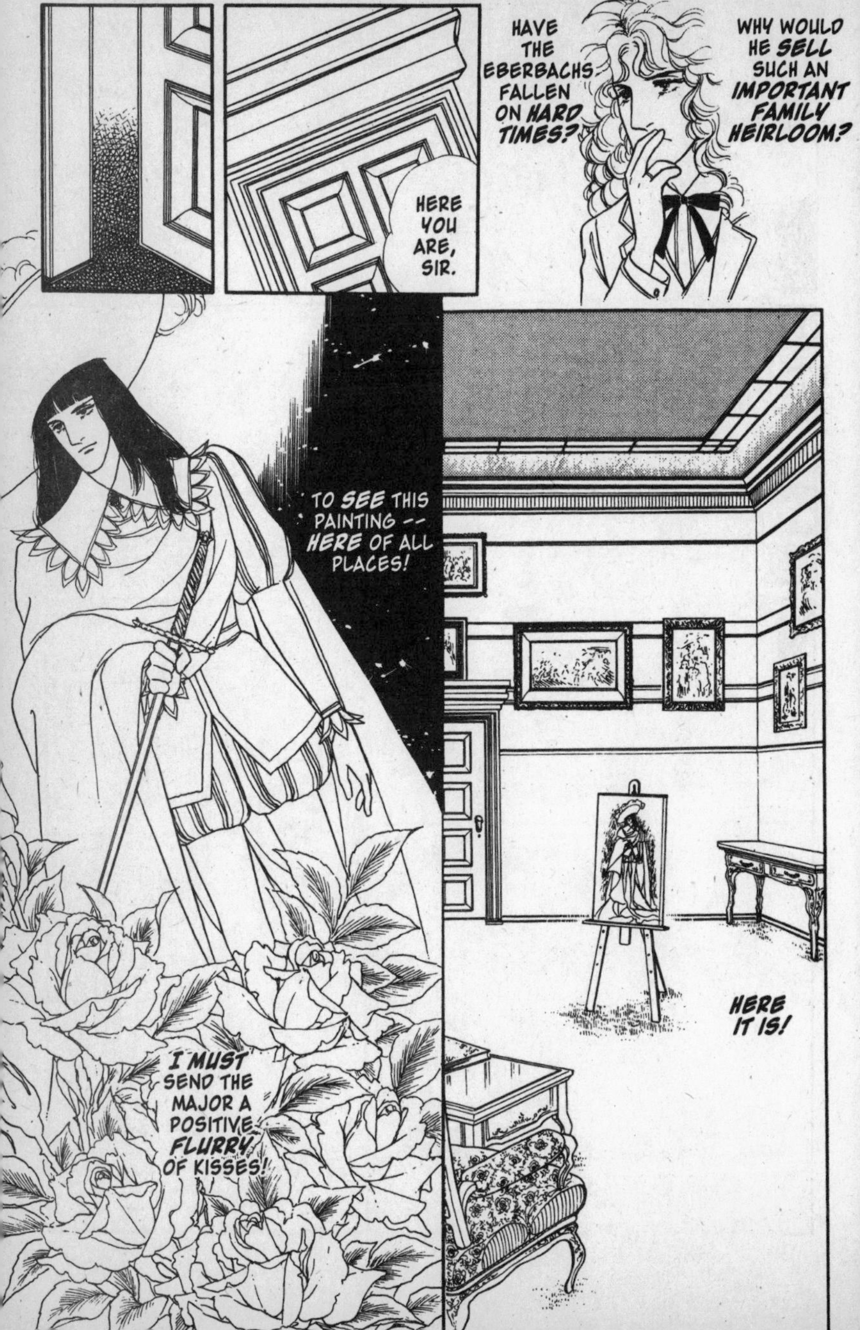
WHY WOULD HE SELL SUCH AN IMPORTANT FAMILY HEIRLOOM?
HAVE THE EBERBACHS FALLEN ON HARD TIMES?
HERE YOU ARE, SIR.
HERE IT IS!
TO SEE THIS PAINTING -- HERE OF ALL PLACES!
I MUST SEND THE MAJOR A POSITIVE FLURRY OF KISSES!

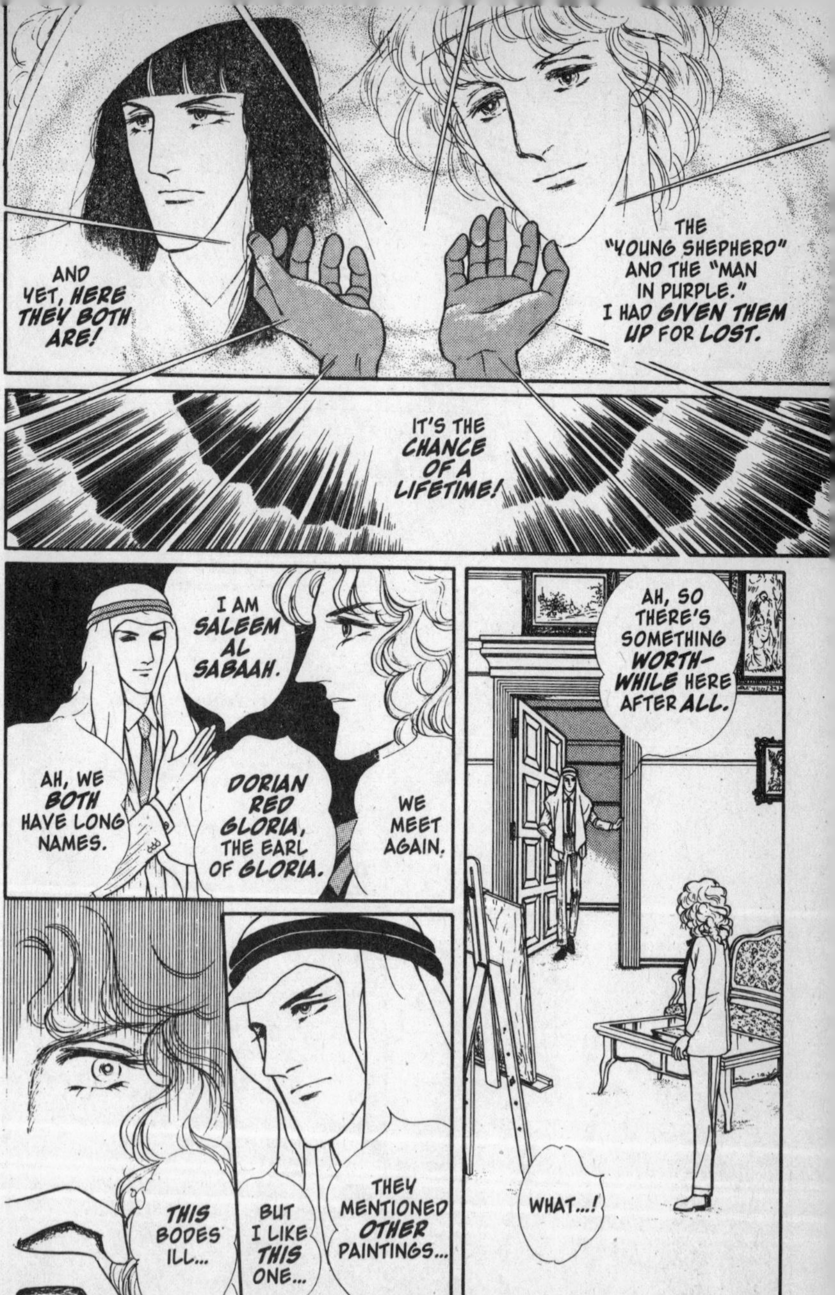
THE "YOUNG SHEPHERD" AND THE "MAN IN PURPLE." I HAD GIVEN THEM UP FOR LOST.
AND YET, HERE THEY BOTH ARE!
IT'S THE CHANCE OF A LIFETIME!
AH, SO THERE'S SOMETHING WORTH-WHILE HERE AFTER ALL.
WHAT...!
I AM SALEEM AL SABAAH.
WE MEET AGAIN.
DORIAN RED GLORIA, THE EARL OF GLORIA.
AH, WE BOTH HAVE LONG NAMES.
THEY MENTIONED OTHER PAINTINGS...
BUT I LIKE THIS ONE...
THIS BODES ILL...

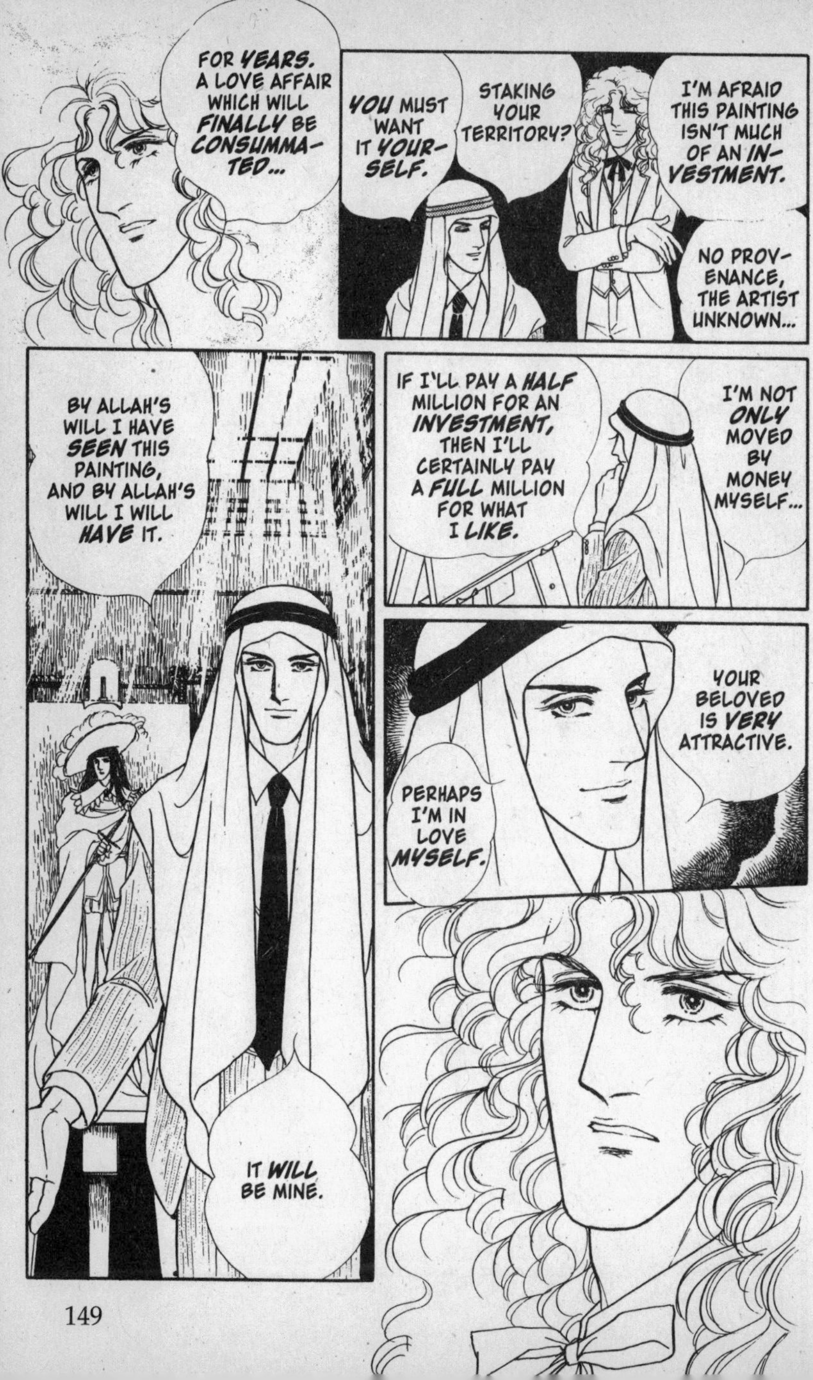
I'M AFRAID THIS PAINTING ISN'T MUCH OF AN IN-VESTMENT.
NO PROV-ENANCE, THE ARTIST UNKNOWN...
STAKING YOUR TERRITORY?
YOU MUST WANT IT YOUR-SELF.
FOR YEARS. A LOVE AFFAIR WHICH WILL FINALLY BE CONSUMMA-TED...
I'M NOT ONLY MOVED BY MONEY MYSELF...
IF I'LL PAY A HALF MILLION FOR AN INVESTMENT, THEN I'LL CERTAINLY PAY A FULL MILLION FOR WHAT I LIKE.
YOUR BELOVED IS VERY ATTRACTIVE.
PERHAPS I'M IN LOVE MYSELF.
BY ALLAH'S WILL I HAVE SEEN THIS PAINTING, AND BY ALLAH'S WILL I WILL HAVE IT.
IT WILL BE MINE.

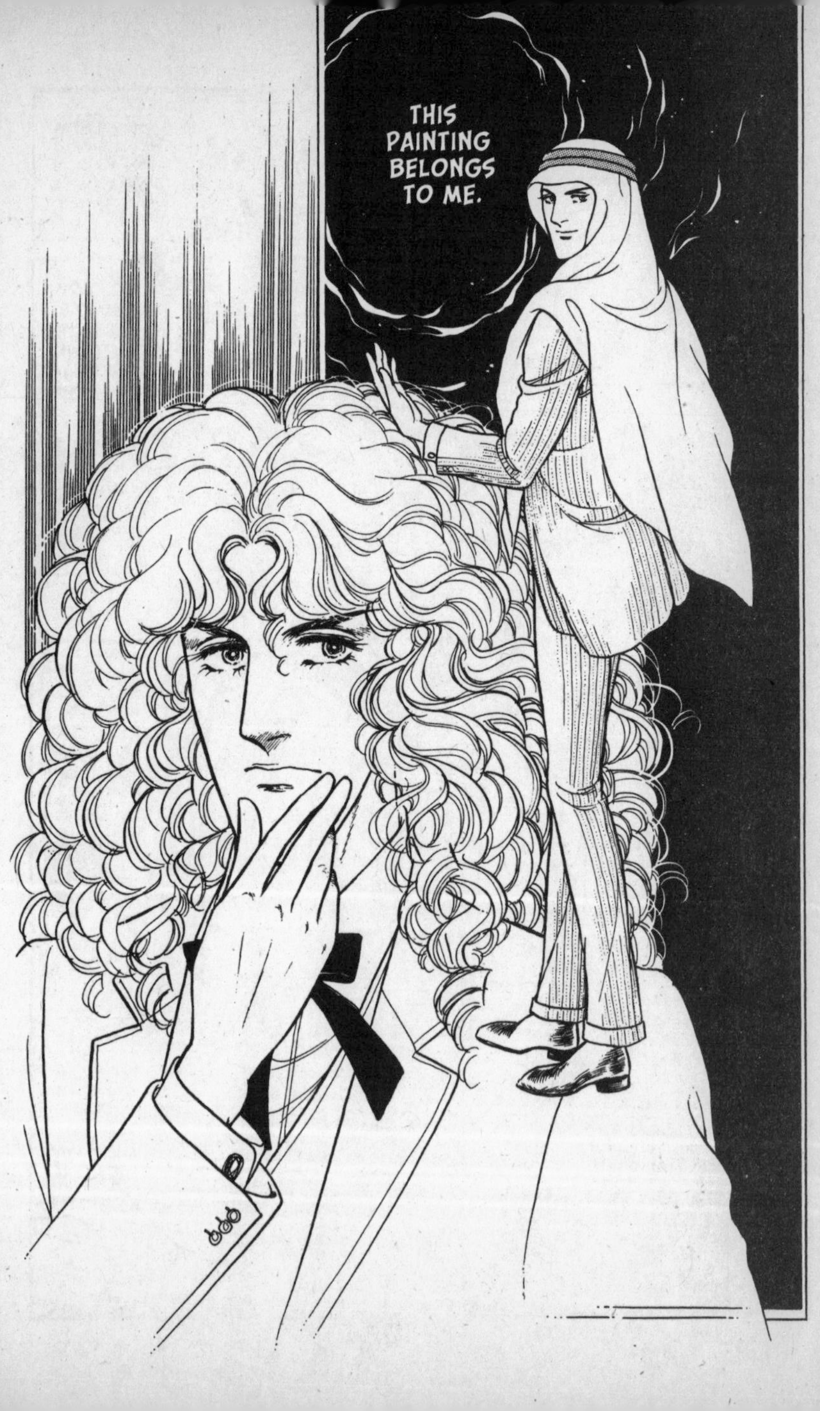
THIS PAINTING BELONGS TO ME.

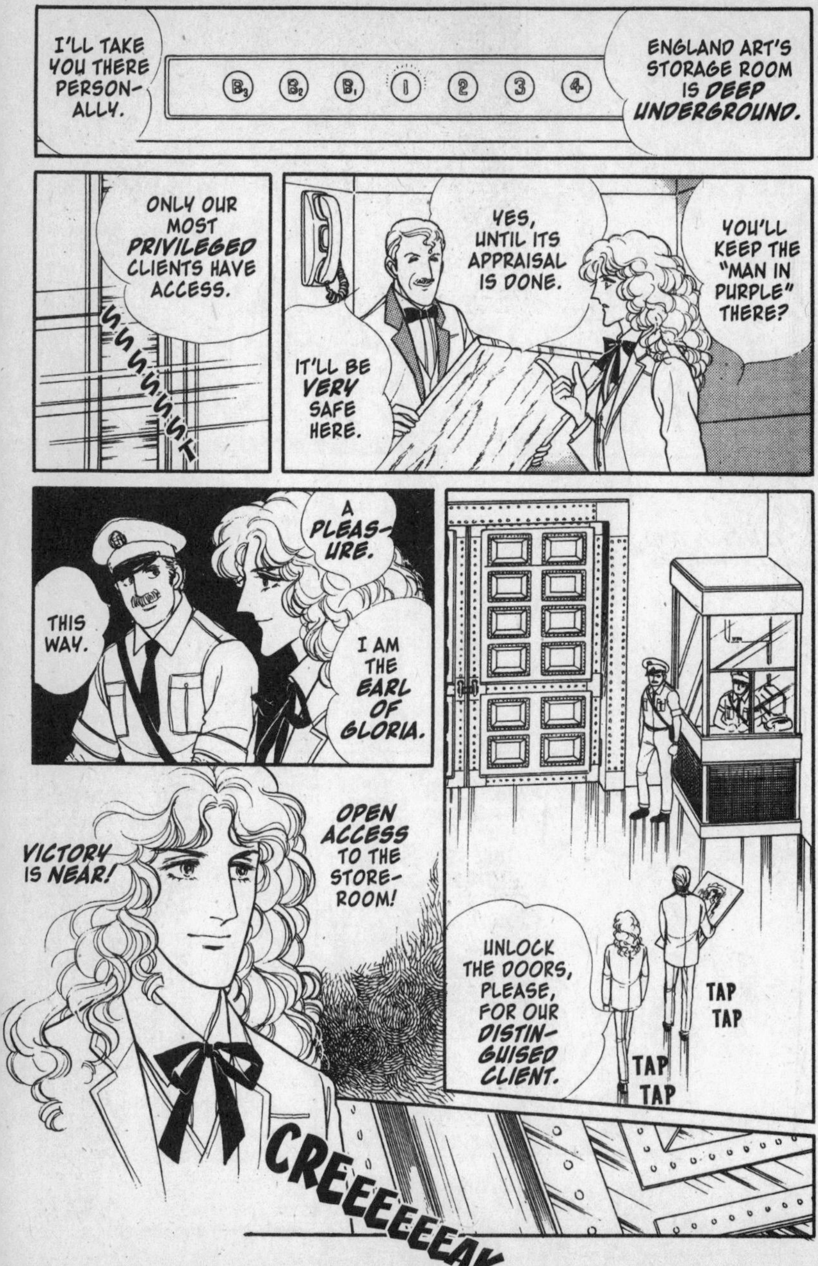
ENGLAND ART'S STORAGE ROOM IS DEEP UNDERGROUND.
I'LL TAKE YOU THERE PERSON-ALLY.
YOU'LL KEEP THE "MAN IN PURPLE" THERE?
YES, UNTIL ITS APPRAISAL IS DONE.
IT'LL BE VERY SAFE HERE.
ONLY OUR MOST PRIVILEGED CLIENTS HAVE ACCESS.
SSSSSSST
UNLOCK THE DOORS, PLEASE, FOR OUR DISTIN-GUISED CLIENT.
TAP TAP
TAP TAP
A PLEAS-URE.
I AM THE EARL OF GLORIA.
THIS WAY.
OPEN ACCESS TO THE STORE-ROOM!
VICTORY IS NEAR!
CREEEEEEEAK

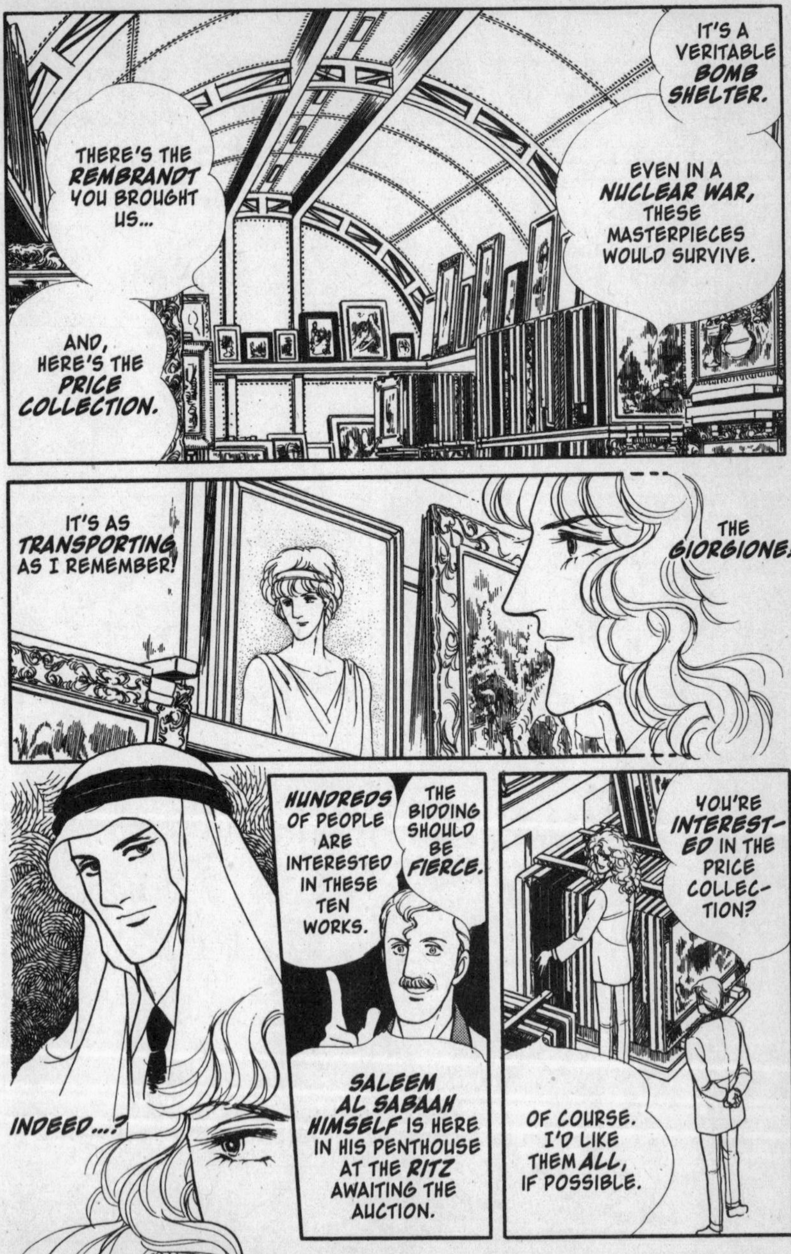
IT'S A VERITABLE BOMB SHELTER.
EVEN IN A NUCLEAR WAR, THESE MASTERPIECES WOULD SURVIVE.
THERE'S THE REMBRANDT YOU BROUGHT US...
AND, HERE'S THE PRICE COLLECTION.
THE GIORGIONE!
IT'S AS TRANSPORTING AS I REMEMBER!
YOU'RE INTEREST-ED IN THE PRICE COLLEC-TION?
OF COURSE. I'D LIKE THEM ALL, IF POSSIBLE.
THE BIDDING SHOULD BE FIERCE.
HUNDREDS OF PEOPLE ARE INTERESTED IN THESE TEN WORKS.
SALEEM AL SABAAH HIMSELF IS HERE IN HIS PENTHOUSE AT THE RITZ AWAITING THE AUCTION.
INDEED...?

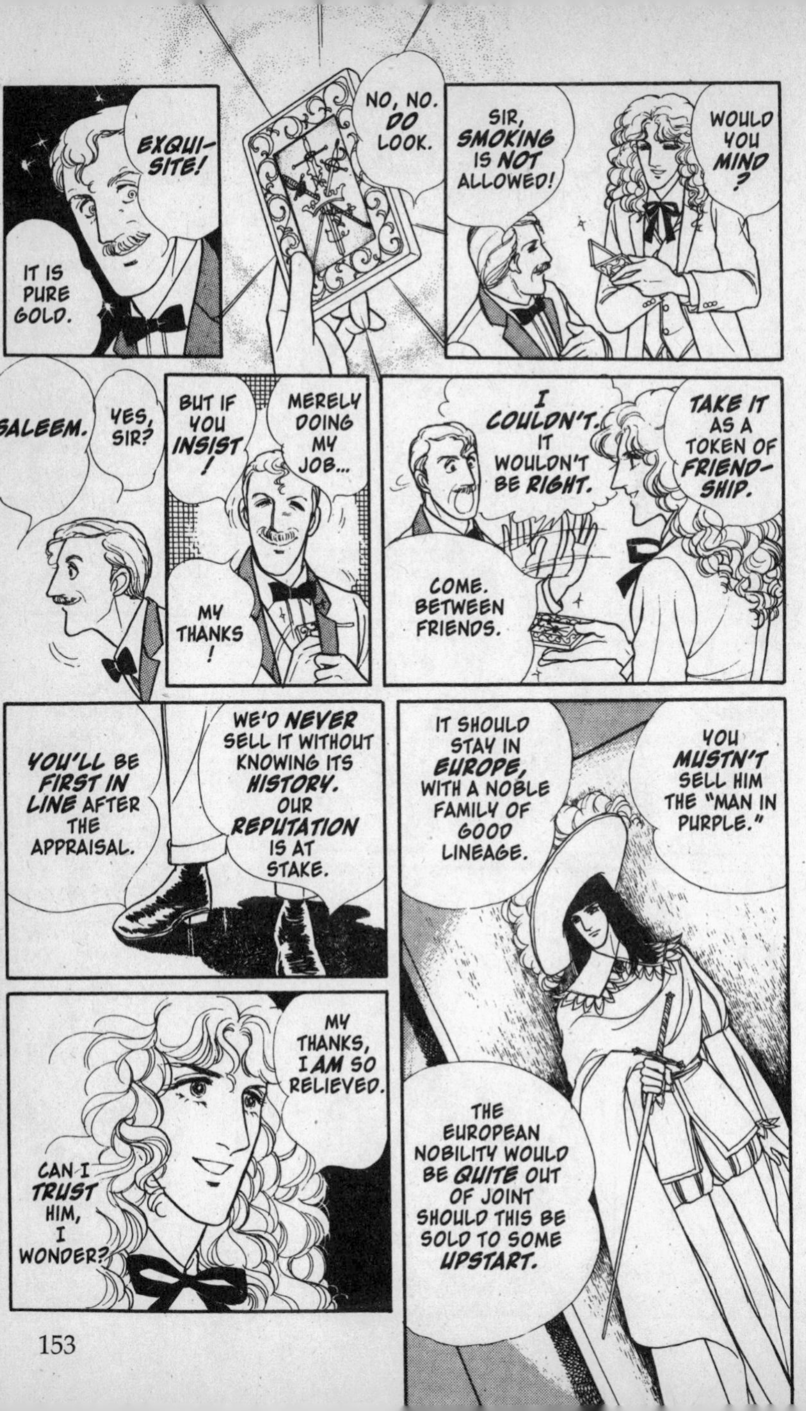
WOULD YOU MIND?
SIR, SMOKING IS NOT ALLOWED!
NO, NO. DO LOOK.
EXQUISITE!
IT IS PURE GOLD.
TAKE IT AS A TOKEN OF FRIENDSHIP.
I COULDN'T. IT WOULDN'T BE RIGHT.
COME. BETWEEN FRIENDS.
MERELY DOING MY JOB...
BUT IF YOU INSIST!
MY THANKS!
YES, SIR?
SALEEM.
YOU MUSTN'T SELL HIM THE "MAN IN PURPLE."
IT SHOULD STAY IN EUROPE, WITH A NOBLE FAMILY OF GOOD LINEAGE.
THE EUROPEAN NOBILITY WOULD BE QUITE OUT OF JOINT SHOULD THIS BE SOLD TO SOME UPSTART.
WE'D NEVER SELL IT WITHOUT KNOWING ITS HISTORY. OUR REPUTATION IS AT STAKE.
YOU'LL BE FIRST IN LINE AFTER THE APPRAISAL.
MY THANKS, I AM SO RELIEVED.
CAN I TRUST HIM, I WONDER?

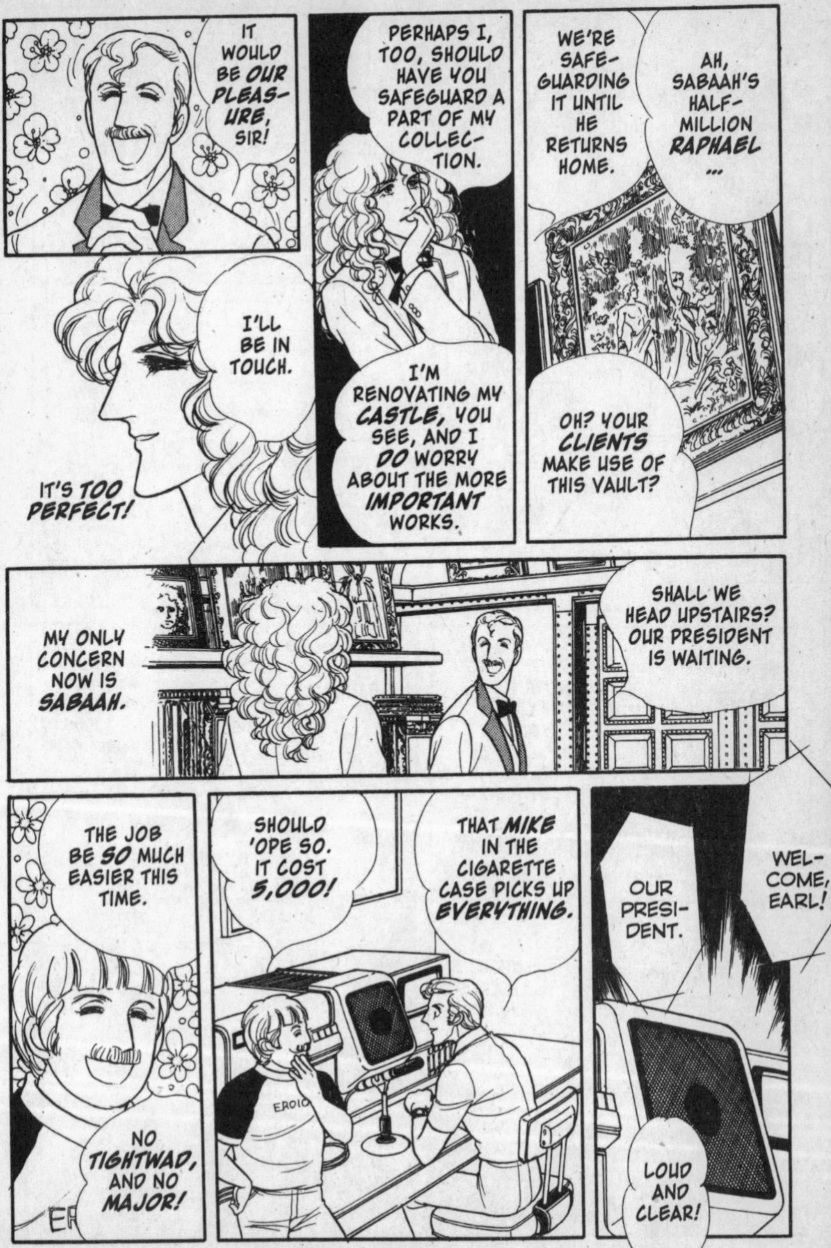

AH, SABAAH'S HALF-MILLION RAPHAEL ...
WE'RE SAFEGUARDING IT UNTIL HE RETURNS HOME.
OH? YOUR CLIENTS MAKE USE OF THIS VAULT?
PERHAPS I, TOO, SHOULD HAVE YOU SAFEGUARD A PART OF MY COLLECTION.
I'M RENOVATING MY CASTLE, YOU SEE, AND I DO WORRY ABOUT THE MORE IMPORTANT WORKS.
IT WOULD BE OUR PLEASURE, SIR!
I'LL BE IN TOUCH.
IT'S TOO PERFECT!
SHALL WE HEAD UPSTAIRS? OUR PRESIDENT IS WAITING.
MY ONLY CONCERN NOW IS SABAAH.
WELCOME, EARL!
OUR PRESIDENT.
LOUD AND CLEAR!
THAT MIKE IN THE CIGARETTE CASE PICKS UP EVERYTHING.
SHOULD 'OPE SO. IT COST 5,000!
THE JOB BE SO MUCH EASIER THIS TIME.
NO TIGHTWAD, AND NO MAJOR!

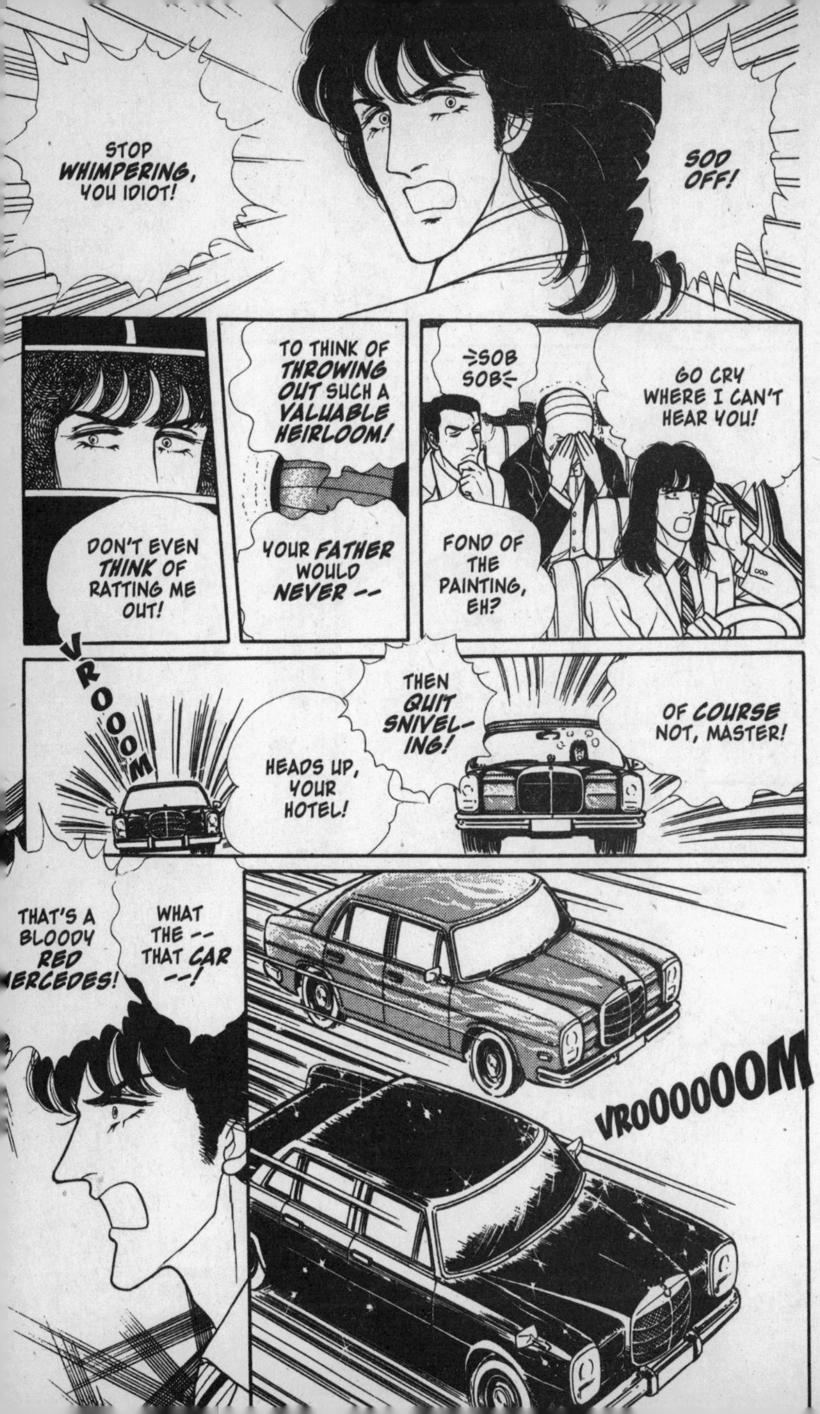
SOD OFF!
STOP WHIMPERING, YOU IDIOT!
GO CRY WHERE I CAN'T HEAR YOU!
SOB SOB
FOND OF THE PAINTING, EH?
TO THINK OF THROWING OUT SUCH A VALUABLE HEIRLOOM!
YOUR FATHER WOULD NEVER --
DON'T EVEN THINK OF RATTING ME OUT!
VROOOOM
OF COURSE NOT, MASTER!
THEN QUIT SNIVELING!
HEADS UP, YOUR HOTEL!
VROOOOOOM
WHAT THE -- THAT CAR --!
THAT'S A BLOODY RED ERCEDES!

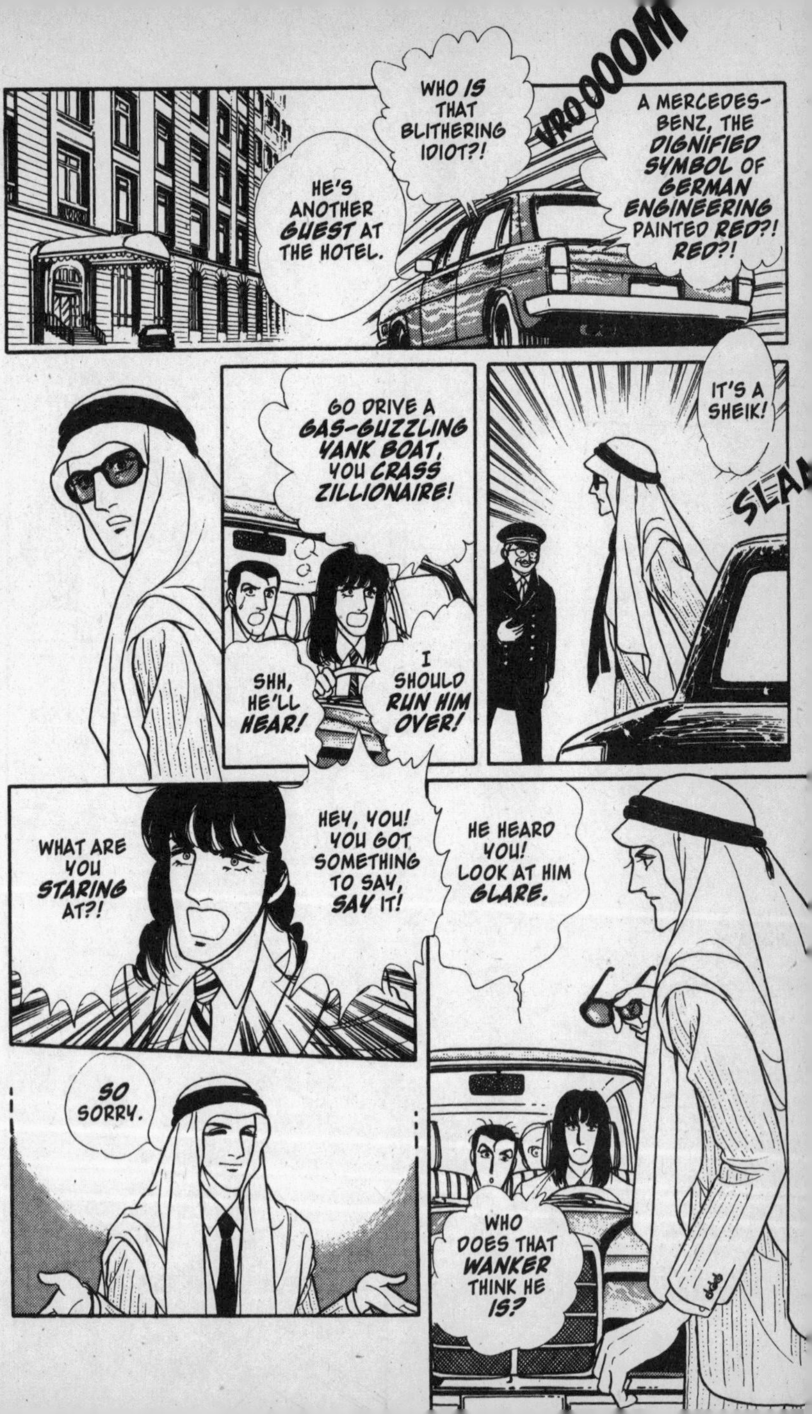
A MERCEDES-BENZ, THE DIGNIFIED SYMBOL OF GERMAN ENGINEERING PAINTED RED?! RED?!
VROOOOM
WHO IS THAT BLITHERING IDIOT?!
HE'S ANOTHER GUEST AT THE HOTEL.
IT'S A SHEIK!
SLAA
GO DRIVE A GAS-GUZZLING YANK BOAT, YOU CRASS ZILLIONAIRE!
I SHOULD RUN HIM OVER!
SHH, HE'LL HEAR!
HE HEARD YOU! LOOK AT HIM GLARE.
WHO DOES THAT WANKER THINK HE IS?
HEY, YOU! YOU GOT SOMETHING TO SAY, SAY IT!
WHAT ARE YOU STARING AT?!
SO SORRY.

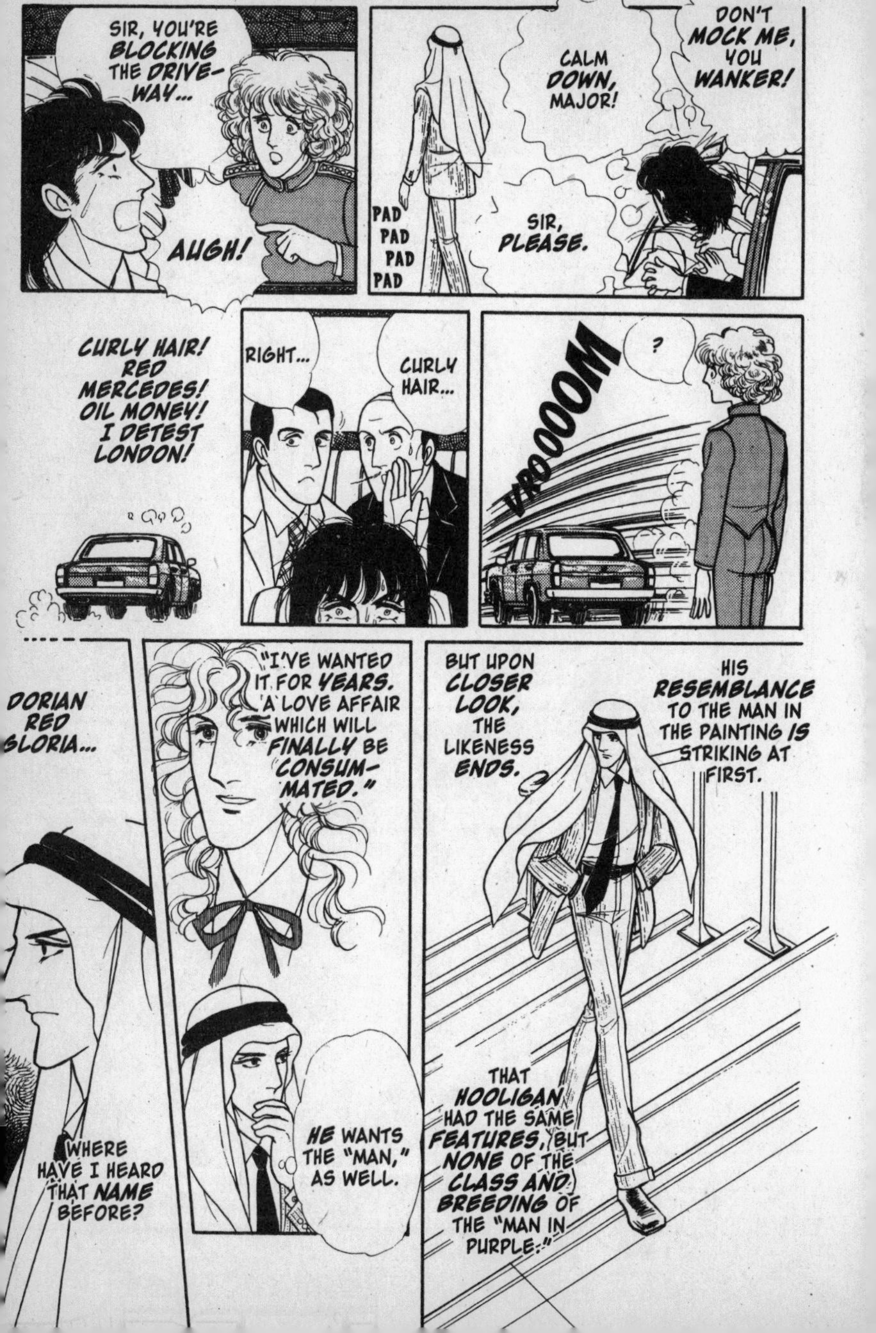
DON'T MOCK ME, YOU WANKER!
CALM DOWN, MAJOR!
SIR, PLEASE.
PAD PAD PAD PAD
SIR, YOU'RE BLOCKING THE DRIVE-WAY...
AUGH!
VROOOOOM
?
CURLY HAIR...
RIGHT...
CURLY HAIR! RED MERCEDES! OIL MONEY! I DETEST LONDON!
HIS RESEMBLANCE TO THE MAN IN THE PAINTING IS STRIKING AT FIRST.
BUT UPON CLOSER LOOK, THE LIKENESS ENDS.
THAT HOOLIGAN HAD THE SAME FEATURES, BUT NONE OF THE CLASS AND BREEDING OF THE "MAN IN PURPLE."
"I'VE WANTED IT FOR YEARS. A LOVE AFFAIR WHICH WILL FINALLY BE CONSUM-MATED."
HE WANTS THE "MAN," AS WELL.
DORIAN RED GLORIA...
WHERE HAVE I HEARD THAT NAME BEFORE?

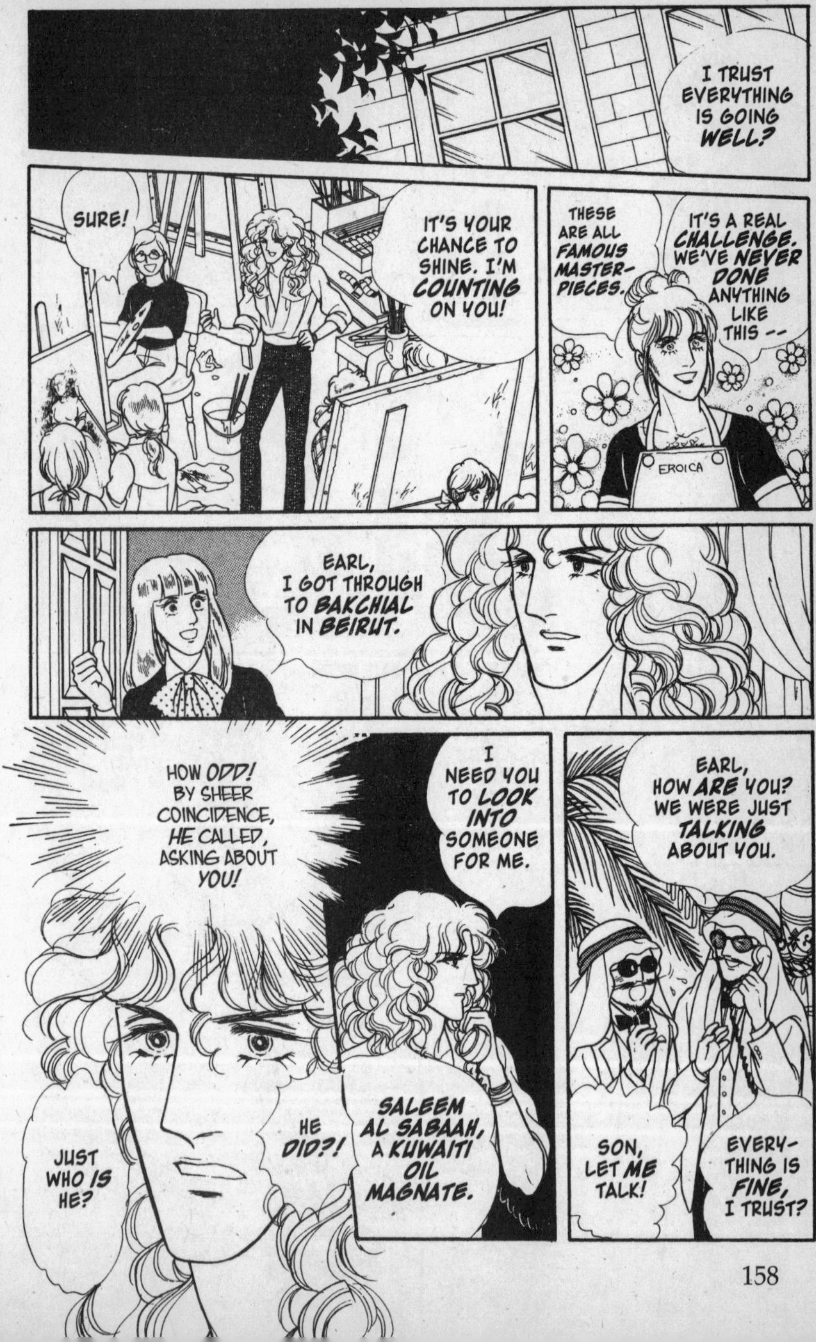
I TRUST EVERYTHING IS GOING WELL?
IT'S A REAL CHALLENGE. WE'VE NEVER DONE ANYTHING LIKE THIS --
THESE ARE ALL FAMOUS MASTER-PIECES.
IT'S YOUR CHANCE TO SHINE. I'M COUNTING ON YOU!
SURE!
EARL, I GOT THROUGH TO BAKCHIAL IN BEIRUT.
EARL, HOW ARE YOU? WE WERE JUST TALKING ABOUT YOU.
EVERY-THING IS FINE, I TRUST?
SON, LET ME TALK!
I NEED YOU TO LOOK INTO SOMEONE FOR ME.
SALEEM AL SABAAH, A KUWAITI OIL MAGNATE.
HOW ODD! BY SHEER COINCIDENCE, HE CALLED, ASKING ABOUT YOU!
HE DID?!
JUST WHO IS HE?

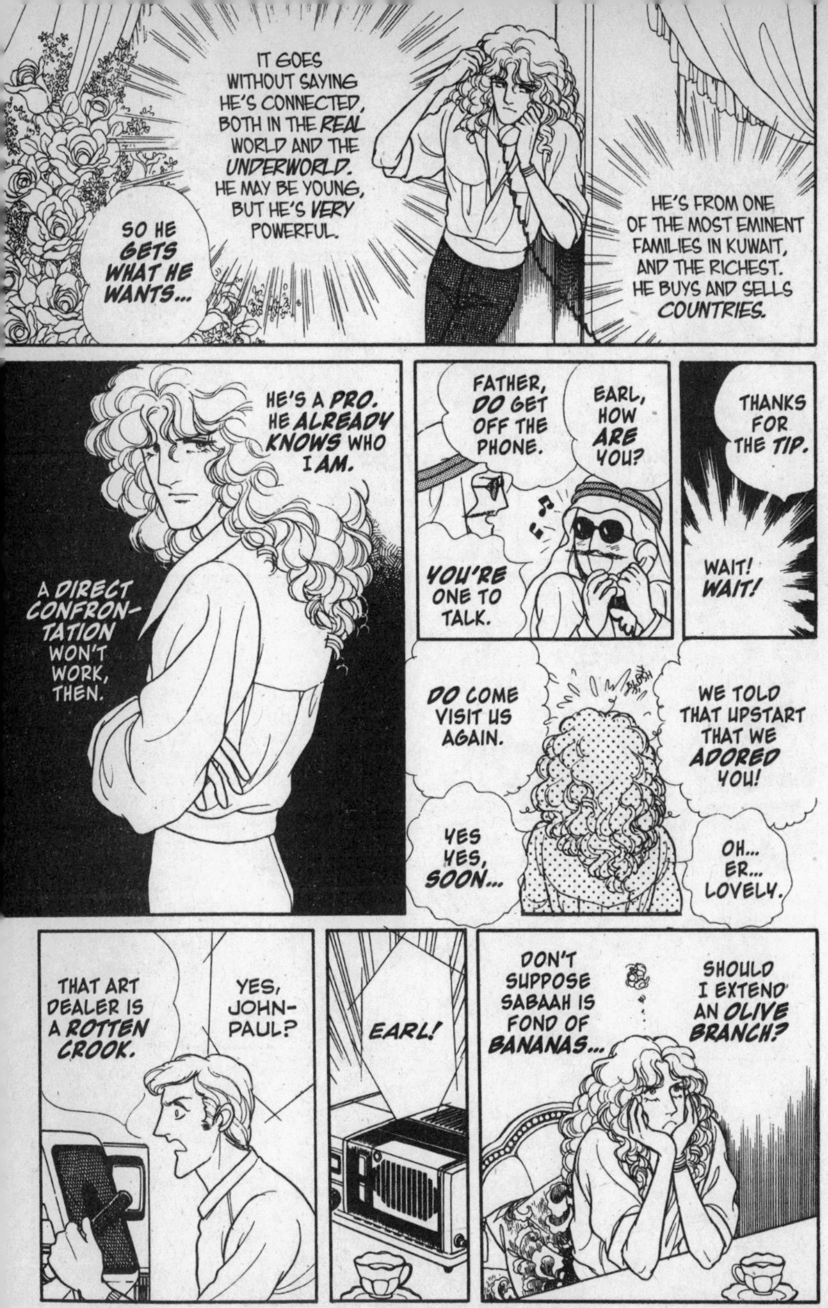
HE'S FROM ONE OF THE MOST EMINENT FAMILIES IN KUWAIT, AND THE RICHEST. HE BUYS AND SELLS COUNTRIES.
IT GOES WITHOUT SAYING HE'S CONNECTED, BOTH IN THE REAL WORLD AND THE UNDERWORLD. HE MAY BE YOUNG, BUT HE'S VERY POWERFUL.
SO HE GETS WHAT HE WANTS...
THANKS FOR THE TIP.
WAIT! WAIT!
EARL, HOW ARE YOU?
FATHER, DO GET OFF THE PHONE.
YOU'RE ONE TO TALK.
WE TOLD THAT UPSTART THAT WE ADORED YOU!
DO COME VISIT US AGAIN.
OH... ER... LOVELY.
YES YES, SOON...
HE'S A PRO. HE ALREADY KNOWS WHO I AM.
A DIRECT CONFRONTATION WON'T WORK, THEN.
SHOULD I EXTEND AN OLIVE BRANCH?
DON'T SUPPOSE SABAAH IS FOND OF BANANAS...
EARL!
YES, JOHN-PAUL?
THAT ART DEALER IS A ROTTEN CROOK.

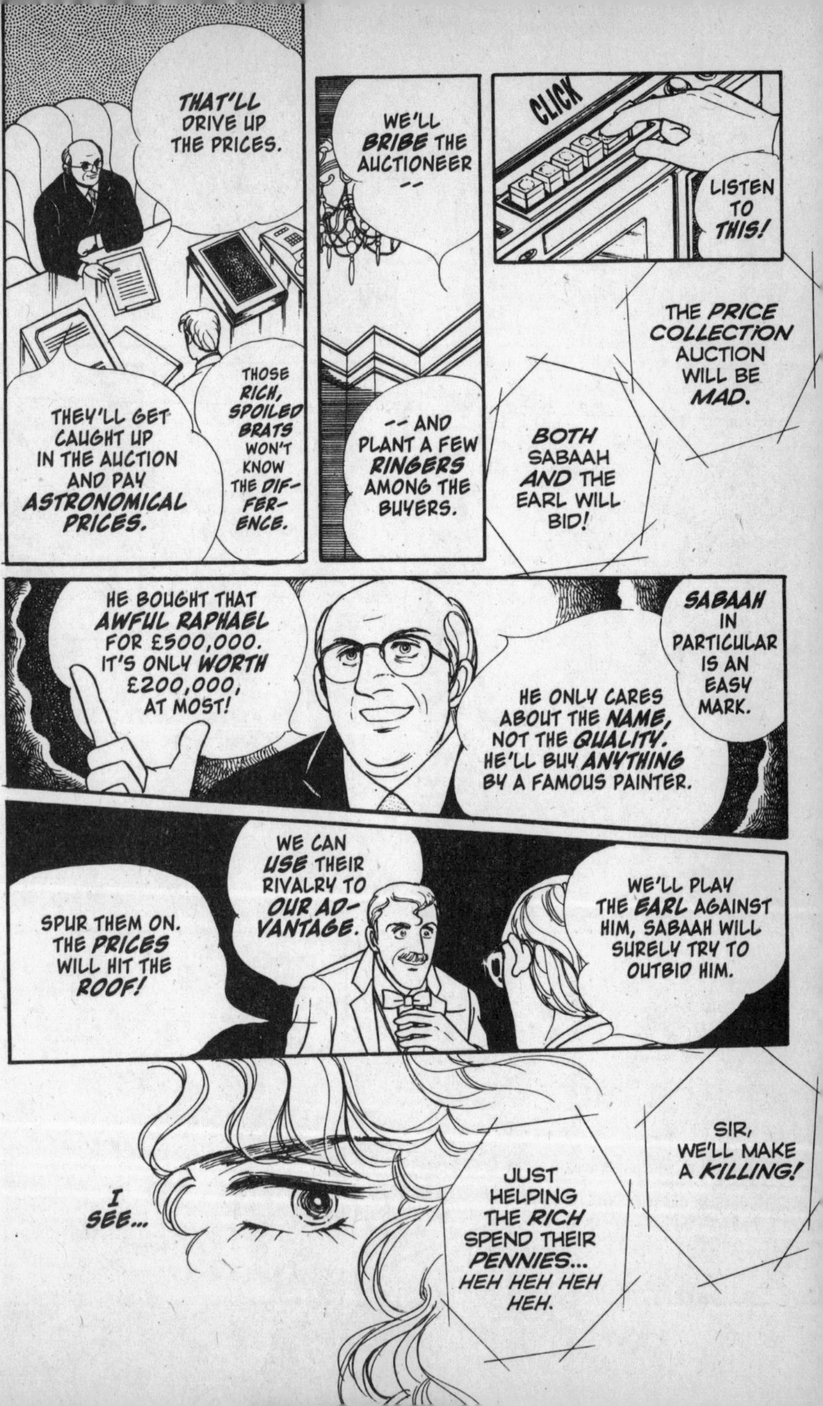
CLICK
LISTEN TO THIS!
THE PRICE COLLECTION AUCTION WILL BE MAD.
BOTH SABAAH AND THE EARL WILL BID!
WE'LL BRIBE THE AUCTIONEER --
-- AND PLANT A FEW RINGERS AMONG THE BUYERS.
THAT'LL DRIVE UP THE PRICES.
THOSE RICH, SPOILED BRATS WON'T KNOW THE DIF-FER-ENCE.
THEY'LL GET CAUGHT UP IN THE AUCTION AND PAY ASTRONOMICAL PRICES.
SABAAH IN PARTICULAR IS AN EASY MARK.
HE ONLY CARES ABOUT THE NAME, NOT THE QUALITY. HE'LL BUY ANYTHING BY A FAMOUS PAINTER.
HE BOUGHT THAT AWFUL RAPHAEL FOR £500,000. IT'S ONLY WORTH £200,000, AT MOST!
WE'LL PLAY THE EARL AGAINST HIM, SABAAH WILL SURELY TRY TO OUTBID HIM.
WE CAN USE THEIR RIVALRY TO OUR AD-VANTAGE.
SPUR THEM ON. THE PRICES WILL HIT THE ROOF!
SIR, WE'LL MAKE A KILLING!
JUST HELPING THE RICH SPEND THEIR PENNIES... HEH HEH HEH HEH.
I SEE...

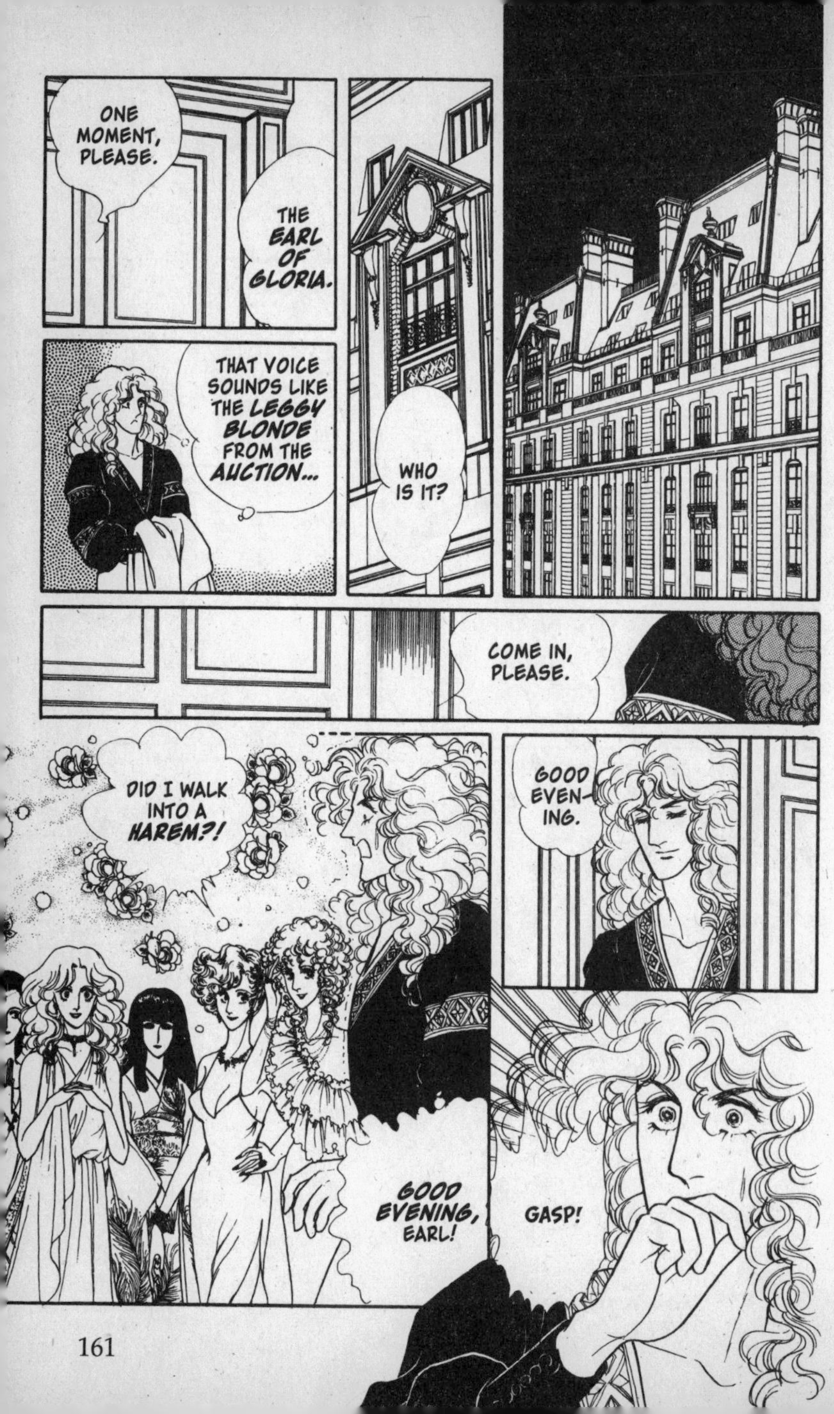
WHO IS IT?
THE EARL OF GLORIA.
ONE MOMENT, PLEASE.
THAT VOICE SOUNDS LIKE THE LEGGY BLONDE FROM THE AUCTION...
COME IN, PLEASE.
GOOD EVENING.
DID I WALK INTO A HAREM?!
GOOD EVENING, EARL!
GASP!

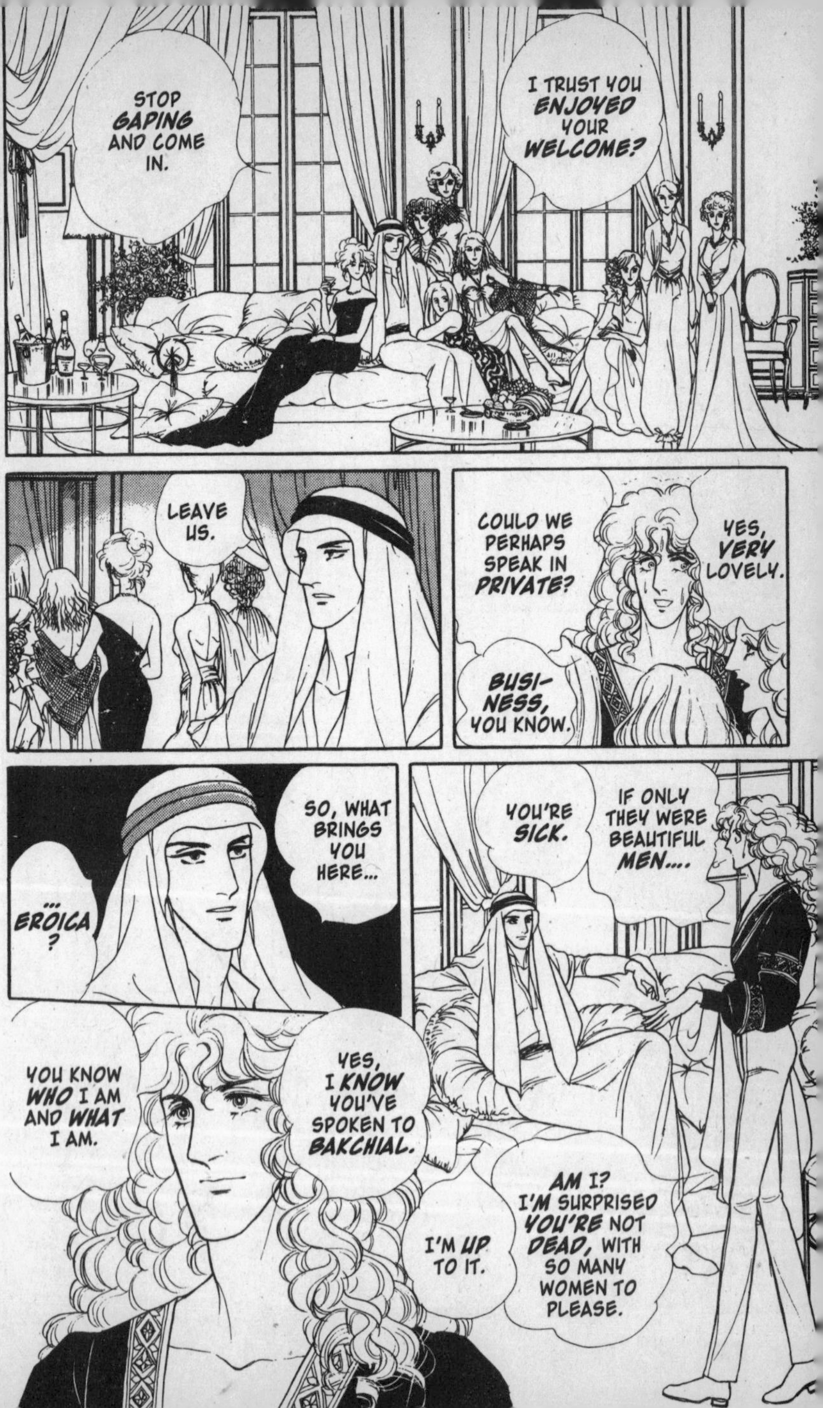
I TRUST YOU ENJOYED YOUR WELCOME?
STOP GAPING AND COME IN.
YES, VERY LOVELY.
COULD WE PERHAPS SPEAK IN PRIVATE?
BUSI-NESS, YOU KNOW.
LEAVE US.
IF ONLY THEY WERE BEAUTIFUL MEN....
YOU'RE SICK.
AM I? I'M SURPRISED YOU'RE NOT DEAD, WITH SO MANY WOMEN TO PLEASE.
I'M UP TO IT.
SO, WHAT BRINGS YOU HERE...
...EROICA?
YES, I KNOW YOU'VE SPOKEN TO BAKCHIAL.
YOU KNOW WHO I AM AND WHAT I AM.

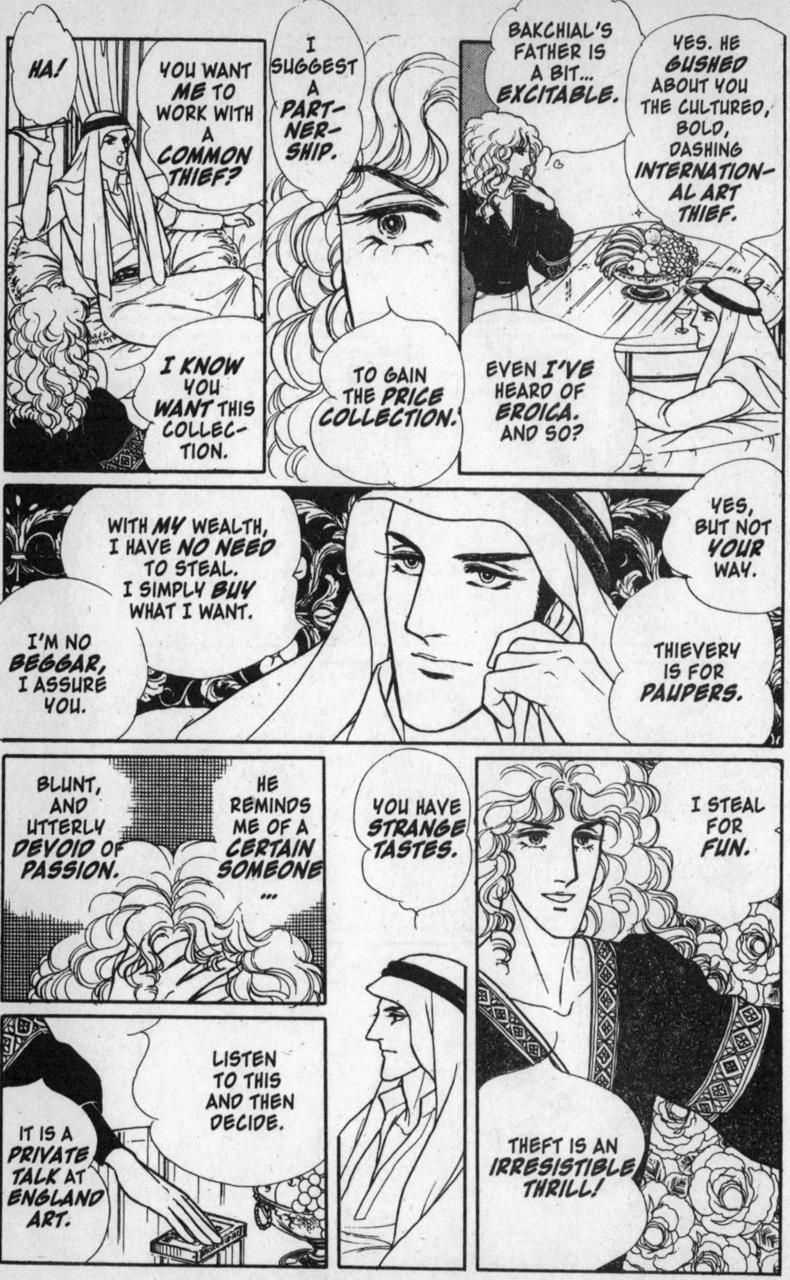
BAKCHIAL'S FATHER IS A BIT... EXCITABLE.
YES. HE GUSHED ABOUT YOU THE CULTURED, BOLD, DASHING INTERNATIONAL ART THIEF.
EVEN I'VE HEARD OF EROICA. AND SO?
I SUGGEST A PARTNERSHIP.
TO GAIN THE PRICE COLLECTION.
HA!
YOU WANT ME TO WORK WITH A COMMON THIEF?
I KNOW YOU WANT THIS COLLECTION.
YES, BUT NOT YOUR WAY.
THIEVERY IS FOR PAUPERS.
WITH MY WEALTH, I HAVE NO NEED TO STEAL. I SIMPLY BUY WHAT I WANT.
I'M NO BEGGAR, I ASSURE YOU.
I STEAL FOR FUN.
THEFT IS AN IRRESISTIBLE THRILL!
YOU HAVE STRANGE TASTES.
HE REMINDS ME OF A CERTAIN SOMEONE ...
BLUNT, AND UTTERLY DEVOID OF PASSION.
LISTEN TO THIS AND THEN DECIDE.
IT IS A PRIVATE TALK AT ENGLAND ART.

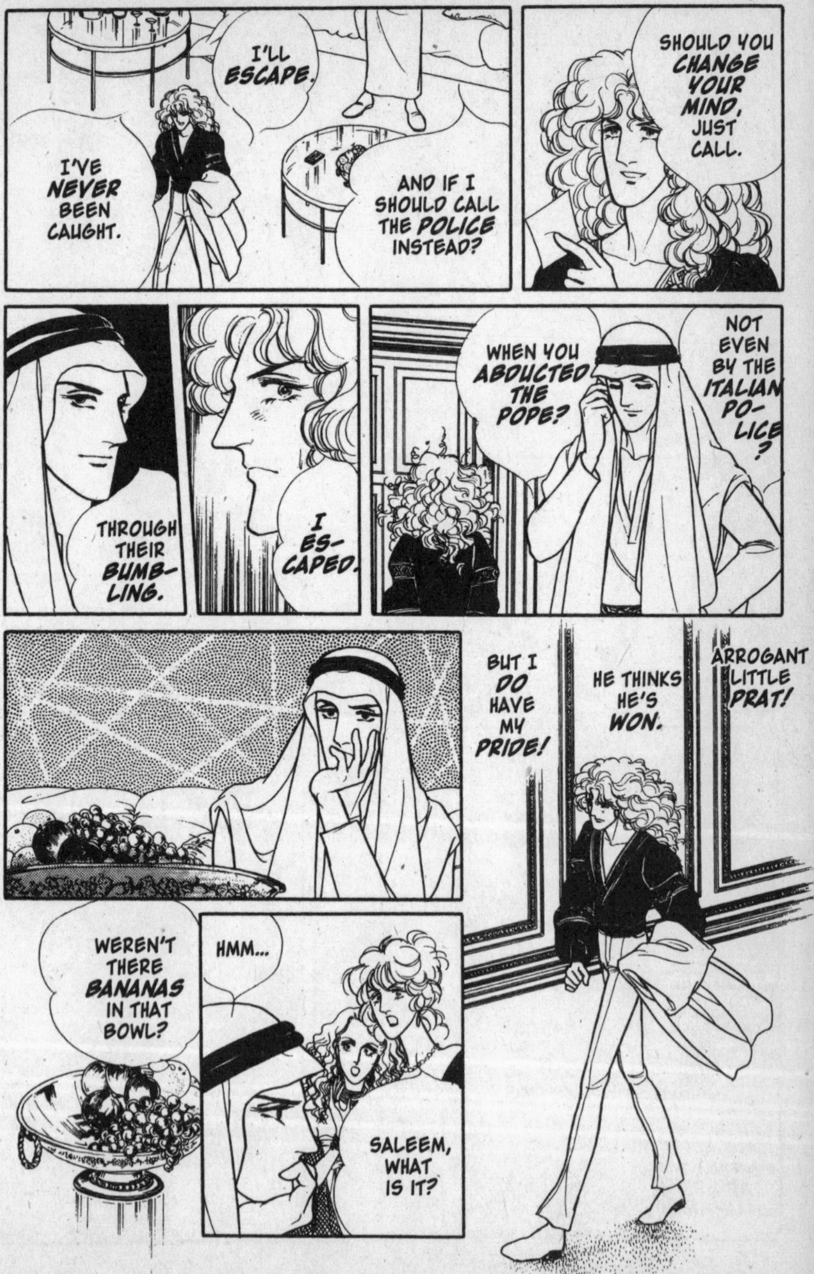

SHOULD YOU *CHANGE YOUR MIND*, JUST CALL.
AND IF I SHOULD CALL THE *POLICE* INSTEAD?
I'LL *ESCAPE*.
I'VE *NEVER* BEEN CAUGHT.
NOT EVEN BY THE *ITALIAN POLICE*?
WHEN YOU *ABDUCTED THE POPE*?
I ESCAPED.
THROUGH THEIR *BUMBLING*.
ARROGANT LITTLE *PRAT!*
HE THINKS HE'S *WON*.
BUT I *DO* HAVE MY *PRIDE!*
HMM...
SALEEM, WHAT IS IT?
WEREN'T THERE *BANANAS* IN THAT BOWL?

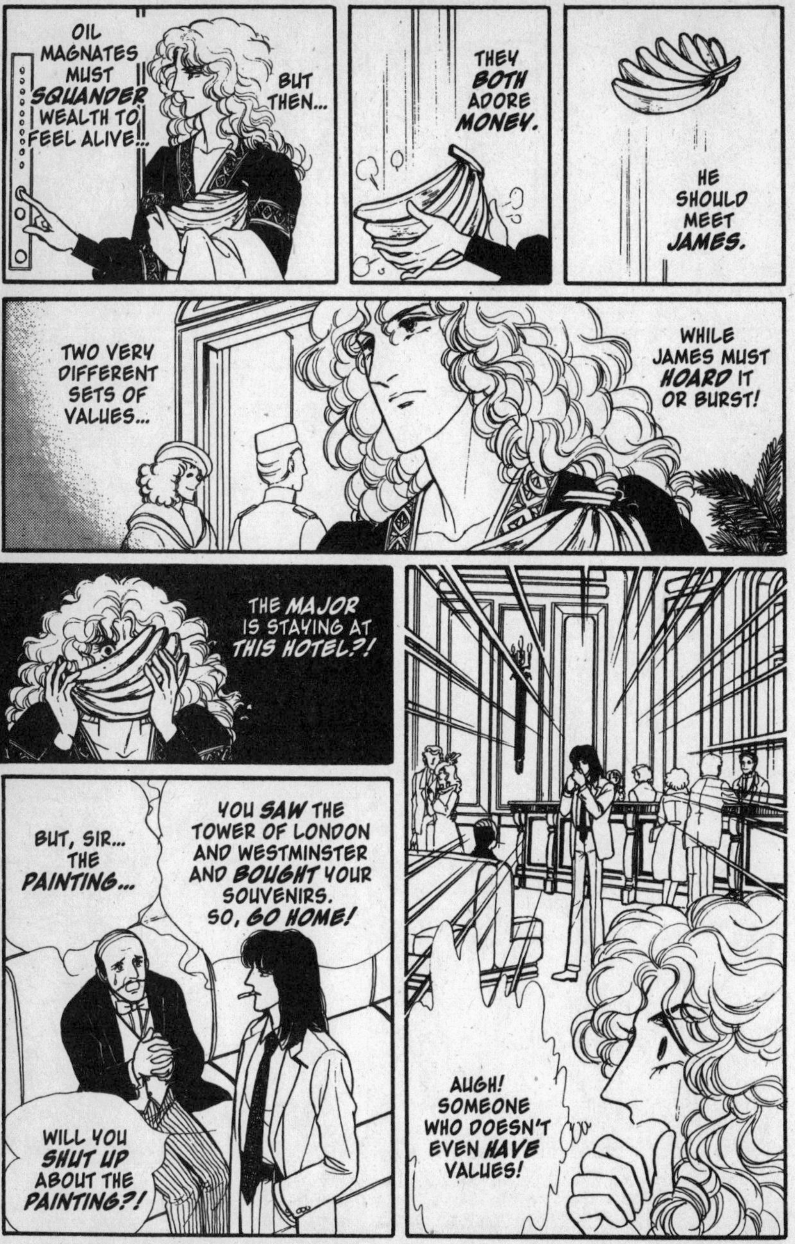
HE SHOULD MEET JAMES.
THEY BOTH ADORE MONEY.
BUT THEN...
OIL MAGNATES MUST SQUANDER WEALTH TO FEEL ALIVE!...
WHILE JAMES MUST HOARD IT OR BURST!
TWO VERY DIFFERENT SETS OF VALUES...
AUGH! SOMEONE WHO DOESN'T EVEN HAVE VALUES!
THE MAJOR IS STAYING AT THIS HOTEL?!
YOU SAW THE TOWER OF LONDON AND WESTMINSTER AND BOUGHT YOUR SOUVENIRS. SO, GO HOME!
BUT, SIR... THE PAINTING...
WILL YOU SHUT UP ABOUT THE PAINTING?!

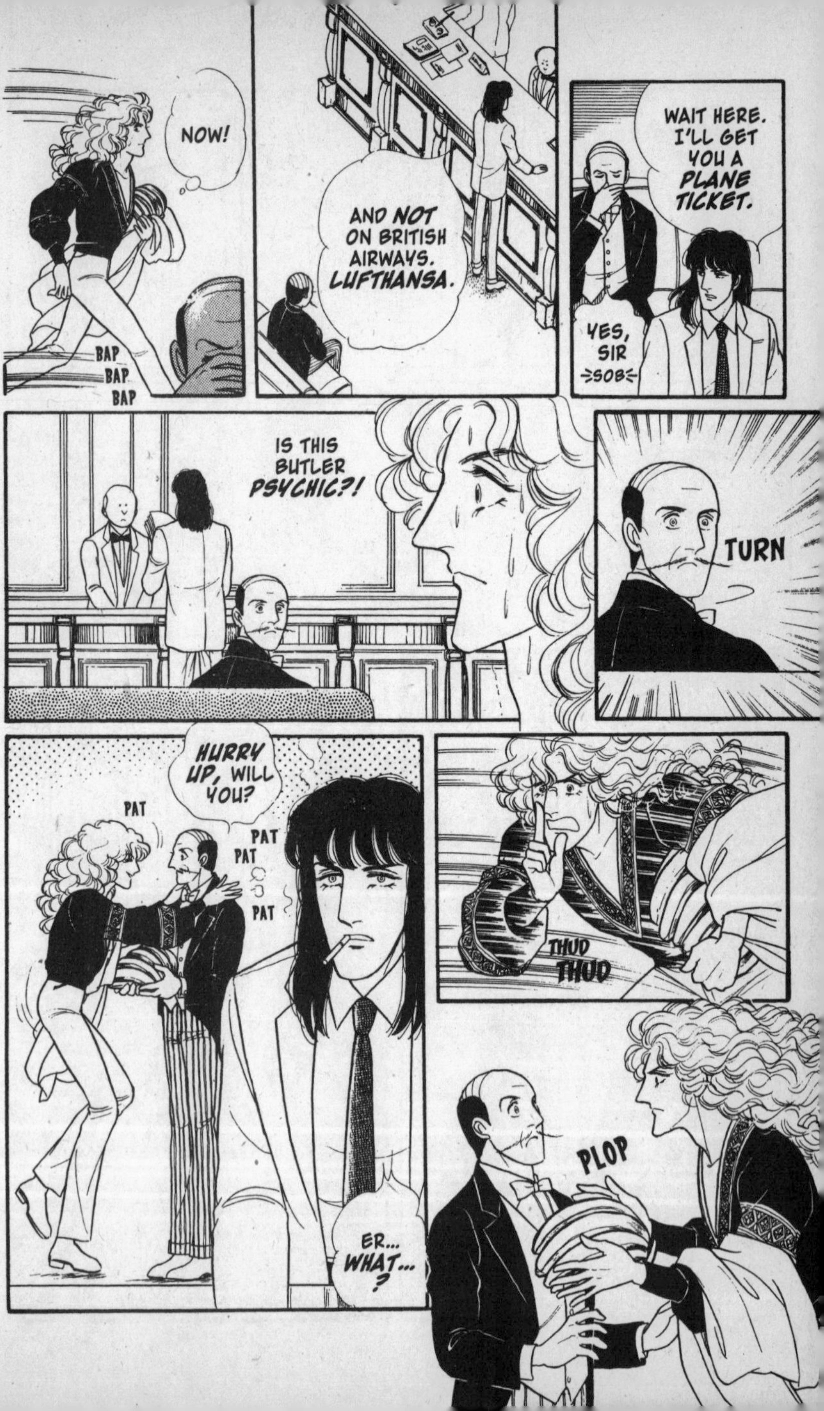

WAIT HERE. I'LL GET YOU A PLANE TICKET.
YES, SIR
SOB
AND NOT ON BRITISH AIRWAYS. LUFTHANSA.
NOW!
BAP
BAP
BAP
TURN
IS THIS BUTLER PSYCHIC?!
THUD
THUD
PLOP
HURRY UP, WILL YOU?
PAT
PAT
PAT
PAT
ER... WHAT...?

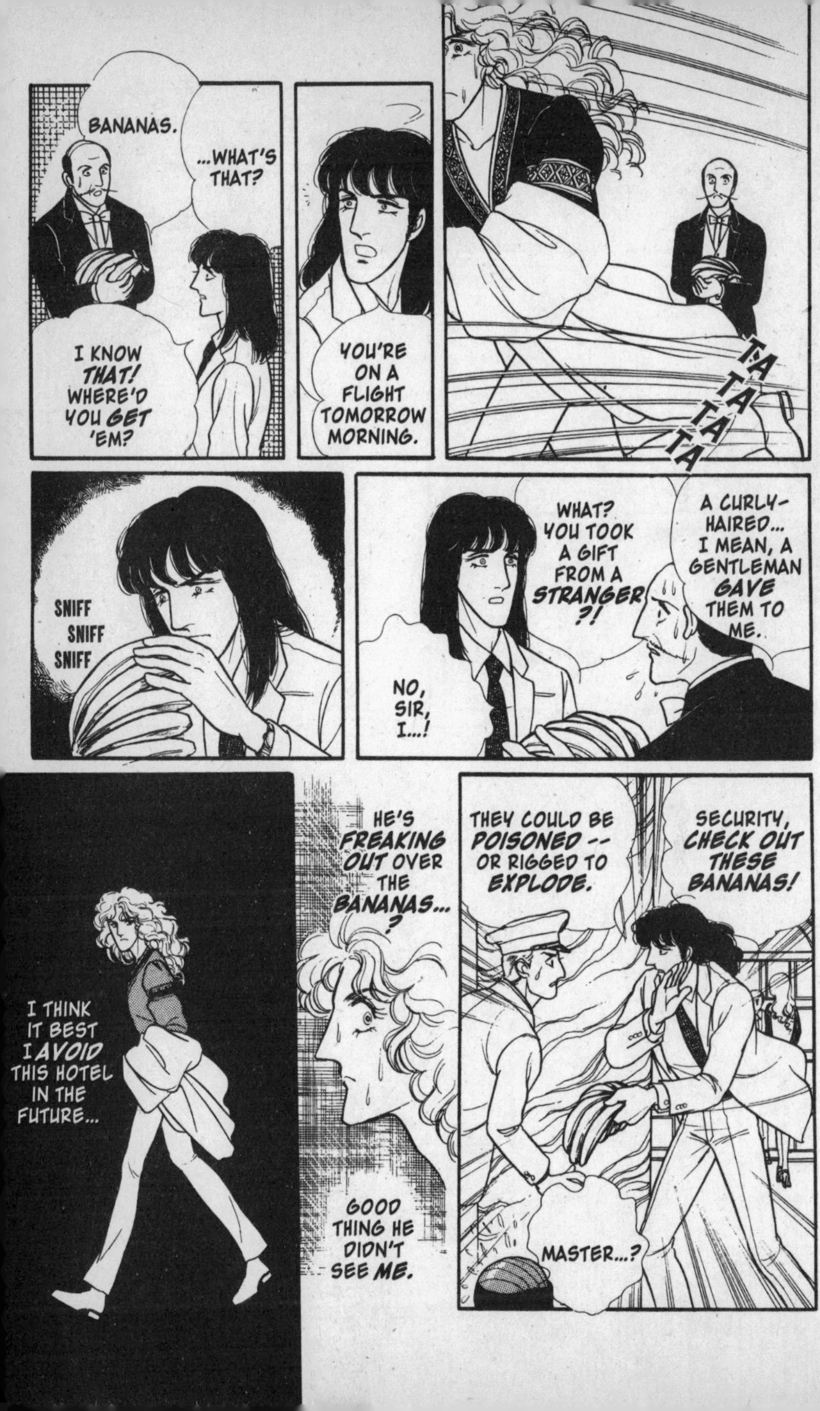
TATATATA
YOU'RE ON A FLIGHT TOMORROW MORNING.
...WHAT'S THAT?
BANANAS.
I KNOW THAT! WHERE'D YOU GET 'EM?
A CURLY-HAIRED... I MEAN, A GENTLEMAN GAVE THEM TO ME.
WHAT? YOU TOOK A GIFT FROM A STRANGER?!
NO, SIR, I...!
SNIFF SNIFF SNIFF
SECURITY, CHECK OUT THESE BANANAS!
THEY COULD BE POISONED -- OR RIGGED TO EXPLODE.
MASTER...?
HE'S FREAKING OUT OVER THE BANANAS...?
GOOD THING HE DIDN'T SEE ME.
I THINK IT BEST I AVOID THIS HOTEL IN THE FUTURE...

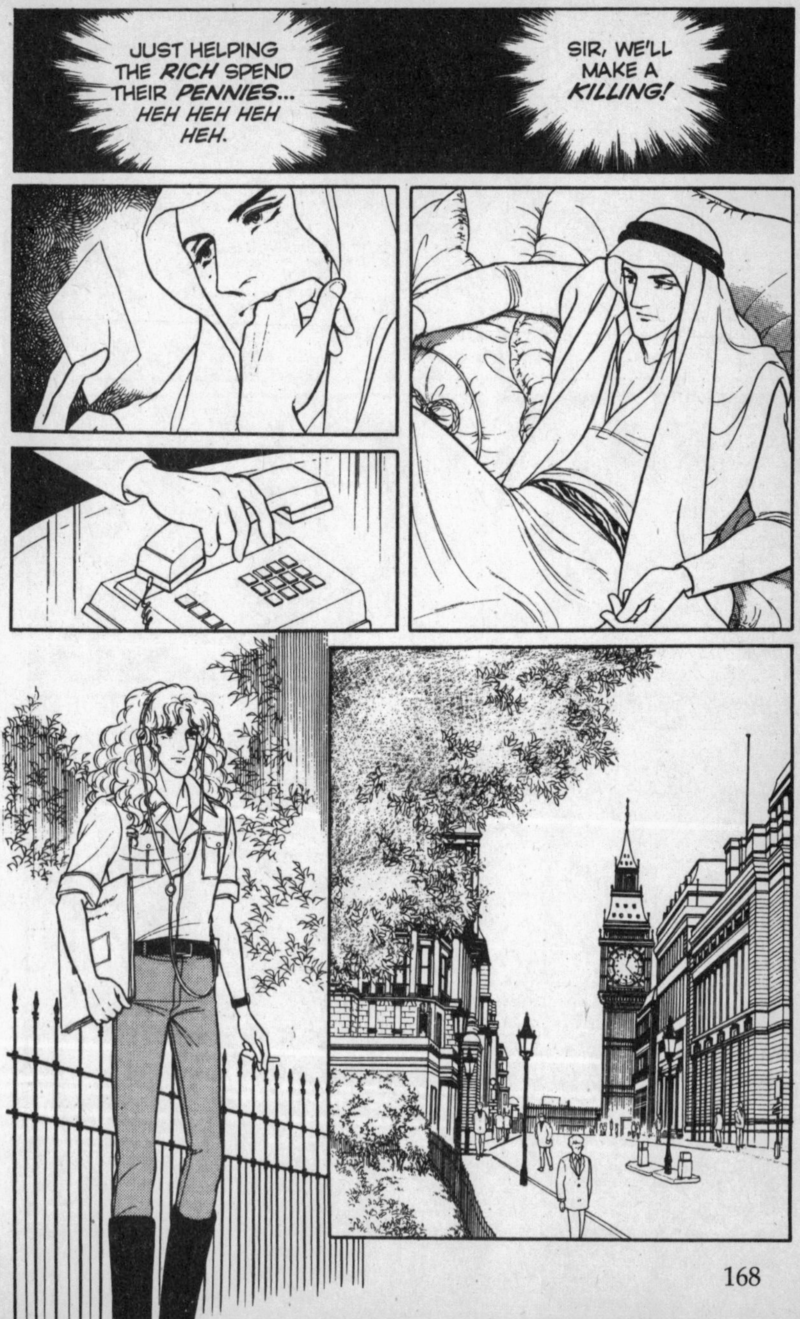
SIR, WE'LL MAKE A *KILLING!*
JUST HELPING THE *RICH* SPEND THEIR *PENNIES... HEH HEH HEH HEH.*

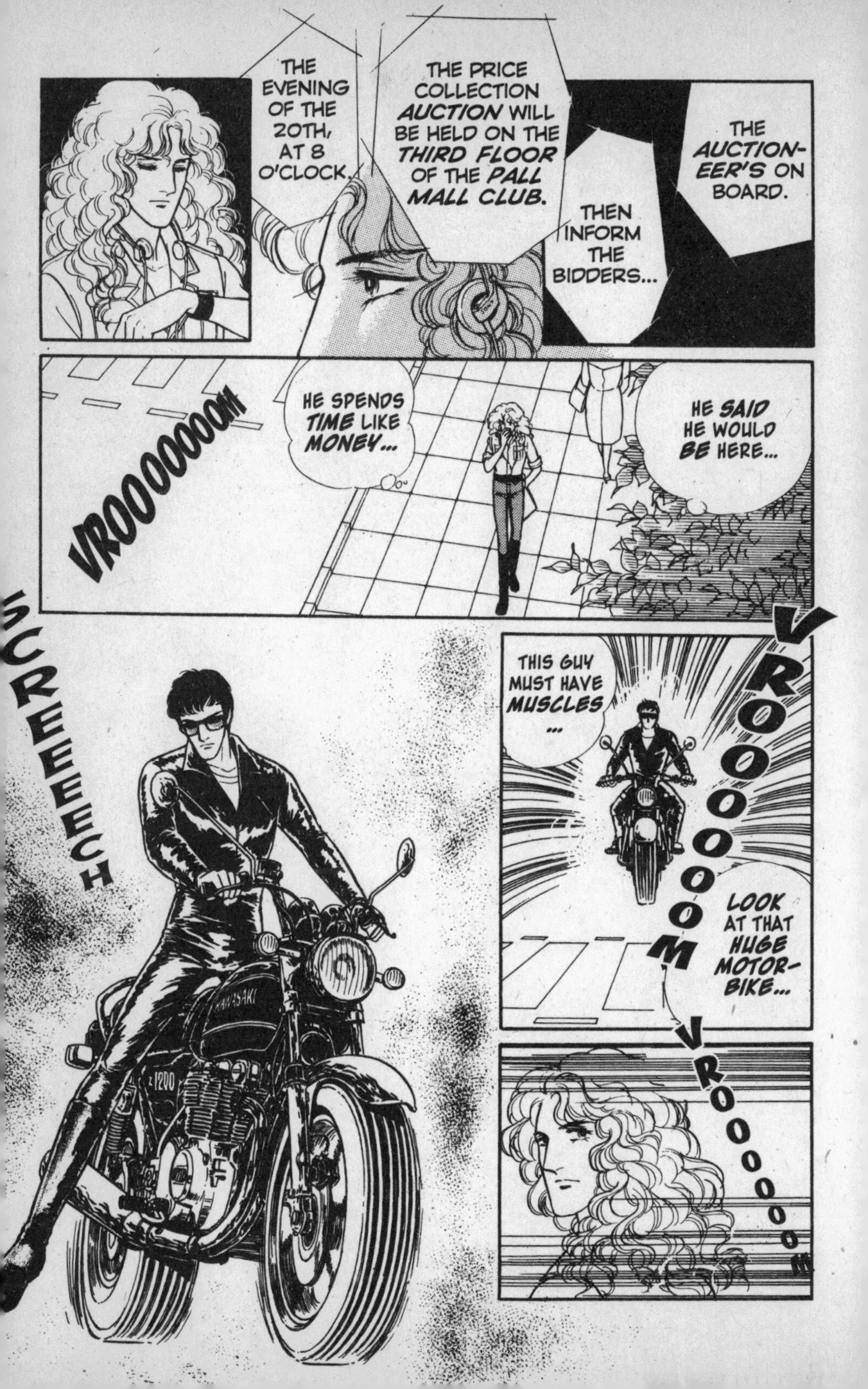
THE AUCTIONEER'S ON BOARD.
THEN INFORM THE BIDDERS...
THE PRICE COLLECTION AUCTION WILL BE HELD ON THE THIRD FLOOR OF THE PALL MALL CLUB.
THE EVENING OF THE 20TH, AT 8 O'CLOCK.
HE SAID HE WOULD BE HERE...
HE SPENDS TIME LIKE MONEY...
VROOOOOOOM
VROOOOOOOM
THIS GUY MUST HAVE MUSCLES ...
LOOK AT THAT HUGE MOTOR-BIKE...
VROOOOOOOOM
SCREEEEECH

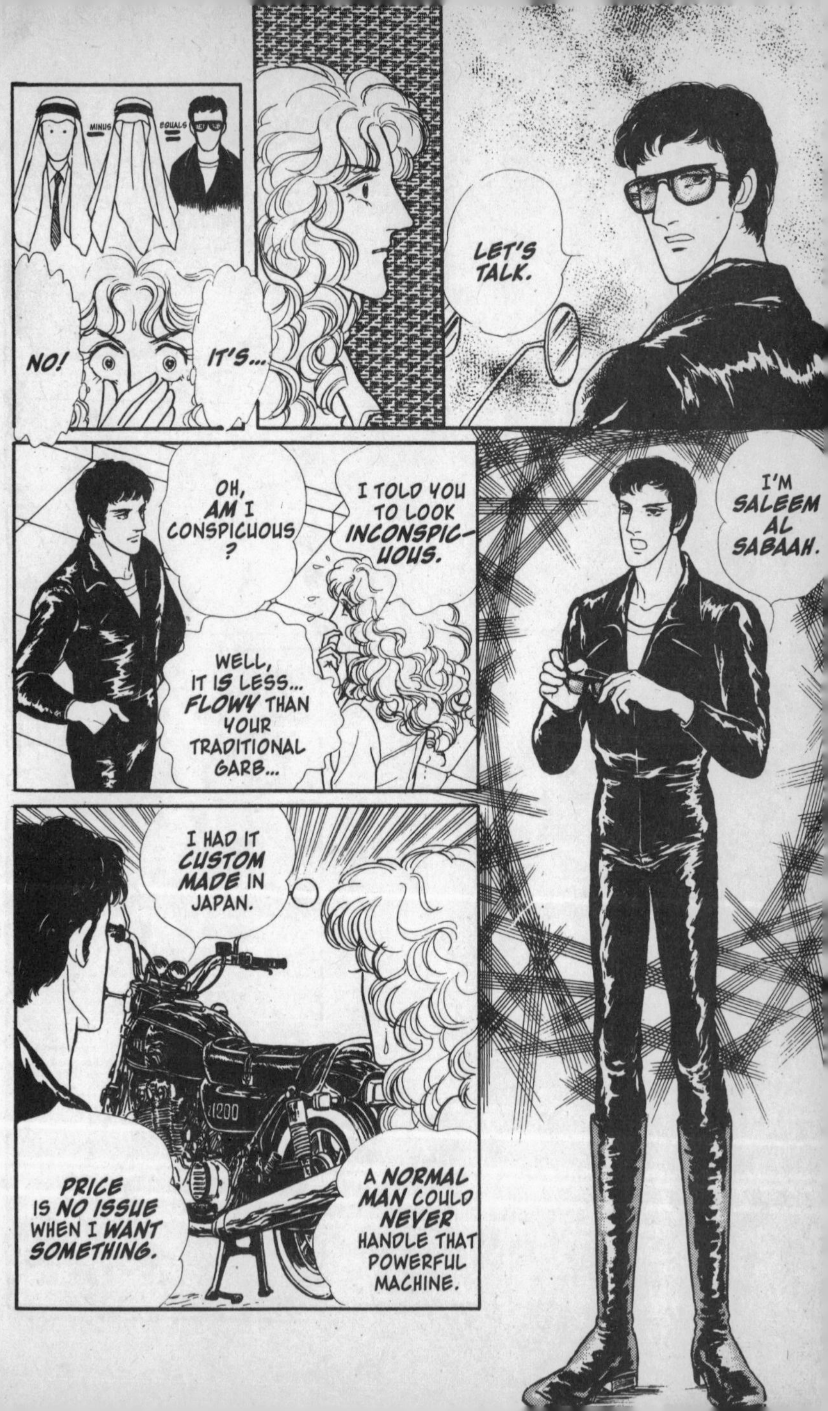
LET'S TALK.
MINUS
EQUALS
IT'S...
NO!
I'M SALEEM AL SABAAH.
I TOLD YOU TO LOOK INCONSPICUOUS.
OH, AM I CONSPICUOUS?
WELL, IT IS LESS... FLOWY THAN YOUR TRADITIONAL GARB...
I HAD IT CUSTOM MADE IN JAPAN.
A NORMAL MAN COULD NEVER HANDLE THAT POWERFUL MACHINE.
PRICE IS NO ISSUE WHEN I WANT SOMETHING.

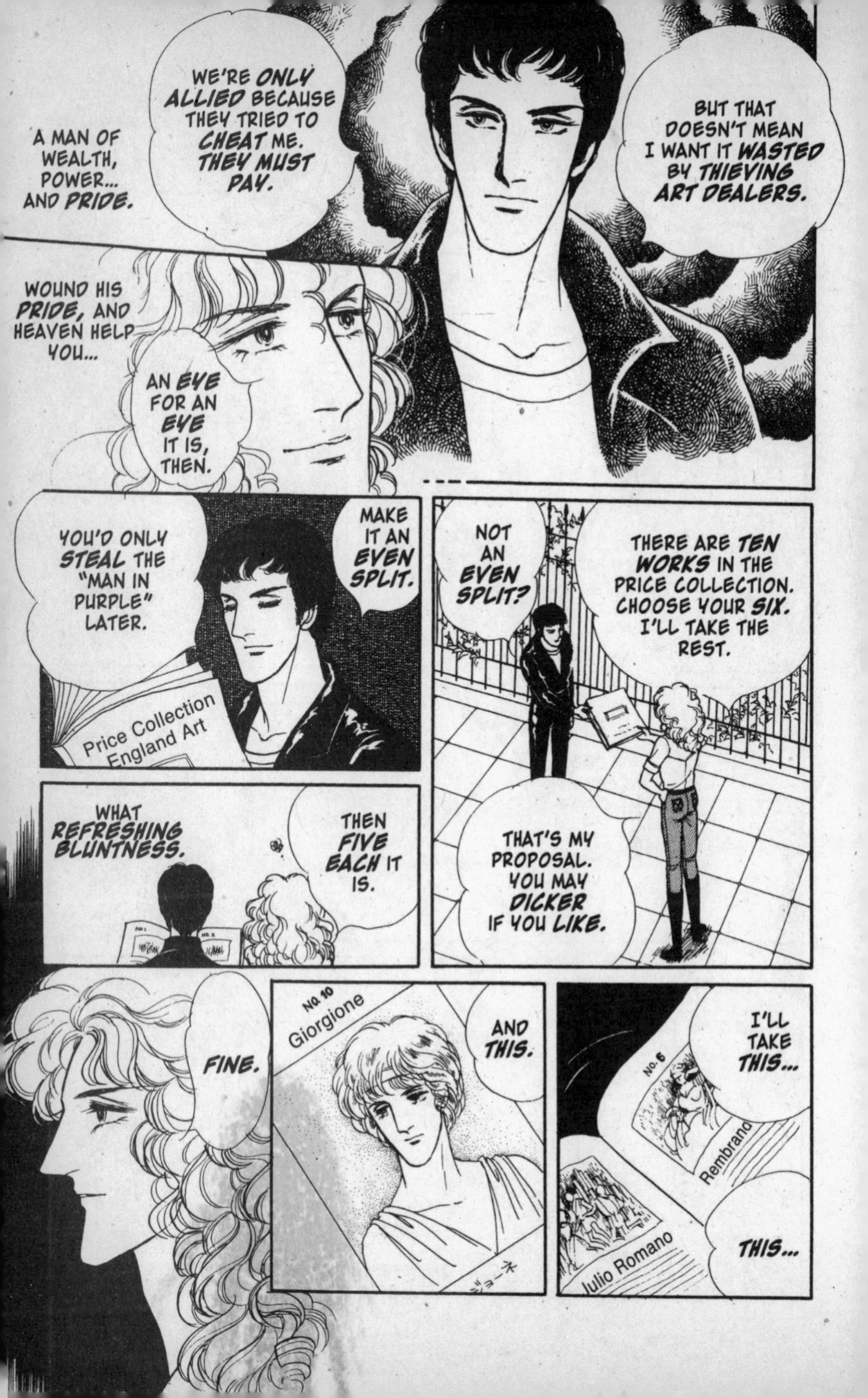
BUT THAT DOESN'T MEAN I WANT IT WASTED BY THIEVING ART DEALERS.
WE'RE ONLY ALLIED BECAUSE THEY TRIED TO CHEAT ME. THEY MUST PAY.
A MAN OF WEALTH, POWER... AND PRIDE.
WOUND HIS PRIDE, AND HEAVEN HELP YOU...
AN EYE FOR AN EYE IT IS, THEN.
THERE ARE TEN WORKS IN THE PRICE COLLECTION. CHOOSE YOUR SIX. I'LL TAKE THE REST.
NOT AN EVEN SPLIT?
THAT'S MY PROPOSAL. YOU MAY DICKER IF YOU LIKE.
MAKE IT AN EVEN SPLIT.
YOU'D ONLY STEAL THE "MAN IN PURPLE" LATER.
Price Collection England Art
THEN FIVE EACH IT IS.
WHAT REFRESHING BLUNTNESS.
I'LL TAKE THIS...
No. 6
Rembrand
THIS...
Iulio Romano
AND THIS.
No. 10
Giorgione
FINE.

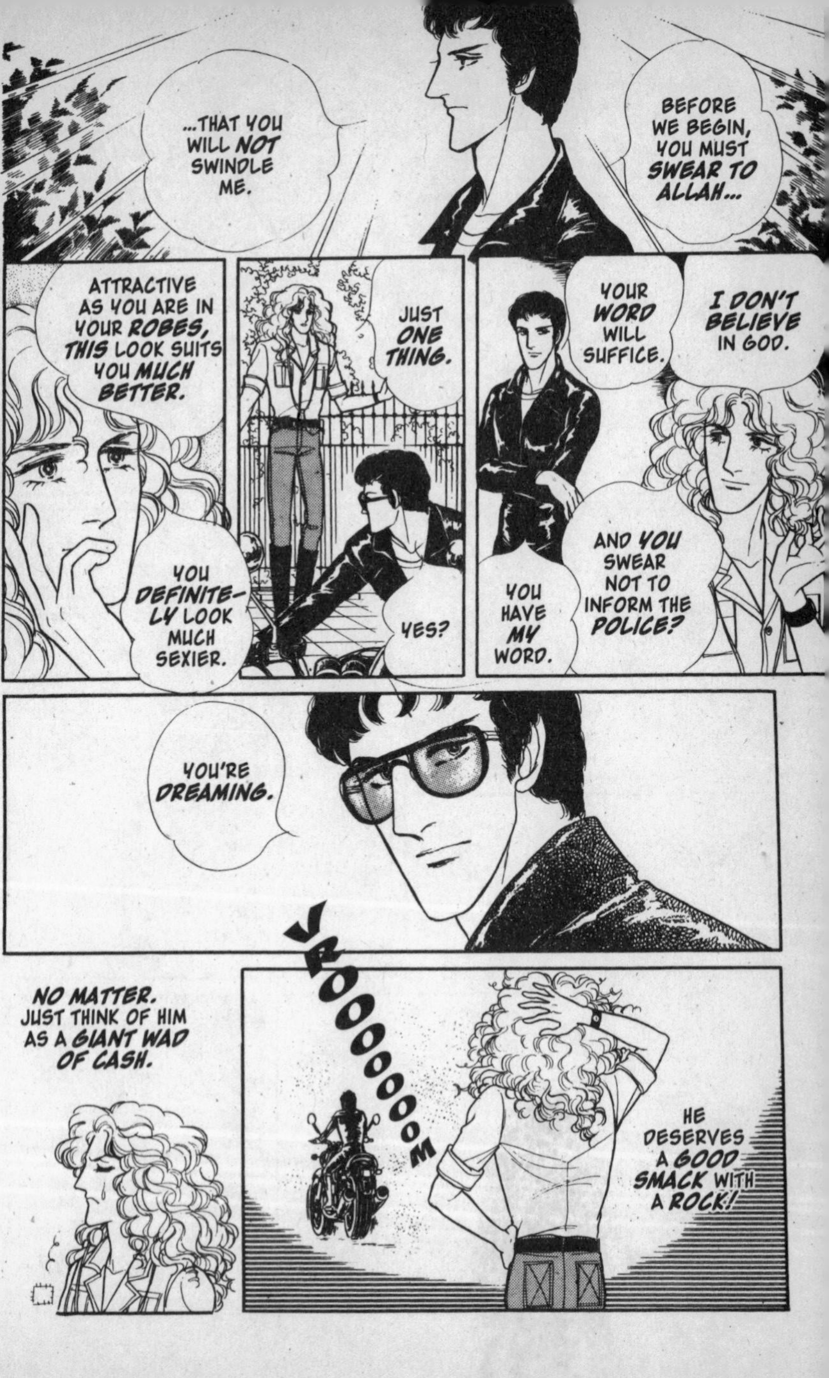
BEFORE WE BEGIN, YOU MUST SWEAR TO ALLAH...
...THAT YOU WILL NOT SWINDLE ME.
I DON'T BELIEVE IN GOD.
YOUR WORD WILL SUFFICE.
AND YOU SWEAR NOT TO INFORM THE POLICE?
YOU HAVE MY WORD.
JUST ONE THING.
YES?
ATTRACTIVE AS YOU ARE IN YOUR ROBES, THIS LOOK SUITS YOU MUCH BETTER.
YOU DEFINITE-LY LOOK MUCH SEXIER.
YOU'RE DREAMING.
VROOOOOOOM
HE DESERVES A GOOD SMACK WITH A ROCK!
NO MATTER. JUST THINK OF HIM AS A GIANT WAD OF CASH.

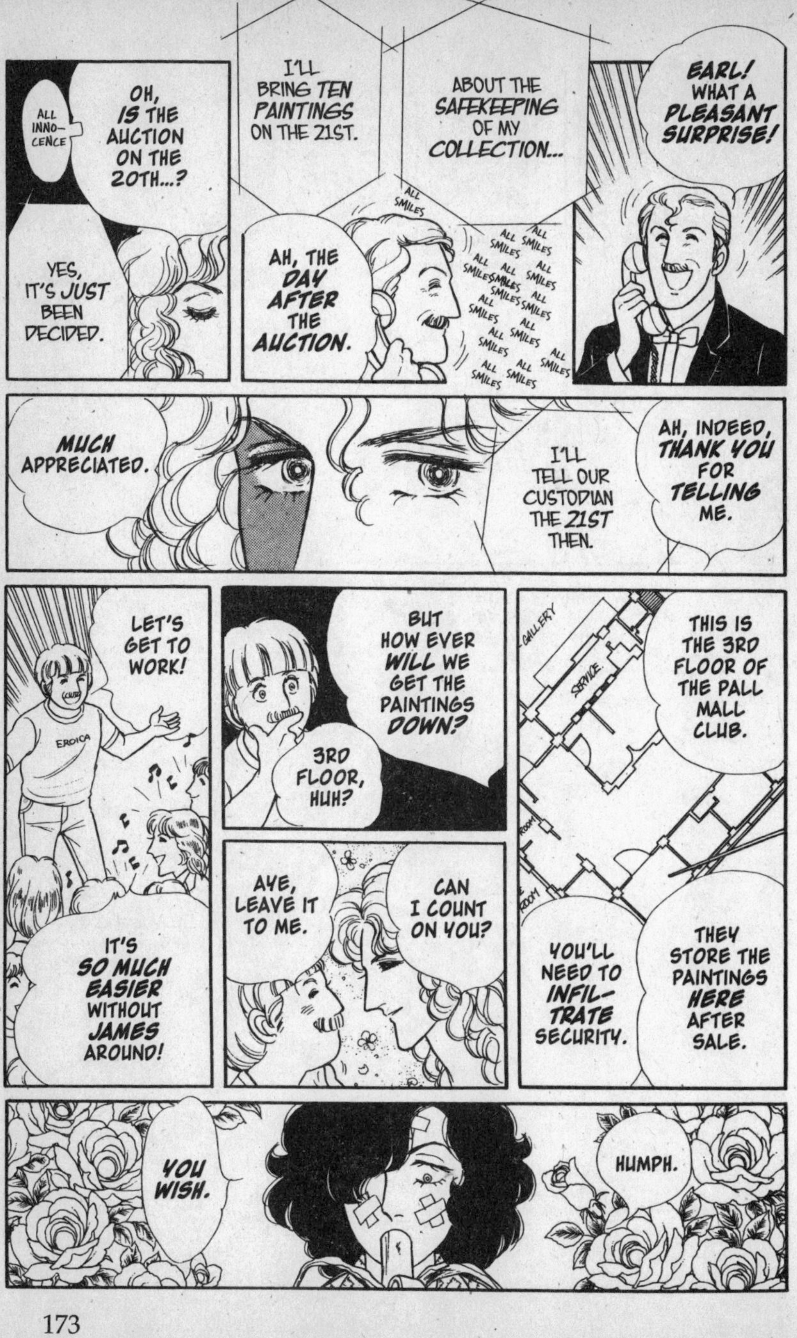

EARL! WHAT A PLEASANT SURPRISE!
ALL SMILES
ABOUT THE SAFEKEEPING OF MY COLLECTION...
I'LL BRING TEN PAINTINGS ON THE 21ST.
AH, THE DAY AFTER THE AUCTION.
OH, IS THE AUCTION ON THE 20TH...?
ALL INNOCENCE
YES, IT'S JUST BEEN DECIDED.
AH, INDEED, THANK YOU FOR TELLING ME.
I'LL TELL OUR CUSTODIAN THE 21ST THEN.
MUCH APPRECIATED.
THIS IS THE 3RD FLOOR OF THE PALL MALL CLUB.
GALLERY
SERVICE
THEY STORE THE PAINTINGS HERE AFTER SALE.
YOU'LL NEED TO INFILTRATE SECURITY.
BUT HOW EVER WILL WE GET THE PAINTINGS DOWN?
3RD FLOOR, HUH?
CAN I COUNT ON YOU?
AYE, LEAVE IT TO ME.
LET'S GET TO WORK!
EROICA
IT'S SO MUCH EASIER WITHOUT JAMES AROUND!
HUMPH.
YOU WISH.

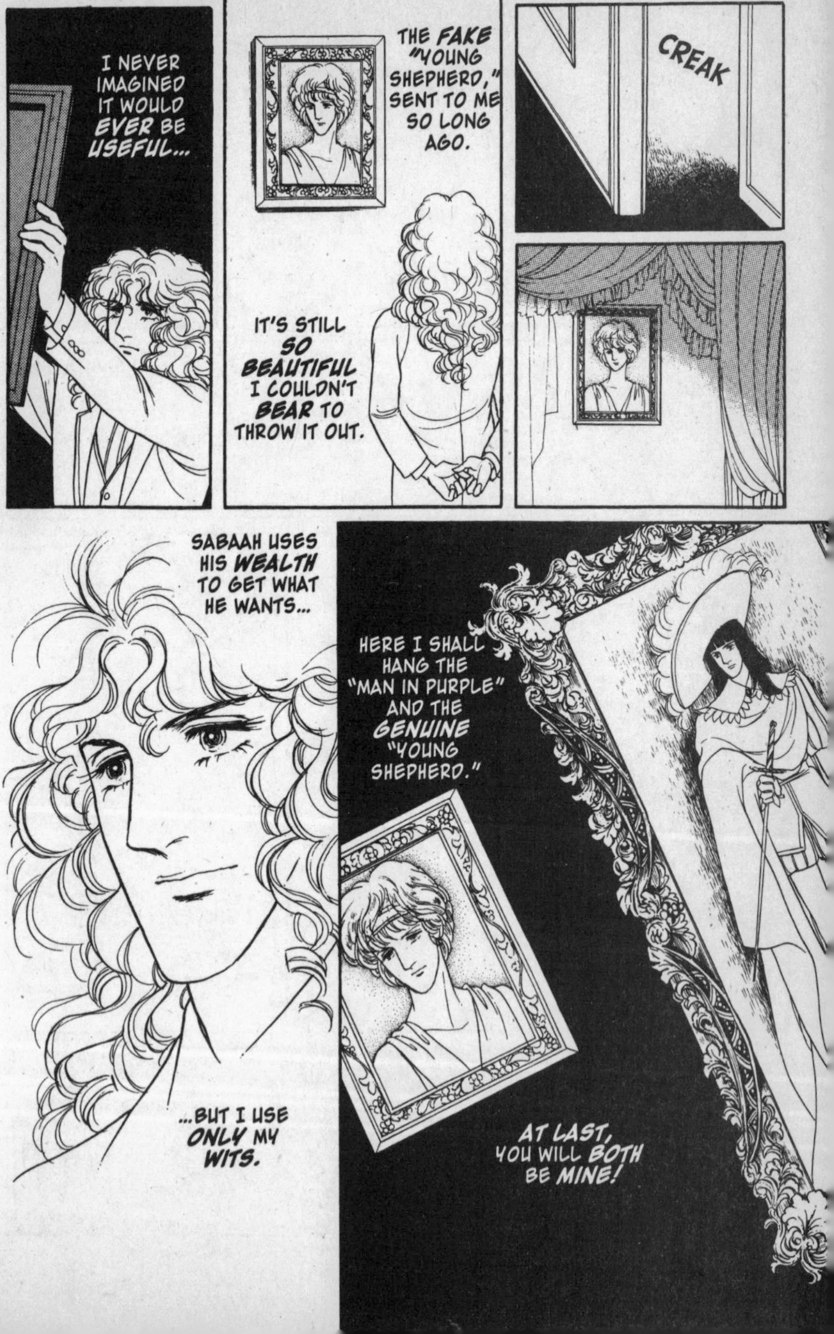
CREAK
THE FAKE "YOUNG SHEPHERD," SENT TO ME SO LONG AGO.
IT'S STILL SO BEAUTIFUL I COULDN'T BEAR TO THROW IT OUT.
I NEVER IMAGINED IT WOULD EVER BE USEFUL...
HERE I SHALL HANG THE "MAN IN PURPLE" AND THE GENUINE "YOUNG SHEPHERD."
AT LAST, YOU WILL BOTH BE MINE!
SABAAH USES HIS WEALTH TO GET WHAT HE WANTS...
...BUT I USE ONLY MY WITS.

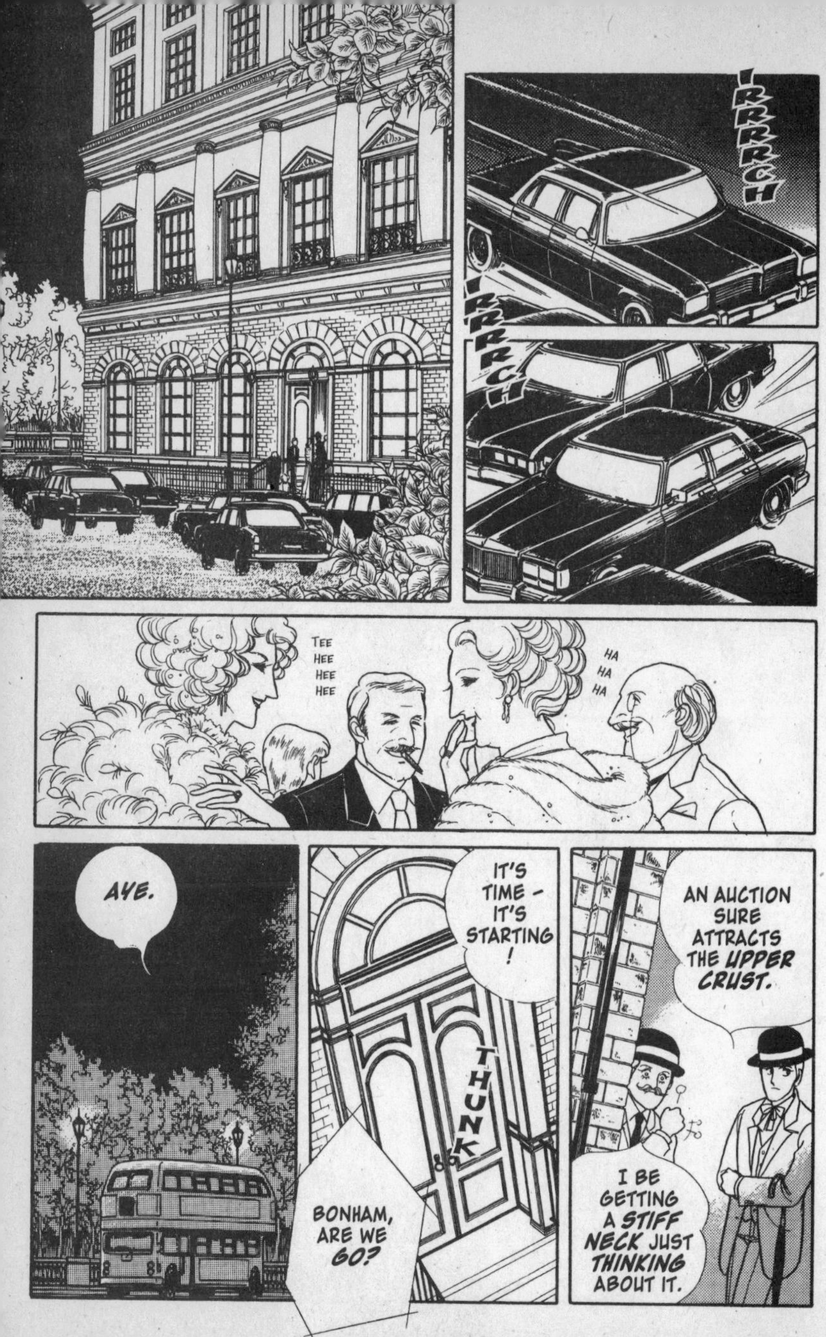
IRRRRCH
IRRRRCH
HA HA HA
TEE HEE HEE HEE
AN AUCTION SURE ATTRACTS THE UPPER CRUST.
I BE GETTING A STIFF NECK JUST THINKING ABOUT IT.
IT'S TIME - IT'S STARTING!
THUNK
BONHAM, ARE WE GO?
AYE.

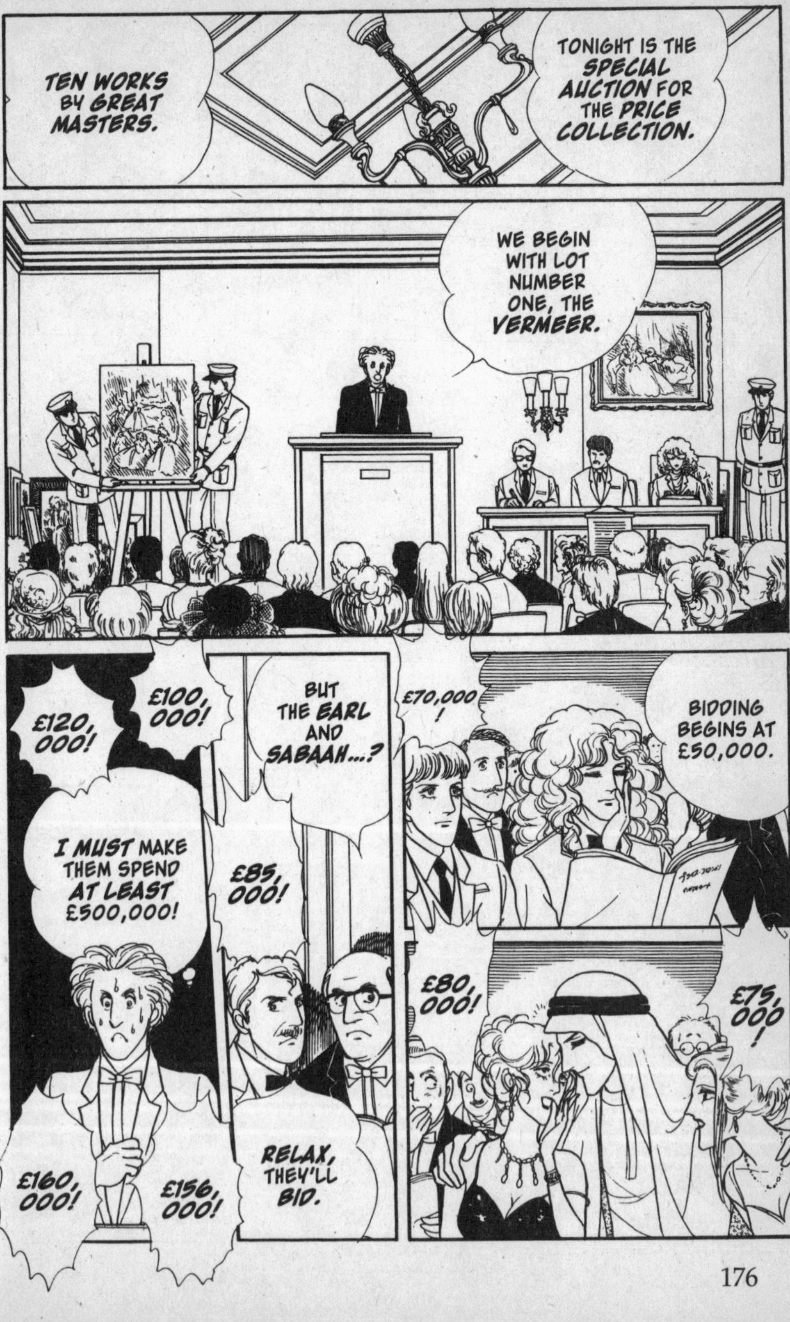
TONIGHT IS THE SPECIAL AUCTION FOR THE PRICE COLLECTION.
TEN WORKS BY GREAT MASTERS.
WE BEGIN WITH LOT NUMBER ONE, THE VERMEER.
BIDDING BEGINS AT £50,000.
£70,000!
£75,000!
£80,000!
BUT THE EARL AND SABAAH...?
£85,000!
RELAX, THEY'LL BID.
£100,000!
£120,000!
I MUST MAKE THEM SPEND AT LEAST £500,000!
£156,000!
£160,000!

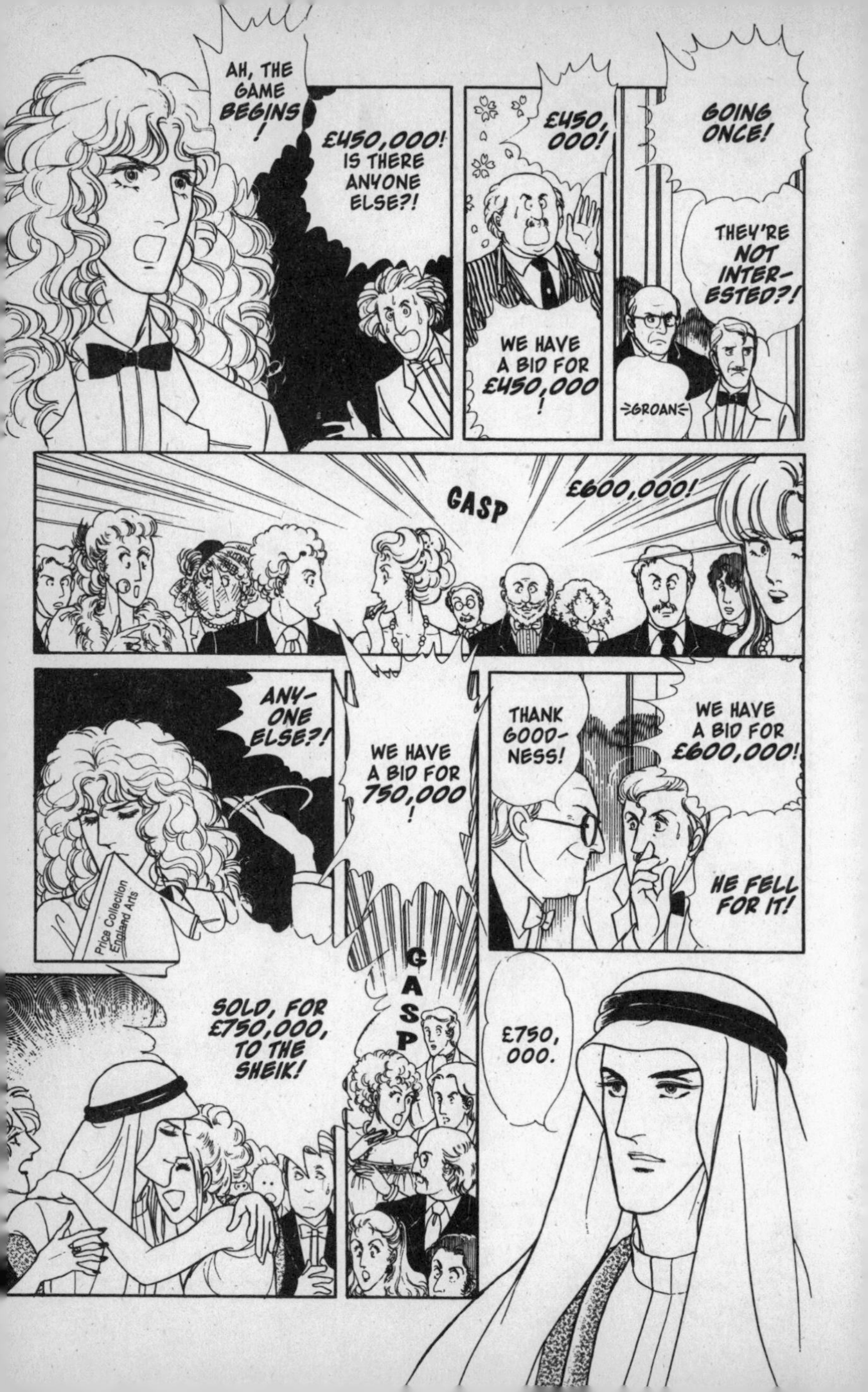
GOING ONCE!
THEY'RE NOT INTER-ESTED?!
GROAN
£450,000!
WE HAVE A BID FOR £450,000!
£450,000! IS THERE ANYONE ELSE?!
AH, THE GAME BEGINS!
£600,000!
GASP
WE HAVE A BID FOR £600,000!
THANK GOOD-NESS!
HE FELL FOR IT!
WE HAVE A BID FOR 750,000!
ANY-ONE ELSE?!
Price Collection England Arts
£750,000.
GASP
SOLD, FOR £750,000, TO THE SHEIK!

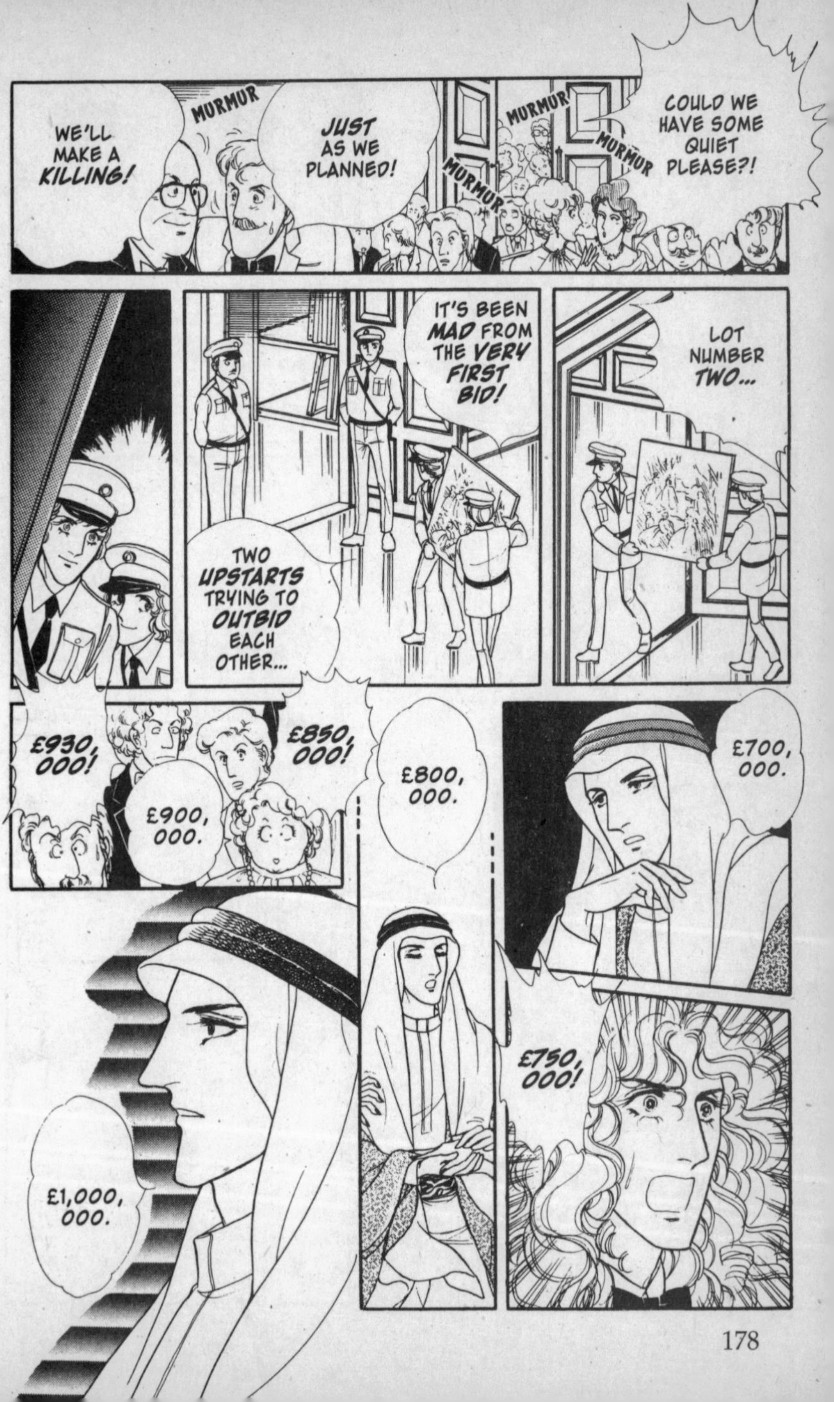
COULD WE HAVE SOME QUIET PLEASE?!
MURMUR
MURMUR
MURMUR
JUST AS WE PLANNED!
MURMUR
WE'LL MAKE A KILLING!
LOT NUMBER TWO...
IT'S BEEN MAD FROM THE VERY FIRST BID!
TWO UPSTARTS TRYING TO OUTBID EACH OTHER...
£700,000.
£750,000!
£800,000.
£850,000!
£900,000.
£930,000!
£1,000,000.

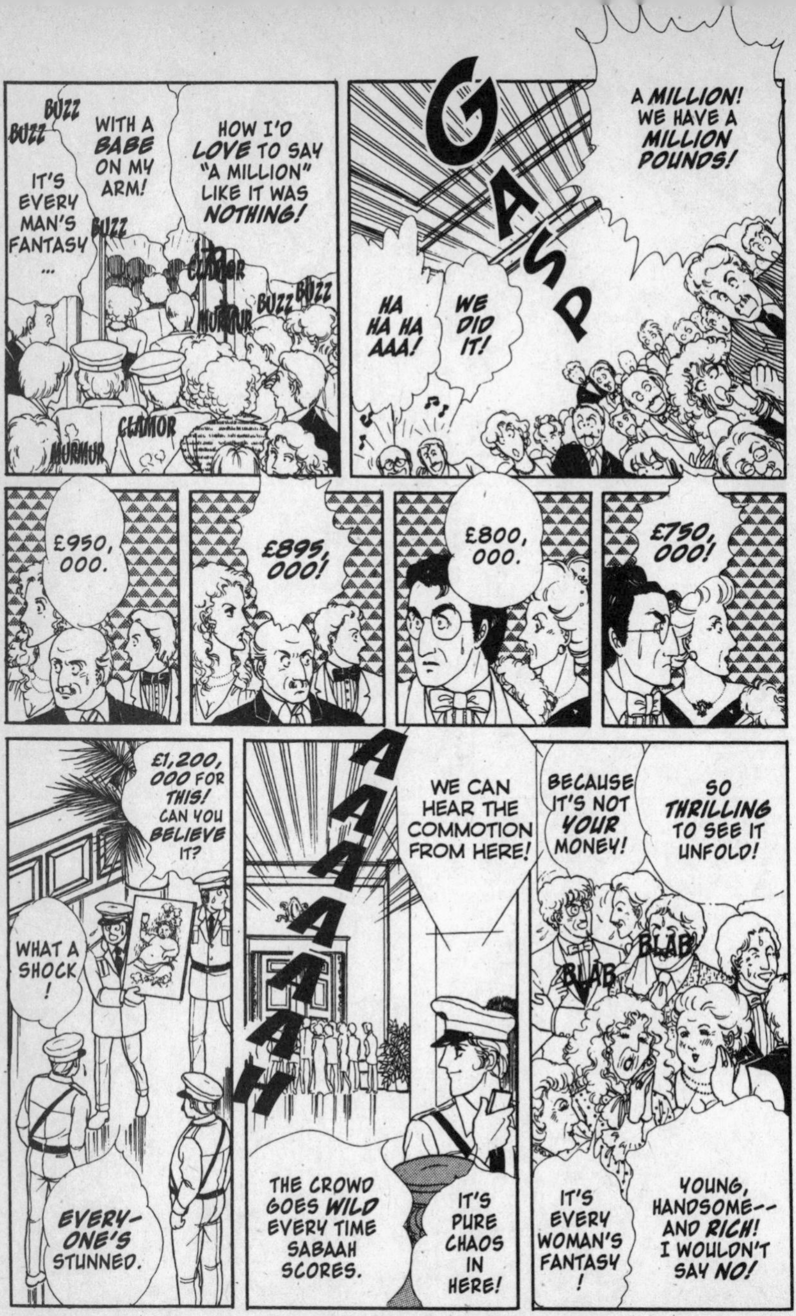
GASP
A MILLION! WE HAVE A MILLION POUNDS!
WE DID IT!
HA HA HA AAA!
HOW I'D LOVE TO SAY "A MILLION" LIKE IT WAS NOTHING!
WITH A BABE ON MY ARM!
IT'S EVERY MAN'S FANTASY...
BUZZ
BUZZ
BUZZ
CLAMOR
MURMUR
BUZZ
BUZZ
CLAMOR
MURMUR
£750,000!
£800,000.
£895,000!
£950,000.
SO THRILLING TO SEE IT UNFOLD!
BECAUSE IT'S NOT YOUR MONEY!
BLAB
BLAB
YOUNG, HANDSOME-- AND RICH! I WOULDN'T SAY NO!
IT'S EVERY WOMAN'S FANTASY!
WE CAN HEAR THE COMMOTION FROM HERE!
AAAAAAAH
IT'S PURE CHAOS IN HERE!
THE CROWD GOES WILD EVERY TIME SABAAH SCORES.
£1,200,000 FOR THIS! CAN YOU BELIEVE IT?
WHAT A SHOCK!
EVERYONE'S STUNNED.

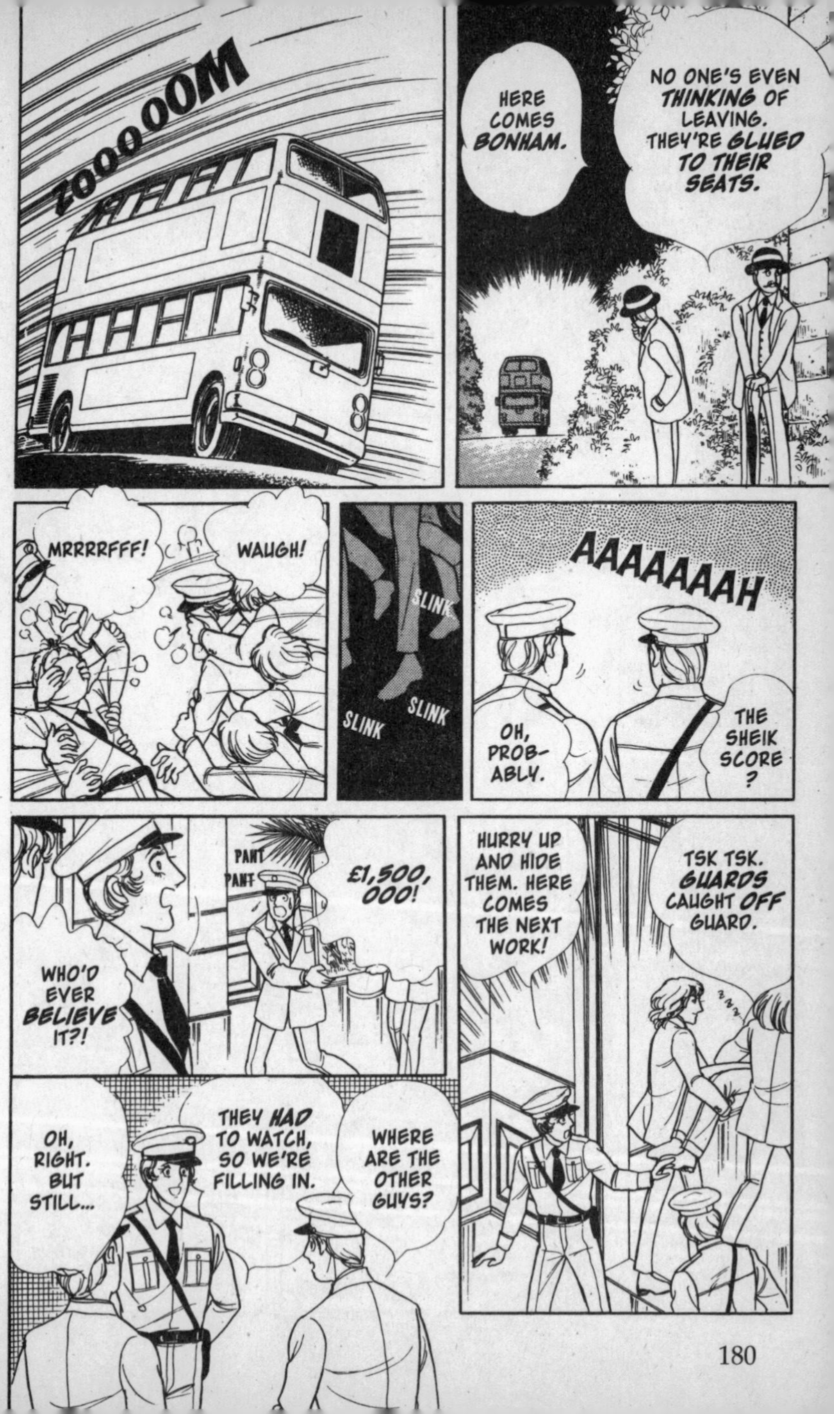
NO ONE'S EVEN THINKING OF LEAVING. THEY'RE GLUED TO THEIR SEATS.
HERE COMES BONHAM.
ZOOOOOOM
AAAAAAAH
THE SHEIK SCORE?
OH, PROB-ABLY.
SLINK
SLINK
SLINK
WAUGH!
MRRRRFFF!
TSK TSK. GUARDS CAUGHT OFF GUARD.
HURRY UP AND HIDE THEM. HERE COMES THE NEXT WORK!
£1,500, 000!
PANT
PANT
WHO'D EVER BELIEVE IT?!
WHERE ARE THE OTHER GUYS?
THEY HAD TO WATCH, SO WE'RE FILLING IN.
OH, RIGHT. BUT STILL...

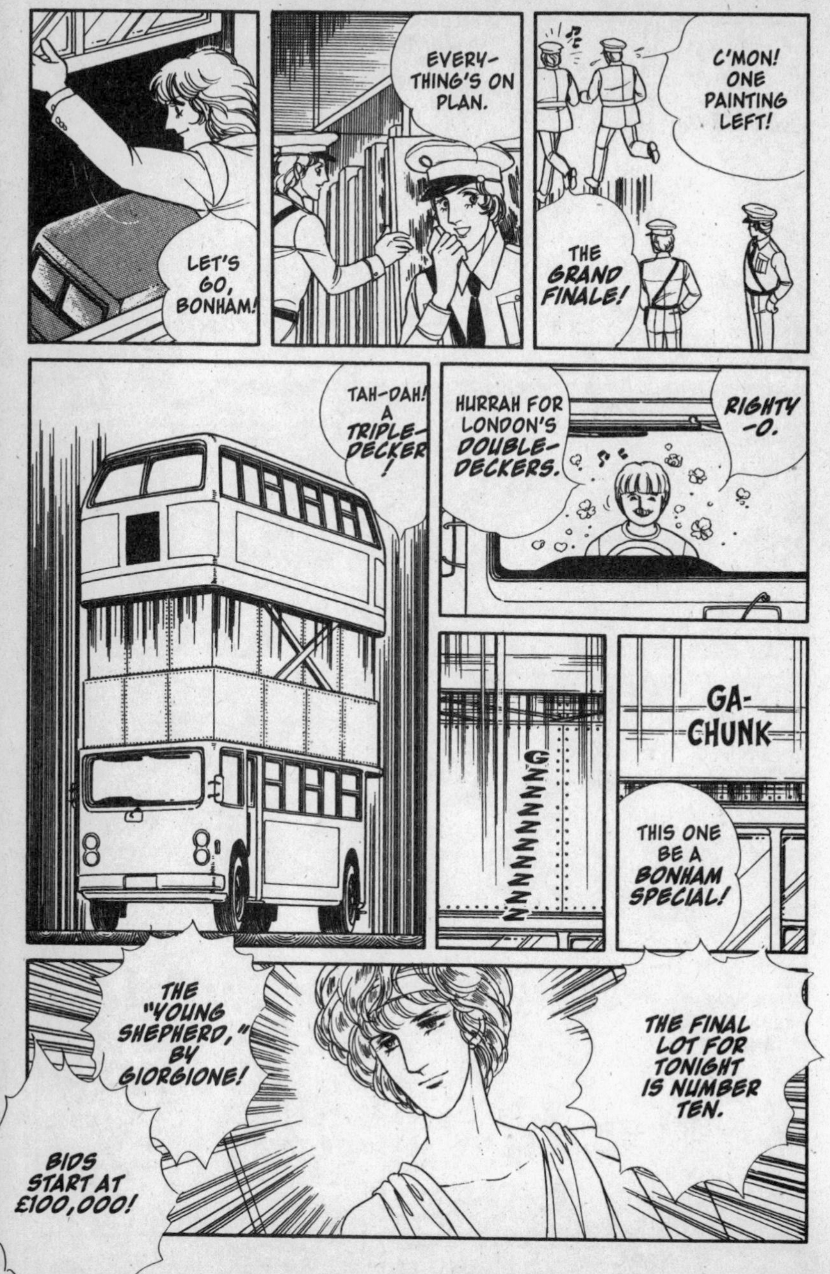
C'MON! ONE PAINTING LEFT!
THE GRAND FINALE!
EVERY-THING'S ON PLAN.
LET'S GO, BONHAM!
RIGHTY-O.
HURRAH FOR LONDON'S DOUBLE-DECKERS.
GA-CHUNK
THIS ONE BE A BONHAM SPECIAL!
GNNNNNNNNN
TAH-DAH! A TRIPLE-DECKER!
THE FINAL LOT FOR TONIGHT IS NUMBER TEN.
THE "YOUNG SHEPHERD," BY GIORGIONE!
BIDS START AT £100,000!

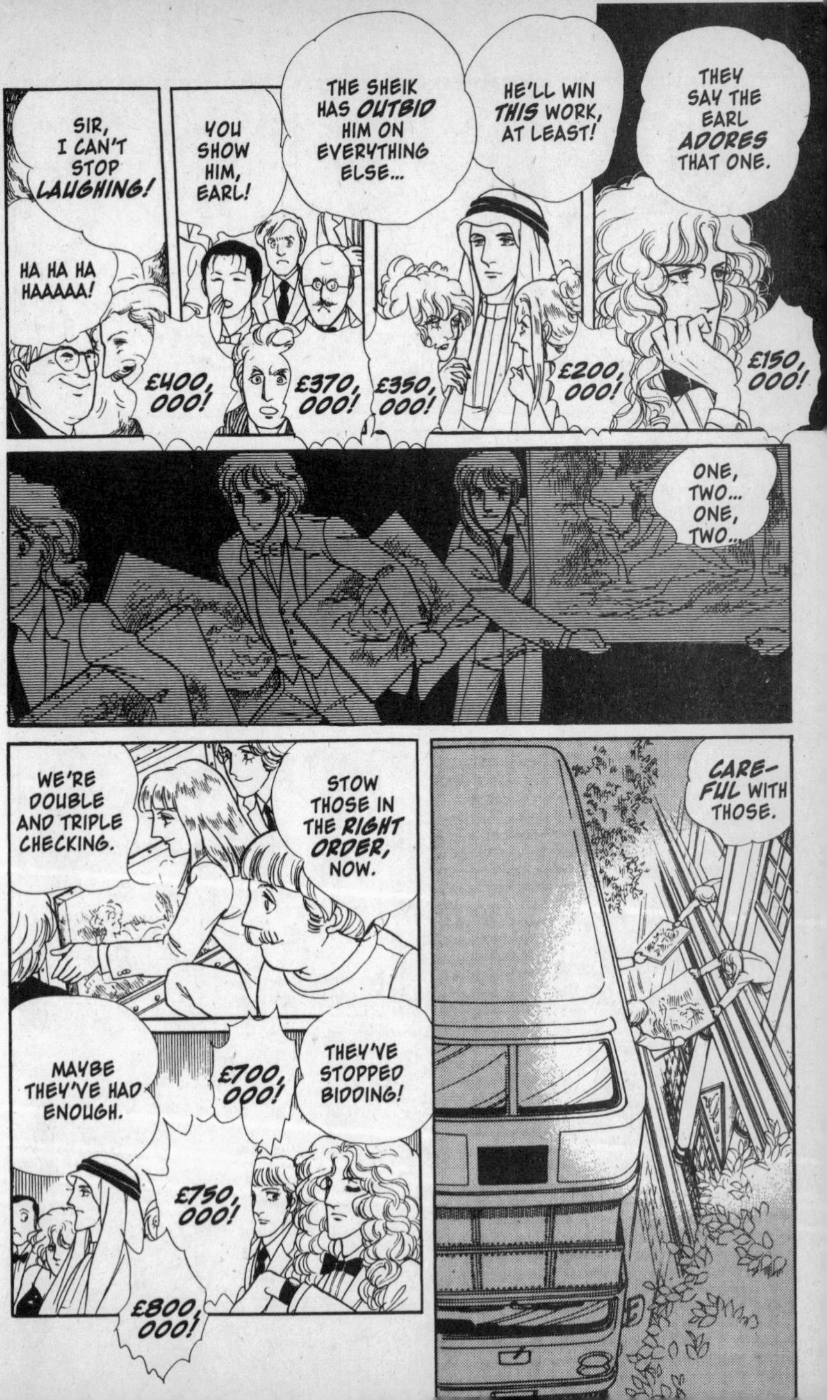
THEY SAY THE EARL ADORES THAT ONE.
£150,000!
THE SHEIK HAS OUTBID HIM ON EVERYTHING ELSE...
HE'LL WIN THIS WORK, AT LEAST!
£200,000!
£350,000!
YOU SHOW HIM, EARL!
£370,000!
£400,000!
SIR, I CAN'T STOP LAUGHING!
HA HA HA HAAAAA!
ONE, TWO... ONE, TWO...
CAREFUL WITH THOSE.
STOW THOSE IN THE RIGHT ORDER, NOW.
WE'RE DOUBLE AND TRIPLE CHECKING.
THEY'VE STOPPED BIDDING!
£700,000!
MAYBE THEY'VE HAD ENOUGH.
£750,000!
£800,000!

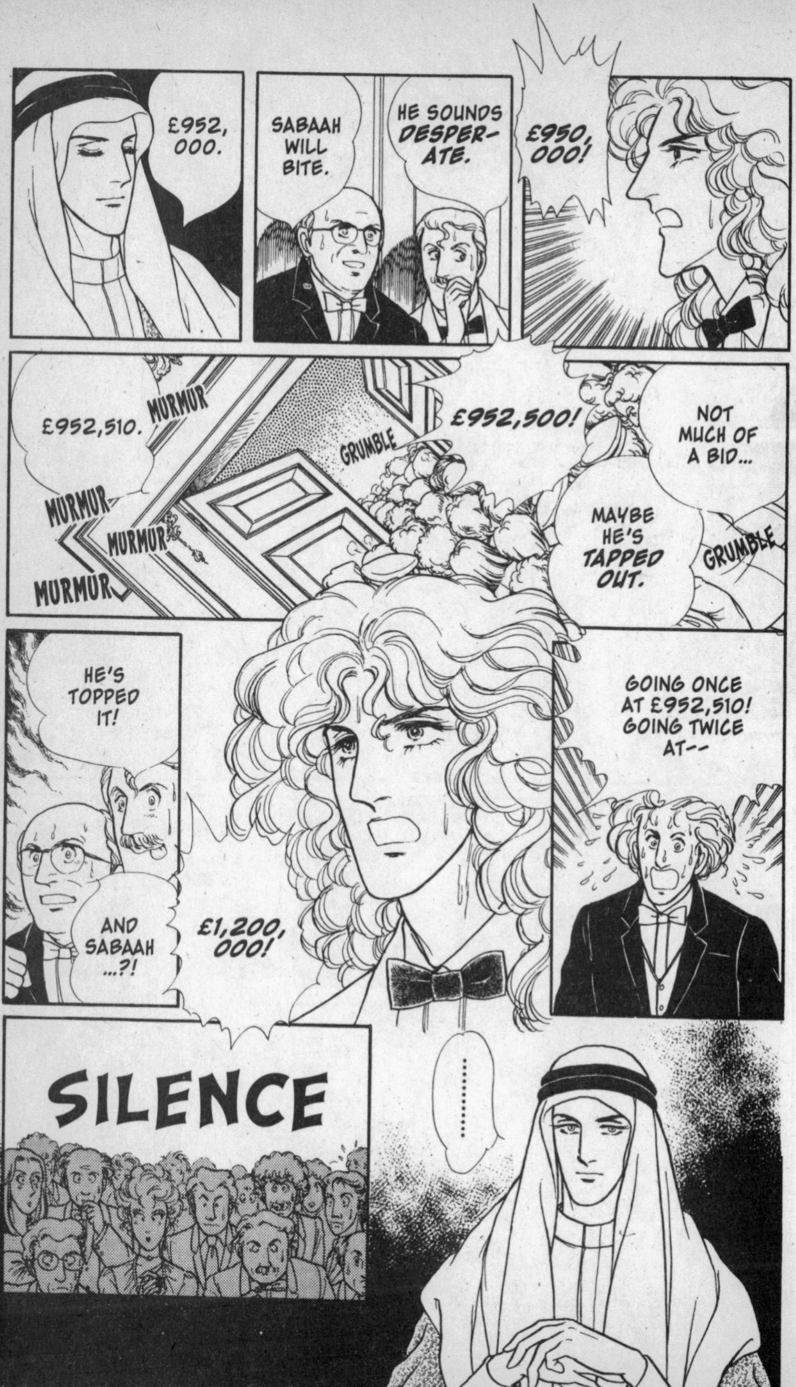
£950,000!
HE SOUNDS DESPERATE.
SABAAH WILL BITE.
£952,000.
NOT MUCH OF A BID...
MAYBE HE'S TAPPED OUT.
GRUMBLE
£952,500!
GRUMBLE
£952,510.
MURMUR
MURMUR
MURMUR
MURMUR
GOING ONCE AT £952,510! GOING TWICE AT--
£1,200,000!
HE'S TOPPED IT!
AND SABAAH ...?!
......
SILENCE

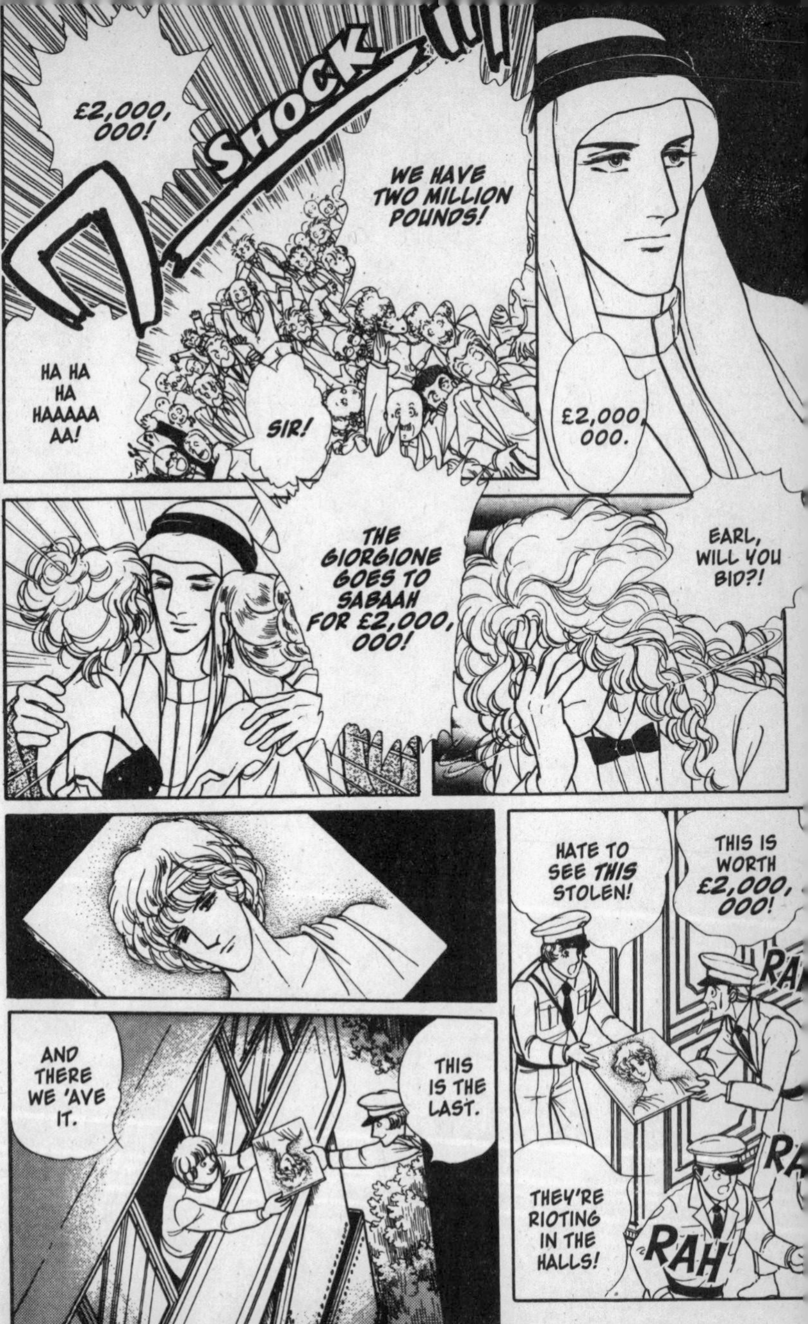

£2,000,000.
SHOCK
WE HAVE TWO MILLION POUNDS!
£2,000,000!
SIR!
HA HA HA HAAAAA AA!
EARL, WILL YOU BID?!
THE GIORGIONE GOES TO SABAAH FOR £2,000,000!
THIS IS WORTH £2,000,000!
HATE TO SEE *THIS* STOLEN!
RA
RA
THEY'RE RIOTING IN THE HALLS!
RAH
THIS IS THE LAST.
AND THERE WE 'AVE IT.

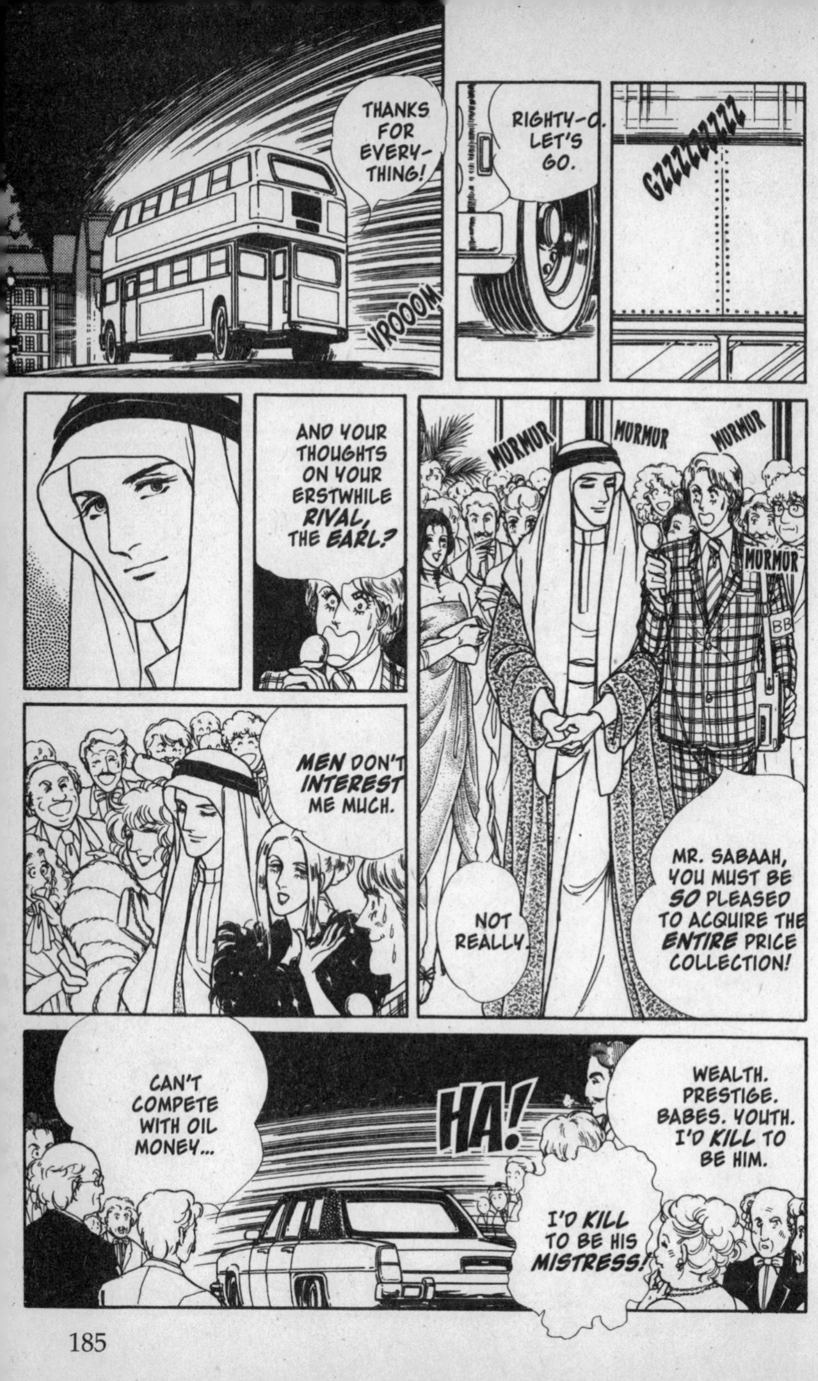
GZZZZZZZZZ
RIGHTY-O. LET'S GO.
THANKS FOR EVERY-THING!
VROOOM
MURMUR
MURMUR
MURMUR
MURMUR
MR. SABAAH, YOU MUST BE *SO* PLEASED TO ACQUIRE THE *ENTIRE* PRICE COLLECTION!
NOT REALLY.
AND YOUR THOUGHTS ON YOUR ERSTWHILE *RIVAL*, THE *EARL?*
MEN DON'T *INTEREST* ME MUCH.
WEALTH. PRESTIGE. BABES. YOUTH. I'D *KILL* TO BE HIM.
I'D *KILL* TO BE HIS *MISTRESS!*
HA!
CAN'T COMPETE WITH OIL MONEY...

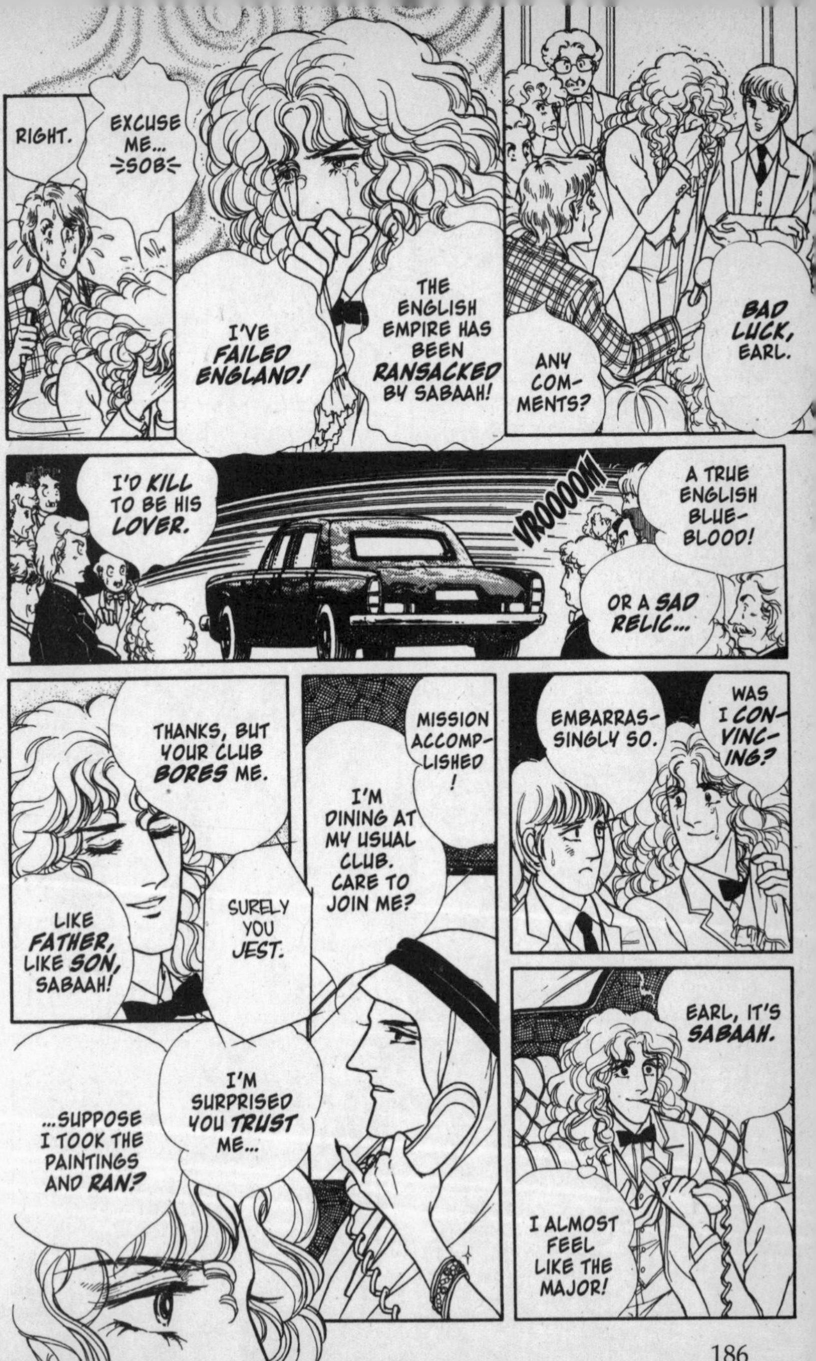
BAD LUCK, EARL.
ANY COMMENTS?
THE ENGLISH EMPIRE HAS BEEN RANSACKED BY SABAAH!
I'VE FAILED ENGLAND!
EXCUSE ME... SOB
RIGHT.
A TRUE ENGLISH BLUE-BLOOD!
VROOOOM
OR A SAD RELIC...
I'D KILL TO BE HIS LOVER.
WAS I CONVINCING?
EMBARRASSINGLY SO.
EARL, IT'S SABAAH.
I ALMOST FEEL LIKE THE MAJOR!
MISSION ACCOMPLISHED!
I'M DINING AT MY USUAL CLUB. CARE TO JOIN ME?
THANKS, BUT YOUR CLUB BORES ME.
SURELY YOU JEST.
LIKE FATHER, LIKE SON, SABAAH!
I'M SURPRISED YOU TRUST ME...
...SUPPOSE I TOOK THE PAINTINGS AND RAN?

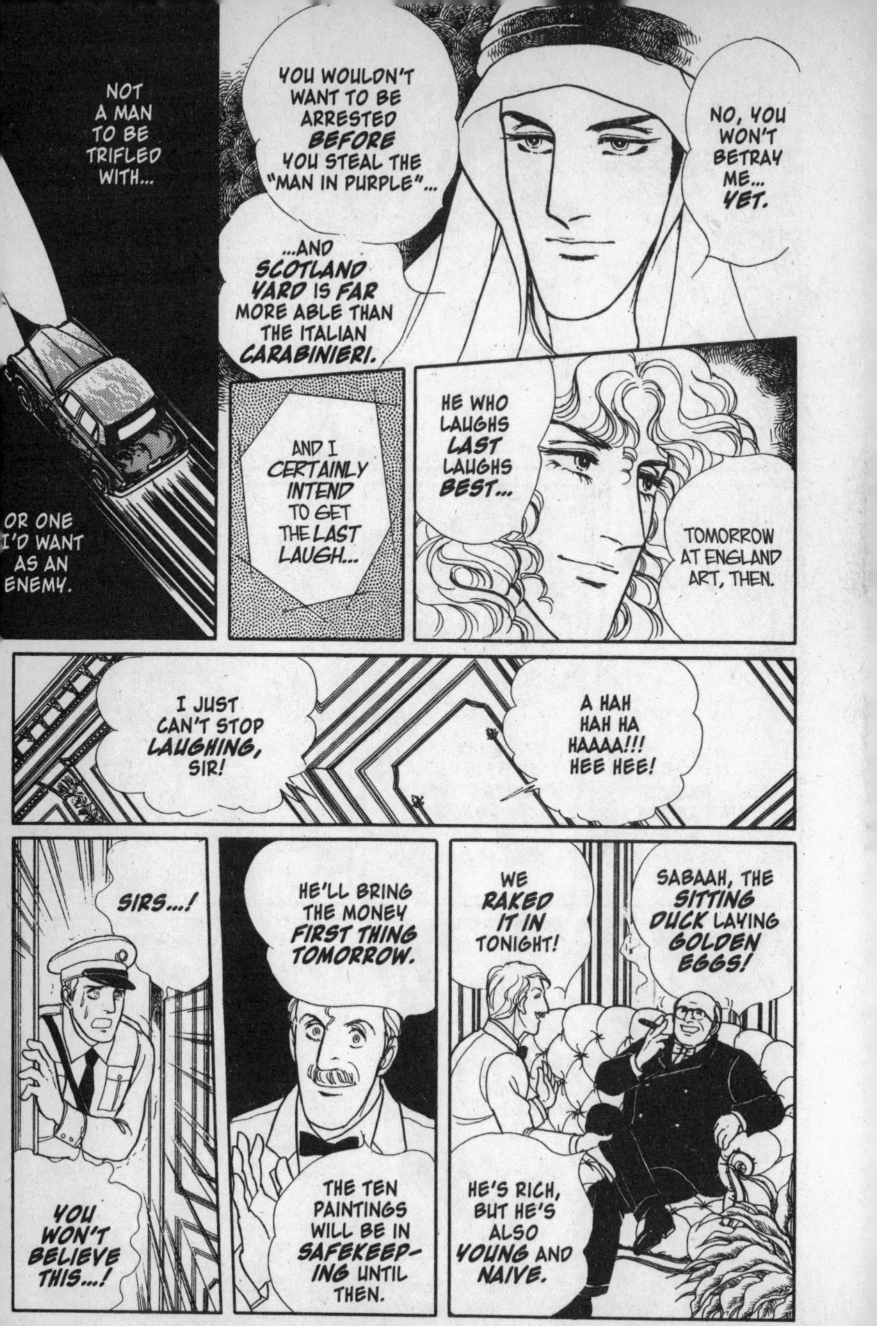
NO, YOU WON'T BETRAY ME... YET.
YOU WOULDN'T WANT TO BE ARRESTED BEFORE YOU STEAL THE "MAN IN PURPLE"...
...AND SCOTLAND YARD IS FAR MORE ABLE THAN THE ITALIAN CARABINIERI.
TOMORROW AT ENGLAND ART, THEN.
HE WHO LAUGHS LAST LAUGHS BEST...
AND I CERTAINLY INTEND TO GET THE LAST LAUGH...
NOT A MAN TO BE TRIFLED WITH...
OR ONE I'D WANT AS AN ENEMY.
A HAH HAH HA HAAAA!!! HEE HEE!
I JUST CAN'T STOP LAUGHING, SIR!
SABAAH, THE SITTING DUCK LAYING GOLDEN EGGS!
WE RAKED IT IN TONIGHT!
HE'S RICH, BUT HE'S ALSO YOUNG AND NAIVE.
HE'LL BRING THE MONEY FIRST THING TOMORROW.
THE TEN PAINTINGS WILL BE IN SAFEKEEPING UNTIL THEN.
SIRS...!
YOU WON'T BELIEVE THIS...!

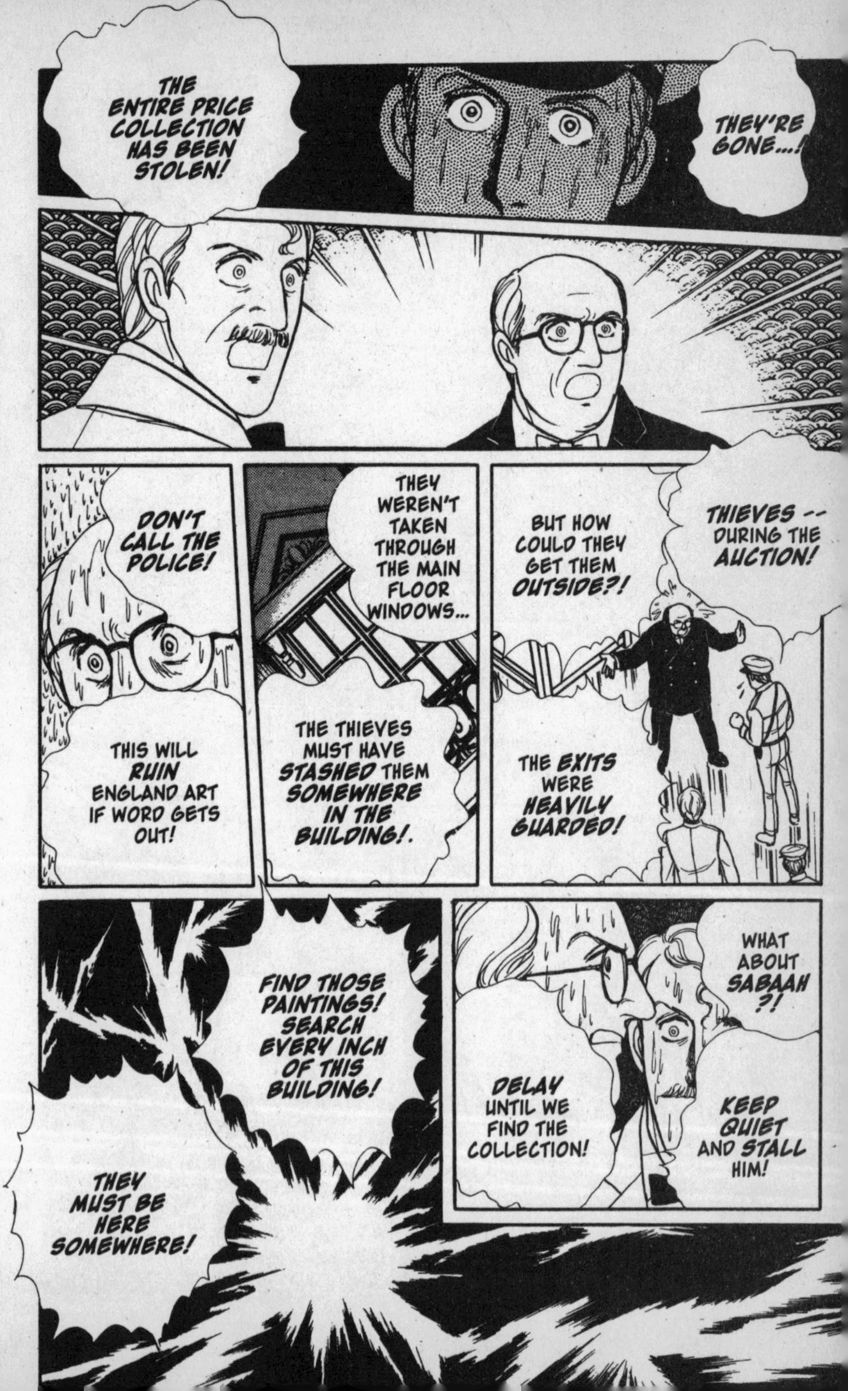
THEY'RE GONE...!
THE ENTIRE PRICE COLLECTION HAS BEEN STOLEN!
THIEVES -- DURING THE AUCTION!
BUT HOW COULD THEY GET THEM OUTSIDE?!
THE EXITS WERE HEAVILY GUARDED!
THEY WEREN'T TAKEN THROUGH THE MAIN FLOOR WINDOWS...
THE THIEVES MUST HAVE STASHED THEM SOMEWHERE IN THE BUILDING!.
DON'T CALL THE POLICE!
THIS WILL RUIN ENGLAND ART IF WORD GETS OUT!
WHAT ABOUT SABAAH?!
KEEP QUIET AND STALL HIM!
DELAY UNTIL WE FIND THE COLLECTION!
FIND THOSE PAINTINGS! SEARCH EVERY INCH OF THIS BUILDING!
THEY MUST BE HERE SOMEWHERE!

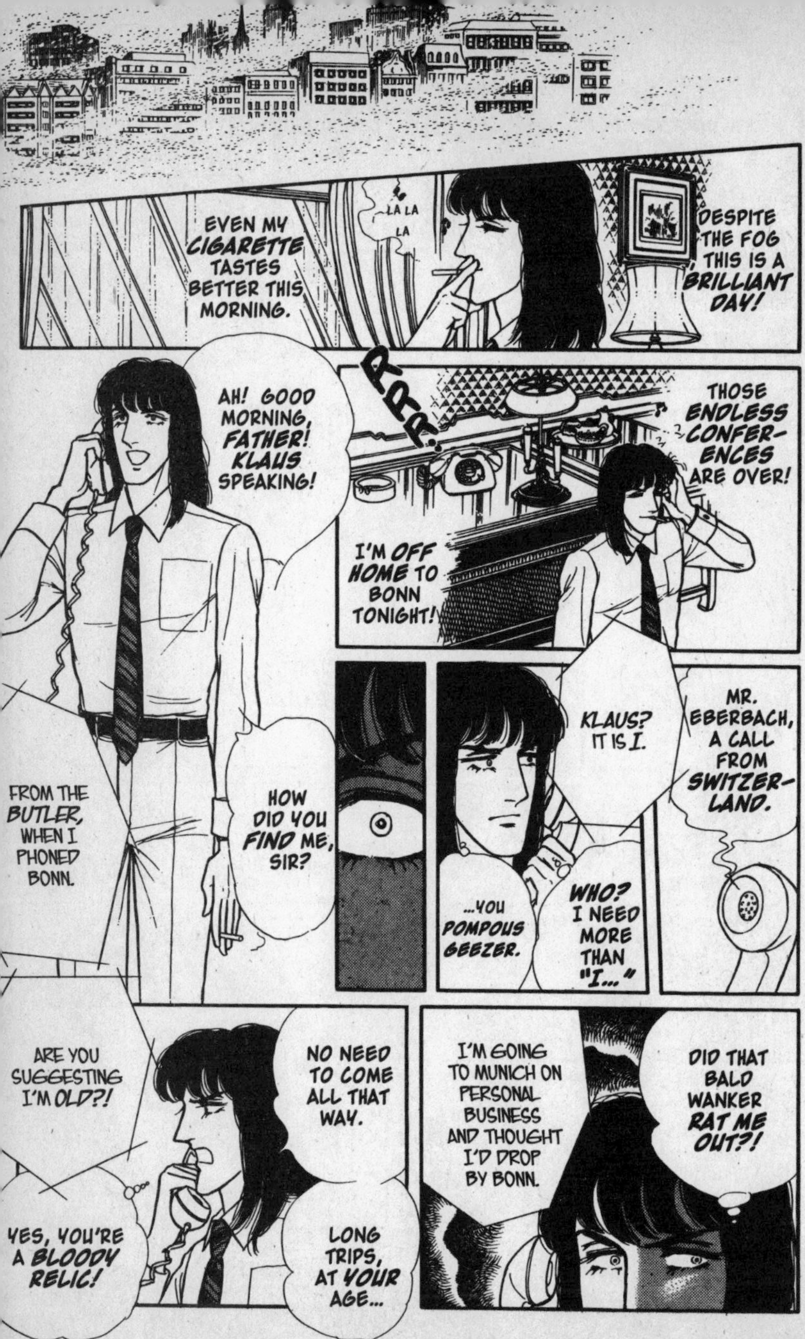
DESPITE THE FOG THIS IS A BRILLIANT DAY!
LA LA LA
EVEN MY CIGARETTE TASTES BETTER THIS MORNING.
THOSE ENDLESS CONFER-ENCES ARE OVER!
RRRR
I'M OFF HOME TO BONN TONIGHT!
MR. EBERBACH, A CALL FROM SWITZER-LAND.
KLAUS? IT IS I.
WHO? I NEED MORE THAN "I..."
...YOU POMPOUS GEEZER.
AH! GOOD MORNING, FATHER! KLAUS SPEAKING!
HOW DID YOU FIND ME, SIR?
FROM THE BUTLER, WHEN I PHONED BONN.
DID THAT BALD WANKER RAT ME OUT?!
I'M GOING TO MUNICH ON PERSONAL BUSINESS AND THOUGHT I'D DROP BY BONN.
NO NEED TO COME ALL THAT WAY.
ARE YOU SUGGESTING I'M OLD?!
LONG TRIPS, AT YOUR AGE...
YES, YOU'RE A BLOODY RELIC!

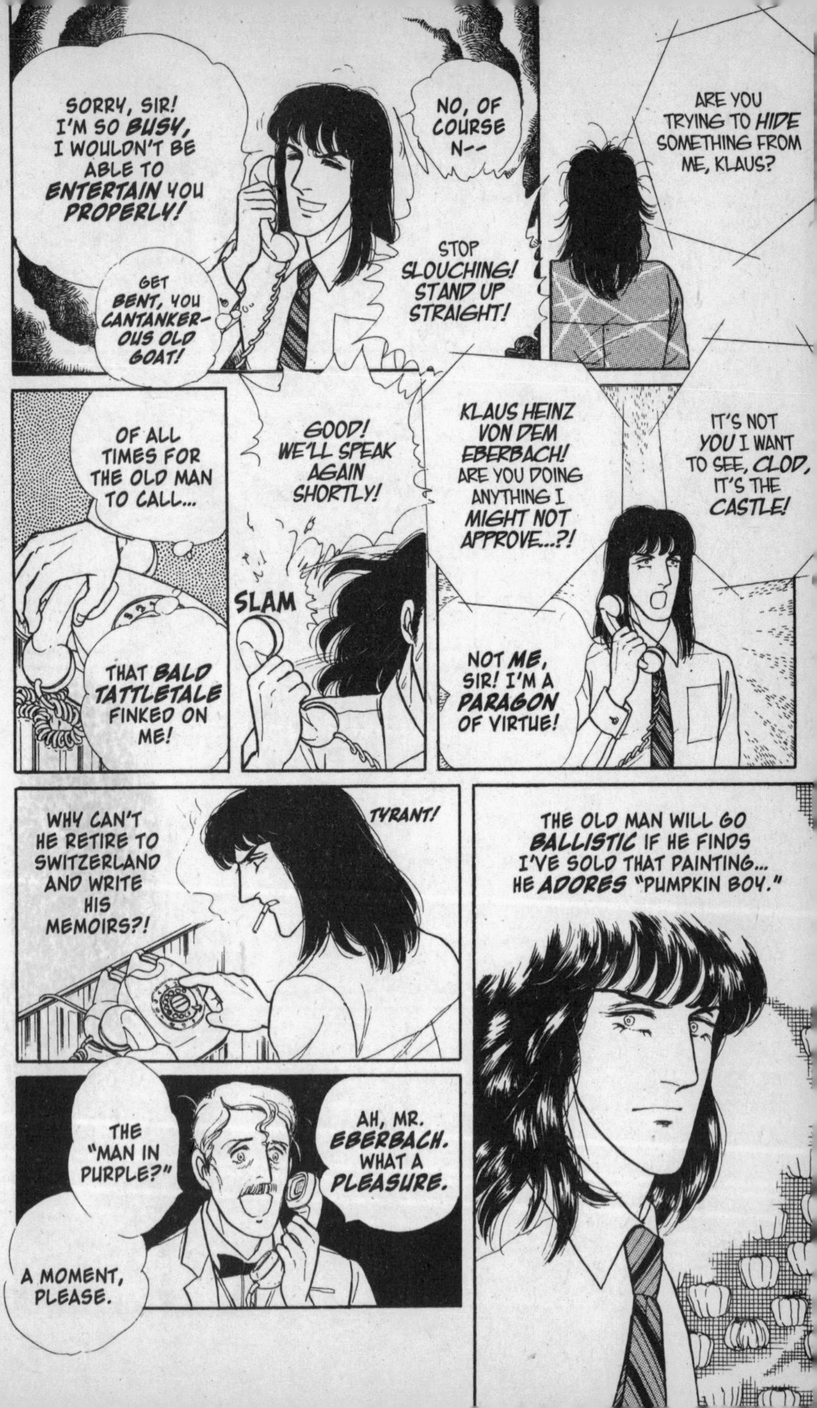
ARE YOU TRYING TO HIDE SOMETHING FROM ME, KLAUS?
NO, OF COURSE N--
STOP SLOUCHING! STAND UP STRAIGHT!
SORRY, SIR! I'M SO BUSY, I WOULDN'T BE ABLE TO ENTERTAIN YOU PROPERLY!
GET BENT, YOU CANTANKEROUS OLD GOAT!
KLAUS HEINZ VON DEM EBERBACH! ARE YOU DOING ANYTHING I MIGHT NOT APPROVE...?!
NOT ME, SIR! I'M A PARAGON OF VIRTUE!
IT'S NOT YOU I WANT TO SEE, CLOD, IT'S THE CASTLE!
GOOD! WE'LL SPEAK AGAIN SHORTLY!
SLAM
OF ALL TIMES FOR THE OLD MAN TO CALL...
THAT BALD TATTLETALE FINKED ON ME!
THE OLD MAN WILL GO BALLISTIC IF HE FINDS I'VE SOLD THAT PAINTING... HE ADORES "PUMPKIN BOY."
TYRANT!
WHY CAN'T HE RETIRE TO SWITZERLAND AND WRITE HIS MEMOIRS?!
AH, MR. EBERBACH. WHAT A PLEASURE.
THE "MAN IN PURPLE?"
A MOMENT, PLEASE.

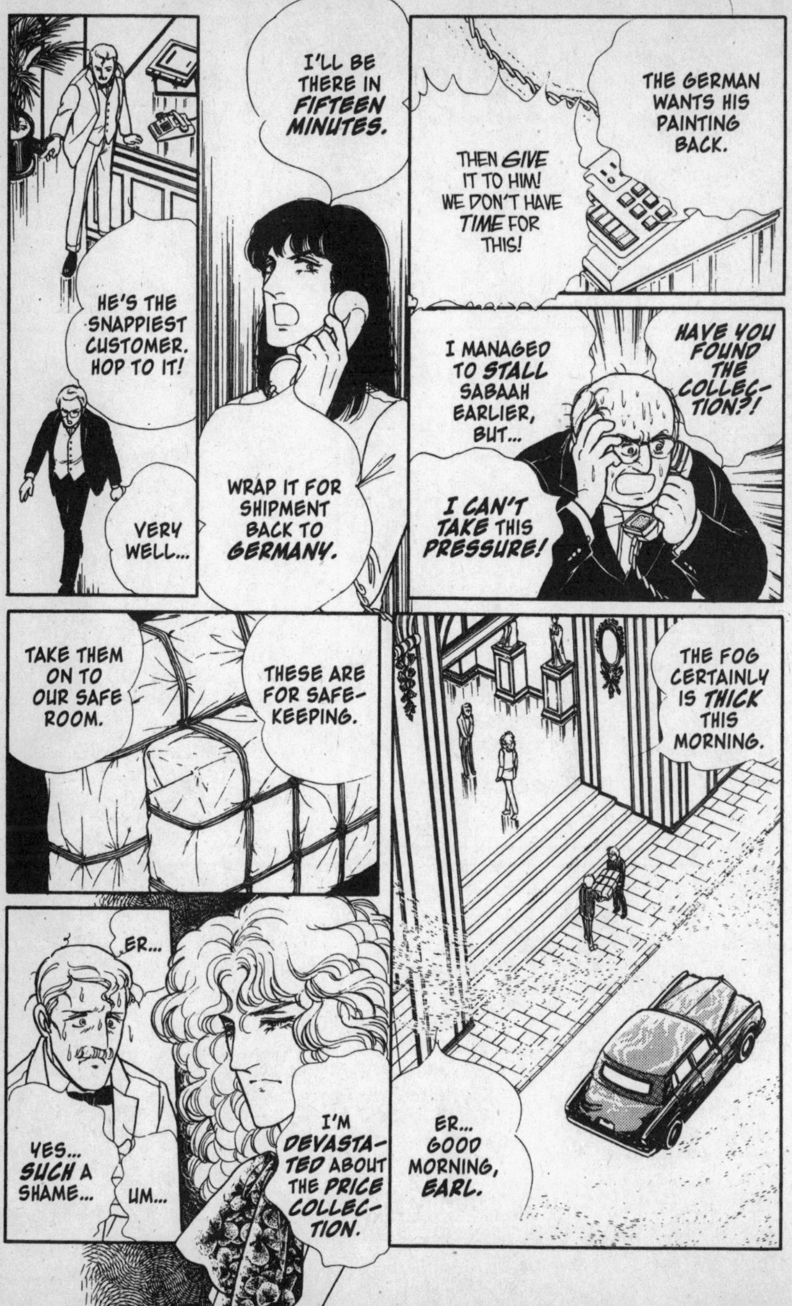
THE GERMAN WANTS HIS PAINTING BACK.
THEN GIVE IT TO HIM! WE DON'T HAVE TIME FOR THIS!
HAVE YOU FOUND THE COLLECTION?!
I MANAGED TO STALL SABAAH EARLIER, BUT...
I CAN'T TAKE THIS PRESSURE!
I'LL BE THERE IN FIFTEEN MINUTES.
WRAP IT FOR SHIPMENT BACK TO GERMANY.
HE'S THE SNAPPIEST CUSTOMER. HOP TO IT!
VERY WELL...
THE FOG CERTAINLY IS THICK THIS MORNING.
ER... GOOD MORNING, EARL.
THESE ARE FOR SAFE-KEEPING.
TAKE THEM ON TO OUR SAFE ROOM.
I'M DEVASTATED ABOUT THE PRICE COLLECTION.
ER...
UM...
YES... SUCH A SHAME...

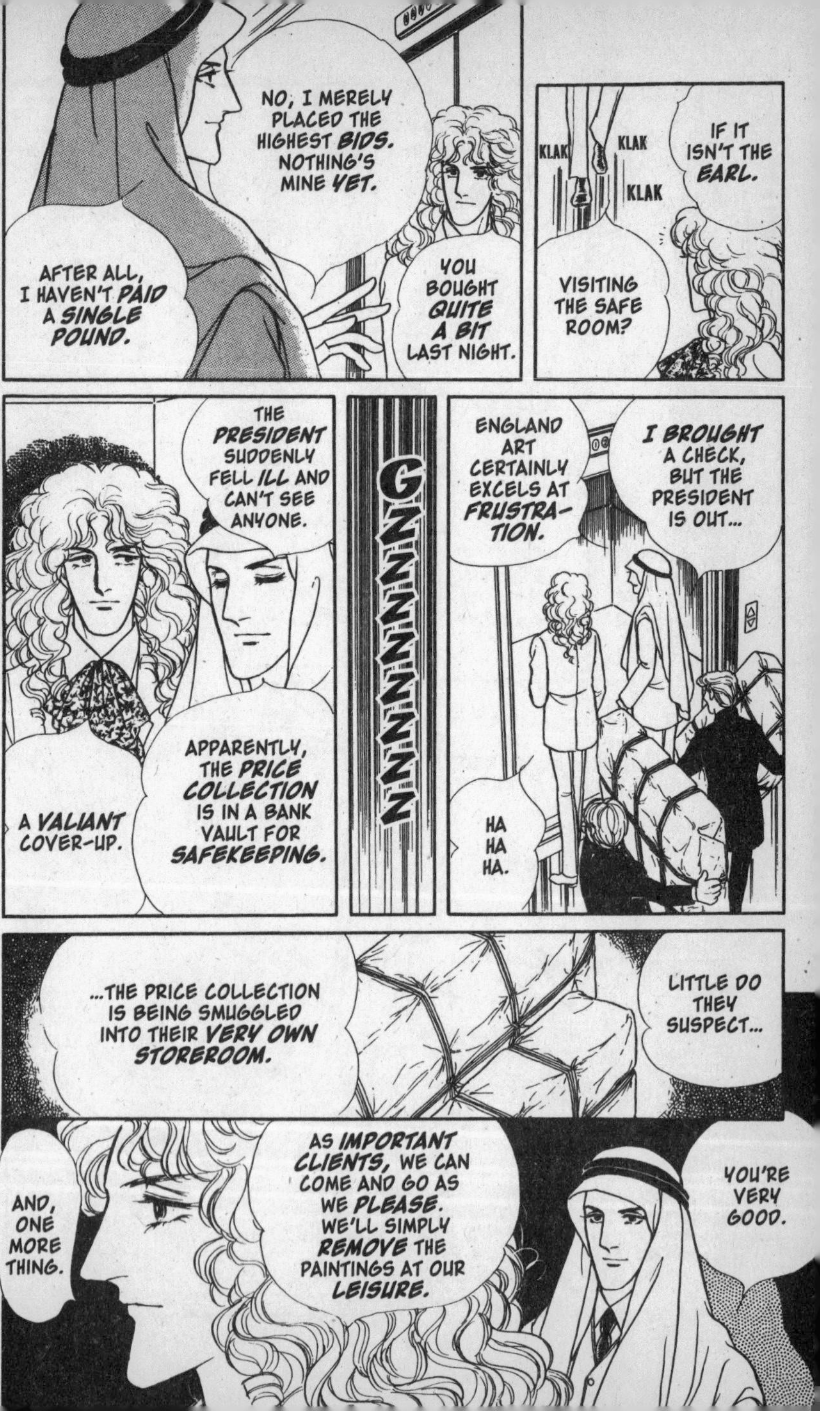
IF IT ISN'T THE EARL.
KLAK KLAK KLAK
VISITING THE SAFE ROOM?
YOU BOUGHT QUITE A BIT LAST NIGHT.
NO, I MERELY PLACED THE HIGHEST BIDS. NOTHING'S MINE YET.
AFTER ALL, I HAVEN'T PAID A SINGLE POUND.
I BROUGHT A CHECK, BUT THE PRESIDENT IS OUT...
ENGLAND ART CERTAINLY EXCELS AT FRUSTRATION.
HA HA HA.
GZZZZZZZZZZZ
THE PRESIDENT SUDDENLY FELL ILL AND CAN'T SEE ANYONE.
APPARENTLY, THE PRICE COLLECTION IS IN A BANK VAULT FOR SAFEKEEPING.
A VALIANT COVER-UP.
LITTLE DO THEY SUSPECT...
...THE PRICE COLLECTION IS BEING SMUGGLED INTO THEIR VERY OWN STOREROOM.
YOU'RE VERY GOOD.
AS IMPORTANT CLIENTS, WE CAN COME AND GO AS WE PLEASE. WE'LL SIMPLY REMOVE THE PAINTINGS AT OUR LEISURE.
AND, ONE MORE THING.

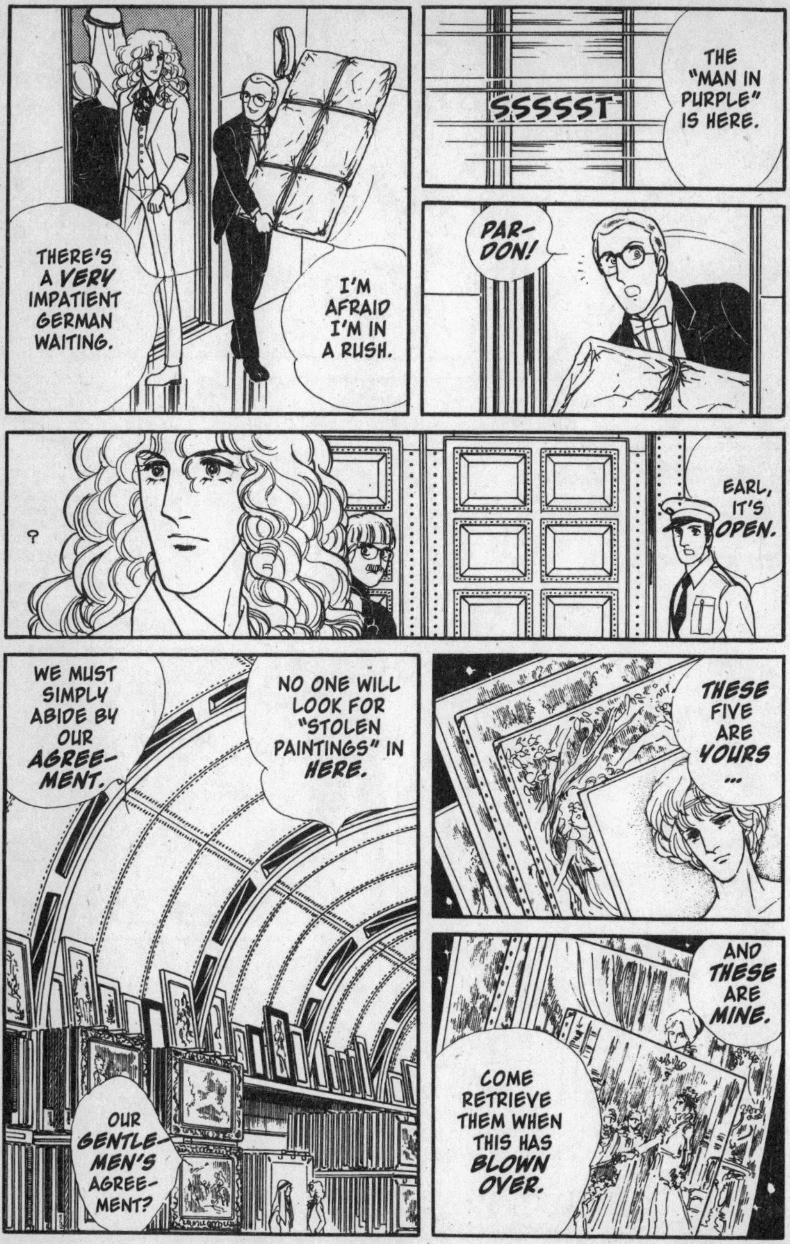
SSSSST
THE "MAN IN PURPLE" IS HERE.
PAR-DON!
I'M AFRAID I'M IN A RUSH.
THERE'S A VERY IMPATIENT GERMAN WAITING.
EARL, IT'S OPEN.
?
THESE FIVE ARE YOURS...
AND THESE ARE MINE.
COME RETRIEVE THEM WHEN THIS HAS BLOWN OVER.
NO ONE WILL LOOK FOR "STOLEN PAINTINGS" IN HERE.
WE MUST SIMPLY ABIDE BY OUR AGREEMENT.
OUR GENTLEMEN'S AGREEMENT?

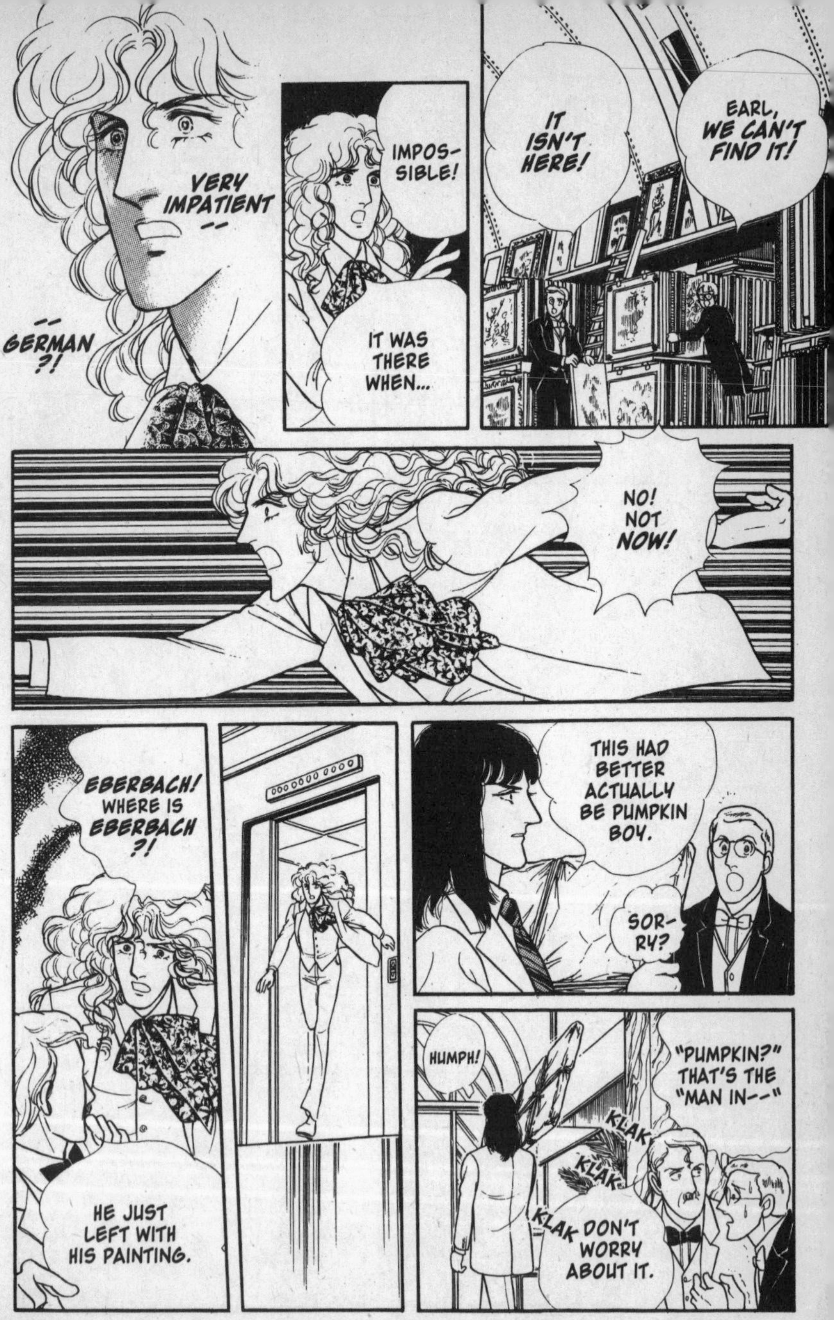
EARL, WE CAN'T FIND IT!
IT ISN'T HERE!
IMPOSSIBLE!
IT WAS THERE WHEN...
VERY IMPATIENT --
-- GERMAN ?!
NO! NOT NOW!
THIS HAD BETTER ACTUALLY BE PUMPKIN BOY.
SORRY?
"PUMPKIN?" THAT'S THE "MAN IN--"
HUMPH!
KLAK
KLAK
KLAK
DON'T WORRY ABOUT IT.
EBERBACH! WHERE IS EBERBACH?!
HE JUST LEFT WITH HIS PAINTING.

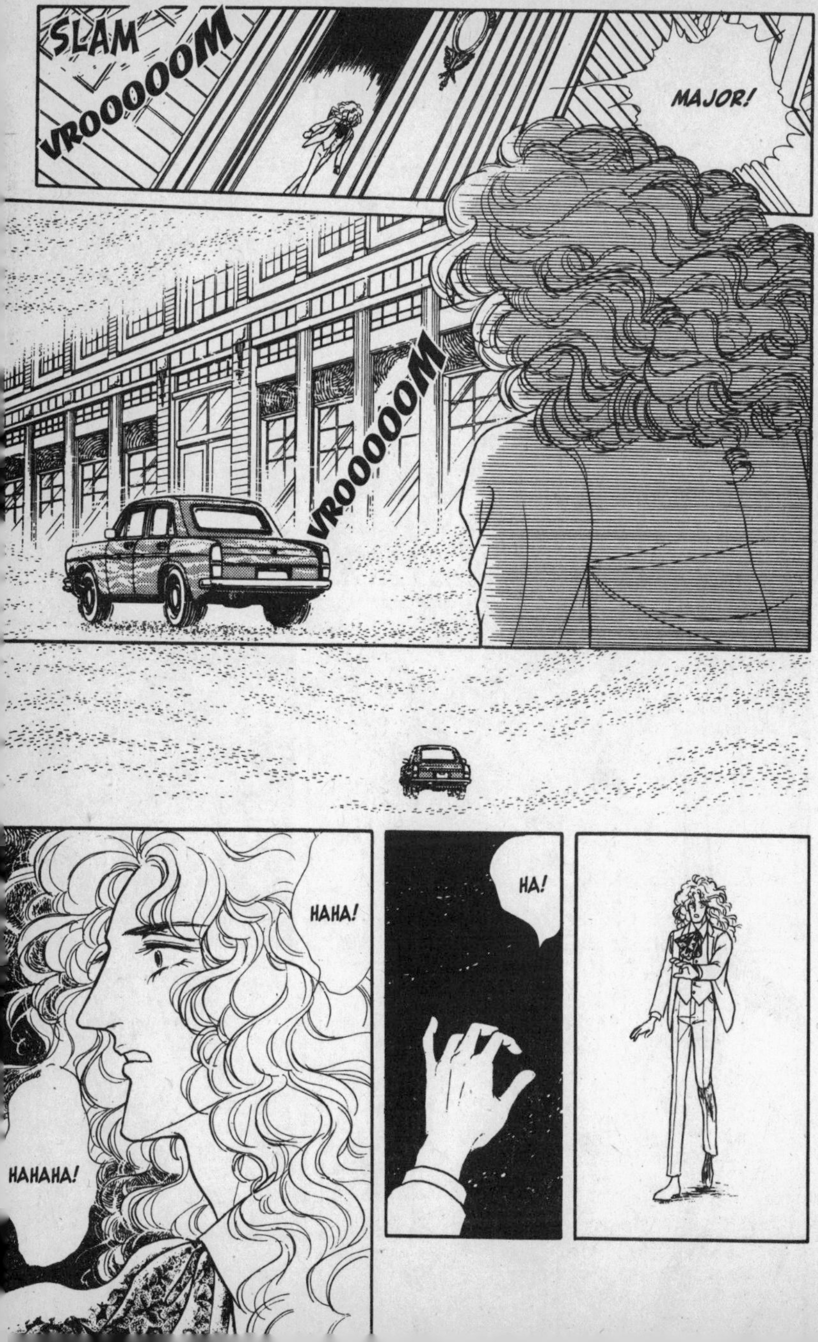
MAJOR!
SLAM
VROOOOOM
VROOOOOM
HA!
HAHA!
HAHAHA!

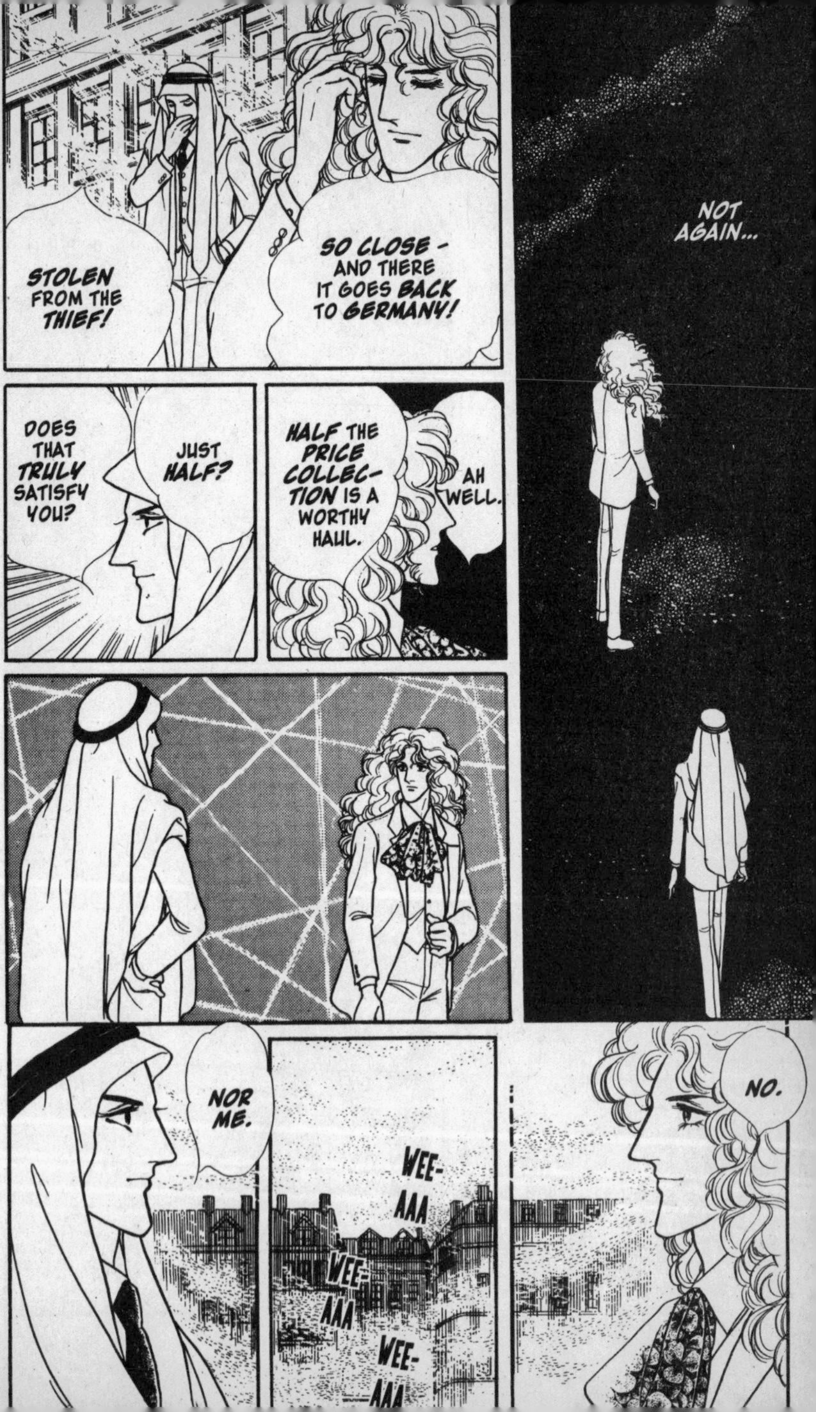
NOT AGAIN...
SO CLOSE - AND THERE IT GOES BACK TO GERMANY!
STOLEN FROM THE THIEF!
AH WELL.
HALF THE PRICE COLLECTION IS A WORTHY HAUL.
JUST HALF?
DOES THAT TRULY SATISFY YOU?
NO.
WEE-AAA
WEE-AAA
WEE-AAA
NOR ME.

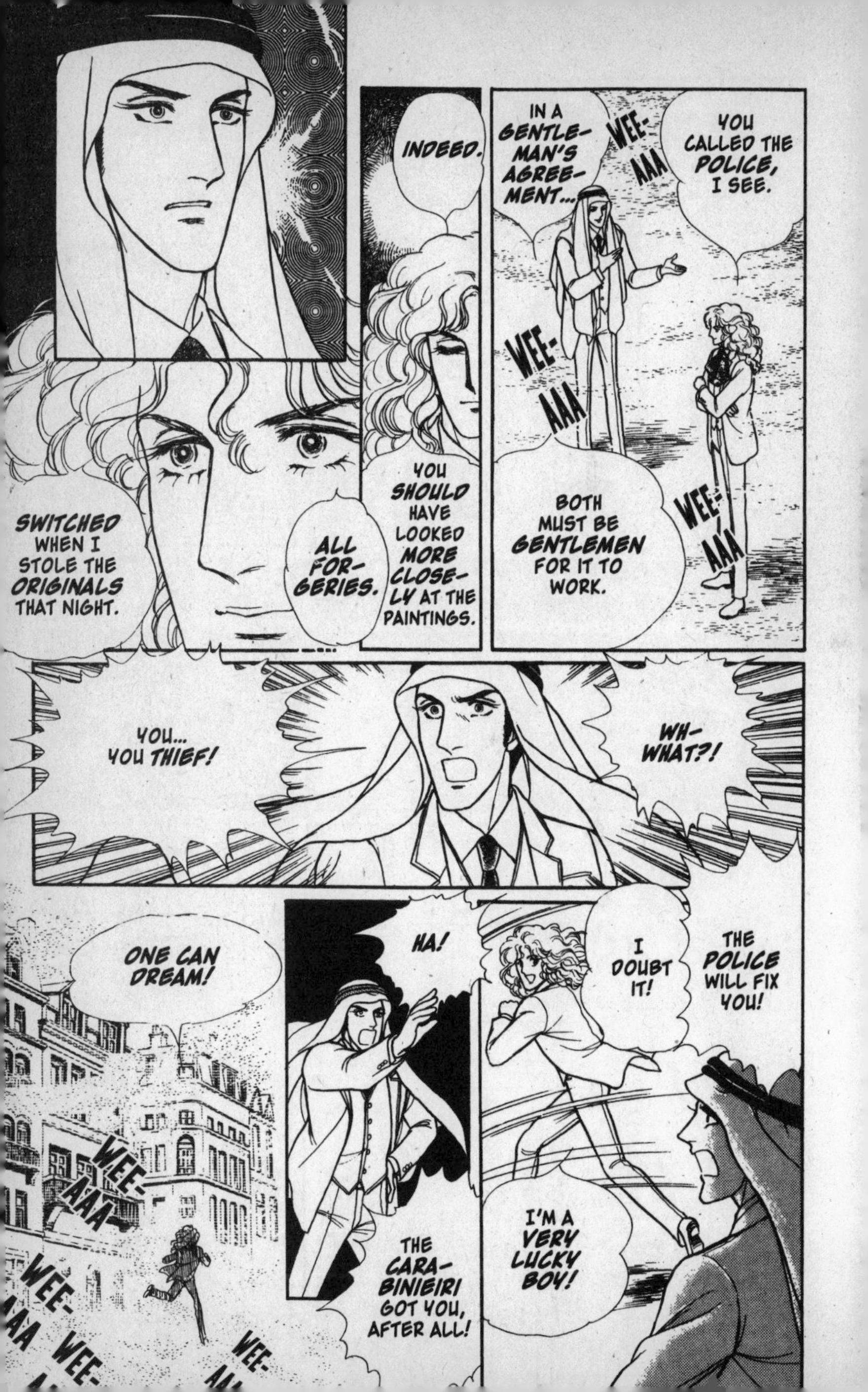

YOU CALLED THE POLICE, I SEE.
WEE-AAA
IN A GENTLE-MAN'S AGREE-MENT...
WEE-AAA
WEE-AAA
BOTH MUST BE GENTLEMEN FOR IT TO WORK.
INDEED.
YOU SHOULD HAVE LOOKED MORE CLOSE-LY AT THE PAINTINGS.
ALL FOR-GERIES.
SWITCHED WHEN I STOLE THE ORIGINALS THAT NIGHT.
WH-WHAT?!
YOU... YOU THIEF!
THE POLICE WILL FIX YOU!
I DOUBT IT!
I'M A VERY LUCKY BOY!
HA!
THE CARA-BINIEIRI GOT YOU, AFTER ALL!
ONE CAN DREAM!
WEE-AAA
WEE-AAA
WEE-
WEE-

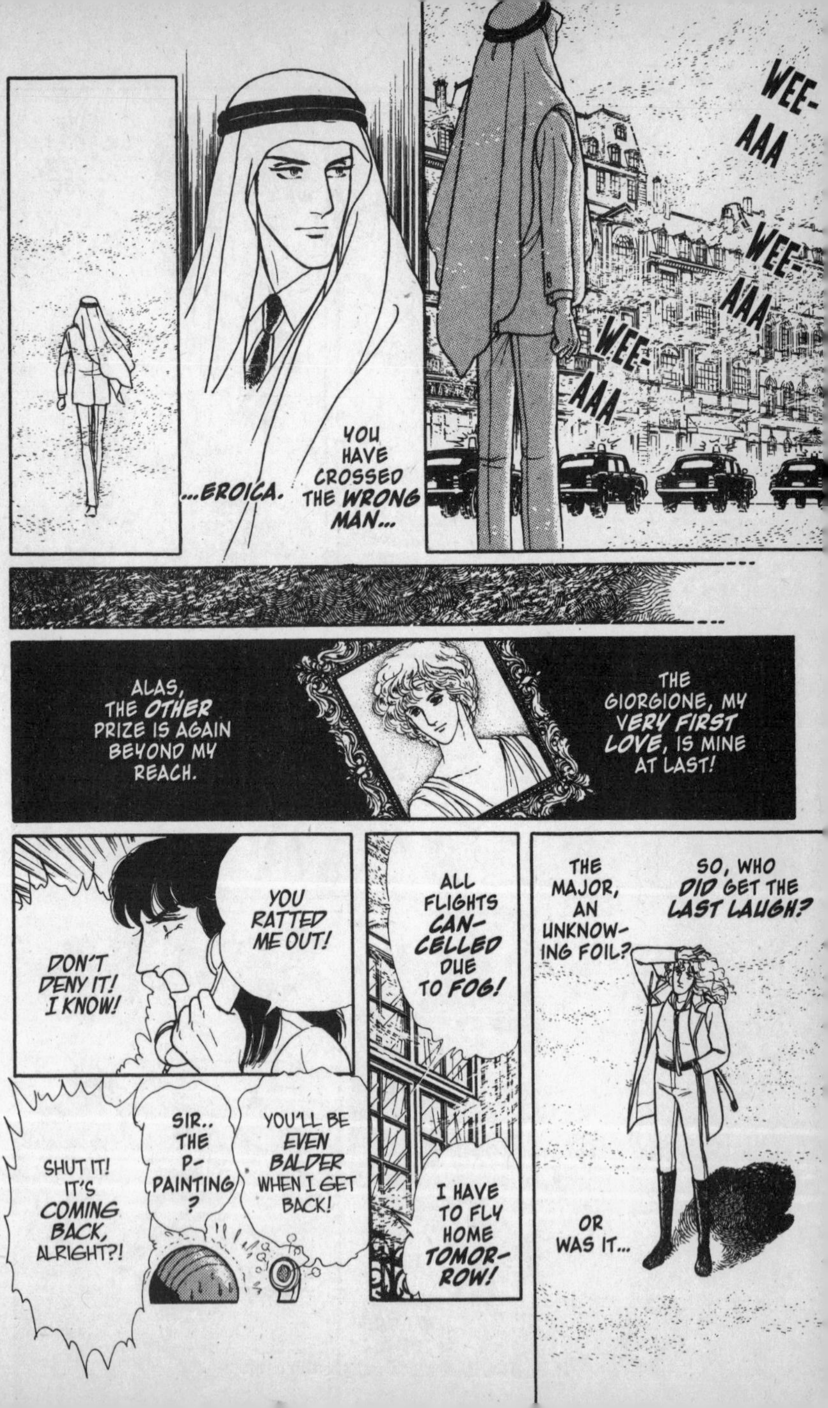
WEE-AAA
WEE-AAA
WEE-AAA
YOU HAVE CROSSED THE WRONG MAN...
...EROICA.
THE GIORGIONE, MY VERY FIRST LOVE, IS MINE AT LAST!
ALAS, THE OTHER PRIZE IS AGAIN BEYOND MY REACH.
SO, WHO DID GET THE LAST LAUGH?
THE MAJOR, AN UNKNOWING FOIL?
OR WAS IT...
ALL FLIGHTS CAN-CELLED DUE TO FOG!
I HAVE TO FLY HOME TOMOR-ROW!
YOU RATTED ME OUT!
DON'T DENY IT! I KNOW!
YOU'LL BE EVEN BALDER WHEN I GET BACK!
SIR.. THE P-PAINTING?
SHUT IT! IT'S COMING BACK, ALRIGHT?!

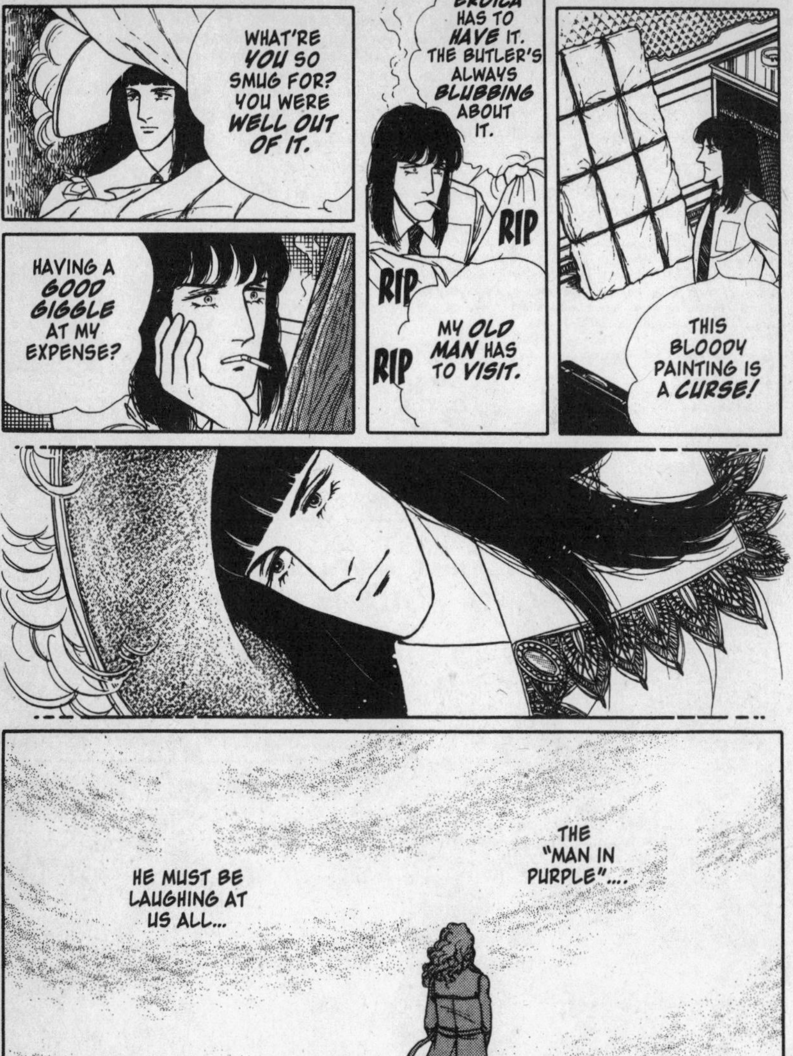

THIS BLOODY PAINTING IS A CURSE!
EROICA HAS TO HAVE IT. THE BUTLER'S ALWAYS BLUBBING ABOUT IT.
RIP
RIP
MY OLD MAN HAS TO VISIT.
RIP
WHAT'RE YOU SO SMUG FOR? YOU WERE WELL OUT OF IT.
HAVING A GOOD GIGGLE AT MY EXPENSE?
THE "MAN IN PURPLE"....
HE MUST BE LAUGHING AT US ALL...

END OF *FROM EROICA WITH LOVE* VOLUME SEVEN

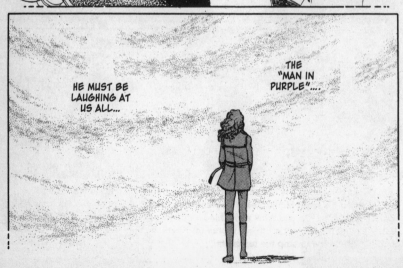

EROICA YORI AI WO KOMETE Volume 7 © 1976 Yasuko Aoike. All rights reserved. First published
in Japan in 1978 by AKITA PUBLISHING CO., LTD., Tokyo.

FROM EROICA WITH LOVE Volume 7, published by WildStorm Productions, an imprint of DC
Comics, 888 Prospect St. #240, La Jolla, CA 92037. English Translation © 2006. All Rights Reserved.
English translation rights in U.S.A. arranged with AKITA PUBLISHING CO., LTD., Tokyo, through
Tuttle-Mori Agency, Inc., Tokyo. The stories, characters, and incidents mentioned in this magazine are
entirely fictional. Printed on recyclable paper. WildStorm does not read or accept unsolicited submissions of ideas, stories or artwork. Printed in Canada.

DC Comics, a Warner Bros. Entertainment Company.

Tony Ogasawara – Translation and Adaptation
Sno Cone – Lettering
Larry Berry – Design   ISBN:1-4012-0876-2
Jim Chadwick – Editor   ISBN-13: 978-1-4012-0876-9

COMING NEXT IN VOLUME 8:
KLAUS AND EROICA SQUARE OFF IN THE SKY!

By Yasuko Aoike. The Major ... document on the KGB to
NATO when his flight ... ies a famous painting that
Eroica lusts after. Do ... a hijacking will stop the
world's most flamboy ... e may just have to join
forces with Eroica to ...